Contemporary Debates in Aesthetics and the Philosophy of Art

Contemporary Debates in Philosophy

In teaching and research, philosophy makes progress through argumentation and debate. *Contemporary Debates in Philosophy* presents a forum for students and their teachers to follow and participate in the debates that animate philosophy today in the western world. Each volume presents pairs of opposing viewpoints on contested themes and topics in the central subfields of philosophy. Each volume is edited and introduced by an expert in the field, and also includes an index, bibliography, and suggestions for further reading. The opposing essays, commissioned especially for the volumes in the series, are thorough but accessible presentations of opposing points of view.

1. Contemporary Debates in Philosophy of Religion *edited by Michael L. Peterson and Raymond J. VanArragon*
2. Contemporary Debates in Philosophy of Science *edited by Christopher Hitchcock*
3. Contemporary Debates in Epistemology *edited by Matthias Steup and Ernest Sosa*
4. Contemporary Debates in Applied Ethics *edited by Andrew I. Cohen and Christopher Heath Wellman*
5. Contemporary Debates in Aesthetics and the Philosophy of Art *edited by Matthew Kieran*
6. Contemporary Debates in Moral Theory *edited by James Dreier*

Forthcoming *Contemporary Debates* are in:

Cognitive Science *edited by Robert Stainton*
Metaphysics *edited by Ted Sider, Dean Zimmerman, and John Hawthorne*
Philosophy of Mind *edited by Brian McLaughlin and Jonathan Cohen*
Social Philosophy *edited by Laurence Thomas*
Political Philosophy *edited by Thomas Christiano*
Philosophy of Language *edited by Ernie Lepore*

Contemporary Debates in Aesthetics and the Philosophy of Art

Edited by

Matthew Kieran

 **Blackwell**
Publishing

© 2006 by Blackwell Publishing Ltd

BLACKWELL PUBLISHING
350 Main Street, Malden, MA 02148–5020, USA
9600 Garsington Road, Oxford OX4 2DQ, UK
550 Swanston Street, Carlton, Victoria 3053, Australia

First published 2006 by Blackwell Publishing Ltd

1   2006

Library of Congress Cataloging-in-Publication Data

Contemporary debates in aesthetics and the philosophy of art/edited by Matthew Kieran.
    p.   cm.–(Contemporary debates in philosophy; 5)
  Includes bibliographical references and index.
  ISBN-13: 978-1-4051-0239-1 (hardcover: alk. paper)
  ISBN-10: 1-4051-0239-X (hardcover: alk. paper)
  ISBN-13: 978-1-4051-0240-7 (pbk.: alk. paper)
  ISBN-10: 1-4051-0240-3 (pbk.: alk. paper)
  1. Aesthetics, Modern–20th century. 2. Aesthetics, Modern–21st century.
3. Art–Philosophy. I. Kieran, Matthew, 1968– II. Series.

  BH201.C585   2005
  111′.85–dc22

                                                    2005009259

A catalogue record for this title is available from the British Library.

Set in 10 on 12.5 pt Rotis Serif
by SNP Best-set Typesetter Ltd, Hong Kong
Printed and bound in the United Kingdom
by TJ International Ltd, Padstow, Cornwall

The publisher's policy is to use permanent paper from mills that operate a sustainable forestry policy, and which has been manufactured from pulp processed using acid-free and elementary chlorine-free practices. Furthermore, the publisher ensures that the text paper and cover board used have met acceptable environmental accreditation standards.

For further information on
Blackwell Publishing, visit our website:
www.blackwellpublishing.com

Contents

Acknowledgments

A collection such as this depends upon the goodwill and talents of many. I would like to thank the authors not just for their contributions but also for their patience and willingness throughout the editorial process. I am grateful to Sarah Kriefman for help in ensuring consistency in the formatting of the manuscript and to Jeff Dean's staff at Blackwell for preparing it so ably for publication. Finally I would like to register my deep appreciation of the help and encouragement given by Jeff Dean at all stages of the editorial process.

Matthew Kieran

The editor and publisher gratefully acknowledge the permission granted to reproduce the following copyright material in this book:

"Beautiful Woman" from *The Really Short Poems of A.R. Ammons* by A.R. Ammons. W.W. Norton, 1992. © by A.R. Ammons. Used by permission of W.W. Norton & Company, Inc.

"This Be the Verse" from *Collected Poems* by Philip Larkin. © 1988, 1989 by the Estate of Philip Larkin. Reprinted by permission of Farrar, Straus and Giroux, LLC.

Every effort has been made to trace copyright holders and to obtain their permission for the use of copyright material. The publisher apologizes for any errors or omissions in the above list and would be grateful if notified of any corrections that should be incorporated in future reprints or editions of this book.

Notes on Contributors

Noël Carroll is the Mellon Professor of Humanities at Temple University, Philadelphia, and the author of *Beyond Aesthetics* (Cambridge University Press, 2001).

Gregory Currie is Professor of Philosophy at the University of Nottingham, UK. His most recent works are a study of the imagination, *Recreative Minds* (with Ian Ravenscroft, Oxford University Press, 2002) and a book of his essays, *Arts and Minds* (Oxford University Press, 2004).

David Davies is Associate Professor of Philosophy at McGill University in Montreal. He is the author of *Art as Performance* (Blackwell, 2004), and of many articles on topics in the philosophy of art, philosophy of mind, and metaphysics.

Stephen Davies teaches philosophy at the University of Auckland. He is the author of *Definitions of Art* (Cornell University Press, 1991), *Musical Meaning and Expression* (Cornell University Press, 1994), *Musical Works and Performances* (Clarendon Press, 2001), and *Themes in the Philosophy of Music* (Oxford University Press, 2003).

George Dickie is Professor Emeritus at the University of Illinois, Chicago. His most recent books are *Art and Value* (Blackwell, 2001), *Introduction to Aesthetics: An Analytic Approach* (Oxford University Press, 1997), and *The Century of Taste: The Philosophical Odyssey of Taste in the Eighteenth Century* (Oxford University Press, 1996).

Marcia Muelder Eaton is Professor of Philosophy at the University of Minnesota. She has written several books and articles in the area of aesthetics and the philosophy of art. Her most recent book is *Merit: Aesthetic and Ethical* (Oxford University Press, 2000). She is a former President of the American Society for Aesthetics.

Berys Gaut teaches in the Department of Moral Philosophy at the University of St Andrews in Scotland. He is author of numerous articles in aesthetics, philosophy of film, and moral philosophy. He is coeditor of the *Routledge Companion to Aesthetics*, and author of *Art, Emotion, and Ethics* (Oxford University Press, forthcoming).

Tamar Szabó Gendler is an Associate Professor of Philosophy and Codirector of the Cognitive Studies Program at Cornell University. Her work focuses primarily on issues in epistemology, philosophical psychology, metaphysics, and aesthetics. She is currently working on a cluster of problems surrounding the relation between imagination and belief.

Alan H. Goldman is the William R. Kenan, Jr., Professor of Humanities and Professor of Philosophy at the College of William & Mary, Williamsburg, Virginia. He is the author of six books, including *Aesthetic Value* (Westview Press, 1995) and *Practical Rules: When We Need Them and When We Don't* (Cambridge University Press, 2002).

Gordon Graham is Regius Professor of Moral Philosophy at the University of Aberdeen in Scotland and Director of the Centre for the Study of Scottish Philosophy. His publications include many articles on aesthetics as well as *Philosophy of the Arts: An Introduction to Aesthetics* (Routledge, 3rd revised edn. 2005). His Stanton Lectures on "Art in an Irreligious World" are to be published in 2006 by Oxford University Press.

Robert Hopkins is Professor of Philosophy in the University of Sheffield, UK. His current research interests include the sensory imagination; the roles of testimony, reason, and experience in aesthetic judgment; and the aesthetics of sculpture. He is author of *Picture, Image and Experience* (Cambridge University Press, 1998), and numerous papers in journals including *Mind* and *Philosophical Review*. In 2001 he was awarded a Philip Leverhulme Prize in recognition of his research.

Gary Iseminger is Stephen R. Lewis, Jr. Professor of Philosophy and Liberal Learning, Emeritus, at Carleton College, Northfield, Minnesota, where he taught from 1962 to 2004, with time out for visiting teaching stints in England, Ireland, Hong Kong, and other parts of Minnesota. He has written and edited articles and books in the philosophy of logic and on the intentional fallacy and other topics in aesthetics. He is the author of *The Aesthetic Function of Art* (Cornell University Press, 2004).

Daniel Jacobson is Associate Professor of Philosophy at Bowling Green State University, Ohio. He works in moral philosophy, broadly construed, and has published on topics in the history of ethics, ethical theory, moral psychology, and political philosophy, as well as aesthetics.

Eileen John is Lecturer in Philosophy at the University of Warwick, UK. Her research concerns moral and epistemological issues in art, focusing on literary fiction, poetry, and film.

Matthew Kieran is Senior Lecturer in Philosophy at the University of Leeds, UK, and Vice-President of the British Society of Aesthetics. He is the author of *Revealing Art* (Routledge, 2004), coeditor of a series of collected papers including *Imagination, Philosophy and the Arts* (Routledge, 2003), and has written numerous articles in aesthetics and ethics.

Carolyn Korsmeyer is Professor of Philosophy at the University at Buffalo, State University of New York. Her recent books include *Making Sense of Taste: Food and Philosophy* (Cornell University Press, 1999), *Gender and Aesthetics: An Introduction* (Routledge, 2004), and an edited collection, *The Taste Culture Reader: Experiencing Food and Drink* (Berg, 2005).

Karson Kovakovich is a doctoral student in the Philosophy Department at Rutgers University, New Brunswick, New Jersey. His research interests are in epistemology, metaphysics, and philosophy of mind.

Peter Lamarque is Professor of Philosophy and Head of Department at the University of York, UK. He is editor of the *British Journal of Aesthetics*, author of *Fictional Points of View* (Cornell University Press, 1996), and coauthor, with Stein Haugom Olsen, of *Truth, Fiction, and Literature: A Philosophical Perspective* (Clarendon Press, 1994). He also edited *Philosophy and Fiction: Essays in Literary Aesthetics* (Aberdeen University Press, 1983), *Concise Encyclopedia of Philosophy of Language* (Elsevier Press, 1997); and, with S. H. Olsen, *Aesthetics and the Philosophy of Art: The Analytic Tradition* (Blackwell, 2003).

Jerrold Levinson is Distinguished Professor of Philosophy at the University of Maryland, College Park. He is the author of *Music, Art, and Metaphysics* (Cornell University Press, 1990), *The Pleasures of Aesthetics* (Cornell University Press, 1996), *Music in the Moment* (Cornell University Press, 1998), and *L'art, la musique, et l'histoire* (Editions de l'Eclat, 1998); editor of *Aesthetics and Ethics* (Cambridge University Press, 1998) and *The Oxford Handbook of Aesthetics* (2003); and coeditor of *Aesthetics Concepts* (Oxford University Press, 2001). A third collection of his essays, *Contemplating Art*, will appear from Oxford University Press in 2006. He is a past President of the American Society for Aesthetics (2001–3) and has been a visiting professor at various places including Johns Hopkins University, Columbia University, and the University of London.

Dominic McIver Lopes is Distinguished Professor of Philosophy at the University of British Columbia, Canada. He is the author of *Understanding Pictures* (Oxford University Press, 1996) and *Sight and Sensibility: Evaluating Pictures* (Oxford University Press, 2005). In addition, he is coeditor of several collections of papers, including the *Routledge Companion to Aesthetics* (2000) and *Philosophy of Literature: An Anthology* (Blackwell, 2003).

Derek Matravers is a Senior Lecturer in Philosophy at The Open University. He is also an Associate Lecturer at Cambridge University, and a Fellow-Commoner of Jesus

Notes on Contributors

College. He is the author of *Art and Emotion* (Cambridge University Press, 1998) and numerous articles in aesthetics and ethics.

Aaron Meskin is Assistant Professor of Philosophy and member of the Fine Arts Doctoral Program at Texas Tech University in Lubbock, Texas. His research interests include the epistemology of artistic value and beauty, the nature of photography, and the intersection of cognitive science and aesthetics.

Daniel O. Nathan is Associate Professor of Philosophy at Texas Tech University. He is the author of articles in aesthetics, the philosophy of law, and ethics, and his current research interest is on interpretation in law and the arts.

Robert Stecker is Professor of Philosophy at Central Michigan University. He is the author of three book in aesthetics: *Artworks: Definition, Meaning, Value* (Penn State Press, 1997), *Interpretation and Construction: Art, Speech, and the Law* (Blackwell, 2003), and *Aesthetics and the Philosophy of Art* (Rowman and Littlefield, 2005).

Jonathan M. Weinberg is Assistant Professor of Philosophy and member of the Program in Cognitive Science at Indiana University, Bloomington. He works in the intersection of cognitive science and philosophy, especially epistemology and aesthetics.

Introduction: A Conceptual Map of Issues in Aesthetics and the Philosophy of Art

Matthew Kieran

Ways of Approach

There are two ways in which people tend to approach problems in aesthetics. The first starts from looking at paradigmatic artworks, aesthetic experiences, or critical practices, and seeing what philosophical questions naturally arise. When thinking about the nature of artistic value, for example, we might start from the kinds of statements we are likely to make in appreciating, evaluating, and judging artworks. The variety tends to be enormous, and attention to the rich complexity of our everyday practice is important. Nonetheless the point of doing so is to abstract relevant types and categories of statements to be sorted. We talk about, amongst other things, doing justice to a work; the vividness or richness of experience involved; the originality of a work; the imaginativeness of the artist; the expressiveness, beauty, or poignancy of a work; savoring or delighting in our experience of a work; and what we may learn from it. Such characterizations are commendatory: in virtue of ascribing them to a work we are evaluating it highly. Looking at such statements we might be drawn to the fact that many of them concern our experiences with a work. If we put the two observations together it is natural to be drawn to the thought that the value of artworks consists in the value of the experiences they afford us. Indeed, this is the conception of artistic value that Gordon Graham's paper argues for. Then we might look at statements that don't seem to tie up so straightforwardly to such a conception and see if they can't be redescribed in such terms, related to such statements, or ruled out. Talk of learning from artworks may be linked to the way in which artworks shape and guide our experiences with them, giving shape to our imaginings, emotions, and perceptions. Talk of originality may be linked to works being experientially valuable because new artistic styles, such as impressionism or cubism, may lead us to see the world in new ways. On the other hand, talk of doing justice to a work, or the downgrading of pastiches and forgeries in favor of originals, tends to pull away from this line of thought. One of David Davies's arguments against such a conception, for example, is that it cannot hope to make sense of one of the distinctive kinds of visual art of the twentieth century, namely ready-mades familiar from Duchamp through to contemporary conceptual art. What both Gordon Graham and David Davies are seeking to do is show how their favored theoretical account of the value of art springs from, and can best make sense of, our deep intuitions about art. Of course this may require giving up some intuitions we have in light of certain putative theoretical benefits a particular account may bring, and its promise to preserve other intuitions that we share. But this does highlight a generic problem with this kind of piecemeal approach. There may be worries about just what is and is not to count as paradigmatic and why. In the case of Gordon Graham's and David Davies's arguments the status of conceptual art is problematic. We need to think about what conceptual art takes itself to be doing, why and how, in order to get a grip on whether its aims are related in the right kind of way to artistic practice. Although we may be persuaded by the range of considerations one rather than another author offers, we can see how this piecemeal approach not only tries to square intuitions with theoretic commitments but naturally leads on to other questions.

The second kind of approach is much more programmatic. It comes at questions either from within aesthetics or from outside, seeking to develop or vindicate a highly systematized conception of things like the nature of the imagination, emotions, artworks, or how we engage with them. Furthermore, it does so in ways that promise to yield answers to a host of related questions derived from what is taken to be the program's most fundamental insight. For example, Gregory Currie has devoted much philosophical energy to developing a general philosophical account of the imagination, construed as the simulation of belief and desire-like states. I don't actually believe that Anna Karenin exists, that she thinks and feels, but in reading Tolstoy's book I imagine that she does. My mental states run similarly to those I would have were I to believe that she did exist and I was reading about what actually happened to her – except of course, because I am simulating the relevant states, I don't then believe or act as if she could be saved. Imagination, according to Gregory Currie, just is the capacity to simulate more straightforward propositional states detached from their normal action-tending outputs. It promises to yield answers to a whole range of fundamental questions ranging from an account of how we can come to know other minds to what exactly is required in engaging with and responding to fiction. The difficulty that tends to beset the piecemeal approach, how to judge which conflicting intuitions to ditch, how to resolve difficult questions before going off to think about further related questions, doesn't arise as much with this approach. By its very nature the programmatic approach works up a theoretical program from a purported fundamental insight and seeks to apply it globally to a whole range of different questions where the basic insight looks as if it will deliver informative answers. But a potential difficulty of this approach stands in contrast to an advantage the piecemeal approach has, namely, sensitivity to the particular. Aaron Meskin and Jonathan Weinberg, for example, argue that the trouble with Currie's account is that it all too quickly flattens out, falsely, the kind of imaginative interactions we have with artworks. It is up to readers to discern for themselves whether there is something to the particular criticisms made. But it shouldn't be assumed that programmatic accounts are neces-

Matthew Kieran

sarily distortive. Both Eileen John and Daniel Jacobson, in different ways, urge us to think of the relationship between the moral character and significance of artworks and their value as art in piecemeal if structured ways. But we might think that such a piecemeal account owes us an explanation as to why we judge that the immoral character of a work may make it less valuable as art in one case and yet not so in another. Indeed, we might say, some kind of theoretical explanation is required if the claims being made are not to be open to accusations of randomness or arbitrariness.

The Integration Challenge

Perhaps which approach one tends to opt for is partly a function of the nature of one's interest in such questions. Differences in approach also partly reflect distinct philosophical temperaments, as does the emphasis given to conceptual analysis, laying out a pattern of thought, precise argument, or attention to artistic phenomenology. Nonetheless, whatever the differences, there are certain challenges we should expect any philosophical approach to give rise to and should legitimately ask them to meet. Christopher Peacocke (1999) has suggested that any area of philosophy needs to reconcile its metaphysical and epistemological claims broadly construed. This is what he has termed the integration challenge. Expanding on this thought, we might say that philosophical questions tend to arise where there is an apparent clash in claims made along at least the four following vectors:

1. Metaphysics. This is a matter of the nature, ontological status, or kind of thing that we are picking out, from the nature of aesthetic properties to the status of artistic evaluations.
2. Epistemology. Here the focus is on how we come to know things within the relevant area, from what the appropriate interpretation of a work is or what the relevant object of appreciation is to how we know that one work is better than another.
3. Semantics. Attention is brought to bear on the contents of our statements and thoughts about works and the ways in which they function in our discourse.
4. Pretheoretic phenomenology. A concern with sensitivity to and discrimination amongst how things seem to us in our experience of creating, engaging with, and appreciating artworks.

Problems arise because of apparent clashes between, or tensions amongst, claims that people want to make in relation to some or all of these concerns, and the challenge is to reconcile them. Given there are at least these four vectors, there are in principle numerous ways in which one may seek to resolve any such challenge.

Consider the status of evaluative claims made with respect to aesthetic experiences and artworks. The kind of epistemic claims that tend to be made look objectivist. We make statements based on the presumption that we are reasonable judges of what is good in certain kinds of music but not in others; we often think we have made mistakes in buying a particular CD or admiring a certain painting; we often think we know people whose taste is better than our own in certain areas, and so on. This also conforms to our epistemic practice. We think we can learn things about appreciation from art critics, teachers, or friends who show us new things. But this is in apparent tension with what we are usually tempted to say about the metaphysical status of aesthetic properties and artistic evaluations. It is common to hear people say about artistic disagreements that such disputes are *merely* a matter of taste. Note that this tension is distinctive of the aesthetic case rather than something that arises in the same manner across all evaluative areas. In the moral case, by contrast, we're inclined to start by assuming the same kind of metaphysical and epistemic objectivity. No-one (at least if they are serious about the nature of moral enquiry) naturally starts from the position of saying that whether cruelty is bad or not is merely a matter of taste.

One way of seeking to resolve the apparent tension is to argue, along the lines George Dickie suggests, that there are objective, generalizable principles of a sort which constrain our aesthetic evaluations. Notice that this may be true even if artistic evaluation is, in Humean terms, based on the warm sentiments of the heart rather than cold reason (i.e., subjective). According to Hume ([1757] 1993), epistemic objectivity only need be secured by reference to the discrimination afforded by standard human nature and the requisite sensitivity of taste, breadth of experience, and critical sympathy (amongst other things) required in being a good judge. On the other hand, it may be that, like Alan Goldman, one thinks reflection on both the phenomenology of aesthetic evaluation and the nature of principles in general shows that epistemic objectivity cannot be secured in such a manner. Perhaps this is where one of the relevant differences between aesthetic and ethical evaluation lies. We expect there to be principles in the moral case, a demand commonly exhibited in ordinary moral discourse, but seem far less bothered about appeal to principles in the aesthetic case. Of course, if epistemic objectivity cannot be secured by principles it doesn't show that the case for it collapses. Aesthetic particularism could in principle be compatible with epistemic objectivity.

One reason for thinking that in the aesthetic case the tension is only apparent involves reflecting on the nature and involvement of the emotions. Given the centrality of emotional responses with respect to many kinds of artworks it shouldn't be surprising if the epistemology of the emotions should play a significant role in appreciating and evaluating artworks. Furthermore, there are objective epistemic constraints that apply with respect to knowing whether or not one is feeling or ought to feel emotions such as anger, sadness, or fear. Of course, as the essays by Derek Matravers and Tamar Gendler and Karson Kovakovich show us, what their role is and what the nature of these constraints are may be controversial. But that there are some such constraints with respect to what the nature of an emotion consists in and that there are criteria that must be met for the emotion to be appropriate is fairly uncontroversial. Thus, at least where emotions are central in appreciating and evaluating artworks, it looks as if we can show how it is that the metaphysical status of evaluative claims could be subjective while nonetheless involving, at least to some degree, an objective epistemology. Even then the complexities of human psychology and our emotional life in particular may be such that we can't know or say within certain broad constraints just what the appropriate inflections are. Perhaps once the general constraints are met there just are many nuanced responses that are appropriate depending on the emotional life brought to bear by the reader. Such matters may speak both to questions concerned with principles of evaluation and the constraints on interpretation spoken to by both Daniel Nathan and Robert Stecker.

In a similar vein consider the nature of aesthetic properties, which range from the wholly evaluative, beauty for instance, to lower level thicker properties including expressive ones such as sadness, joy, or melancholy. How are we to approach the problem of what it is for something to be beautiful? There's a natural tendency, perhaps given its most forceful articulation in Immanuel Kant, to think of beauty as something pure and uncontaminated. The beautiful just is that which gives rise to pleasure in our apprehension and contemplation of the form of the thing in our experience of it aside from any other concern (Kant [1790] 2000). This squares with much of our talk about beauty. Yet, as Marcia Eaton is keen to point out, this conception is at apparent odds with epistemic factors that seem to influence our capacity to delight in what appears to be delightful. In certain cases we seem unable or unwilling to savor the appearance of something where we know that what brought it about was immoral or destructive. How should this apparent clash be resolved? Carolyn Korsmeyer too sets out to resolve a certain tension arising from the standard conception of beauty, albeit from a different angle. There is a particular species of the beautiful in which delight is commingled with terror, horror, or fear. In such cases are the negative feelings merely coincidental with a pure delight that is the mark of the beautiful or is there some deeper internal relation? And if so what does that tell us both about this particular kind of beauty and the nature of beauty in general?

Descending down toward thicker properties such as expressive ones, fundamental questions arise in similar fashion. Epistemically speaking we seem to be on sure ground when we say that a novel expresses (or at least can express) pessimism, a painting vitality, or music melancholy. At least when we consider representational works, though there are questions to be asked about what the nature of expressiveness consists in, that works can be expressive initially looks unproblematic. We can perceive that people express emotional states, hence works that are representational can represent characters that do so. But when we consider pure music, or indeed abstract visual works, even this basic epistemic certainty is threatened. For how can nonrepresentional marks on a canvas or harmonies express emotions or more general cognitive-affective states of mind when they don't represent anything or anyone? Is there something to the idea, as Stephen Davies is inclined to hold, that we hear in musical structures characteristics which resemble the perceived behavior and appearance of people in whatever states we take the music to express? Alternatively is there, as Jerrold Levinson suggests, a fundamental link between perceived expressiveness and hearing the music as the personal expression of the mental life of some indefinite underlying persona? However the question is to be resolved in the case of pure music it cannot but shed light on the nature of expressiveness in general.

Where there is a clash between the vectors amongst some set of claims we naturally make, it can be tempting to reconstrue one of the fundamental notions that we started with or, alternatively, to become a deflationist about one of them. In a tradition stemming from Kant, though in some ways a distortion of Kant's actual views, the notion of aesthetic experience was given a psychological twist at the start of the twentieth century. Aesthetic experience was said to involve some sort of distinct perceptual attitude, had certain ineffable properties or affective unity that give it a distinct feel from other more mundane kinds of experience. Although this squared with the way people often spoke of aesthetic experience, no doubt influenced by the aestheticism of figures like Walter Pater and Oscar Wilde, it sat at odds with our pretheoretic phenomenology. Paradigmatic aesthetic experiences, ranging from noticing certain color relations in a painting and following the narrative structure of a film to appreciating dissonant music, hardly seem to involve experiences which include any of these features. A natural way to go in the face of this problem is to tie the notion of aesthetic experience into the idea of aesthetic reward, at least where such gratification involves the correct or appropriate apprehension of its object. Such a move lends itself to reconstruing the notion of aesthetic experience in epistemic terms, as Gary Iseminger argues we ought to do, rather than thinking about the notion as a distinct kind of experience as such. By contrast, Noël Carroll argues that there is greater reason to go for a more deflationary conception according to which aesthetic experience just is the apprehension of a work's formal, expressive, or design properties and their interrelations. Either way the important point here is that such contrasting approaches arose as distinct ways of handling the same challenge: how to integrate the demands made upon the notion of aesthetic experience when considered in terms of the four vectors delineated above.

An Aesthetic Triad

We've seen how the integration challenge arises in relation to various issues, but there is more to be said about the subject matter of aesthetics and the philosophy of art. We can think of it as constituting a triad:

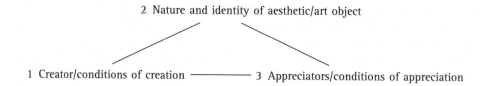

2 Nature and identity of aesthetic/art object

1 Creator/conditions of creation ——————— 3 Appreciators/conditions of appreciation

This triad constitutes the subject matter of aesthetics and the philosophy of art. Challenges that arise, and indeed answers to them, tend to presuppose the prominence of one point of the triad over the others or of certain relations between the points of the triad. For example, consider how we might go about answering a question as to what kind of values are appropriate to the evaluation of art. The nature of the question focuses on the third point of the triad. We might start by looking at the nature of critical practice: how informed appreciators engage with works and come to judgments, and the nature of their underlying reasoning. We might yet go further and consider, as both Peter Lamarque and Berys Gaut in their different ways do, certain metaphysical constraints tied up with what it is for something to be an artwork. If it is in the nature of something as art to preclude considerations of truth then it might be difficult to see how praising a work in cognitive terms such as insight or profundity could be proper to the evaluation of it *as* art. But in order to evaluate such a claim we have to think about matters concerning the nature of art and its possible

Matthew Kieran

relations to matters such as truth, imagination, and understanding. Alternatively, if we are thinking about something on the second point of the triad, say in considering the nature of visual representation, then following Robert Hopkins's and Dominic Lopes's contrasting essays, the differences in claims at the third point of the triad – concerning how we come to process visual information – look crucial. Alternatively the relations between the first and the third points may be thought to be crucial for a particular question. Robert Stecker and Daniel Nathan, to take one example, differ over the ways and degrees to which this is so in appropriately constraining our interpretation of artworks.

It is true that the terms aesthetic object and artwork are not coextensive. Many aspects of nature are aesthetic objects, and crafted utensils, furniture, or religious idols may be aesthetic without necessarily constituting art works. Conversely, it is far from obvious that all artworks – good, bad, or indifferent – must be aesthetic in their nature or appeal. But whether we are dealing with art objects or aesthetic ones the triad in principle remains the same. After all, even in the case of a natural landscape how it came to be the way it is or our understanding of what it is that we are looking at may be important for our appreciation of it.

This collection is not so much a survey but a series of pairs of essays engaging in some of the central questions that preoccupy contemporary philosophers in the field. In one sense then, though there are interrelations, as one would expect given what I have said above, some seem closer to or further removed from the concerns of others. There is, however, a dominant tendency that reflects something about the nature of the contemporary field. Most of the essays' questions and concerns cluster around the second and third points of the triad. Furthermore it is the third point on the triad, the focus on the nature and conditions of audience appreciation, that is the most dominant. In this general feature, as in much else, the collection reflects a dominant emphasis in contemporary philosophical approaches to aesthetics and the arts. What is taken to be known or understood at the third point of the triad is directed toward the other points in the triad to gain insight and form conclusions. In some ways this is understandable. The emphasis on audience reception arose partly as a reaction against the Romantic conception of art, which was bound up with an artist-orientated approach concentrating on matters such as genius, creativity, the personal history of the artist and the importance of artistic expression (often taken to be *the* defining feature of art). On the one hand Romanticism was found guilty of conflating personal and historical interests with artistic ones and, on the other, it was thought to embody a too rarified, partial, and exclusive conception of art (in terms of both the questions it addressed about art and those it failed to recognize). Once the shackles of Romanticism had been removed, it suddenly seemed as if a host of questions – from the nature of fiction, interpretation, evaluation, and the cognitive value of the arts, to the role of the imagination – could be explored in terms of the nature and conditions of audience response. No doubt much progress has been made in those terms. Yet there does remain an important kernel of truth in the Romantic vision (Kieran 2004). A striking feature of contemporary aesthetics is that the first point on the triad has almost entirely been eclipsed. It is especially strange when we bear in mind general philosophical considerations in other areas that would suggest its centrality. Artworks are, standardly at least, intentionally made artifacts produced with many aims in mind, and are the end result of actions. Considerations about action in general suggest then that there is an internal link to the psychology of the makers – their states, intentions, and character. Furthermore, as in the moral case, it is not just the nature of what has been done that is so linked but, at least in part, how the action is to be evaluated. Hence artistic evaluation looks as if it will often refer back to the psychology of the artist(s). It is surprising, therefore, how little attention contemporary aesthetics and the philosophy of art has paid to the nature of artistic character. I only point this out as one direction in which the area may develop in the future. For, as the essays in this collection show, there are presently many others.

References

Hume, D. ([1757] 1993). "Of the Standard of Taste." In David Hume, *Selected Essays*, ed. Stephen Copley and Andrew Edgar (pp. 133–54). Oxford: Oxford University Press.

Kant, I. ([1790] 2000). *Critique of the Power of Judgement*, trans. P. Guyer and E. Matthews. Cambridge, UK: Cambridge University Press.

Kieran, M. (2004). *Revealing Art*. London: Routledge.

Peacocke, C. (1999). *Being Known*. Oxford: Clarendon Press.

HOW ARE ARTISTIC EXPERIENCE AND VALUE INTERRELATED?

Aesthetic Empiricism and the Challenge of Fakes and Ready-mades

Gordon Graham

When the painting *Disciples at Emmaus* was found to be by van Meegeren and not by Vermeer, the world's estimation of its artistic value fell dramatically. A "great master" became a mere "fake" (see Werness 1983). And yet nothing in the picture itself changed. In fact, strictly, it was not even a fake, because there never was any real *Disciples at Emmaus* by Vermeer, and from this it follows that van Meegeren's could not have been a fraudulent copy. Rather, his picture, though certainly in the style of Vermeer, and intentionally so, was an original both in conception and in execution. But if it was an original work, and nothing in it changed as a result of the revelation of its true creator, why did the world's estimation of its value fall? That it did so is evidence of a general belief that the value of a painting derives not merely from its internal properties but from the reputation of the palette or studio from which it originated.

Fakes

From another point of view, however, this belief could only be the result of prejudice, the mindless worship of great names. If the picture was at one time good enough to be exhibited, and if nothing in the picture itself was altered by the identity of its creator becoming known, how could the facts about its provenance make it any the less worth exhibiting? Surely the value of pictures lies in what there is to see in them, and not in their causal origins. And indeed, even if it had been a fake in the proper sense – a copy of a real painting by Vermeer, now lost perhaps – once exposed as a fake it would nevertheless retain the aesthetic properties that made it worth exhibiting.

This sort of case raises a serious question about the relation between the integrity and independence of estimations of artistic worth and the pressures brought to bear upon them by conventional reaction to the exposure of "copyists" like van Meegeren. It is a question that has been widely discussed in the philosophy of art and considerations have been brought on both sides which taken in isolation prove both persuasive and inconclusive, it seems. (For a helpful summary of the arguments see Stalnaker 2001.) Yet, while philosophers can have their doubts about the supremacy of "authenticity," the exposure of a fake (or even, as in the case of Van Meegeren, a pastiche) inevitably leads to its downgrading. No director of a significant gallery could retain a picture in a position of prominence once it had been shown to have been fraudulently produced. The significance of this fact about the artworld is one of the things this essay aims to assess.

Ready-mades

For the moment though, I want to point to a parallel between the phenomenon of the fake and another phenomenon that has also provoked a good deal of discussion in the philosophy of art and in art criticism more generally, namely the art of the "ready-made." Duchamp's *Fountain* is the first and certainly the most famous example of this phenomenon. In response to a declaration by the organizers of an art exhibition in New York that they were open to any and every submission, the French artist Marcel Duchamp (1887–1968) submitted a manufactured urinal. There seems little question now but that this was intended as a jocular way of putting the organizers' self-professed freedom from convention to the test. They meant, no doubt, that they were resolved not to be dictated to by aesthetic presupposition and orthodox opinion, and Duchamp (probably) meant only to point up the carelessness with which they articulated this intention. In a sense the organizers failed his test, since they did indeed reject his urinal. But the joke, if that is what it was, turned out to have a serious outcome. Notwithstanding *Fountain*'s rejection, perhaps because of it in fact, the artworld came to embrace the thought that ready-mades could indeed be viewed as art and accordingly ready-mades began to be exhibited in the same way as creative works. Duchamp may have meant his "submission" to be whimsical, but it brought about a great change in aesthetic mores, one upon which he himself was to capitalize. By the time the turn of Andy Warhol's Brillo Boxes (1969) came round, ready-mades were an accepted art form (though Warhol's boxes were copies rather than the real thing). So, for example, the much heralded Tate Modern's opening exhibition included Michael Craig-Martin's *An Oak Tree*, which despite its name was a half glass of water on a bathroom shelf, both easily purchased from any DIY store.

Were the organizers of the New York exhibition really mistaken in rejecting Duchamp's urinal? Can ready-mades be art? These questions raise precisely the same issue as the earlier one about fakes and pastiche, though in the opposite direction. The urinal, when it lay in the factory, had no aesthetic merits, nor were any claimed for it. (I leave aside here the important and interesting topic of the aesthetics of design.) But once placed in an art exhibition, it assumed (or was accorded) a different role, as something to be "appreciated." Yet how could mere change of location effect this dramatic transformation from the functional to the aesthetic? Is it possible for ordinary objects from everyday life to be transformed into artworks not by the addition of any intrinsically artistic properties but by a mere change of place?

Here too, though, while we can ask whether there is any satisfactory philosophical or aesthetic justification for the art of the ready-made, it is simply to be recorded as a fact about the contemporary artworld that ready-mades have long been accepted and assigned a respected place within it. The opinion of the artworld is not the last word, of course. In so far as it is inarticulate, which it often is, it rests upon an intuitive judgment or feeling rather than a theoretical understanding, and this means that it can be confronted by, and in itself is no better than, a contrary judgment or feeling – usually the feeling and judgment of the "man in the street."

This conflict is not based solely upon intuitive conviction. Both sides can call upon considerations that do something to support them. The modern artworld is quick to make use of the category of the "challenging" in defense of its productions. According to this defense, since all great art challenges the general public's preconceptions, we should expect truly novel art to be rejected by those whose minds are formed by and constrained within ordinary ways of thinking and feeling; and it was always thus. Now while there is a frequent tendency for this line of defense to commit the fallacy of affirming the consequent – all great art offends ordinary sensibilities, therefore all that offends ordinary sensibilities is great art – it is certainly reasonably easy to assemble a large number of historical instances when genuinely innovative art has been rejected by the viewing (and listening) public, only to be succeeded first by acceptance and then by adulation. Beethoven's music was found "difficult" by contemporary audiences; today it is one of the best program choices from the point of view of filling the concert hall.

On the other side of the debate, however, defenders of "the public's" response to "modern" art can point to the fact that it is only recently (in that same art history) that painters, composers, and writers have assumed to themselves what we might call the superautonomy of "art for art's sake." It is thus only recently that art has run any serious risk of intellectual and social isolation. When art was sponsored by patrons and bought by customers, its justification with the public beyond the artworld was secure; it was wanted. Of course it is true that the artist's public (like every other public) tends to be conservative in its tastes, with the result that quite often innovative styles have taken time to be accepted. But "modern" art in many of its forms faces a new sort of inward looking isolation. Who cares about the Turner Prize (for example) now that it is given *by* artists *to* artists, who reserve to themselves the sole authority to declare it to be art of importance and value? It may or may not be significant that this is a condition in large part confined to the "conceptual" movement in visual arts and music. Notoriously, audiences drop dramatically when the program is exclusively the "modern" classical music favored by composers and critics, and the public will not pay to see the winner of visual art competitions in the way that it will pay to see the winner of the Cannes Film Festival *Palme D'Or* (Tarantino's *Pulp Fiction*, for example) or buy the novel that takes the Booker Prize (Ishiguro's *Remains of the Day*, say).

These too are facts that the defenders of "the man in the street" can call upon. Yet they have little bearing on the issue of fakes, and indeed with respect to the two cases under discussion – fakes and ready-mades – there is some dissimilarity between the view of the artworld on the one hand and that of the general public on the other. The artworld rejects fakes and accepts ready-mades. In the world beyond artists and professional critics, attitudes to fakes on the one hand and ready-mades on the other tend to differ. It is quite generally supposed that fraudulent pictures hitherto thought to be from the studios of great masters ought indeed to be removed from positions of admiration and repute, even if they retain considerable interest. By contrast, there is deep suspicion of ready-mades and an inclination to think that they too are frauds (of a different kind) and should be removed from galleries and other places of public approval.

Those who are more in sympathy with contemporary art than they are with the mindset of "the man in the street" can plausibly claim that the public's attitude to fakes is hardly consistent with its attitude to ready-mades. If translation to the gallery cannot bestow artistic value on ready-mades, mere removal from the gallery cannot deprive erstwhile exhibitable paintings of it. The general public cannot have it both ways. Of course, if this is indeed a contradiction it could be readily resolved. Just as the art world consistently rejects fakes and accepts ready-mades, so the common opinion of the viewing public could be made consistent by accepting fakes at the same time as rejecting ready-mades, and refusing to see paintings (or other artworks) relegated on the basis of extrinsic facts about them. Yet this solution to the inconsistency is unlikely to be taken up. The truth is that the viewing public wants it both ways. Can it have what it wants? Can the rejection of fakes and the rejection of ready-mades be consistent?

Aesthetic Empiricism

In answering this question it is obvious that intuitive judgment and feeling are not enough since these are usually equally strong and equally able to call upon a supporting rhetoric. We need to dig deeper, to uncover and resolve the philosophical differences that lie beneath. There may in fact be several such differences, but the one I want to explore at some length relates to the doctrine known as "aesthetic empiricism." This is the view that any estimation of the artistic merits of a work must be based upon the intrinsic properties of that work and not upon facts external to it. Plainly, those who want to defend the attitude of the art world will do best to reject aesthetic empiricism. Both the rejection of fakes and the acceptance of ready-mades depends upon its being the case that facts extrinsic to the works in question can rightly be called upon in the assessment of artistic merit. However, it is important that there be no question begging here. The acceptance of ready-mades as works of aesthetic interest and merit presupposes the falsehood of aesthetic empiricism; it does not show it to be false.

This is the weakness in an argument advanced by David Davies (2000). Davies's essay aims to show that indirect arguments against aesthetic empiricism (such as are to be found in Currie 1989) are not decisive. Instead he appeals to the rejection of fakes and the acceptance of ready-mades as a direct refutation; the actual practice of the art world shows aesthetic empiricism to be false. This contention begs the question however. The acceptance of ready-mades *presupposes* the falsehood of aesthetic empiricism, for the simple reason that if it is true, the acceptance of ready-mades by the art world or any one else is based upon error. The existence of the practice cannot be taken as a decisive "fact" independent of the beliefs underlying it. In short, as far the logic of Davies's "refutation" is concerned, what we have is a case of "one person's *modus ponens* is another person's *modus tollens*."

What Davies's argument does do, however, is point up a weakness in the alternative view that wants to reject ready-mades and at the same time reject fakes, because it presents it with a dilemma. If aesthetic empiricism is false the most obvious ground upon which to reject ready-mades is lost, while if it is true, the rejection of fakes seems irrational. Either way the view of the art world wins out. Or so it seems. We need to consider the philosophical issues more closely.

Contextualism

Those who doubt the truth of aesthetic empiricism generally believe it to be inadequate to our experience of art. Works of art are not to be considered in isolation. Each of them has a history and a context and if we are to see or to hear them as works of art we have to be aware of this context and history. The aesthetic empiricist supposes falsely, this critic alleges, that aesthetic appreciation is best served by an "innocent" eye, one uncontaminated by anything other than the "pure" experience of the work. But "innocence" here could only mean the sort of naivety that depends upon ignorance. This is not something peculiar to the arts. Students coming new to philosophy, for example, can be impressed by an argument their teacher advances; they will be less impressed once they learn that the argument in question has been the stock in trade of philosophers since the time of Plato, say. Had they known this already, they would not have been much impressed at all. So too with painters and composers. Music in the style of Handel is attractive and sophisticated. Composed two centuries later, it lacks the originality of imagination and conception that is a large part of the reason that we praise Handel and his contemporaries. Pastiche differs from that of which it is a pastiche not in terms of its intrinsic properties, but in terms of its place in a creative sequence.

It also differs in intention, and necessarily so. A contemporary composer could not write baroque music *de novo*. To be able to compose with such sophistication he or she must have a knowledge of composition, and such knowledge inevitably brings with it an awareness of the tradition out of which it has grown. But precisely because of this knowledge, the resultant "baroque" compositions must be, not copies of works certainly, but imitations of a style. And this is their artistic defect. Modern "baroque" composers will have failed, as the original baroque composers did not, to find an authentic voice of their own. This is a serious limitation of creative imagination, and hence an artistic and aesthetic defect. But we the audience can only know this if we hear the works in historical context. Listening to them in isolation will not reveal this. The same point can be made about painting. Painters like van Meegeren, even if they are not in the strict sense forgers, are copyists who have to master the style and methods of the past in order to create their copies. Accordingly, they both lack originality and, since they knowingly do so, lack authenticity.

Now neither the judgment of unoriginality nor inauthenticity can be "read off" the painting or the score by mere acquaintance. By the same token, once we know of them, we cannot look at the painting or hear the music with the same ears. It is difficult to say whether this "cannot" is a psychological or a logical one. Does our knowledge of context alter the content of the experience, or merely the judgment we base upon it? This is an issue that might repay further examination, but for present purposes it is enough to observe that there is this impossibility, that we cannot view a pastiche in the same way once we know it to be a pastiche.

I shall dub this the "contextual" objection to aesthetic empiricism, and it certainly seems a strong one. Authenticity, originality, and imagination are unquestionably important concepts in aesthetic judgment and artistic evaluation and if what has been said is correct, they inevitably imply a context. However, while the contextual objection appears to show that there is reason to re-evaluate fakes in the light of newly discovered extrinsic facts about them, it cannot be made to support the acceptance of ready-mades so easily. Indeed, on the contrary, the very same point can, in a different way, be made to reveal a deficiency in the art of the ready-made.

The Kantian Aesthetic

Aesthetic appreciation is not best secured by an "innocent" eye. This is the heart of the contextualist objection, and it takes exception to the idea that aesthetic experience and evaluation are confined to the viewer in the presence of the work. It rejects, in effect, the long-dominant Kantian conception of aesthetic experience as essentially a contemplative attitude that "plays upon" the object of contemplation. In the *Critique of the Power of Judgement* Kant locates aesthetic judgment halfway between the logically necessary and the purely subjective. "The judgement of taste is . . . not a cognitive judgement, hence not a logical one, but is rather aesthetic, by which is understood one whose determining ground cannot be other than subjective" (*Critique* §1). On the other hand, aesthetic apprehension is not merely subjective for while

> the person making the judgement feels himself completely free with regard to the satisfaction that he devotes to the object, he cannot discover as grounds of the satisfaction any private conditions, pertaining to his subject alone, and must therefore regard it as grounded in those that he can presuppose in everyone else; consequently he must believe himself to have grounds for expecting a similar pleasure of everyone. Hence he will speak of the beautiful as if beauty were a property. (*Critique* §6)

This aesthetic pleasure or feeling of approval is to be contrasted both with the feeling that something is "agreeable" and with the feeling that something is "good." The mark of the agreeable is that it is purely a matter of personal taste (Kant's now familiar example is a preference for Canary-wine), and those who make such appraisals have no reason to expect others to share their preference. By "the good" Kant here means what is useful and accordingly holds that judgments of this sort arise "from the concept" of the end that is to be served; given an end in view, whether something is good (i.e., useful to that end) is not a matter of taste but a matter of fact. It follows that the peculiar value of aesthetic delight lies in this: it is composed of a judgment that is disinterestedly free, free that is to say from both practical and cognitive determination. It is not a judgment of either personal liking or general usefulness but a judgment arising from the "free play of the imagination" (§9).

How is such a judgment possible? How is a judgment based upon subjective feeling to command universal assent in the way that a claim to knowledge does? The answer lies in a *sensus communis* or shared sensibility among human beings, which is both awakened and invoked when a judgment of taste is made (§§22 and 40). However, if this shared sense is not to be converted into the affirmation of objectively verifiable propositions about classes of things, and thereby lose its distinctive aesthetic character, judgments of taste must be "invariably laid down as a singular judgement upon the Object" (§8). This is why "delight" in the beautiful takes the form of the contemplation rather than the intellectual classification of objects.

This Kantian account has been enormously influential, and there are a number of elements in it that have virtually assumed the status of the self-evident – the aesthetic as a mode of contemplation, and the autonomy of art as purpose without purposiveness, for instance. But in the present context, the aspect most worth focusing on is the supposition that aesthetic judgment is a distinctive mental act – the free play of the imagination. Now if this is indeed the nature of aesthetic judgment, then within the bounds set by the *sensus communis* the imagination is free to play where it will. This would imply that the relation between art and the aesthetic is a purely contingent one. No doubt it is also a fortuitous one – artifacts deliberately intended to be "art objects" are those upon which the imagination finds it easiest to play – but the point is that there is no intrinsic connection between works of art and aesthetic appreciation. Even if the aesthetic attitude is more easily assumed with respect to art objects, evidently it is not confined to them.

This is the importance of the Kantian conception for present purposes. Precisely because it does not confine aesthetic judgment to intentional works of art, it licences the art of the ready-made. Encouraged to let its imagination play upon a manufactured urinal, the mind may discover within itself the feeling of approval that is to be contrasted both with the feeling that something is "agreeable" and with the feeling that something is "good." In short, the removal of the urinal or the Brillo box from the hardware store to the exhibition hall is a signal to the imagination to let itself play freely, and the fact that neither was originally intended as an art object is no bar to its doing so.

In short, the art of the ready-made has an ally in the Kantian aesthetic, and consequently one line of defense for aesthetic empiricism is to contest that aesthetic. And it does indeed seem contestable, for while it shows aesthetic judgment to be possible, it cannot give us a satisfactory account of aesthetic criticism. What I mean is this. If aesthetic judgment is indeed a mode of contemplation, in sharp contrast to other types of judgment, it cannot arise from or be based upon inference. When I judge the accused to be guilty of the crime, for example, my judgment is based upon, and inferred from evidence. So too when I judge a scientific hypothesis to have been refuted by experiment, or when I judge the experiment designed to test it to have failed. It is not always the case that such patterns of reasoning are conclusive, and so not always the case that the judgment is logically compelling. Nevertheless, it is the existence of such patterns of reasoning that enables us to discriminate between better and worse judgments and to question the judgment of others. None of this seems possible on the Kantian conception. What is possible is a kind of analysis by which we identify specific features of an object that the imagination may play freely upon. Thus the form of "criticism" is not "X is aesthetically good *because* a, b, and c," but "a, b, and c in X are the elements at which to direct aesthetic attention."

It seems then, that within the Kantian scheme of things aesthetic judgment is quite unlike other kinds of judgment, to the point where it can scarcely be thought of judgment at all, since it is not a kind of thinking but a kind of looking. This radical difference, in my view, should lead us to wonder whether the underlying philosophical project of trying to identify a distinctive "aesthetic" mental state is not mistaken. A legal judgment is to be distinguished from a scientific judgment not in terms of the kind of mental act it is, but in terms of the kind of object it judges. If we deploy the same concept of "judgment" in the case of the aesthetic then it seems that we will locate its distinctiveness in the nature of the object contemplated, and not in a special attitude of contemplation. On this view there is no identifiable psychological experience to be described as "aesthetic" any more than there is a "philosophical experience" which arises when the mind encounters a philosophical argument. Judgment is judgment. Not all objects are art objects. From this it follows, *pace* Kant, that aesthetic judgment is not a matter of the imagination playing freely where it will.

Aesthetic Engagement

It is time to return to the main issue, and show how the rejection of Kantianism bears upon aesthetic empiricism and the issue of fakes and ready-mades. The connection is to be made through what I earlier labeled "contexualism." Contextualism is the view that aesthetic appreciation and evaluation often requires us to locate a work of art in an art historical tradition. Only by so doing can we properly evaluate the originality and authenticity of a work of art and avoid the danger of acclaiming fakes. This means that aesthetic appreciation must go beyond contemplating the intrinsic properties of a work and make reference to extrinsic facts about the history of its creation. It must therefore reject the Kantian concept of free play of the imagination as an adequate account of aesthetic judgment.

But by the same token, ready-mades are to be rejected as works of art because it is precisely a Kantian-style aesthetic that the art of the ready-made assumes. Duchamp's *Fountain* ceased to be a joke or a whimsy when it came to be believed that we could take up towards it the same sort of attitude that we normally reserve for intentionally created artworks, that we could "contemplate" it aesthetically. The same idea is at work in John Cage's (silent) *4'33"* which invites us to give to the sounds around us the same sort of attention that we give to the deliberately produced sounds in the concert hall. (The fact that Cage wrote a piece entitled "Music for Duchamp" shows that he was aware of the affinity and meant to draw attention to it.) But the mistake is the same in both cases. Aesthetic judgment is a form of *engagement*, not just a form of *attention*, and the trouble with the sounds around us or the ready-made urinal is that there is nothing in them to engage us aesthetically.

Why not? This distinction between "engagement" and "attention" is plainly crucial. What it is meant to convey is the idea that aesthetic experience is a meeting of minds – the mind of the artist and the mind of the audience – and not the activity of a single mind "playing" upon an object. This means that an art work is the embodiment of aesthetic purpose, and the activity of aesthetic appreciation is one of both understanding and evaluating that purpose. Since neither the chance sounds around us, nor a purely functional urinal, has any intentional aesthetic purpose, neither will repay aesthetic attention, properly so called, even though either might be made to generate a certain measure of contemplative interest.

Aesthetic Cognitivism

This cognitive alternative to the Kantian conception has several important implications. For instance, it inevitably raises a doubt as to whether nature can be appreciated aesthetically, a subject much discussed of late, and it further implies that we can identify a specific aesthetic purpose among the various purposes human beings pursue. Nor have I done much more than assert its superiority in the light of the difficulties in Kantianism briefly alluded to. But these are issues that must remain unexplored here.

The position we have arrived at is this. Contextualism explains why the rejection of fakes makes sense, and in its turn this seems to imply the falsehood of aesthetic empiricism. But if aesthetic empiricism is indeed false, there appears to be no ground for rejecting ready-mades as art. The consequence is that the inclination many people have to reject both fakes and ready-mades as aesthetically worthless is inconsistent. When it comes to fakes and ready-mades the most coherent position seems to be that of the contemporary artworld – that fakes are to be rejected but ready-mades can be regarded as works of art. Upon further analysis, however, it emerges that the idea of the art of the ready-made relies upon a Kantian aesthetic which the belief in contextualism will also lead us to reject. In short, contextualism underwrites the public's inclination, and endorses the rejection of both fakes and ready-mades. Where though does this leave aesthetic empiricism?

The cognitivist alternative to Kantianism construes aesthetic appreciation and evaluation as a form of understanding rather than contemplation. When we stand in front of a Jackson Pollock action painting, or one of the extraordinary productions of Juan Miró, it is certainly possible to let our eye run along lines and over colors in a sort of aesthetic "savoring," something akin to tasting wine on the tongue. But such an attitude gives us no ground to ask, and no means of answering, what seems like an obvious critical question: what is Pollock or Miró about here? What is the meaning or the point of their paintings? At the same time, the aesthetic purposes we seek to understand must be realized *in* and not merely *through* the works of art. The appeal of Kantianism derives in part from an important insight incorporated within it – that aesthetic judgment is essentially sensual. This is why there is something odd about the idea of conceptual art, at least as some of its exponents interpret it. Conceptual art in many of its manifestations quickly implies the elimination of art since it seems to represent the medium as merely causally related to the message, a sort of psychological "prompt" that awakens thoughts in the viewer. This is the difference my distinction between "in" and "through" is intended to capture.

If we are to preserve the essentially sensual nature of art in what I have called the cognitive alternative to Kantianism, therefore, what is required is a conception of aesthetic understanding for which the sensual – the sound of the music, the line and color of the painting, the rhythm of the poetry, and so on – is ineliminable. There is much more to be said (and asked) about such a conception than would be strictly pertinent here. The point to be emphasized for present purposes is this. Kantianism construes aesthetic judgment as a form of contemplation, partly because it sees that aesthetic judgment applies to sensually rather than intellectually apprehended objects; the proper objects of aesthetic judgment are not concepts or propositions but sights, sounds, and so forth. Now the view I have called "contextualism" rejects the first of these contentions but not the second. It holds that aesthetic judgment is not a matter of "playing upon" a presented object, since there are occasions when it can and ought to involve appeal to facts extrinsic to the object. The relevance of such extrinsic facts, however, can still lie in their bearing upon the apprehension and evaluation of the sensual object, how we see it and hear it.

It is easiest to illustrate the point with an example. Suppose that towards the end of a piece of music a melody is repeated but with a different orchestration – in the woodwind rather than the strings, say. The second time round the music is different, but to apprehend the structure of the whole piece, it is essential that we hear the passage in the woodwind as a repeat of the earlier passage in the strings. To identify the second passage as a different version of the same melody is to hear it in the light of something that is strictly speaking extrinsic to it – the first version of the melody. No one, I imagine, would think this an odd claim to make; we do hear things differently when we hear them as repeats. Yet this example is simply another instance of "contextualism." As in the case of the van Meegeren, there is a sense in which the music does not change when placed in context, and another sense in which it does. Its being a repetition, however, is an aesthetically relevant property of the composition. And so too, I would say, the van Meegeren's being a pastiche of Vermeer is an aesthetically relevant property, and to apprehend it correctly, which is to say sensually, is to see (literally) it in light of this fact.

The same cannot be said about ready-mades. The move from the hardware store shelf to the gallery wall is a change of context, certainly, but it is not a context that has a bearing on the aesthetic purposes realized in the ready-made, for the simple reason that there are no aesthetic purposes realized in the ready-made; the purposes of its creator were entirely functional. Of course, it might be contended that Warhol (for example) had an aesthetic purpose when he put the Brillo box on display, and perhaps he had. But whatever these purposes they were not realized in the sensual properties of the box. They could not be, since Warhol had no part in giving it those properties. We can say, certainly, that its being put on display makes us see it in a different way, but even when this really is the case, it makes no aesthetic difference, and we are only inclined to think it does insofar as we assume an erroneous view of something called "aesthetic experience."

So aesthetic empiricism is defensible at least to this extent. If aesthetic judgment is comparable with other forms of judgment it must be inferential, and the basis of the inference is the sensual properties of the object. Such a contention, I have argued, is consistent with the contextualist objection to what we might call the naive version of aesthetic empiricism, which accepts too easily a Kantian assumption about aesthetic experience. In turn this implies that there is a distinction to be drawn between fakes and ready-mades such that, contrary to initial appearances, the attitude that rejects both fakes and ready-mades as artistically worthwhile objects can be made consistent. And the same conclusion implies that the contemporary artworld still has some work to do to show that ready-mades have a real claim on aesthetic attention.

Against Enlightened Empiricism

David Davies

The inaccessibility of much late modern art to otherwise competent receivers is arguably traceable to the fact that they bring to bear upon late modern works a broadly "empiricist" conception of artistic appreciation and artistic value. Works, it is assumed, are given for appreciation in an experiential encounter with a perceptible entity – a canvas on a gallery wall, for example, or the sequence of sounds produced by an orchestra – and artistic value is essentially a matter of the kind of experience elicited in such an experiential encounter. A number of arguments have been offered in the last two decades against naive or sophisticated versions of "aesthetic empiricism," as Currie termed the common-sense account of artistic appreciation. Opponents of aesthetic empiricism maintain that the properties rightly ascribable to artworks in our critical and appreciative practice are not confined to manifest properties, or properties that supervene on manifest properties, or properties that supervene on manifest properties and the category of art to which a work belongs. Rather, a work's artistic properties depend in part upon broader features of the art-historical context in which an artist was working. Thus only if our encounter with a manifest work is informed by a proper understanding of this context can we grasp the distinctive artistic properties of the work so manifested, and thereby come to properly appreciate it.

One might think that empiricist axiology of art stands or falls with empiricist epistemology of art. Certainly, the notions of artistic value and artistic appreciation seem to be intimately related. Artistic value is presumably the value that a receiver can determine through a proper appreciation of an artwork, and a proper appreciation is one that enables a receiver to determine a work's artistic value. However, empiricist axiology has proved more resilient than its epistemological counterpart. Indeed, we may detect such a residue of empiricism even in the writings of philosophers who have been among the most trenchant critics of empiricist theories of appreciation. Such philosophers presumably believe that taking appropriate account of the episte-mological relevance of provenance does not call into question the basic principle of empiricist axiology, that the artistic value of a work resides in qualities of the experience it elicits in an appropriately primed receiver. What is called for, it seems, is a *refinement*, but not a repudiation, of the empiricist view.

Following a suggestion by Matthew Kieran, I shall term this view, which combines an antiempiricist epistemology of art and an empiricist axiology of art, "enlightened empiricism." Proponents of enlightened empiricism include Malcolm Budd (1995), Matthew Kieran (2001), though his more recent work (2004, 2005) takes a turn away from this position, Roman Bonzon (2003), and (arguably) Jerrold Levinson (1996). Most recently, Gordon Graham espouses a form of enlightened empiricism in chapter 1 of this volume in challenging the artistic credentials of ready-mades such as Duchamp's *Fountain*. My principal purpose in this paper is to understand the attractions of enlightened empiricism, and to suggest why such attractions should nevertheless be resisted.

The Case Against an Empiricist Account of Artistic Properties

Before turning to this task, it will be useful to reflect on the kinds of arguments that have led many philosophers to repudiate empiricist conceptions of the properties of works that bear upon artistic appreciation, such a repudiation being one component of enlightened empiricism. Suppose (in the spirit of Currie 1989) we term those properties of an artwork that can be brought in support of a judgment on its artistic merits the "artistic properties" of the work. The distinctive feature of an empiricist epistemology of art, then, is the claim that a work's artistic properties are identical to, or intimately related to, what is "manifest" to receivers who engage in a direct experiential encounter with an instance of the work. Proponents of aesthetic empiricism so construed may indeed grant the relevance, for appreciation, of some nonmanifest features of a work – for example, the category of art to which a work belongs (Walton 1970) which may depend upon provenance. But they oppose the idea that artistic properties depend upon other facts about provenance – for example, facts about the art-historical context in which the work was created – not accessible in such an encounter. Two kinds of arguments have been offered against aesthetic empiricism. First, there are "indirect" arguments that appeal to hypothetical cases where differences in artistic *value* supposedly require differences in artistic properties not explicable in empiricist terms (e.g., Currie 1989: chapter 2). Second, there are "direct" arguments, that point to purported ascriptions of such nonempiricist artistic properties in our appreciative and critical discourse about art (e.g., Danto 1981, Binkley 1977).

In chapter 1 Graham comments on a paper of mine (Davies 2000) which, he rightly notes, identifies problems with indirect antiempiricist arguments, and, he further claims, endorses the following "direct" argument against aesthetic empiricism: since we reject fakes and accept ready-mades, the actual practice of the artworld shows aesthetic empiricism to be false. Such an argument, he maintains, effectively begs the question since, if aesthetic empiricism is true, then the acceptance of ready-mades as art is mistaken. I agree that such an argument would be seriously flawed. However

(1) considerations raised later in Graham's paper undermine the idea that the argument begs the question against the empiricist, and (2) I did not in fact mean to offer such an argument in the paper cited, although I grant that my argument might be read in the way Graham reads it. First, as he goes on to point out, one can defend the artistic enfranchisement of ready-mades if one adheres to a Kantian aesthetic according to which the appreciation of artworks is a matter of adopting a particular kind of contemplative attitude towards an object and thereby being moved to a distinctive kind of approval of that object. Since the Kantian aesthetic seems perfectly compatible with an aesthetic empiricist conception of a work's artistic properties, a proponent of aesthetic empiricism who also subscribes to the Kantian aesthetic can accept ready-mades as legitimate art. (For reasons I shall come to at the end of this chapter, I think this would misconstrue what artistic appreciation of a ready-made involves, but this doesn't bear on the present point.)

Second, the kind of direct argument that I tentatively endorsed does not assume that whatever is accepted as art by the artworld is thereby art. (In chapter 3 of Davies 2004, I offer what I think is a more satisfactory argument against aesthetic empiricism.) It depends, rather, upon a methodological assumption that I termed the "critical practice constraint" (or, in Davies 2004, the "pragmatic principle"). This principle holds the ontology of art accountable to the epistemology of art by making both answerable, *not* to our actual artistic practice, but to something like a Rawlsian codification of that practice that seeks a reflective equilibrium between critical judgments made and a philosophical representation of the principles that govern those judgments. While these aspects of the critical practice constraint are only implicit in the argument of Davies 2000, I have spelled out and defended this constraint in much greater detail elsewhere (most recently in chapter 1 of Davies 2004). Two things bear noting here, however. First, for the direct argument against aesthetic empiricism as I understand it, only through such a process of rational reflection on our artistic practice does the *acceptance* of works such as ready-mades bear upon their *acceptability* as works, and upon more general issues in the philosophy of art. Second, what matters are the practices and judgments of those involved, in a broad sense, in the relevant artistic community. These practices and judgments can be challenged by rational reflection of the sort just noted, but *not* by the judgments of the "man in the street" unless he belongs to the relevant community. The underlying intuition, here, is that "work of art," "artistic appreciation," and "artistic value," in the sense in which these terms interest us as philosophers of art, are *not* part of the ordinary vocabulary of competent speakers of a natural language, but terms that get their sense through a distinctive set of practices, with a particular tradition, and a distinctive discourse employed by those who broadly participate in those practices. As Danto long ago argued (1964), to see something as art requires, in this sense of the term, an artworld.

In fact, direct arguments against aesthetic empiricism of the sort described closely resemble the argument Graham himself presents for a contextualist alternative to aesthetic empiricism. Rational reflection on the kinds of judgments made by informed participants in artistic practices identify properties, cited in discussions of a work's artistic merits, that seem to depend upon features of provenance inadmissible on empiricist grounds. Warhol's *Brillo Boxes*, as discussed by Danto (1981), possess such properties, but, interestingly, so do more standard works such as those found in

Danto's gallery of perceptually indistinguishable but artistically very different "red rectangles." This places the burden of proof on the aesthetic empiricist to account for these features of our practice, either by showing how the relevant properties can be understood in empiricist terms, or by arguing that, on rational reflection, we are justified in disqualifying our practice in this respect. Barring a discharging of this burden of proof, the cited features of practice count as anomalies for aesthetic empiricism.

How to be an Enlightened Empiricist

I shall henceforth assume for present purposes that contextualist objections defeat an aesthetic empiricist conception of artistic properties. This is common ground between enlightened empiricists and myself. The question, then, is whether empiricist axiology can be maintained in the face of this conclusion. In order to answer this question, we must first clarify how empiricist axiology of art conceives the experiences that are supposed to enter into determining artistic value, and how their bearing on artistic value is to be understood.

In its simplest form, the idea behind empiricist axiology of art is that the value of an artwork resides in the experiences it elicits in the receiver. A crude form of empiricist axiology might take account only of experiences elicited directly in a perceptual encounter with a work. The view becomes more plausible, however, if we include not only those experiences directly elicited in such an encounter, but also those exercises of the imagination prompted by that encounter. As it stands, however, this characterization is still inadequate. For it is surely not the case that *all* of the experiences elicited through imaginative engagement with an instance of a work bear upon its artistic value. Standing in front of a painting, an art thief may experience great pleasure as a result of imagining just how he or she might be able to remove the painting from the gallery and sell it to a collector, but this clearly does not reflect upon the artistic value of the work. To clarify which experiences are relevant to the artistic value of a work, we will need to appeal to something like the very slippery Kantian notion of a "disinterested" response. We will also have to tie the work to the experience in an intimate manner to avoid a purely instrumental conception of artistic value. It would surely be unacceptable to maintain that artistic value consists in some *detachable* experience elicited by a work, which we could imagine being elicited in other ways. The experiences must be properly grounded in experienced qualities of the work, and they must be inseparable from engagement with the work so that a proper characterization of the experience in question cannot be given without referring to details of the work. (See Budd 1995 and Kieran 2001 for good discussions of these issues.)

We may also ask how a work's eliciting certain kinds of experiences can confer *value* upon the work. If the experiences are those directly elicited in a perceptual encounter with an instance of a work, then it might be argued that the value-conferring experiences are elicitings of an inherently valuable "aesthetic emotion" (Bell 1914). If, however, one's empiricist axiology also embraces those exercises of the imagination prompted by an encounter with an instance of a work, one is more likely to hold that the experiences elicited by works are valuable in a number of different ways bearing upon the artistic value of the works themselves. Kieran and Levinson each take such a line. Kieran, while acknowledging the importance of the purely "aesthetic" response to a work, argues that it is often hard to distinguish this from other valued features of the experiences elicited by works – for example, their emotional depth or the kinds of cognitive understanding they afford (2001: 220). In the case of representational and narrative works, what matters is that the imaginative experience is not only aesthetically appealing but also enlightens and deepens our understanding of the kinds of characters and states of affairs represented.

A similar pluralism is espoused by Levinson (1996). Examining the view that artistic value is a matter of the enduring pleasures to be found in active engagements with works, he cautions that the experiences engendered by artworks have value for us not merely in virtue of their being pleasurable or yielding some other immediately affective reward. Rather, they may be intrinsically valuable

> because one's cognitive faculties are notably exercised or enlarged; because one's eyes or ears are opened to certain spatial and temporal possibilities; because one is enabled to explore unusual realms of emotion; because one's consciousness is integrated to a degree out of the ordinary; because one is afforded a distinctive feeling of freedom or transcendence; because certain moral truths are made manifest to one in concrete dress; or because one is provided insight, in one way or another, into human nature. (Levinson 1996: 18–19)

It is indisputable, I think, that these sorts of cognitive and affective values are among the things for which we value works of art, and that the imaginative experiences elicited in receivers in their encounters with instances of works – objects in galleries, performances of musical and theatrical works, films projected in auditoria, copies of literary works – are crucial to the realization and appreciation of those values. What is distinctive of empiricist axiology, however, is the claim that artistic value is to be *equated* with the value that resides in such imaginative experiences. It is this claim that may seem difficult to reconcile with the repudiation of empiricist epistemology of art. If the appreciation of artworks requires that we take account of the history of making of the artistic vehicle with which we engage in our encounter with an instance of a work, why should we think that the only sort of artistic value properly ascribed to works in our appreciation of them is empiricist in nature? Our first question, therefore, is how enlightened empiricists achieve such a reconciliation of nonempiricist epistemology and empiricist axiology.

The key to being an enlightened empiricist lies in a particular way of understanding the case against empiricist epistemology of art sketched above. Consider, for example, Levinson, who argues from the rejection of an empiricist epistemology of art to an ontology of art that views features of provenance as partly constitutive of the artwork – musical works and literary works being not structure-types but structure types as indicated under specified circumstances. On such an account, empiricist epistemology is flawed because it fails to take account of the manner in which the history of making of a given artistic vehicle partly determines *properties of the appreciable object or structure* that results from the artist's activity – what is represented or expressed, for example. If one wishes to identify the work with an object or structure *as specified in a particular context*, knowledge of features of provenance is necessary for the proper appreciation of works because provenance determines salient features of that object or structure.

But if this is how we understand the argument against empiricist epistemology of art, then there is no reason to question the basic empiricist axiological thesis that the value of a work is a function of the experiences elicited in a receiver. We need only refine this thesis to make explicit the requirement that the receiver take account of those properties of the product of the artist's activity that are not given in an uninformed encounter with the manifest work, but that require knowledge of provenance. Levinson, for example, addressing the idea that the value of an artwork is a function of the qualities of the imaginative experiences it engenders in receivers, stresses that

> the pleasure proper to an object as art is one that is fully cognisant of the background from which a work emerges, the process whereby it came to have the exact shape that it does, the challenges inherent in the medium and material employed, the problems with which the work is wrestling, and so on. The proper pleasure of art is an *informed* pleasure, and understands that its object – unlike the beauties of nature – is an artifact, has a history, and represents something done and achieved. (Levinson 1996: 16–17; see also Kieran 2001: 217)

And Graham, granting the contextualist case against aesthetic empiricism, reconciles this with the claim that the proper objects of aesthetic judgments are "sights, sounds, and so forth" by maintaining that the relevance for aesthetic judgments of the extrinsic facts to which the contextualist draws attention lies in "their bearing upon the apprehension and evaluation of the sensual object, how we see it or hear it."

Why Not to be an Enlightened Empiricist

There is no denying the intuitive appeal of enlightened empiricism. On the one hand, in offering a broad range of affective and cognitive values to be located in the experiences elicited by artworks, it promises to accommodate the diversity of artistic values that we ascribe to the works themselves. On the other hand, the "enlightened" nature of the empiricism ensures that the works to which such values are ascribed are properly contextualized. Even for such an enlightened empiricism, however, all artistic value must ultimately reside in characteristics of the experiences elicited in receivers in a suitably informed engagement with an instance of a work. This is the sense in which enlightened empiricism still comprises an *empiricist* theory of artistic value. Thus it is open to challenge if there are factors that enter into our assessments of artistic value that are not reducible to the experienced effects of works. Reflection on some examples provides us with the basis for such a challenge.

Consider, first, Kenneth Clark's account, in his book *Looking at Pictures*, of Turner's *Snowstorm*. Clark maintains that, whereas in earlier attempts to represent the power of nature Turner relied on design and composition, in *Snowstorm*,

> the dramatic effect of light is not achieved by contrast of tone . . . but by a most subtle alternation of colour. As a result, oil paint achieves a new consistency, an iridescence,

which is more like that of some living thing . . . than a painted simulacrum. The surface of a late Turner is made up of gradations so fine and flecks of colour so inexplicable that we are reminded, whatever the subject, of flowers and sunset skies. (Clark 1960: 146)

It is not implausible to think that the artistic values of the painting to which Clark alludes could be captured by the enlightened empiricist analysis. But Clark continues: "to substitute colour for tone as a means of observing enlightened space could not be achieved by mere observation: it was a major feat of pictorial intelligence and involved Turner in a long struggle," a struggle involving years of "experiments" (p. 146). Turner's *Snowstorm* represents "a major feat of pictorial intelligence" because of what was involved in articulating a particular artistic content by finding novel ways in which to employ the physical medium of oil paint to realize certain artistic aims.

If we think that the artistic value of Turner's painting is at least in part a matter of its involving such a "major feat of pictorial intelligence," is it plausible to say that this value resides in features of the imaginative experience elicited in us when we contemplate the picture in light of what Clark has told us? It is certainly conceivable that my "informed" experience differs in certain respects from my relatively "uninformed" experience. But surely this is because I am now aware of a value that the picture has. The difference in experience is to be explained in terms of a *prior recognition* of a value ascribable to the work. This value does not itself consist in the difference in experience, as the enlightened empiricist must say, but itself accounts for the difference in experience. And even if the informed experience were to be identical, qua imaginative experience, to the uninformed experience, this would not affect the value rightly ascribable to the work in virtue of what Turner achieved in virtue of his experimentally based innovations in the use of the medium for artistic ends.

A similar example is the "staining" technique discovered by Morris Louis, as described by Clement Greenberg: "Louis spills his paint on unsized and unprimed cotton duck canvas, leaving the pigment almost everywhere thin enough, no matter how many different veils of it are superimposed, for the eye to sense the threadedness and wovenness of the fabric underneath" (Greenberg 1960: 28). In exploiting new materials in this way, Louis was able to produce canvases described by Edward Lucie-Smith as "veils of shifting hue and tone: there is no feeling that the various colour configurations have been drawn with a brush" (1976: 106). Clearly, again, the enlightened empiricist has no trouble accounting for artistic values that are a function of the imaginative experiences elicited by the observable features of the paintings to which Lucie-Smith alludes. But, as with the preceding example, it is surely not the case that any artistic value ascribable to the work in virtue of Louis's ingenious exploitation of novel resources is a function of the imaginative experience elicited in us when we contemplate the canvas in light of what we know about its history of making. Again, it seems that any difference in our imaginative experience does not ground, but is grounded in, a recognized difference in artistic value.

As a third example, consider Michael Nyman's score to Peter Greenaway's film *Drowning by Numbers*, which Nyman explicitly acknowledges to be a development of a number of passages in the slow movement of one of Mozart's *Sinfonia Concertante*.

David Davies

To the uninformed ear, the relevant passages in the two works sound very similar and might be expected to elicit similar imaginative experiences bearing on the artistic values of the works. To the informed ear, the works manifest very different valuable qualities, however, in part because one of the things one listens for in Nyman's piece is the way in which he has used the piece by Mozart as a vehicle for articulating a very different kind of artistic content. But the different artistic values ascribable to the two works surely do not reside solely in the different experiences elicited in the informed receiver who listens to performances of the works. Rather, much of what we value in Mozart's piece – the compositional skills and structural sensitivities upon which he drew – informs our enlightened listening, as a value of which we are cognitively aware, while a recognition of the different postmodernist values ascribable to Nyman's work are again things that we bring to our listening experience rather than derive from it.

Finally, consider a case that Graham discusses, van Meegeren's *Disciples at Emmaus*. As Graham rightly notes, one virtue of rejecting an empiricist epistemology of art and admitting the relevance of provenance to the appreciation of works is that we can explain why our assessment of this canvas changes when we take it to be the work of a twentieth-century journeyman painter rather than the work of Vermeer. But the difference between the value ascribed to the work when attributed to Vermeer, and the value ascribed to the work when attributed to van Meegeren, is surely *not* grounded in the different experiences elicited in us, as receivers, when our perceptual engagements with the canvas are "informed" first by one piece of information about provenance and then by the other. That our experiences differ *reflects* the value we find in the work on each occasion. It isn't the *ground* of that difference in value.

Relatedly, if recent claims about the use of optical devices such as the *camera obscura* by Vermeer and other artists are to have any bearing on the artistic values ascribable to the paintings they produced by such means, that bearing is surely not entirely mediated by the different imaginative experiences elicited in viewers who do or do not accept the sort of case presented by writers such as Steadman (2001) and Hockney (2001). If, to use an example of Hockney's, we conclude that the precise rendering of perspective in the representation of a highly complex chandelier in van Eyck's *Arnolfini Marriage* is not the result of astonishing skill in draftsmanship but of a more mechanical technique employing optical devices, this may affect some of the value judgments that we make with respect to the painting, but this change in assessment of artistic value is not exhaustively, or even primarily, to be explained in terms of the different imaginative experiences elicited in us when we come to believe Hockney's account of how the painting was produced.

A recent paper (Sharpe 2000) might be thought to offer a similar challenge to enlightened empiricism. However, my arguments differ from Sharpe's in two crucial respects. First, he takes the intrinsic value of artistic experience that, for the empiricist, determines artistic value, to reside in *affective* qualities of that experience, its yielding "pleasure" of some kind for the receiver. But, as the passage from Levinson (1996: 18–19) cited earlier clearly indicates, the empiricist may hold that the intrinsic value of artistic experience involves both cognitive and affective dimensions of that experience. Secondly, Sharpe argues that, in clarifying *which* experiences determine artistic value, the empiricist must beg the question by defining "appropriate reception" in terms of a grasping of *objective properties* of the work. But this is not, in itself, a problem, for the empiricist may insist that artistic value resides in qualities of the experiences elicited by these objective properties. My own argument, on the other hand, maintains that the experiences elicited by artworks may involve a grasping of artistic *values* that the work is taken to possess independently of those experiences.

I said earlier that enlightened empiricism follows from a particular way of understanding the argument against empiricist epistemology. For enlightened empiricists, the problem with empiricist epistemology is that it fails to take adequate account of the role that a history of making plays in determining properties of the object or structure specified by the artist. But there is another way of understanding the antiempiricist argument, upon which I have tacitly drawn in setting out the foregoing examples. What reflection on our critical and appreciative practice demonstrates, it can be argued (e.g., Dutton 1979, Currie 1989, Davies 2004), is that the object of critical appreciation is not merely the manifest or contextualized properties of the product of the artist's endeavors per se, but rather the artist's *achievement* in producing such a product. It is because we cannot determine the nature of an artist's achievement without referring the manifest work to a history of making that the empiricist account of artistic appreciation is mistaken.

If one's critique of empiricist epistemology takes this line, however, enlightened empiricism is no longer an attractive option. For, on this way of viewing things, provenance bears upon the appreciation of works not only because it partly determines salient properties of a specified object or structure, but also because knowledge of provenance is essential if we are to grasp *what the artist has done* in bringing such an object or structure into existence. In appreciating a work, we appreciate a particular performance or doing on the part of an agent. In the examples discussed above, it is such doings on the part of Turner, Louis, Mozart, Nyman, Vermeer, van Meegeren, and van Eyck that enter significantly into the artistic value of their works. Differences in elicited experiences, in such cases, are the result of acknowledged differences in ascribed achievements.

Two Empiricist Counterarguments

How might the enlightened empiricist respond to this sort of argument? One strategy is to argue that such assessments of the artist's achievement are not rightly brought to bear in determining the artistic value of works. The *enlightened* empiricist is unlikely to find this response attractive in its traditional empiricist garb, where it involves an appeal to the distinction between "artistic value" and "art-historical value." But another empiricist line of argument has found favor with at least some enlightened empiricists. This line of reasoning is to be found in Alfred Lessing's "empiricist" treatment of forgeries. Lessing argues that the "originality" which we ascribe to *The Disciples at Emmaus* understood as Vermeer's work, but not to *The Disciples at Emmaus* understood as by van Meegeren, is not something that would confer an artistic value on the former that is lacking in the latter. Originality is not an artistic value distinct from the sorts of aesthetic merit celebrated by the empiricist. Rather, whatever value originality has for us as lovers of art is parasitical upon our proper concern with aesthetic merit: "We must not forget that the search for originality is, or ought to be, but the means to an end. That end is, presumably, the production of aesthetically valuable or beautiful works of art." We value originality only because, without it, "the possibilities for the creation of aesthetically pleasing works of art would soon be exhausted" (Lessing 1995: 20).

The enlightened empiricist can attempt a similar line of defense, holding that we value artistic achievements of the sort canvassed in the above examples only insofar as they enhance the possibilities for the kinds of valuable experiences comprised by the enlightened empiricist axiology of art. Levinson's status as an enlightened empiricist depends upon whether one reads the following passage as an expression of such a defense, or as an attempt to distance himself from empiricism. (Levinson attempts to distance himself from empiricism in more recent papers, in particular in his discussion of "problem-solving value" and "originality-value" (1998: 97–8).) Considering the claim that "an art work is valuable, ultimately, only insofar as *experience* of it is in some way worthwhile," he comments in a footnote that

> Even this may be unduly restrictive. Artworks may be valuable to us artistically in ways that go beyond their value in experience to us, strictly speaking. Part of an artwork's value might reside in its art-historical relations to other artworks, e.g. ones of anticipation, or originality, or influence, independent of the value of experiencing the work in the appropriate manner. In other words, part of a work's value as art may consist in how the work is connected to an important artistic tradition. However, it will remain true that the value of such traditions themselves – what we might call *cultural value* – is not ultimately explicable except in terms of the enrichment of human experience. (Levinson 1996: 12)

Matthew Kieran has suggested a similar defense of enlightened empiricism (in private correspondence).

This line of reasoning is open to a number of different responses. First, we might question whether all of the "achievement properties" cited in the above examples are matters of "cultural value" in Levinson's sense. It is far from apparent, for example, that the value we ascribe to Turner's *Snowstorm* in virtue of his "feat of pictorial intelligence," or the value we ascribe to Louis's works in virtue of his innovative painting techniques, are values that stem from the contributions that each painter made to a developing tradition that has served to enrich human experience. In neither case is the innovation one that has spawned a "school" or "tradition" of other painters whose works have realized the sorts of experiential values proposed by the enlightened empiricists.

Second, if it is said that in the Turner and Louis cases the "experiential" payoff of the artistic achievement is to be found in the very works themselves – the paintings by Turner and Louis where the innovations yield valuable experiences for receivers of the works – it is not obvious that even this must be the case in order for a work to have artistic value in virtue of what was done by the artist. Certain early twentieth-century "experiments" in performance, such as the "bruitism" of Marinetti and Russolo (see Goldberg 2001: chap. 1), possess neither cultural value, in Levinson's sense, nor obvious merit through directly enriching human experience. Yet what was done by the artists at this time has genuine artistic interest, of the same sort as the interest we take in those artistic doings that do have experiential value.

Third, and most important, even if it be granted that the artistic value that resides in what an artist does or achieves is always ultimately accountable to the ways in which artworks can "enrich human experience" through the various channels canvassed earlier, this will not save enlightened empiricism. For the artistic value ascribable to a work in virtue of what an artist has done in the sorts of case considered above is in no way a function of the experiences elicited in encounters with instances of that *particular* work. As argued earlier, the dependence, if any, in such cases runs in the opposite direction: it is through our recognition of the artistic value of what was done that we come to experience the work differently.

Another possible defense of enlightened empiricism might maintain that all judgments of artistic value depend upon the experiences elicited in us by works, because all such judgments involve the *projecting* of value onto the works as a result of such experiences. To say that a work has a particular artistic value is just to say that we are disposed to respond to it, or be affected by it, in certain ways. There are no artistic values "in the world" to which our judgments are accountable, on such a view.

The first question we might ask, of one who offered such an argument, is whether what is being proposed is a general antirealism or quasi-realism about values. For example, does the same apply to claims about scientific or other kinds of human achievements? If so, then we might be relatively unperturbed by the claim that, in ascribing value to Turner's *Snowstorm* on the basis of what Turner achieved, we are not discovering an independent value in the world but merely projecting our own response onto the work. If the value ascribed to Turner's work is no less objective than the value we ascribe to the scientific work of Einstein, we can perhaps rest happy with that conclusion.

More significantly, philosophical debates about the objectivity of values are largely orthogonal to the debates that currently concern us between empiricist and non-empiricist theories of artistic value. For the enlightened empiricist's claim is that artistic value is dependent *in a very specific way* upon our responses to works. More specifically, the artistic value of a work is supposedly entirely reducible to features of the imaginative experiences elicited in receivers in their engagements with instances of that work. The antiempiricist is one who denies this thesis, and maintains that at least some elements that go into artistic value are not so reducible. Such elements – the examples cited are "achievement properties" of works – are not reducible to differences in such imaginative experiences, but, rather, can be appealed to in explaining some such differences. The judgment that a particular work involves an artistically valuable achievement is, so the antiempiricist claims, something that is brought to our imaginative experience of a work, not something derived from it. But this leaves open the status of this judgment concerning the value of the achievement. There is no reason to rule out an explanation of this judgment in response-dependent or projectivist terms. All we rule out is that the "response" in terms of which it is to be elucidated is the imaginative experience elicited by the work.

David Davies

Reflections on Ready-mades

I began this chapter by suggesting that commitment to an empiricist conception of art presents an obstacle to properly appreciating much late modern art. It might seem appropriate, then, to conclude by bringing the lessons drawn from the discussion of enlightened empiricism to bear upon the sorts of modern artworks – in particular ready-mades – whose status as art is called into question by Graham. However Graham's argument in fact requires only a "minimal" kind of empiricist axiological premiss, one not called into question by my antiempiricist arguments. For his charge is that ready-mades are *incapable* of having the sort of experiential value celebrated by empiricists, and this can be brought against the artistic pretensions of ready-mades as long as we grant that an artwork must have, or be in principle capable of having, *some* value grounded in the imaginative experiences elicited in a direct experiential encounter with one of its instances. His contention is that, by definition, ready-mades cannot be valued in this way. So, even if we grant that the sorts of artistic values countenanced by the enlightened empiricist do not exhaust the modes of artistic value, we can artistically disenfranchise the ready-made as long as the capacity to possess such values is a *necessary* condition for being an artwork.

We may paraphrase Graham's argument as follows. The artistic pretensions of ready-mades are grounded in the idea that, by transporting a mass-produced object into a gallery, we make it available for the sort of contemplative attention that, on a Kantian aesthetic, is the basis for aesthetic judgments on the merits of artworks. But aesthetic judgments, whereby the artistic merits of artworks are assessed, should be viewed not as merely contemplative but as cognitive, requiring not merely attention to but also engagement with the essentially sensual entity that is an instance of a work. Engagement is to be understood as involving not just attention to the sensual properties of such an instance, but attention informed by a grasp of the aesthetic purposes realized in that instance. Since a ready-made is an object whose creator had merely functional purposes, however, no aesthetic purposes of the person exhibiting the ready-made can be realized in the sensuous properties of the object, so the work cannot be engaged aesthetically, and cannot be a subject of aesthetic judgment.

A full response to this argument goes beyond the confines of this chapter. Let me suggest, however, what form such a response should take. Take, first, the claim that the artistic pretensions of ready-mades reside in their capacity, when transported into the artworld, to function as objects of aesthetic contemplation. This view, while it has its defenders, is optional at best. We do indeed find such a view expressed by Clement Greenberg, who takes Duchamp's lesson to be "that anything that can be experienced at all can be experienced aesthetically, and that anything that can be experienced aesthetically can also be experienced as art" (1971: 19), and by Monroe Beardsley (1983: 25), who takes the inability of ready-mades to connect with "the aesthetic interest" as the reason why they are not artworks but merely art criticism pursued by nonstandard means. But this reading of ready-mades has been strongly denied by both philosophers of art (e.g., Danto 1981, Binkley 1976) and historians of art (de Duve 1996), and is surely not applicable to later artists such as Warhol. A central contention of Danto (1981) is that the "transfiguration" of commonplace objects when they are exhibited as artworks involves their being used for artistic purposes in virtue of which they acquire representational and expressive properties in no way reducible to the manifest properties they share with their untransfigured counterparts.

Second, the identification of artistic properties and artistic value with *aesthetic* properties and value, conceived as properties embodied in the sensuality of art-objects to which we attend either in a Kantian fashion or in the manner proposed by Graham, has been a principal target of contemporary artists, as noted by philosophical commentators (e.g., Binkley 1977). To appeal to such an identification in arguing against the artistic pretensions of late modernism therefore requires at least argument. While we may indeed wish to uphold the idea that there is an essential aesthetic component to the functioning of artworks, it seems more promising to try to rethink that component in something like the manner proposed by Goodman in his talk of "symptoms of the aesthetic" that are characteristics of the way an entity functions as a symbol, broadly construed (Goodman 1978: 67–8).

Finally, it may be necessary to rethink the common-sense idea that ready-mades, as works, are properly identified with the mass-produced objects exhibited in galleries. For, as Graham notes with respect to Warhol, there seems clearly to be an artistic purpose that underlies the exhibiting of the mass-produced object, and while that artistic purpose is not realized in any manipulative activities responsible for the manifest properties of that object, it is realized in the action of doing something with the object. If the action itself serves to realize that purpose in a manner that functions aesthetically in something like Goodman's sense, then we may find it more illuminating to think of the focus of our appreciative engagement as an action performed with an object rather than the object per se. This suggests an analogy between ready-mades, as works, and other artworks that use readymade material to realize artistic purposes – for example, the collages of synthetic cubism contemporaneous with Duchamp's ready-mades and the later constructions of Eva Hesse.

These remarks obviously call for much fuller elaboration and defense, something I have attempted elsewhere (Davies 2004). But they suggest how we might sustain a minimalist empiricist axiological premiss of the sort suggested above while both accommodating late modernist art and repudiating the more thoroughgoing enlightened empiricism that was the target of earlier sections of this chapter.

Note

This chapter developed out of a very lively and enjoyable exchange of ideas with Matthew Kieran. I should also like to thank Berys Gaut and Jerry Levinson for helpful discussions of the issues in this chapter.

References for Chapters 1 and 2

Beardsley, M. (1983). "An Aesthetic Definition of Art." In H. Curtler (ed.), *What is Art?* (pp. 15–29). New York: Haven.

Bell, C. (1914). *Art.* London: Chatto and Windus.

Binkley, T. (1976). "Deciding about Art." In L. Aagard-Mogensen (ed.), *Culture and Art* (pp. 90–109). Atlantic Highlands, NJ: Humanities Press.

Binkley, T. (1977). "Piece: Contra Aesthetics." *Journal of Aesthetics and Art Criticism,* 35: 265–77.

Bonzon, R. (2003). "Fiction and Value." In D. M. Lopes and M. Kieran (eds.), *Imagination, Philosophy, and the Arts* (pp. 160–76). London: Routledge.

Budd, M. (1995). *Values of Art.* Harmondsworth, UK: Penguin.

Clark, K. (1960). *Looking at Pictures.* London: John Murray.

Currie, G. (1989). *An Ontology of Art.* New York: St Martin's Press.

Danto, A. (1964). "The Artworld." *Journal of Philosophy,* 61: 571–84.

Danto, A. (1981). *The Transfiguration of the Commonplace.* Cambridge, MA: Harvard University Press.

Davies, D. (2000). "Aesthetic Empiricism and the Philosophy of Art." *Synthesis Philosophica,* 15: 49–64.

Davies, D. (2004). *Art as Performance.* Oxford: Blackwell.

De Duve, T. (1996). *Kant after Duchamp.* Cambridge, MA: MIT Press.

Dutton, D. (1979). "Artistic Crimes: the Problem of Forgery in the Arts." *British Journal of Aesthetics,* 19: 304–14.

Goldberg, RoseLee (2001). *Performance Art,* revised and expanded edn. London: Thames and Hudson.

Goodman, N. (1978). *Ways of Worldmaking.* Indianapolis: Hackett.

Greenberg, C. (1960). "Louis and Noland." *Arts International,* 4: 26–9.

Greenberg, C. (1971). "Counter-avant-garde." *Arts International,* 15: 16–19.

Hockney, D. (2001). *Secret Knowledge.* London: Thames and Hudson.

Kant, I. ([1790] 2000). *Critique of the Power of Judgement,* ed. P. Guyer, trans. E. Matthews. Cambridge, UK: Cambridge University Press.

Kieran, M. (2001). "Value of Art." In B. Gaut and D. M. Lopes (eds.), *Routledge Companion to Aesthetics* (pp. 215–25). London: Routledge.

Kieran, M. (2004). *Revealing Art.* London: Routledge.

Kieran, M. (2005). "Value of Art." In B. Gaut and D. M. Lopes (eds.), *Routledge Companion to Aesthetics,* 2nd edn. London: Routledge.

Lessing, A. ([1965] 1995). "What is wrong with a forgery?" In A. Neill and A. Ridley (eds.), *Arguing About Art* (pp. 8–21). New York: McGraw-Hill.

Levinson, J. ([1992] 1996). "Pleasure and the Value of Works of Art." In J. Levinson (ed.), *The Pleasures of Aesthetics* (pp. 11–24). Ithaca, NY: Cornell.

Levinson, J. (1998). "Evaluating Music." In P. Alperson (ed.), *Musical Worlds* (pp. 93–107). College Park, PA: Penn State Press.

Lucie-Smith, E. (1976). *Late Modern.* New York: Praeger.

Sharpe, R. A. (2000). "The Empiricist Theory of Artistic Value." *Journal of Aesthetics and Art Criticism,* 58: 321–32.

Stalnaker, N. (2001). "Fakes and Forgeries". In B. Gaut and D. M. Lopes (eds.), *Routledge Companion to Aesthetics* (pp. 395–407). London: Routledge.

Steadman, P. (2001). *Vermeer's Camera.* New York: Oxford University Press.

Walton, K. (1970). "Categories of Art." *Philosophical Review,* 79: 334–67.

Werness, H. P. (1983). "Han van Meegeren *Fecit*." In D. Dutton (ed.), *The Forger's Art: Forgery and the Philosophy of Art* (pp. 1–57). Berkeley: University of California Press.

Further Reading for Chapters 1 and 2

Bowden, R. (1999). "What is Wrong with an Art Forgery?: an Anthropological Perspective." *Journal of Aesthetics and Art Criticism*, 57: 333–44.

Goodman, N. (1976). *Languages of Art*, 2nd edn., Chapter III. Indianapolis: Hackett.

Hoaglund, J. (1976) "Originality and Aesthetic Value." *British Journal of Aesthetics*, 16: 46–55.

Neill, A. and Ridley, A. (eds.). (2002). *Arguing about Art*, 2nd edn., Part 3. London: Routledge.

IN WHAT DOES TRUE BEAUTY CONSIST?

Beauty and Ugliness In and Out of Context

Marcia Muelder Eaton

I ask you to teach me properly what beauty is by itself, answering my question with the utmost precision you can attain.

(Socrates, in Plato, *Greater Hippias*, 286e)

Conflicting Intuitions

Like many of the most common words in any language, the words "beautiful" and "ugly" are used in a great variety of ways. They are employed to describe everything from seashores to mornings to symphonies to human bodies and actions to mathematical theorems and physics experiments. If someone describes all of these different things as "beautiful," is he or she claiming that there is some property that they all have in common? And if they are said to be "ugly" do they just lack whatever is it that beautiful things have, or do they have some other special feature that all and only ugly things have? Or suppose individuals use "beautiful" and "ugly" to say something about their own feelings and do not intend to ascribe some intrinsic properties to objects. Do they imply that there is something similar about the way they feel in the presence of particular flowers or some mornings or some pieces of music and so on that are said to be beautiful? Does "ugly" refer to a special negative feeling no matter what object is being criticized?

It is interesting, but puzzling, to consider many of the "sayings" in which the word "beauty" figures:

- Beauty is as beauty does.
- Beauty is in the eye of the beholder.
- Beauty is truth, truth beauty.
- Beauty is only skin deep.

- You can neither eat beauty nor make flannel out of it.
- Eyes can never see the heart's beauty.
- Beauty is its own excuse for being.
- Beauty provoketh thieves sooner than gold.
- A thing of beauty is a joy forever.

Readers undoubtedly can add items to this list. Which of these claims is true? What happens if "ugliness" is substituted for "beauty" in these sentences? If the meaning of "beauty" (or "ugliness") is the same in each statement then, obviously, not all of them can be true. Still each statement seems to make an important observation – to capture interesting, perhaps even essential, features of human experience.

With all due respect to Plato, I am inclined to think that it is philosophical folly to try to link "beauty" or "ugliness" to a single, precise definition or to attempt to restrict the number or kinds of jobs for which individuals use these words. Instead I shall try to point to some of the different directions in which we seem to feel pulled in the attempt to make aesthetic sense of the world and I shall argue that many, if not all, of the uses of "beautiful" and "ugly" depend upon connections these properties have to other features of the contexts in which they are employed.

The sayings I have listed above indicate some of the intuitions – conflicting as they are – that people have about beauty. Perhaps one of the most widespread attitudes is that expressed in "Beauty is in the eye of the beholder." We have all made judgments with which others disagree – find a French rococo vase garish that others exclaim with delight about, for example. Wherein lies the explanation for such discrepancies? "It's just a matter of taste" very quickly seems to lead to "There's no accounting for taste."

Other expressions that have made their way into standard repertoires of ordinary aesthetic conversation, for example "Beauty is truth" or "Eyes can never see the heart's beauty" or "A thing of beauty is a joy forever," seem to belie the intuition that what is beautiful depends wholly on an individual's personal response. Do we believe that a thing of beauty is a joy forever depending on who the beholder is? Truth, surely, is not in the eye of the beholder, nor is the inner beauty we find in the hearts of the pure in spirit the sort of thing we consider simply a matter of taste. Although there is no denying widespread disagreement about what is beautiful or ugly, there do seem to be some areas of agreement. How could anyone find a Monet watercolor painting ugly or cringe at the sound of The Three Tenors or look with contempt at a sunset? How could anyone delight in a garbage dump or a deformed frog or a choir singing off key?

Taking Beauty and Ugliness Out of Context

This dilemma – feeling on the one hand that beauty or ugliness is strictly a matter of personal preference and yet on the other hand feeling that all human beings must respond the same way to at least some sights and sounds – is hard, perhaps in the end impossible, to resolve. One of the most brilliant attempts was made by Immanuel Kant near the end of the eighteenth century (Kant [1790] 1997). His answer to the

Marcia Muelder Eaton

question, "How can one, with rational consistency, believe both that judgments about the beautiful are subjective and at the same time that they are universally true?" has had a profound influence on aesthetic theories ever since.

When I say, "Spinach is delicious," I am perfectly aware of the fact that I am saying only something about myself and, perhaps, about other people who, like me, respond to this vegetable with pleasure. I know that I am not making a universal claim about spinach for it is widely disliked. Kant correctly pointed out that "beautiful" does not work like "delicious," nor do we want it to. Terms describing personal preference do a quite different job from those used to attribute beauty (and at least some other aesthetic descriptions). Of course, when I say that a rose is beautiful or a composition chaotic or a waterfall sublime, I *am* saying something about my own personal response. But unlike my reports about my finding spinach delicious, when I use "beautiful" or "chaotic" or "sublime" I feel that somehow I am doing more than just making an autobiographical remark: I believe that I am saying something about the rose or composition or waterfall with which everyone will agree. But how can one have it both ways? How can I at one and the same time say something about my own personal pleasure or pain and yet make a general claim about the way the world is?

Kant proposed that judgments about what is beautiful are subjective in the sense that they say something about the subject judging (i.e., *me* when I say, "That rose is beautiful") and not something about the object (i.e., *that rose*), for we feel that the property beauty is in my experience, not in the object per se. An important part of the meaning of sentences containing the world "beautiful" is a statement about the pleasure felt by the person uttering the sentence. But unlike sentences containing terms like "delicious," whose meaning totally resides in reports about a subject's pleasure, the meaning and logic of beauty-sentences includes implications about how others will also respond. When I say, "That rose is beautiful" I expect that others will also take pleasure in the flower, and that expectation is, according to Kant, part of the very meaning of my utterance. We use the word "beauty" to do a special job, and its special meaning reflects this. Kant believed that we reserve the word "beautiful" to say things about how persons qua persons respond to certain things. Responses to spinach are the responses of a particular individual with a particular past, particular tastes, and so forth, and when someone says, "Spinach is delicious," the speaker and hearer both know the words "to me" are understood. But responding with pleasure to a beautiful rose is not like this. When someone utters, "That rose is beautiful," the words "to me" are not part of the meaning. All that seems to matter is the fact that one is a human being. Unlike the spinach case where one doesn't expect even widespread agreement, when I say something is beautiful, I expect universal agreement. I am saying something like this: "I am responding with pleasure and nothing about my pleasure is idiosyncratic, so everyone else ought to respond as I do." Thus Kant claimed that judgments about the beautiful are at one and the same time subjective and universal.

But when do we respond with the special sort of pleasure that Kant insists leads to our judging that something is beautiful? He answered that aesthetic pleasure is occasioned simply by what have come to be called "formal qualities" of things – colors, shapes, lines, and the relationships between these. And it is the mere apprehension of form that excites aesthetic pleasure. We respond to *how* something appears;

we don't care what something is, Kant thought, or who made it, or what it's made of, or when or where it was made. Aesthetic pleasure is felt immediately upon the perception of some things and is independent of any scientific beliefs or ethical attitudes that we may have or come to have. If the color and shape of a wallpaper design pleases me aesthetically, I don't care, for example, how much it costs, or whether it is a baroque or rococo design. If I am pleased by a flower as I walk through a forest, my pleasure in no way depends upon my knowing what species it is, whether or not it has medicinal powers, or even if it is real. I just feel pleasure, "period," – and realize that others will respond the same way.

Kant does recognize that sometimes concepts are involved when we have aesthetic pleasures, but he insists that these concepts do not "determine" our experiences. If I find a particular flower beautiful, I may judge that it is a beautiful rose, for instance. But it's being a *rose*, if my pleasure is aesthetic, is not the *cause* of the pleasure. That is, I do not like it because it is a rose but because the form pleases me. I would be equally pleased by the same form were the flower to belong to another species. And we are all free to play around with and enjoy applying other concepts – to think of the flower as a dancing maiden or bleeding heart or whatever might seem apt. Having this freedom is part of Kant's reason for insisting upon the indeterminacy of any concepts that play a role when we have aesthetic experiences. I can also be sure that individuals who do not know what kind of flower they are looking at or who apply other concepts will find it pleasing. The irrelevance of particular belief sets or moral attitudes is part of what accounts for my sense that everyone else ought to respond as I do. Kant, then, would have agreed wholeheartedly with several "sayings" about the beautiful, for example, beauty is in the eye of the beholder – but, he would add, in the eye of all beholders if in any at all – and with all of those old sayings that imply that beauty is its own excuse for being.

Kant's views have been extremely influential. For a large part of the twentieth century formalist critics in the Kantian tradition had the upper hand and many went even farther than Kant himself had in ruling out the relevance of particular concepts, beliefs, or moral values. Although Kant had himself distinguished between natural and artistic beauty, recognizing that part of the appreciation of art is responding to things as having been created by another human being, formalists extended his decontextualized views of beauty to art generally. "A poem should not mean/ But be," wrote the poet Archibald MacLeish in "Ars Poetica." The theorists Monroe Beardsley and W. K. Wimsatt called reference to artistic intentions or any other external information about works of art a "fallacy" (Wimsatt and Beardsley 1954). Roger Fry maintained that subject matter, for instance, is irrelevant to the beauty or ugliness of a work of art. "Rembrandt expressed his profoundest feelings just as well when he painted a carcass hanging up in a butcher's shop as when he painted the Crucifixion or his mistress," he wrote (Fry [1927] 1970: 297). Clive Bell insisted that, "To appreciate a work of art we need bring with us nothing but a sense of form and color and a knowledge of three-dimensional space" (Bell 1914: 25). In other words, nothing about the context of a work matters; a work's *aesthetic* value depended only on what one could directly perceive. Something like the following is at the heart of such formalistic theories of beauty:

Marcia Muelder Eaton

X is beautiful if and only if attention to intrinsic properties of X yields pleasurable perceptual experiences.

Many artists, critics, and aestheticians have taken such a position – but not everyone has agreed.

Putting Beauty and Ugliness Into Context

Writing about a century after Kant, at the end of the nineteenth century the famous novelist Leo Tolstoy worried that aesthetic value cannot be wholly explained in terms of pleasure, for so doing deprives art of much of its importance within communities (Tolstoy [1898] 1930). Confusing the value of art with pleasure is like confusing the value of food with pleasure, he wrote. Just as the genuine value of food lies in its nutritional capacities, so the genuine value of art lies in its power to nourish the souls of individuals and communities. Great art actually improves societies, he thought, and concentrating on formal properties alone can never have this effect. One might expect Tolstoy to agree with those who say, "Beauty is as beauty does." However, he feared that the tendency to associate beauty with pleasure precluded its being either a serious aesthetic or ethical concern.

Developments in the history of art also led many people to believe that beauty no longer played the only or even the most important role in aesthetics. Movements from abstract expressionism to dadaism led many critics to talk more about the importance of the arousal of human emotion or the workings of unconscious psychology than about pleasurable titillation. A work's being "moving" or "compelling" or just plain "interesting" mattered more than (or at least as much as) its being appealing. In the twentieth century, two horrific world wars and several more local but similarly brutal conflicts caused many artists to attempt to do "more" than just please their audiences. Some theorists went so far as to exclaim that beauty was "dead."

But at the end of the twentieth century more and more artists, critics, and aestheticians began to take renewed interest in beauty, and to argue that it is (or can be) relevant and that it does (or can) matter to the value of art and thus to art's importance in communities. Undeniably a strong formalist strain still exists in art and aesthetics, but increasingly as people turn again to investigating beauty they couch it in contextual terms. More writers share the view that beauty and ugliness, and their relevance to art, can only be understood and appreciated as a cultural or communal phenomenon. Explicit and implicit is the fear that failure to recognize this has had, and may continue to have, harmful consequences in the twenty-first century with respect to social, environmental, and political problems.

One area of aesthetics where contextualization of beauty has become particularly strong is environmental aesthetics. Our aesthetic preferences, many argue, are not and should not be construed as independent of scientific and moral beliefs and theories. That they *are* not independent is an empirical claim. That they *should not be* is an ethical claim. Both claims demand justification.

Kant, remember, thought that all that is necessary for feeling aesthetic pleasure is one's humanity. There is something about being a person per se that makes us delight in a particular rose or a waterfall. And it is hard to deny this. We have prototypical beauties and "uglies," roses and garbage dumps, for instance. But aesthetic prototypes also vary across cultures. Like ethical paradigms such as "Always tell the truth," or "Do not kill," aesthetic paradigms are shaped by particular histories, geography, economics, religion, and so forth. Some tastes must be acquired. They develop as we have more and more experience or change as one becomes more educated. In the absence of practice in reading, people often fail to "get" and hence to enjoy a complex poem or novel. Appreciating a fugue, for instance, requires considerable music training. Recently several aestheticians have argued that what and how much one knows plays a crucial role in the appreciation of nature as well.

Kant does recognize that tastes must be developed and refined – that our early judgments of taste are often "crude and uncouth" (Kant [1790] 1997: section 32). But he thinks refinement comes via exemplars, that we attend to those things that have "enjoyed the longest-lasting approval in the course of cultural progress." But he still insists that what we may learn in the process does not *determine* our experiences. What we know about a flower or a musical composition is not what accounts for the pleasure or pain we may feel when apprehending it.

Contextual theorists disagree. Sometimes at least, they insist, the pleasures of beauty or the pains of ugliness are determined by what one knows about the objects apprehended. Allen Carlson, for example, insists that we must adopt a *cognitive* model of nature appreciation, one that makes room for the role of knowledge as well as the role of a kind of unmediated pleasure of the sort Kant associated with beauty. Just as it is not possible to judge an epic as a *beautiful epic* unless one know what an epic is, so one cannot judge a particular natural environment as beautiful unless one knows what sort of environment it is that one is judging. It would be absurd to maintain that a landscape is ugly because there are so few trees if one is looking at a desert scene. Deserts have their own kind of beauty – and one realizes this only when one knows something about deserts. Indeed, the more one knows about deserts the more one is in a position to know whether this one is more or less beautiful than that one. Or if one knows that a species of plant or animal lives only under very special conditions, it is more likely that one will aesthetically appreciate that organism when one sees it. Carlson writes: "If to aesthetically appreciate art we have to have knowledge of artistic traditions and style within those traditions, to aesthetically appreciate nature we must have knowledge of the different environments of nature and of the systems and elements within those environments" (Carlson 1979: 273). As knowledge is acquired, judgments develop and change.

But one can go even further. Sometimes one's aesthetic pleasure or pain is the result of realizing that one is attending to a particular sort of thing, contextualists argue. Kant denies this. Some people think fur coats are ugly, not because they exhibit displeasing formal properties but precisely because they are what they are: coats made from the fur of animals. Or one may delight in landscapes that one believes sustainable – maintained via sound ecological practices – precisely because one is aware of this fact.

Several of the "sayings" with which we began this discussion suggest something general about beauty that has particular applications within environmental aesthetics, applications that cognitivists draw upon. "Beauty is only skin-deep," for instance,

Marcia Muelder Eaton

implies that one should guard against being seduced by things that are beautiful. What appeals to us aesthetically may not, this saying warns, turn out to be genuinely valuable. There are beautiful but evil people, elegant-looking but sloppily made cars or faucets, and so on. Another saying on this list, "Eyes can never see the heart's beauty," is, I think, closely related to the warning about the possibly shallow character of at least some beautiful-seeming things. An apparently beautiful person may turn out to be morally ugly. A person's or object's real value, these sayings assert, lie in something like true character or successful functioning in areas that really matter. Human beings are too easily taken in by a pretty face or a sleek design. The connotation of these sayings might be expressed in another way: there is a difference between *appearing* and really *being* beautiful or ugly. Particularly with respect to people, we are warned, what is seen by the eye should not be confused with what can be discovered by the heart. Cognitivists, of course, would say that what is seen by the eye should not be confused with what can be discovered by the mind. And, they would add, it can be dangerous to allow attitudes about what looks beautiful in nature to be the basis of environmental practice.

Above I referred to disagreements about the value of fur coats and ecologically sound landscapes. It is helpful to consider examples of what we might call "dangerous beauty" and "safe ugliness" in environmental practices and policies.

- Many people find large expanses of green, closely mown lawns quite beautiful. But maintaining such lawns requires fertilizers and herbicides that pollute groundwater, and the use of mowing machines that pollute the air.
- Most people are awed by the beauty of the huge statues that dot the coast of Easter Island. It turns out that getting the stones to these sites required cutting down so many trees (used to roll the stones) that within a generation the island was deforested and a thriving community was replaced by a destitute populace.
- Driving through the countryside one can't help but admire neat contour planting, which was established as a popular conservation practice in the early twentieth century. These fields are also considered visually appealing by most farmers. But like suburban yards, the practices required to maintain such rural landscapes (weed killers, fertilizers, huge machinery) often destroy the land.
- Burning forests endanger lives and often destroy the elegant homes of individuals who built in the forest in order to enjoy its beauties. But fires are a stage in the cycle of forest renewal; some seeds germinate, for instance, only when temperatures reach the very high levels that are reached during prolonged burning.
- Many people think that wetland areas are ugly swamps that smell bad and breed mosquitoes. But they are an invaluable means of filtering groundwater and sustaining a diversity of wildlife.

If one agrees that correctly judging nature or works of art depends upon whether one has the necessary and appropriate knowledge, it will then follow that one can be wrong about what one thinks is beautiful or ugly. Positive attitudes may turn into negative attitudes and vice versa. If I learn that a "swamp" provides valuable filtration and wildlife habitat I may come to see it as a lovely "wetland" or "water meadow."

When I consider the harmful effects of having a large green lawn I may begin to see it as a blight on the landscape rather than a jewel. When I fully understand its context, what I first took to be a lovely home may begin to become an eyesore.

It would be foolish to deny that the term "beauty" is often used to report on what individuals find immediately pleasing – that beauty is in the eye of whoever beholds something that causes them sensual pleasure. But cognitivists or, more generally, contextualists draw our attention to the fact that we also sometimes reserve the use of "beautiful" or "ugly" to describe experiences in which knowledge shapes and informs the pleasures or pains of perceptual experience. Here what is *really beautiful* is reserved for the experiences of informed observers, that is, experiencers whose hearts or minds are, as it were, in the right place. Cognitivists do not deny that sensory pleasure plays a core role in experiences of beauty, but they insist that knowledge plays a core role as well. Thus their theories of beauty take this form:

> X is beautiful if and only if attention to intrinsic properties of X yields pleasurable perceptual experiences in an informed observer who is observing X.

Obviously there are degrees or levels of informedness. But the fact is that at least sometimes as people's beliefs change so do their responses change, and this includes those pleasurable responses that are associated with the beautiful. Sometimes when one realizes that a particular practice is unhealthy for the environment one continues to enjoy its products. One may continue to take pleasure in looking at large, closely mown lawns, for instance, but decide that one must no longer have such a lawn oneself and even urge others to get rid of theirs. An individual might confess to longing for a "trophy house" in a forest but forego buying one because he or she realizes that such houses are not compatible with sound forest management practices. Similarly we may decide to support healthy environmental practices even if we don't particularly like the look of a swamp or burnt forest. Knowledge can and does affect *action*.

But knowledge also can change *response*. That is, when one learns that a practice is healthy one's perceptual pleasures may be increased. One may even go from finding an area ugly to finding it beautiful and vice versa. Joan Nassauer has found that suburban dwellers do change their minds about what is beautiful or ugly after being instructed about the consequences of certain landscaping practices. Using the technique of computer imaging, she has used photographs of streets displaying alternative strategies, for example, with different amounts of vegetation. When asked which of the scenes they prefer, most persons who live in midwestern American suburbs initially opt for a street scene in which there is mainly grass, with a few trees, short shrubs, some flowers, sharp contours, obvious curbing, smooth sidewalks. She then explains to groups that several of these features are environmentally unfriendly. Curb-lined streets, for instance, permit more rapid run-off of rainwater; thus fertilizers and herbicides used to keep lawns so green and uniform make their way more quickly into the groundwater than they would were curbs absent. She explains that lawn-mowers are among the most polluting machines ever invented and that exotic plants require excessive amounts of water. Nassauer has found that in groups with which she works, many individuals gradually begin to change their aesthetic preferences –

Marcia Muelder Eaton

they revise their prototypes of what counts as beautiful. As they learn more about sound ecological practices, they actually begin to see their own lawns as less attractive. They begin to find yards with less mown turf more visually appealing, come to prefer curbless streets, and so on (Nassauer 1988).

I am not claiming that everyone's attitudes about what counts as beautiful changes as they learn more about sound ecological practices. Different sorts of values weigh more or less heavily in different individuals. On some occasions economic concerns or religious beliefs or ecological worries may matter so much that questions about the beauty or ugliness of something matters very little. Being able to look out at a vast expanse of green lawn may override concern for groundwater. Some people say they don't want to know certain things. They consider it irrelevant or distracting to be told that an author was mean to his children or that a painter beat his models or that a composer was born in France. Similarly some people insist that they want to experience nature "unfettered by knowledge." The philosopher Ronald Moore told me about a date he had as a teenager when he invited a girl to walk with him in a forest. "All she wanted to do was to tell me the names of wildflowers," he complained. Now, questions about what Ron wanted to do aside, he asked whether too much naming can get in the way of communing aesthetically with nature. My answer is that something gets in the way if it prevents one's responding with pleasure to what one perceives. Naming does not necessarily have this effect. Indeed, many people experience heightened pleasure from knowing the names of plants and animals. Something like the pleasure of recognition adds to one's sensory pleasure and it is hard, usually impossible, I think, to separate these two sorts of pleasure and insist that only the latter is genuinely aesthetic. Further, there are times when one is likely to have the pleasure of seeing only when one knows what to look for. Suppose one knows that the flower *calypso bulbosa* grows only in some moist soils where one also finds stands of old white cedar trees. I suggest that knowing that one is in such a biosystem will cause one to look for the flower; lack of this knowledge may cause one to miss the bloom altogether. Put simply, the more you know, the more you see, and the more you see the more you feel. The less you know, the greater the chance that you will not see the very things that would cause sensory pleasure were you to perceive them. And absence of certain bits of information, as we have seen, can lead to instilling aesthetic preferences that are actually harmful. Undeniably it is possible to enjoy nature without knowing the names of species or soil types or climatic conditions, and so forth. But being informed can and does heighten enjoyment.

Limiting Cognitive Contextualism

Some cognitivists argue that it follows from their position that nothing in nature can be ugly. Allen Carlson writes that natural environments have "mainly positive aesthetic qualities . . . All virgin nature . . . is essentially aesthetically good" (Carlson 1984: 5). From understanding, appreciation follows. So how could there be anything in nature that is ugly? Strong cognitivists admit that some landscapes – slag heaps or parking lots – are ugly, but insist that if we limit ourselves to environments that have not been spoiled by human beings, then due understanding of nature entails appreciation of at least all pristine landscapes. I think that in saying this they go too far.

To begin with, I have problems with the interpretation of the term "natural" that applies it only to landscapes untouched by humans. High-rise apartment buildings may be as "natural" as beaver dams; parking lots may be as natural as forests burned because of lightning strikes. But this issue aside, there are still problems with a strong form of cognitivism that insists that there is nothing in nature that is not beautiful.

Just as economic or religious or scientific or other values may override perceptual aesthetic pleasures or pains, so responding to the look of something may diminish or even eliminate an appreciation based in nonaesthetic values. If the term "beautiful" is to do any work, then there must be some things that are not beautiful. I think there are some obvious examples of ugly natural objects. Deformities in plants and animals are one example. Or consider the shells that people collect. Ugly shells are left behind as shellers gather the ones they prefer. And the discards are described as "ugly" or at least "unattractive" or "unappealing." One guidebook to shells on the Florida coast describes the pen shell as follows: "A large, dark, brittle, spiny, unattractive shell, most folks ignore the saw-toothed pen shell (*altina serrata*) . . . . Even uglier on the outside, the stiff pen shell (*altina rigida*) hides a . . . beautiful iridescent lining, in a rainbow of colors. (Neal 2002: 105–6). Would a strict cognitivist insist that the shell's exterior is beautiful but the inside even more beautiful, or must one who understands the shell and its role in ocean environments determine that the inside and outside are equally beautiful? Both positions seem absurd to me. Admittedly, some people may delight in the brutal shape of the pen shell, may even describe it as "beautiful." What I insist is that a majority of people will describe it as the guidebook authors do: "unattractive," and "ugly." An adequate environmental aesthetics must account for this – or at least allow for it. Strict cognitivists seem to forget that knowledge by itself does not insure sensory pleasure. Consider again this theory:

> X is beautiful if and only if attention to intrinsic properties of X yields pleasurable perceptual experiences in an informed observer who is observing X.

This leaves out the possibility of unpleasant sensory experiences. Cognitivists are right to insist that we should respect all natural objects or systems. It does not follow that all of them yield pleasurable sensations. Kantians, as we saw, left out the central role that knowledge can play. But too strict a cognitive contextualism may unduly dismiss the role perception plays. Any adequate theory of beauty must account, I think, for both the roles of sensation and of knowledge.

Conclusion

Knowledge about what is helpful or harmful to the environment will not affect people's aesthetic preferences and actions unless they also have appropriate values. As I have argued elsewhere, our encounters in and with the world are not such that different sources of value act as viewing stands separated from one another (Eaton 2001). Specifically, one must *care* about having a healthy environment before what one learns translates into what one does. In general, it is a combination of beliefs and values that affect aesthetic preferences and corresponding actions in all human realms. This is reflected in some of our "sayings," for example, "Beauty is as beauty does," or "Beauty provoketh thieves sooner than gold."

In the Rodgers and Hammerstein musical *Carousel*, one of the characters sings about how her responses to a fisherman she has fallen in love with have changed over time. She reports that the smell of the fisherman's clothes initially nearly made her pass out but that after falling in love with him fish has become her "favorite perfume." There are analogs to this olfactory change for all the sensations. Where beauty is concerned, it is sight and sound, of course, that are most relevant. (People do, however, sometimes speak of beautiful smells, tastes, and touches.) It is common to be told by someone that he or she initially found another individual ugly, but that after coming to know that person began to see him or her as beautiful.

Knowledge plays a significant role in determining whether one feels pleasure or pain when looking or listening to art works. As Dorothea says in George Eliot's novel, *Middlemarch*,

> You know, uncle, I never see the beauty of those pictures which you say are so much praised. They are a language I do not understand. I suppose there is some relation between pictures and nature which I am too ignorant to feel – just as you see what a Greek sentence stands for which means nothing to me. (Eliot [1872] 1994: 78)

Moral values can also have a profound affect on aesthetic evaluations. If I come to see someone as beautiful that at first I found unattractive, it is both because of what I learn about that person and what I myself value in human character. Princess Diana and Mother Teresa coincidentally died in the same week, and this led to many comparisons between them. Whether one woman or the other was described as the more beautiful depended, of course, on what one knew about their lives and on one's moral values.

So is the following definition true?

> X is beautiful if and only if attention to intrinsic properties of X yields pleasurable perceptual experiences in an informed observer who is observing X and who also believes that X is morally valuable.

I don't think so. I am not claiming that one's beliefs or moral values always determine one's opinions about what is beautiful and what is not beautiful. Sometimes we continue to see people as visually appealing even if we think they are mean-spirited or unkind, perhaps even when we think they are cruel or tyrannical. It makes perfectly good sense to refer to someone as a handsome scoundrel or gorgeous hussy. We often enjoy seeing or hearing works of art that admittedly demonstrate values that we abhor (sexism or racism, for instance) – sometimes in spite of ourselves.

Still a context of belief and moral value does often change opinions about whether something is beautiful or not. Let us return to the first definition we considered:

> X is beautiful if and only if attention to intrinsic properties of X yields pleasurable perceptual experiences.

Cognitivists insist that the perceiver must be informed, but we have seen that is too strong. It is also too strong to insist that the perceiver morally approve of X. However, since what we enjoy is sometimes affected by beliefs and nonaesthetic values, beauty cannot be completely nor adequately explained in terms of a Kantian insistence on a strict separation of the beautiful from the scientific and ethical.

Thus we must repeat that "beautiful" and "ugly" are used in a variety of ways, sometimes in ways tightly connected to knowledge and moral values but sometimes only loosely connected or not connected at all. What is stable, however, seems to be the inclusion in their definitions of *sensory* responses. But is even this correct?

Some "sayings," such as "Eyes can never see the heart's beauty," seem to put aside perception in favor of reflective insight. Would Mother Teresa have been more beautiful if she had looked like Princess Diana? Some people might answer affirmatively. But others might object that the very question does not make sense. In order to look as good as she did, they would assert, Princess Diana had to have her hair styled, and spend hours on make-up and dressing – all of which required extravagant expenditures. It was precisely Mother Teresa's refusal to waste time or money in such ways that contributed so fundamentally to her beauty.

Another possible source of nonsensory beauty is the sort of beauty that many people attribute to laws of mathematics and science and legal systems. Surely these are not described as beautiful or elegant because of the way they look or sound. Instead people point to economy of conception or ingenuity or ways experiments have of changing the way we look at the world. Here it seems that everything depends upon what one knows and understands (Crease 2002).

As I have said repeatedly above, I do not think we can attach a single meaning to the terms "beauty" or "ugliness." But I am inclined to believe that when they are used to describe purely conceptual entities like laws or theories, they are being used metaphorically. It is the way the parts of a system relate and fit together that is being praised or condemned in these cases. But it is that certain "fit" in objects of perception that seems to be the source of the pleasures of beauty, and lack of it that makes us say something is ugly. Kant was surely correct that no laws or principles or formulas capture this relation. One study of male preferences for particular female faces reported as follows: "Using composite faces, we show here that, contrary to the averageness hypothesis, the mean shape of a set of attractive faces is preferred to the mean shape of the sample from which the faces were selected. In addition, attractive composites can be made more attractive by exaggerating the shape differences from the sample mean" (Perrett, May, and Yousikawa 1994: 239).

But at best such findings report preferential tendencies. Even if one could mathematically capture measurements of faces that please a particular population's rankings, there is no guarantee that a person replicating the look through plastic surgery would be found beautiful after members of the group got to know the individual to whom the new visage belonged. The complex mix of sensation, belief, and value defies formulaic, universal, acontextual assignment of a definition of "beauty." And this means that Socrates' wish for a precise definition of "beauty itself" must go unfulfilled.

CHAPTER FOUR

Terrible Beauties

Carolyn Korsmeyer

Despite their many differences, most of the theories of beauty to be found in the history of philosophy connect the experience of the beautiful with pleasure – with a positive and enjoyable "aesthetic experience" that rivets attention with delight. Indeed some theories actually identify beauty as a type of pleasure, such as the influential seventeenth- and eighteenth-century treatments beginning with empiricists such as John Locke and culminating with Immanuel Kant. George Santayana famously characterized beauty as "pleasure regarded as the quality of a thing" (Santayana [1896] 1955: 31). The connection is also articulated in platonic theories that consider beauty a property of objects that is independent of appreciative response, for objective beauty still delivers pleasure when it is recognized. Common parlance often connects beauty with pleasure as well, that is, with enjoyment of the presentation of an object to the senses and to the imagination. This all may seem obvious and psychologically uninteresting, for why ever should a positive quality such as beauty *not* be linked with pleasure, attraction, and allure?

However, on second thought both philosophy and ordinary usage also hesitate about that easy association, for it is evident that beauty is equally present in art that demands confrontation with discomforting subjects such as loss, grief, and death. In other words, while pleasure and beauty are hard to sever, it is also the case that *pain* mingles with both the subject matter and the affective appreciation of some profound exemplars of beautiful artworks: Shakespeare's *King Lear*, Britten's *War Requiem*, Rodin's *The Burghers of Calais*, Donatello's *Mary Magdalene*. Some theorists have tried to reconcile the apparent contradiction between "pleasure" and "pain" by surmising that beauty redeems painful content, sugar-coating a bitter pill. As the Roman poet Horace observed long ago in his theoretical poem *Ars Poetica* (lines 343–4), hard lessons are better learned when they are well-expressed, when "instruction" mingles with "delight." Doubtless there is some truth to this insight: a beautiful rendering of a difficult truth can make that truth easier to comprehend, even perhaps to accept;

thus pleasure taken in the beauty of difficult art softens the pain of its message. However, if this suggests that the "pleasure" of beauty is distinct from the "pain" of its subject, it is far from a complete picture, for art can be beautiful not despite its painful import, but because of it. This essay explores the perplexing phenomenon of what I shall call "terrible beauty," that is, beauty that is bound up with the arousal of discomforting emotions. In the course of this discussion, I shall try to push the parameters of beauty somewhat further than their usual recognized limits, discovering whether even an aversion such as disgust might find some quarter in beautiful art.

In a way this discussion is a throwback to earlier concerns in aesthetics, for as many have noted, beauty as an artistic value has not been at the center of either art practice or critical appraisal since the mid-twentieth century (Shiner 2001: 221, Brand 2000: 6). But its renewed or continued pertinence is evident in the recent books that mourn its departure (Steiner 2001) or revive older ways of considering the role of beauty in ordinary life (Scarry 1999). Venerable questions about the ontological status of beauty – the kind of quality it is, its relation to aesthetic appraisal, its dependence on other qualities – remain recalcitrant problems for philosophers (Zangwill 2001, Zemach 1997, Mothersill 1984). And most importantly for my focus in this essay, beauty presents a zone of puzzlement for our understanding of any art that pains while appealing, no matter when or under what aesthetic fashion it was produced.

Some of the puzzle about terrible beauties might be cleared up if we could wean ourselves away from employing the rather crude dichotomy of "pleasure" and "pain" when discussing value and disvalue. As many have noted, overreliance on this pair of terms flattens out the nuances of real aesthetic valuation and neglects the range of qualities and experiences that deliver satisfaction and insight (Walton 1993). Later in this discussion I shall have some suggestions about refining this language, for indeed it is fraught with problems and misleading implications. I shall eventually argue that aesthetic pleasure is better understood as a kind of affective absorption, and that the language of emotions provides more illumination than the language of sensation. However, to begin with I shall stick with the pleasure–pain terminology, for not only is it a continuous thread that binds together disparate theories of beauty, it seems to some degree to be inescapable.

Defining Beauty

Before reaching the subject of terrible beauty it is necessary to consider the idea of beauty more generally. Defining beauty is a formidable undertaking, some would say doomed. There are two assessments that feed this pessimistic attitude, one concerning the objects called beautiful, and the other concerning those who find them so. Examples of beautiful art are so diverse that the prospect that they share a definable set of beauty-making qualities is dim. And this is the case even if we stick with more or less indisputably beautiful art, such as the sculptures of Praxiteles or Bernini, the paintings of Monet or Morisot, the music of Mozart or Dvorak. (I say "more or less" to indicate a reasonable generalization about aesthetic appraisals; there is no such thing as unanimity in aesthetic judgments, despite Kant's efforts to find grounds for universality and necessity for pure judgments of taste.) The multiplicity of beautiful things is one of the main reasons that philosophers often conclude that the only trait beautiful objects share is the ability to arouse a distinctive type of pleasure – which is why, incidentally, it is hard to dispense altogether with the language of pleasure and pain. Consequently, aesthetic judgments have a necessarily subjective component: they involve reports of responses. Calling something "subjective" does not entail relativism, for it is clearly not the case that all subjective responses are matters of individual preference: the pain of burning flesh keeps most of us from leaning on stoves. But taste for design, fashion, and art do not have the same physiological foundation that governs sensations, and the sheer variety of aesthetic responses bolsters the idea that beauty is in the eye of the beholder. Even so, beholders often see similarly, and there are many examples of beauty that few would disagree with: sunny spring days, the stars appearing at twilight, flower gardens. These things are easy to find beautiful, and they give pleasure to nearly everyone.

While there are certainly diverse preferences for landscapes and objects of nature, it is especially as we enter the worlds of art that consensus begins to shrink and aesthetic judgments to fragment. Consider the range of responses to objects such as Indian raga, Greek tragedy, postmodern architecture; or to individual works within a genre, such as Bartok's music or the paintings of Anselm Kiefer. Tastes for particular kinds of art differ among cultures, historical periods, and individuals. This demonstrable variety of aesthetic opinion might seem to lead to the conclusion that beauty is merely culturally dependent or individually idiosyncratic. A good many philosophers have attempted to establish grounds for standards of taste and warrant for the convergence of critical opinion, although this will not be my focus here. Rather, I shall consider one aspect of art that contributes to the divergence of aesthetic judgments: the arousal of unpleasant emotions, which many find too taxing to tolerate, as part of the aesthetic response.

To get to that subject, however, requires an indirect route. Strenuous aesthetic experiences (when Oedipus blinds himself, for example) do not immediately spring to mind as central examples of beauty, and therefore one might think that a concentration on such "terrible" beauty displaces the discussion to an area that is aberrant or marginal. I don't think this is the case, and indeed I believe that terrible beauties represent beauty in its most profound dimensions. But to make that case I need first to review some other aspects of beauty. I shall start with a subject that might seem to refer to the simplest kind of aesthetic pleasure: formal beauty.

Beauties of Form

Many attempts to correlate beauty with the regular presence of qualities in beautiful objects concentrate on the *form* of objects, such as intricacy and balance of composition or harmony of parts. We can find this approach in mathematical theories of beauty from Pythagoras to the present; and we can also find it in empiricist attempts to ground aesthetic pleasure in objective properties. The English painter and engraver William Hogarth, for example, concluded that beauty always has a mathematical basis that is best exemplified in a spiral line twisting around a cone from apex to base (Hogarth [1753] 1997). His "line of grace" was invoked by Edmund Burke, who speculated that the appeal of beauty has an erotic origin in the curves of the ideal female body (Burke [1757] 1968). Somewhat earlier, Francis Hutcheson offered a more flexible formula: the pleasure of beauty is aroused by a "compound variety of uniformity amidst variety," that is, by the balance between complexity and simplicity of design (Hutcheson [1725] 1994). Such formulae have contemporary versions as well, such as Monroe Beardsley's general canons for aesthetic judgment: unity, complexity, and intensity (Beardsley 1958).

There is nothing wrong with these speculations inasmuch as they describe certain beautiful objects. However, no formula aptly describes all beautiful objects unless its meaning and application are broadened to the point of vacuity. Eero Saarinen's Gateway Arch in St. Louis has a good deal of uniformity but little variety, as it makes only one enormous, sweeping turn. Yet many would single it out as a beautiful architectural gesture. The church of Santa Maria della Vittoria in Rome is encrusted with so much statuary and decorative detail that by any of these gauges it ought to be a jumble – and it is splendidly beautiful.

The availability of counterexamples to the various attempts to ground beauty in objective correlates may seem to defeat the definitional enterprise altogether. But the fact that a single essence of beauty is elusive does not mean that these attempts have failed to identify relevant features of some beautiful objects. The diversity of beautiful things does not entail that beauty is occult or indefinable, nor that it is merely relative to the beholder. Rather, it means that its sources are multiple. The elaborate flower arrangements painted by Severin Roesen fit Hutcheson's compound ratio; a severe, single bud in a vase is more aptly described by the line of grace. These formulae have not defined beauty itself, but they do single out the qualities of various kinds of beautiful things.

This point is illuminated with a culinary parallel, a comparison that is especially apt because the core metaphor for the ability to make judgments about beauty is "taste" (this metaphor is employed in many European languages and in traditions of Indian aesthetics). All food has taste qualities, and when they are especially pleasing they are called "delicious," which we can understand as a gustatory equivalent of "beautiful." Chocolate is considered by many to be delicious; so is crème brûlée; so is eggplant parmesan; so is cheese soufflé. Note the absence of any theoretical rush to discover some delicious-making property that all these foods share – though admittedly this sensible restraint is probably a symptom of the fact that philosophers traditionally have not considered eating and tasting important enough to merit their concerns (Korsmeyer 1999). When one enjoys a chocolate mousse, one praises the smooth texture of the pudding, the hint of bitter that deepens the sweet, dark flavor and so on. When one enjoys the eggplant dish, one notices the creamy texture of the vegetable, the peppery bite of the sauce. From the fact that neither tastes like the other it does not follow that enjoyment is mysteriously subjective and relative, nor that there are no identifiable properties that justify the claim that these foods are delicious. As it happens, the dishes on this list do share a few relevant properties: they are smooth on the tongue, for instance. But it is obviously inappropriate to try to claim that the common smooth texture must be the quality in virtue of which they are all delicious. Besides, if we did so, we could not accommodate popcorn or carrots on the spectrum of delicious things. The moral of the comparison is this: perceptual values such as delicious and beautiful are subjective inasmuch as they involve positive responses, and often we are moved to try to figure out the basis for those positive responses. But the qualities that make an object beautiful are as various as those that make foods tasty. The fact that there are multiple – indeed myriad – sources of beauty, precludes the formulation of general criteria for this aesthetic value, an insight captured in Kant's observation that aesthetic judgments are *singular*. It does not follow that beauty is *merely* idiosyncratic pleasure, for responses are still dependent on the presence of relevant properties (Zangwill 2001: 19). We may now firmly close two doors opening onto the investigation of beauty: the door that Plato chose – the theory that beauty names a shared trait of all beautiful objects; and the empiricist version of this – that all beautiful objects are correlated with some objective quality that arouses aesthetic pleasure. I shall not search for such commonalities.

This review of formalist theories has been more than a sidebar, for an additional observation about beauties of form leads us closer to consideration of difficult and even painful instances of beauty. Formal properties of objects appeal to sense experience: to the way that an object is presented to its appropriate organ of perception. But even at this surface level of presentation to the senses there are degrees of significance that are relevant to identifying the darker aspects of beauty. Consider these comments by the painter Henri Matisse.

> Supposing I want to paint the body of a woman: First of all I endow it with grace and charm but I know that something more than that is necessary. I try to condense the meaning of this body by drawing its essential lines. The charm will then become less apparent at first glance but in the long run it will begin to emanate from the new image. This image at the same time will be enriched by a wider meaning, a more comprehensively human one, while the charm, being less apparent, will not be its only characteristic. It will be merely one element in the general conception of the figure.
>
> Charm, lightness, crispness – all these are passing sensations. I have a canvas on which the colors are still fresh and I begin work on it again. The colors will probably grow heavier – the freshness of the original tones will give way to greater solidity, an improvement to my mind, but less seductive to the eye. (Matisse [1908] 1953: 257)

Matisse deepens the appreciation of his lines and shapes by making them less immediately pleasant and easy to look at. His remarks illuminate a transition between what is merely "pretty" and what marks a more profound visual value, perhaps something that qualifies as beautiful. Evidently part of the transformation of an appearance from pretty to beautiful requires making appreciation somewhat more strenuous, "less seductive to the eye."

A similar point may be observed about the physical beauty of human beings. No one living has ever laid eyes on the disastrous beauty of Helen of Troy, of whom Homer said, "Small wonder that Trojans and Achaeans should endure so much and so long, for the sake of a woman so marvelously and divinely lovely" (*Iliad* III: 156–8). But in 1971 when Michael Cacoyannis scripted and filmed Euripides' *The Trojan Women*, it was the severe-featured Irene Papas who was cast in the role of Helen. Mere prettiness cannot carry the weight of such a role.

Both these examples indicate that formal appearance alone conveys significance and meaning. The more demanding the conveyance, the more that which is sweet, pretty, or charming edges toward the beautiful and delivers an experience that recognizes implicit moral or existential weight distilled into an art work – or a face. But this also means that beauty begins to move away from the simpler and easier varieties of aesthetic pleasure. And as it moves away, it nears territories of taxing appreciation for qualities that might almost seem to qualify as opposites to beauty: that which is grotesque, harsh, sublime, or even ugly.

Complicating Contrasts

Other attempts to come to grips with the nature of beauty postulate that it might be easier to identify this quality with reference to things that it is not. There is precedent for approaching axiological or normative properties this way, for the idea of the aesthetic itself is classically defined in terms of its contrasting values: aesthetic pleasure is pleasure taken in the intrinsic properties of objects as they are present to sense and imagination, rather than pleasure in or approval of their moral significance, practical use, appeal to erotic desire, and so forth. Beauty seems to have its own opposites that might help pinpoint just what it is. There are several candidates for being "opposites" to beauty, such as things that are monotonous or dull, insignificant, or ugly (Lorand 1994). Such qualities either fail to strike up any aesthetic pleasure at all (such as things that are dull); or they arouse aesthetic displeasure (things that are repulsive, perhaps); or the pleasure they arouse needs to be classed in a different category. Certain kinds of ugliness, for instance, can be savored in art that is grotesque – which can be appraised as excellent on its own terms (Kieran 1997, 2004: 75–86). Indeed sometimes that which is ugly is wonderful just for being ugly – such as a toad, that small monster beloved of fairy tales. While it is hard to imagine a beautiful toad, that is not the same as denying all aesthetic appeal for toads, a twist of appraisal that turns ugly itself into a positive aesthetic property. This informs us that beauty does not have the monopoly on either aesthetic or artistic excellence, and that not all of the contrasts between the beautiful and the not-beautiful serve to separate aesthetic value from disvalue.

This observation acknowledges a difficulty that freights discussions of beauty, namely that the scope of the term expands and contracts in different contexts. If we want to consider "beauty" equivalent to "aesthetic excellence," or even to the slightly more focused "artistic excellence," then inevitably it labels an omnivorous category about which one simply must accept quite a lot of ambiguity and vagueness – for it is shorthand for the entire multitude of aesthetic "goods." The contrast with this usage is just between "beautiful" and "aesthetically discountable." But if we want to think of beauty as a special element of the many aesthetic or artistic excellences that there can be, then we must recognize that there are some contrasts with beautiful that are themselves equally excellent. Indeed most of the interesting contrasts between beautiful and not-beautiful are contrasts with other aesthetically valuable phenomena. And still, as we are about to see, narrowing our focus just to these does not avoid ambiguity, indeterminacy, or ambivalence.

The competing aesthetic value that has received the most theoretical attention is sublimity, which also helps to illuminate the "terrible" elements of beauty. The stan-

Carolyn Korsmeyer

dard distinctions between the beautiful and the sublime are set down in the treatises of the eighteenth century, that period which oversaw intense interest in the expansion of aesthetic categories. In Burke's representative catalogue, that which is beautiful is small, contained, curved, delicate; that which is sublime is vast, unbounded, jagged, and harsh. The sublime presents to the senses and the imagination things that are powerful and terrifying to such a degree that they actually may threaten annihilation of the spectator. Only when there is a margin of safety – physical and psychological – between the sublime object and the spectator can the terror aroused by vast or fearsome objects be converted into a deep and thrilling awe. The rapture of the sublime delivers both aesthetic thrill and insight, for it confronts one with the most dreadful subjects, including what Burke calls the "king of terrors" – death. Because sublimity is so difficult to enjoy, Burke refrains from calling the response to it "pleasure," a tamer appreciation he reserves for beauty; he does, however, claim that it arouses "delight," an experience that eclipses the temperate pleasures of beauty because of the existential significance of its circumstances.

With the sterner category of the sublime available to account for extreme aesthetic value, the scope of beauty tends to shrink: beautiful things are contained and lovely; sublime things are powerful, unbounded, emotionally challenging. Especially with Burke, this division lends itself to a gender divide as well: beautiful things are feminine; in comparison, sublime things are masculine. Their shapes are stronger and harsher than beautiful things, and their enjoyment is suited for the more robust temperament of males. It is only a short step further to suggest that beautiful things are less momentous than sublime things. The "merely beautiful" relinquishes to sublimity objects with greater moral and existential significance. Quite apart from the gender asymmetry, which can be examined for its own import, the implications for beauty itself are a problem, for this venerable value is diminished and retreats back to something close to pretty. Unless "pretty" and "beautiful" are to become synonymous, a strict distinction between beauty and sublimity is hard to sustain without drawing arbitrary divisions. While pretty things have an undeniable aesthetic appeal, they are often avoided by artists because they do not seem able to sustain attention or to support meaning to the same degree as other aesthetic qualities. (We have already seen this suggested in the examples from Matisse's painting and the legendary figure of Helen.) The contrast between pretty and beautiful has been somewhat less explored by philosophers, but it yields as many insights about beauty as do the comparisons between beauty's more familiar counterparts such as the sublime and grotesque. In certain respects pretty and beautiful can be considered points on a continuum of aesthetically pleasing appearance, and considering what goes into assigning an object (or a face or body) its place on this continuum illuminates something of the role of the *difficult* in the formation of beauty.

Easy and Difficult Beauty

In *Three Lectures on Aesthetic* the English philosopher Bernard Bosanquet identifies two classes of things that are beautiful: *easy* beauty, which is pleasant to almost everyone: simple melodies, pretty faces, things that yield "straightforward pleasure"; and *difficult* beauty – in which he includes the sublime – which can present barriers to appreciation "amounting for some persons to repellence" ([1915] 1963: 47). Several features can make beautiful things difficult, including intricacy of pattern that requires attentive focus; tension that "demands profound effort and concentration" (1963: 48); and width of vision present in art that treats unpleasant subjects often considered beneath aesthetic consideration. Comedy is his chief example of art that challenges with its width. While width might encompass qualities that are antithetical to easy beauties, intricacy and tension actually heighten those qualities: "In all this difficult beauty, which goes beyond what is comfortable for the indolent or timid mind, there is nothing but a 'more' of the same beautiful, which we find prima facie pleasant, changed only by being intensified" (1963: 49). Ironically, the "intensification" of beauty actually propels it towards its opposites. Bosanquet offers a somewhat enigmatic comment about aesthetic pleasure that illuminates a kind of paradox of beauty: the fact that it may be found in the most painful of subjects: "Beauty," he says, "is essentially enjoyed; it lives in enjoyment of a certain kind. But you cannot make it up out of enjoyments of any other kind" (1963: 51). Some aspect of this enjoyment stems from the expansion of understanding that takes place in the compressed apprehension that is aesthetic. That is, beauty signals an insight that is of a piece with finding an art work beautiful and aesthetically moving. It is not a conclusion of research or inference, but a clarity of vision embodied in art. And this is quite consistent with the fact that art ponders the most painful subjects.

The Paradox of Beauty

What I am proposing now as a "paradox" of beauty is a variation on more familiar aesthetic paradoxes that note the peculiar appeal that pain and aversion can exert when they are aroused by art. The classic aesthetic paradoxes of tragedy and sublimity, to which we should add horror, a riveting if seldom beautiful genre, make reference to two sources of "unpleasantness": subject matter and emotion. The earliest and most familiar version of this is Aristotle's treatment of tragedy in the *Poetics*, where he wonders how it is that poetry that enacts gruesome plots can also deliver pleasure. The marvel of art is its ability to present formidably difficult subjects in ways that fascinate, charm, amuse, or compel. Aristotle attributed this capacity to the transformative power of mimesis: "We delight in contemplating the most exact likenesses of things which are in themselves painful to see, e.g. the shapes of the most dishonored beasts and corpses" (1961: 1448b, 11–14). The paradox of tragedy notes the pleasure audiences take in the dramatization of difficult subject matter and the arousal of the tragic emotions, identified by Aristotle as pity and fear, but also including dread, sorrow, and recognition of one's own vulnerability and helplessness. He surmises that the desire to learn is pleasurably satisfied with poetry that delivers understanding of terrible truths about worlds divine and human. Aristotle thus furnishes the founding text for so-called cognitive theories of the paradoxes of aversion, which explain appreciation of difficult subjects and discomforting emotive engagement by reference to the pleasure of the knowledge gained from them.

Carolyn Korsmeyer

The paradox of the sublime centers on the deep aesthetic thrill that can be brought about through first arousing one of the most uncomfortable emotions one can experience: terror. Kant ([1790] 1997: 98) calls the sublime a "negative pleasure," a telling oxymoron since pleasure is the exemplar of that which is subjectively positive. He attributes to the sublime a redemptive insight: the realization of human freedom from the bonds of natural law. Both tragedy and sublimity deal with important subjects, indeed with ultimate subjects concerning the meaning of human life, and therefore the insights they disclose may be interpreted as redeeming the discomfort of their encounters. By comparison, art that is categorized as grotesque or horror engenders perhaps even more perplexity, for it is frequently not elevated with the nobility or important content that offsets the strain of tragedy or sublimity. This is one reason, perhaps, that horror and the grotesque mingle less frequently with beauty, though beauty is not altogether excluded from these genres.

Beauty itself is usually not considered to present a paradox; what is there about beauty that could repel? But in fact it does have an enigmatic side, which becomes evident when we compare the concepts of beauty and prettiness: for we have seen how prettiness gives way to beauty as the more important value. The conversion of pretty to beautiful requires a dose of something difficult that arrests attention and causes it to linger. This might be induced by formal complexities, as both Bosanquet and Matisse observe. But with terrible beauty attention is arrested by elements that strain the heart – and yet they induce us to linger over them and savor them in all their heartache and woe. If there is beauty here, is it still to be understood as pleasure?

Pleasure and Emotional Depth

This is the point to look more closely at the appropriateness of pleasure–pain language in this discussion. Reference to pleasure and pain, as we have seen, furnishes a simple way to ground the mysteries of axiological qualities in familiar experiences and to clarify the phenomenon of beauty: since the nature of beauty is obscure, it helps to think of it as the occasion for a kind of pleasure, because we are clearer about the nature of pleasure. Or so it seems at first. But terrible beauties thoroughly complicate what is meant by "pleasure," and the dichotomy with which we started demands closer scrutiny.

Pleasure and pain are not the opposites that they might appear to be. This is the case even with the most basic uses of these terms to refer to bodily sensations or simple feelings. Pain is the name for the type of physical sensation that occurs when the body is injured and nerve endings called nociceptors are aroused; but pleasure may not be a sensation at all in the sense of being an identifiable physical feeling. Although the reference to nociceptors draws from recent physiological science, the suspicion that pleasure is not a sensation has ancient ancestry; Aristotle, for one, raised doubts about the status of pleasure. Certainly we speak of bodily pleasures, and some sensations (such as a caress) are pleasant, but there is no type of sensation that is "pleasure" itself (Zemach 1997). Thus the original opposition is asymmetrical. Calling an experience a pleasure means that there is an appeal or magnetism or attraction to an experience; but it is not identifying a feeling that accompanies experience. The language of aesthetic pleasure is especially misleading for terrible beauties; indeed, not all beauties are even enjoyed, strictly speaking, though they are – to use a sadly anemic expression – appreciated.

Gilbert Ryle proposes that what we term pleasure is an indicator of the intensity of attention and absorption in an activity or event rather than anything distinguishable in itself (Ryle 1954: 60). His characterization is not appropriate for all phenomena that are labeled "pleasure," but it provides a useful lead in sorting through the paradoxes of aversion. From this approach we can see pleasure as indicating that attention is focused and experience intensified, which helps to diminish the paradox implied by taking pleasure in pain. Perhaps even more usefully, it reminds us that there are other mental states that focus attention on the relevant features of objects, for this describes emotions in general and the arousal of emotions by art in particular.

It is significant that the paradoxes of aversion are largely emotional paradoxes, and that beauty and other aesthetic virtues are tangled in the web of emotional responses to art. I think it is misleading to call strenuous emotions such as sorrow or terror "pains," though it is certainly true that they are uncomfortable and that we tend to avoid them in life, despite their appeal in art. Burke refers to the pain of terror, but this is a shorthand way of noticing the stress that terror exerts and – most significantly – the fact that difficult emotions are a means by which we register difficult features of our world. Just as intense pains make us strive to get away from the cause of the pain, uncomfortable emotions lead to recoil and avoidance in practical life. Fear makes us flee; anxiety is so uncomfortable we take pills for it; grief can be unbearable. At the same time, emotions are capable of the same enhancement of attention attributed to pleasures – especially when they are aroused by means of art, with its form and containment. To follow Bosanquet's language, one way to note the emergence of the beautiful out of the merely pretty is in terms of the intensification of experience. Emotions can intensify experience without colliding with some notional "opposite," which is the case with pleasure and pain.

Emotions have a mixed reputation in aesthetic theory, for they are sometimes set aside as merely sentimental engagement. But some of them – especially those at the center of the great paradoxes such as pity, terror, and dread – are recognized for their own aesthetic weight and the understanding they afford. Insight often demands that one face truths that one would rather were otherwise, but a "painful" emotion cannot be considered negative if it is the only means by which one may understand something important. Fear, for example, is negative insofar as it notices something dangerous and terrible; it is also supremely uncomfortable. But it is positive inasmuch as it alerts one to impending threat. Pity strains the heart, but without it one would not notice the grief of others. Art does not avoid difficult subjects, and this requires that emotions be part of aesthetic arousal and the recognition of artistic quality. Aesthetic emotions absorb us in rapt attention, with just enough distance supplied by the containment of art that we reap the intense insight available by means of emotion without turning away from that which arouses it. By these observations I do not mean to endorse the cognitivist perspective according to which disagreeable emotions and perceptions become redeemed by the pleasurable understanding that they enable (Carroll

1990). This position suggests a separability of the aesthetic emotion from the aesthetic insight, as though the aversion were but a regrettable stepping stone to knowledge. While the aversions aroused by some art may be aptly so described, this account fails to capture the kind of art that is capable of rendering the most awful experiences beautiful – not as a step leads to a destination, but as a lens produces clarity.

Can all emotions be transformed by art into a positive aesthetic encounter, perhaps amounting even to beauty? Certainly fear can, and grief, sorrow, and melancholy, as the examples of sublime and tragic art demonstrate. Anger can as well, for anger has a noble side which allies itself with honor and justice. No one has tested all emotions as they are aroused by art, if one could even come up with a complete list of such multifarious mental phenomena. But for most of the history of debates over this subject, some emotions have been deemed unworthy of aesthetic transfiguration. And there is one emotion that has resolutely resisted accommodation in positive aesthetic terms: disgust. This emotion will serve us, therefore, as a test case for the limits of difficult beauty.

Aesthetic Disgust

While fear, pity, grief, and other discomforting emotions have a long history in philosophy of art, disgust has no such ancestry. In fact, it is frequently singled out as the one emotion utterly incompatible with beautiful art. As Kant famously asserts: "There is only one kind of ugliness that cannot be presented in conformity with nature without obliterating all aesthetic liking and hence artistic beauty: that ugliness which arouses *disgust*" (Kant [1790] 1997: 180). His comment echoes ideas earlier expressed by other theorists; indeed, there was a fair convergence of opinion on this subject at this formative period of aesthetics (Menninghaus 2003).

A good deal of the skepticism meted out to disgust as an apt companion to beauty has to do with the typical objects of disgust. This emotion is a response to objects that represent the gross and squalid aspects of life: the putrefaction and rot that ensue after death; reminders of organic being such as blood and mucus, excrement and vomit; bodies eviscerated or taken apart (Miller 1997). One thing that disgust has going against it is that the objects that arouse this emotion tend to be incompatible with dignity and honor. Unlike the circumstances that promote fear or grief, disgust dangerously truncates sympathy and admiration. A description of blood gushing from a wound, for example, may be somewhat disgusting but consistent with the dignity of the injured person. Description of a running nose is not. It must be granted that most art that trades on disgust is not beautiful, nor is it intended to be. There are numerous rewards from the presentation of disgusting subjects, including satisfaction of curiosity, propelling interest in plot, and admiration of virtuoso treatment. Horror genres, war narratives, the horrific cautionary pictures of hell by Hieronymus Bosch are all examples of art that arouses profound disgust as part of understanding and appreciation. It would be foolish to try to cram all of their immense aesthetic impact into the category of "beauty." If there is beauty with the arousal of disgust, it has to be located in more plausible examples, and I think there are at least a few.

Insects that feed off human flesh are pretty good examples of disgusting objects. And yet John Donne elevates a flea that bites two lovers into a weirdly compelling image of union: ("It sucked me first, and now sucks thee,/ And in this flea, our two bloods mingled be.") Emily Dickinson evokes the perspective of a woman who hears a fly buzz as she dies and who glimpses in her final moment the vermin that will consume her corpse: ("With blue, uncertain, stumbling buzz/ Between the light and me;/ And then the windows failed, and then/ I could not see to see.")

Caravaggio's painting, *The Doubting of St. Thomas* (1601–2) captures an event from the story of Christ just after his crucifixion, when he has returned to his disciples to show them proof of his resurrection. When Thomas heard the news of Jesus's return, he was skeptical of its truth: "Unless I see in his hands the print of the nails, and place my finger in the mark of the nails, and place my hand in his side, I will not believe" (John 20: 25). Caravaggio has rendered the apostles a scruffy bunch with unkempt hair and torn robes, free from any signs of holiness such as halos. The curious doubting Thomas actually probes the wound in Jesus's side, inserting his fingers into the gaping skin. Now penetration of the protective covering of the body is one of the standard exemplars of the disgusting according to psychological analysis, for wounds, dismemberments, and blood all signal death and the immanence of decay. There is no gore in the painting, but the sight of dirty fingers intruding into violated flesh quite likely induces a visceral frisson and a spasm of disgust in the viewer. The initial recoil this picture prompts may seem inappropriate for a religious subject. But not only does it render Christ and his followers familiarly human, this aesthetic disgust heightens and enhances recognition of the mystery of the incarnation: the mortality of Jesus the man and the Christian doctrine of everlasting life. The disgust component, I believe, performs the job of intensification that Bosanquet refers to when he says that beauty is an enjoyment that is not composed of other enjoyments.

One may surmise that the absence of gore or decay in this painting controls the disgust response sufficiently that it does not interfere with beauty, but we can find other artworks that push the emotion closer to its trademark grossness. Some, of course, have no claims for beauty, but others do. I offer the example of an episode at the end of Robert Stone's novel *A Flag for Sunrise* (1977) in which a young nun is tortured to death by means of beating and electric shock. It is a harrowing scene that manages to present the sickening effects of torture without flinching, and to do so with a kind of poetry that I believe qualifies as beauty of the most difficult sort. A short passage:

> When he began, she thought: I must do this, I must finish this, not him. She cast the compassing of her mind as high and wide as she could reach toward strength and mercy. She cried because, at first, there was nothing at all. Only the blows falling.
>
> Though he beat her beyond fear, she kept trying. Until she was awash in all the shameful juices of living and she still kept on. Though she forgot in time who he was and what the pain was about she was able to think of the tears, the blood, and mucus and loose teeth in her mouth: these are not bad things, these are just me and I'm all right. (Stone 1977: 415–16)

Carolyn Korsmeyer

One can discover in literature scenes that graphically present brutality and its wreckage, and some of them we would probably prefer to call powerful, admirable, or vivid rather than beautiful; but with some we may also recognize beauty. Such images transfigure the disgusting into the beautiful just as terror transforms into the sublime. And they become beautiful not just because the rendering is deft or poetic, but also because they capture in a breathtaking manner something terrible that we may also recognize as true.

These examples are intended to demonstrate that when beautiful art arouses aversive emotion, the aesthetic effect need not be parsed as a mingling of a negative and a positive affect. There are not two things but one dense and complex phenomenon; even disgust itself becomes an experience of beauty.

But these examples also leave some questions dangling. While terrible beauty is fairly obviously distinguished from what is pretty, what differentiates this aesthetic value from deft grotesquerie or powerful horror? This question raises a problem endemic to aesthetic judgments: the singularity of beauty mentioned earlier. The matter has to be addressed case by case, and decisions are complicated because the border between terrible beauty and the grotesque or horrid is hazy. Just as prettiness shades into beauty, so terrible beauty shades towards horror and other difficult aesthetic categories. The examples I have offered hover at that border, and one might object to calling all of them beautiful. (Perhaps Donne's flea is just too weird for beauty.) The complexity of aversive emotions bound up with artistic beauty creates a zone where terror and horror, beauty and sublimity and ugliness, can be difficult to distinguish. But that is why some beauty is truly terrible.

References for Chapters 3 and 4

Aristotle. (1961). *Poetics*, trans. K. A. Telford. Chicago: Henry Regnery.

Beardsley, M. (1958). *Aesthetics*. New York: Harcourt, Brace.

Bosanquet, B. ([1915] 1963). *Three Lectures on Aesthetic*. Indianapolis: Bobbs-Merrill.

Bell, C. (1914). *Art*. London: Chatto and Windus.

Brand, P. Z. (ed.) (2000). *Beauty Matters*. Bloomington: Indiana University Press.

Burke, E. ([1757] 1968). *A Philosophical Enquiry into the Origin of Our Ideas of the Sublime and the Beautiful*. Notre Dame, IN: University of Notre Dame Press.

Carlson, A. (1979). "Appreciation of the Natural Environment." *Journal of Aesthetics and Art Criticism*, 37: 267–75.

Carlson, A. (1984). "Nature and Positive Aesthetics." *Environmental Ethics*, 6: 5–34.

Carroll, N. (1990) *The Philosophy of Horror, or Paradoxes of the Heart*. New York: Routledge.

Crease, R. (2002). "The Most Beautiful Experiment." *Physics World*, September: 19–20.

Eaton, M. M. (2001). *Merit: Aesthetic and Ethical*. New York: Oxford University Press.

Eliot, G. ([1872] 1994). *Middlemarch*. Harmondsworth, UK: Penguin.

Fry, R. ([1927] 1970). "The Artist and Psychoanalysis." In L. S. Woolf and V. Woolf (eds.), *The Hogarth Essays*. Freeport, NY: Books for Libraries Reprint Series.

Hogarth, W. ([1753] 1997). *The Analysis of Beauty*. New Haven, CT: Yale University Press.

Homer (1942). *The Iliad*, trans. Samuel Butler. New York: Walter J. Black.

Hutcheson, F. ([1725] 1994). "Inquiry Concerning Beauty." In *Philosophical Writings* (pp. 7–44). London: Everyman.

Kant, I. ([1790] 1997) *Critique of Judgement*, trans. W. S. Pluhar. Indianapolis: Hackett.

Kieran, M. (1997). "Aesthetic Value: Beauty, Ugliness and Incoherence." *Philosophy*, 72: 383–99.

Kieran, M. (2004). *Revealing Art*. London: Routledge.

Korsmeyer, C. (1999). *Making Sense of Taste*. Ithaca, NY: Cornell University Press.

Lorand, R. (1994). "Beauty and its Opposites." *Journal of Aesthetics and Art Criticism*, 52: 399–406.

Matisse, H. ([1908] 1953). "Notes of a Painter." In E. Vivas and M. Krieger (eds.), *The Problems of Aesthetics* (pp. 255–61). New York: Holt, Rinehart and Winston.

Menninghaus, W. (2003). *Disgust: Theory and History of a Strong Sensation*, trans. H. Eiland and J. Golb. Albany, NY: State University of New York Press.

Miller, W. I. (1997). *The Anatomy of Disgust*. Cambridge, MA: Harvard University Press.

Mothersill, M. (1984). *Beauty Restored*. Oxford: Clarendon Press.

Nassauer, J. (1988). "Landscape Care: Perceptions of Local People in Landscape Ecology and Sustainable Development." In *Landscape and Land Use Planning* (pp. 27–41). Washington, DC: American Society of Landscape Architects.

Neal, J. and Neal, M. (2002). *Sanibel and Captiva: A Guide to the Islands*. Sanibel, FL: Coconut Press.

Perrett, D. I., May, K. A., and Yousikawa, S. (1994). "Facial Shape and Judgments of Female Attractiveness." *Nature*, 368, March 17: 239–42.

Plato. (1961). *Greater Hippias*. In *Plato: the Collected Dialogues*, trans. B. Jowett, ed. E. Hamilton and H. Cairns. Princeton, NJ: Princeton University Press.

Ryle, G. (1954). *Dilemmas*. Cambridge, UK: Cambridge University Press.

Santayana, G. ([1896] 1955). *The Sense of Beauty*. New York: Dover.

Scarry, E. (1999). *On Beauty and Being Just*. Princeton, NJ: Princeton University Press.

Shiner, L. (2001). *The Invention of Art*. Chicago: University of Chicago Press.

Steiner, W. (2001). *Venus in Exile*. New York: Free Press.

Stone, R. (1977). *A Flag for Sunrise*. New York: Ballantine Books.

Tolstoy, L. ([1898] 1930). *What is Art? and Essays on Art*, trans. A. Maude, London: Duckworth.

Walton, K. (1993). "'How Marvelous! Toward a Theory of Aesthetic Value." *Journal of Aesthetics and Art Criticism* 51: 499–510.

Wimsatt, Jr. W. K. and Beardsley, M. C. (1954). "The Intentional Fallacy." In W. K. Wimsatt, *The Verbal Icon* (pp. 3–18). Lexington: University of Kentucky Press.

Zangwill, N. (2001). *The Metaphysics of Beauty.* Ithaca, NY: Cornell University Press.

Zemach, E. M. (1997). *Real Beauty.* University Park: Pennsylvania State University Press.

Further Reading for Chapters 3 and 4

Carlson, A. (2000). *Aesthetics and the Environment.* New York: Routledge.

Eaton, M. M. (1998). *What About Beauty?* Minneapolis: University of Minnesota Department of Art.

Heidegger, M. (1971). "On the Origin of the Work of Art." In *Poetry, Language, Thought* (pp. 15–86), trans. A. Hofstader. New York: Perennial Library.

Hume, D. ([1757] 1993) "Of the Standard of Taste." In *Selected Essays* (pp. 133–54). Oxford: Oxford University Press.

Moore, R. (1988). "Ugliness." In M. Kelly (ed.), *The Encyclopedia of Aesthetics* (vol. IV, pp. 417–21). New York: Oxford University Press.

Murdoch, I. (1991). *The Sovereignty of Good.* London: Routledge.

Osborne, H. (1952). *Theory of Beauty: an Introduction to Aesthetics.* London: Routledge.

Plato. (1961). *Symposium.* In *Plato: the Collected Dialogues*, trans. M. Joyce, ed. E. Hamilton and H. Cairns. Princeton, NJ: Princeton University Press.

Ross, S. D. (1998). "Beauty." In M. Kelly (ed.) *The Encyclopedia of Aesthetics* (vol. I, pp. 237–44). New York: Oxford University Press.

WHAT IS THE NATURE OF AESTHETIC EXPERIENCE?

Aesthetic Experience: A Question of Content

Noël Carroll

Introduction

For many philosophers, the notion of aesthetic experience is so central to the philosophy of art that they are inclined to call the entire field of inquiry "aesthetics." They believe that art can be defined in terms of aesthetic experience – for them, an artwork just is something produced with the intention to promote aesthetic experience. And they believe that the degree of excellence found in an artwork can be measured in virtue of aesthetic experience – that is, an artwork is good exactly in proportion to the amount of aesthetic experience it affords. For such philosophers – called aesthetic theorists of art – aesthetic experience is the philosopher's stone, the charm that discloses all the secrets of the philosophy of art. But obviously before those mysteries can be unlocked, one must first offer an account of the nature of aesthetic experience. So in those precincts where the aesthetic theory of art presides, the first order of business for the philosopher of art is to deliver such an account.

Of course, not all philosophers of art regard aesthetic experience as so utterly central to the field as do aesthetic theorists. I, for example, do not. Nevertheless, inasmuch as artists, art lovers, and philosophers are constantly talking about aesthetic experience – in ways that are generally converging and reciprocally intelligible – it seems likely that they have something definite in mind, rather than something chimerical or mythic – something, moreover, alluded to so frequently that it is significant enough to warrant the attention of any philosopher committed to elucidating the prevalent concepts of the artworld. That is, even if one does not believe, as aesthetic theorists do, that aesthetic experience is the philosophical cornerstone of the artworld, insofar as one is a philosopher of art, one has an obligation to attempt to clarify the concept of aesthetic experience.

The purpose of this chapter is to do just that – to characterize aesthetic experience, notably with respect to the aesthetic experience of artworks. In this regard, questions about whether the notion of aesthetic experience can be dragooned to define art or to calculate artistic value will be put to one side.[1] Similarly, the issue of the aesthetic experience of nature will be deferred, for the most part, until after I have sketched a positive account of the aesthetic experience of art.

The notion of *aesthetic experience* has two components: the aesthetic and experience. Assuming that we have some inkling of what comprises an experience, the pressing issue for us is what to make of "the aesthetic." The word was introduced in the eighteenth century by Alexander Baumgarten, initially to stand for sensitive knowledge, knowledge delivered by the senses, or sensations which, following Descartes, Leibniz, and Wolfe, Baumgarten regarded as a matter of clear but indistinct ideas. However, even in Baumgarten's hands, the aesthetic came to be associated with the experience of artworks, where artworks appeared to be objects paradigmatically directed at sensitive cognition. This may seem strange to us, considering that literature or poetry is a leading artform, but one that is not primarily addressed to the senses. Yet, insofar as the reigning theories of art in the eighteenth century were representation theories, and insofar as literature/poetry could be thought of provoking inner images (percepts for the imagination) by means of their representations/descriptions, literature could be construed as affording sensitive knowledge at one step removed, so to speak.[2]

However, even if much of what we call aesthetic experience corresponds to what is sensed – either perceived outwardly or "sensed" inwardly – the way the concept has come to be applied exceeds its original usage. For example, the discovery and apprehension of the complex form of a novel like Joyce's *Ulysses* is today regarded as an exemplary instance of having an aesthetic experience, but it barely counts as a robust instance of the exercise of our powers of sensation.

Consequently, in order to develop an adequate account of aesthetic experience, we need to look beyond Baumgarten. In the period since Baumgarten, four major approaches to defining aesthetic experience have emerged. They can be called: the affect-oriented approach, the epistemic approach, the axiological approach, and the content-oriented approach. Historically, elements of these approaches have been combined in various ways, resulting in a diversity of theories of aesthetic experience. In this essay, however, I will be concerned exclusively with these approaches in their pure forms, asking whether any of them can provide an adequate account of aesthetic experience. For clearly if one of these approaches is satisfactory in its pure form, then there is scant reason to cobble together a combinatory theory.

In what follows then, we will assay the strengths and weaknesses of these four approaches to characterizing aesthetic experience. Nevertheless, before proceeding any further, it is perhaps only fair to admit that I prefer a version of the content-oriented characterization of aesthetic experience. Thus the shape this chapter takes is fundamentally that of a disjunctive syllogism, setting out the four alternative approaches as the basic options in this arena of debate and then finding the content-oriented approach to be the last one standing.[3]

The Affect-Oriented Approach

Affect-oriented approaches to the characterization of aesthetic experience take it to be marked by a certain experiential quale, or pulsation, or peculiar feeling tone which is sometimes referred to gingerly in the French tradition by the circumlocution *je ne sais quoi*; Clive Bell thought of it as a highly distinctive feeling with which every true lover of art is intimately familiar. Undoubtedly, the affect-oriented approach derives from Baumgarten's correlation of the aesthetic with sensitive knowledge – perception, sensation, and, in short, feeling. Thus, on this view, aesthetic experience is thought to be a sort of feeling or affect.

This suggestion, needless to say, provokes an inevitable question – namely, "what sort of feeling?" There are so many different kinds of feelings that might attend an experience of a work of art – claustrophobia and a sense of oppressiveness in response to a *film noir* or elation while watching Ruth St. Denis's choreography for *Soaring*, and so on. Perhaps at one time or another virtually every feeling that a human can undergo might figure as an ingredient in some aesthetic experience. But then saying that aesthetic experience is marked by some feeling is of no use, unless the field of relevant feelings can be appreciably narrowed. Simply having feelings, in other words, will not differentiate aesthetic experiences from other sorts.

At this point, it is often suggested that whatever other feelings aesthetic experience involves, it is always comprised of pleasure – either pleasure undiluted, or pleasure in response to or in combination with the other feelings in play in the experience. That is, something, it might be said, is an aesthetic experience if and only if it is pleasurable.

Yet obviously pleasure is not a sufficient condition for aesthetic experience, since sex, drugs, drink, and food, among other things, elicit feelings of pleasure, though indulging in these delights are not typically regarded as aesthetic experiences. Indeed, they are sometimes treated as the very antitheses to aesthetic experience. So it is unlikely that if an experience involves pleasure, then it is automatically an aesthetic experience, rather than some other kind of experience.

But maybe pleasure is a necessary condition for aesthetic experience. However, the proposal that something is an aesthetic experience only if it involves pleasure is suspect from several directions. First, many aesthetic experiences, even though they involve feelings, need not be defined by feelings of pleasure. As one circulates around the statue of "The Prince of the World" in St Sebald in Nürnberg, one sees that behind his comely facade is a mass of decay; beneath that surface handsomeness, the opening in the back of his cloak reveals the corruption of the flesh. Normal viewers do not feel, nor are they intended to feel, pleasure at this manifestation of bodily decomposition. They are meant to be disgusted which, in turn, is intended to remind them that earthly existence is both fleeting and foul, and that corporeal delights are futile and vain. The statue is a *memento mori*. This is also the intended or mandated affect of the death's heads that appear on tables laden with luscious comestibles throughout the *vanitas* tradition of painting, as well as the design behind many contemporary works by artists like Damien Hirst, who compose works that encourage the contemplation of mortality.

In such cases, the feelings of disgust have a legitimate claim to the title of aesthetic experience, since the disgust in question is connected to the percipient's detection of and immersion in the salient aesthetic properties of the pertinent works. But disgust is not pleasurable nor is it plausible to suggest that the informed viewer of "The Prince of the World" takes pleasure or is intended to take pleasure in being disgusted, since not only is the feeling of disgust displeasurable, but delight in the statue would, from the artist's point of view, defeat the mandated purpose of his design. Similar kinds of observations can be made about the affect elicited by many instances of transgressive art of the modern period. Consequently, it is extremely improbable that pleasure is a necessary condition for having aesthetic experience.

Moreover, not only are there artworks that are intended to engender aesthetic experiences involving affects inconsistent with pleasure; displeasure is also the result of many artworks that are originally designed to delight. Here I have in mind defective artworks. For example, the performance of the sonata might have been intended to cause pleasure; but the execution is so inept that it engenders boredom and even pain. What are we to call the experience of sitting through such a performance, attempting to follow its formal and expressive development, but being defeated in the process? Surely the experience of following or trying to follow the form of an artwork is an aesthetic experience. What else would it be? But inasmuch as an incompetent work may frustrate our efforts to derive pleasure from its formal design, and yet the experience still has a claim to being called aesthetic, then pleasure cannot be an essential feature of aesthetic experience.

To the extent that pleasure is regarded as *prima facie* good, to stipulate that pleasure is a necessary condition of aesthetic experience makes the concept of aesthetic experience a commendatory concept; aesthetic experience in this view would be valuable by definition. However, aesthetic experience is arguably a descriptive concept – attending to the form of an artwork, whether it is pleasurable or valuable or not is ostensibly an aesthetic experience. How else would we classify it? So the commendatory use of the concept is not its primary use; the descriptive usage would appear to be more fundamental. Thus, again, it seems that pleasure is not a necessary condition for having an experience categorized as aesthetic.

So far the notion that pleasure is a necessary condition for aesthetic experience has been challenged on the grounds that aesthetic experiences, properly so called, may involve feelings other than pleasure – indeed, feelings that preclude pleasure. However, an even deeper objection to the thesis is that there may be aesthetic experiences that involve no feelings or sensations at all. That is, some aesthetic experiences may not only be bereft of pleasure, but may lack affect altogether. For example, one might take note of the angularity of Katherine Hepburn's body, her gestures, her facial structure, and her way of speaking and, in addition, realize how this all "fits" with the "edginess" that her characters are meant to project; and yet one may take no pleasure, nor suffer any other affect while doing so. On what grounds would it be denied that this is an aesthetic experience? And if it is not an aesthetic experience, what sort is it?

The objection that aesthetic experiences may be affectless cuts more deeply than our previous objections, since it not only undermines the hypothesis that pleasure is a necessary condition for aesthetic experience; it contests the very presupposition of affect-oriented approaches to aesthetic experience. For if there are aesthetic experiences without feeling, sensation, or affect, as there seem to be, then visceral commotion of any sort is neither a necessary nor sufficient condition for aesthetic experience.

One, of course, might claim that in cases of aesthetic experience that appear affectless, there really always are feelings, but very minute ones. However, that gambit gives every indication of being egregiously *ad hoc*. Similarly, the suggestion that simply apprehending the aforementioned properties of Katherine Hepburn, and grasping their coherence together, requires affect is empirically false and, in any case, begs the question.

It might be said that seeing how these properties go together – that is, "getting it" – can be an occasion for pleasure. I would not wish to deny that possibility. But suppose that someone scrupulously discerns the relevant properties and makes out the appropriate relationships here, and yet does not feel pleasure? This is certainly a possible case. Why deny that it is an aesthetic experience? And if it is not an aesthetic experience, what other kind of experience might it be?

By this point in the discussion, the proponent of the affect-oriented approach might complain that the view that pleasure is the mark of aesthetic experience is not being given a fair shake. For this strategy for characterizing aesthetic experience does not make pleasure *simpliciter* the criterion of aesthetic experience, but, rather, something more complex – namely, *disinterested* pleasure. Perhaps this special sort of pleasure can evade some of the objections posed so far. This, of course, will depend upon what the notion of disinterested pleasure signifies. Unfortunately, it signifies different things for different theorists. Nevertheless, I do not think that, on any of its better known variants, it lends any credence to the affect-oriented approach to aesthetic experience.

The idea of disinterest, as propounded early on by Lord Shaftesbury, meant "not motivated by self-concern." On this understanding, a pleasure is disinterested if its object is not my own well-being, but something else. I take pleasure in the look of the landscape and not in the fact that my ownership of it is worth millions to me. In this sense of disinterested pleasure, the pleasure at issue is not the sort of peculiar feeling tone that the affect-oriented approach is searching for. The high I derive from seeing the property and the high derived from the recognition that I own something valuable as sensations of euphoria are pretty much the same. So the concept of disinterested pleasure does not locate a specific feeling, categorically distinct from other feelings of pleasure, and, therefore, capable of hiving off aesthetic experience, parsed as a phenomenologically discriminable affect, from other sorts of pleasures and their corresponding experiences (e.g., gustatory or sexual experiences).

Historically, the conjunction of aesthetic experience with pleasure appears to occur initially in the context of discussions of judgments of taste or positive aesthetic judgments, of which "This rose is beautiful" is paradigmatic. Here the experience of pleasure is regarded as the ground for the judgment of beauty. This pleasure should be disinterested in the sense that it should not be biased personally. But three things need to be noticed about disinterested pleasure here.

First, though it may be plausible (though possibly false) to conjecture that a feeling of pleasure is required in order for a percipient to advance a legitimate judgment of beauty, not all aesthetic experiences are reducible, without begging the question, to experiences of beauty. Thus, there may be aesthetic experiences that do not track beauty and, therefore, do not require feelings of pleasure – thereby eliminating the affect-oriented approach's best candidate for the quale that constitutes a necessary condition for aesthetic experience.

Second, aesthetic experiences should not be conflated with aesthetic judgments. Though aesthetic judgments may presuppose aesthetic experiences, the two are different. So even if positive aesthetic judgments mandate some feeling of pleasure (a dubious hypothesis in my book), it would not follow that aesthetic experiences do. That the tedium of the concert is an unpleasurable aesthetic experience is not contradicted by the fact that a positive judgment or assessment of such a concert might be said to require some palpitation of pleasure in the breast of the percipient. For aesthetic experiences are not the same as positive aesthetic judgments. That is, even if positive aesthetic judgments (or, at least, those involving attributions of beauty) must rest upon a pleasurable aesthetic experience, an experience can be aesthetic without being pleasurable.

And lastly, as we've already seen, disinterest is not, in its primary usage, an affect; it has no phenomenological tone of its own. A self-interested pleasure does not feel any differently than a nonself-centered one. Consequently, saying that aesthetic experience is marked by disinterested pleasure does not supply the wherewithal to distinguish these sorts of experiences from others. The pleasure taken in looking at the orchard cannot be differentiated in virtue of qualia from the twinge of pleasure born of owning the orchard.

Of course, within the tradition that speaks of disinterested pleasure, the idea of disinterestedness became more extensive than merely "not to one's own advantage"; it came to stand for the disavowal of any advantage whatsoever – moral, political, social, religious, and so on. Yet even with this expansion, the concept of disinterested pleasure is still of no use to the affect-oriented approach to characterizing aesthetic experience, since it does not discriminate between pleasures at the level of feeling. The sensation of exultation felt in response to a striking sunrise is not, in terms of its tonal qualities, discriminable by introspection from exultation in response to the resurrection of Christ or to the victory of the oppressed. Since disinterest in its primary use does not specify any particular affective tingle or tremor, disinterested pleasure is not going to supply the theorists who aspire to define aesthetic experience by means of certain felt affective qualities (especially ones thought of in terms of phenomenologically discriminable kinds of pleasure) with what they need to achieve their purposes.

There is, however, within the tradition, at least one way of developing the idea of disinterest that does intersect with a discernible quality of feeling. For Kant, disinterested pleasure is pleasure not caused by the prospect of advantage. It is a way of describing from whence the pleasure comes. It comes free of considerations of advantage for either self or society. But perhaps beginning with Schopenhauer, there emerges the view that aesthetic experiences are those in which in the very process of having them we are freed or liberated from the cares of self and society, that is, from every ordinary concern to which flesh is heir. This is a particular kind of pleasure – one with its own affective tone. It is a feeling of release from the everyday – a sense of relief. For Clive Bell, it is the experience of being lifted out of the quotidian; for Edward Bullough, it is a feeling of being distanced; Monroe C. Beardsley calls it felt freedom. In this way of thinking, aesthetic experience does come suffused with its own variety of affect, a specifiable modality of pleasure, namely a sense of release from mundane, human preoccupations with respect to oneself, one's tribe (both narrowly and broadly construed), and humanity at large.

This suggestion, of courses, faces some of the difficulties already encountered with other variations of the affect-oriented approach. Is release from worldly concerns a sufficient condition for aesthetic experience? Wouldn't the state of nirvana count as aesthetic experience then? But that seems wrong.

Moreover, if release of any sort is taken to be a necessary condition for aesthetic experience, then we are back to the problem of flawed artworks – for instance, the infelicitous performance of the Wagnerian opera that leaves us feeling trapped in the concert hall. In such a case, we feel no pleasure, let alone relief. But once again this experience is certainly an aesthetic one, unless we unadvisedly stipulate that aesthetic experiences are always necessarily rewarding affectively – always occasions of pleasure, delight, or enjoyment in terms of release. But surely most of the life of aesthetes willing to explore the wide range of the art on offer is spent encountering artworks whose forms and qualities leave them either indifferent or disgruntled. Yet to discount as aesthetic most of the experience of those who approach the formal and aesthetic properties of artworks correctly smacks of arbitrariness.

Moreover, another problem with the present extension of the notion of disinterested pleasure is that it appears unlikely that the appropriate aesthetic experience of successful artworks always involves an episode of felt release – not even release from moral and political concerns. Sartre's *No Exit* (*Huis Clos*) as its title suggests, is not intended to, nor does it, engender a sense of release in the prepared spectator, but rather the feeling of inescapability it invites contributes to an aesthetic experience of the play, since that sense of hopelessness is an appropriate response to both the form and the expressive qualities of the play, a way of detecting or apprehending and then assessing them (or appreciating them).[4]

Likewise, rather than abetting an air of release, an artwork might call forth burdensome feelings with practical, moral, and/or political overtones. If performed correctly, Friedrich Durrenmatt's *The Visit* should leave audiences with the recognition that they would have behaved as the villagers in the play behaved. That is, a sense of guilt and a felt weight of moral responsibility is mandated by the play; the experience is not one of being lifted out of the everyday world, but a feeling of being brought down to earth and confronted with who we really are and are not, and of whom instead we should become morally. In other words, the play does not engender release from our everyday lives; it returns us to our everyday lives and reminds us of our moral obligations, while, at the same time, the sense of guilt it instills puts us in touch with the dominant expressive qualities of the play.

Likewise, Kafka's *The Trial* imparts a sense of being irredeemably lost within the snares of bureaucracy in way that encourages socially significant reflection on the inhuman systems of (ir)rationalization we endure under modernity. That frustrating experience of being mystified and the fear and indignation that comes with it involve neither a feeling of liberation in particular nor pleasure more generally; they register

Aesthetic Experience: A Question of Content | 75 |

soberingly our sociopolitical plight. But they are no less legitimate ingredients of our aesthetic experience for their implication with real world concerns, since these affects, though not the sort typically favored by affect-oriented theorists, connect us with salient formal and expressive features of *The Trial*. Indeed, these feelings of imprisonment (rather than release) disclose essential artistic structures and properties of *The Trial* to us, enabling us to apprehend, interpret, and weigh them.

In short, supposing that the idea of release from the everyday (including the practical, the moral, and the political) is an intelligible one, it does not appear to be the hallmark of every aesthetic experience. For we have seen examples of aesthetic experience that are at odds with the putative fugues from the ordinary concerns that affect-oriented theorists often advance as necessary conditions of aesthetic experience. Moreover, there are also, I would maintain, cases of aesthetic experience where no palpitation of relief obtains – I note, for instance, how solidly the pyramid sits on the horizon with no flash of buoyancy in my chest, or I take in how sharply articulated the musculature of the statue is with no glimmering of a transition within my inner states whatsoever. These seem unquestionably to be aesthetic experiences. Therefore, aesthetic experiences can obtain without attending feelings of liberation.

Of course, at this juncture, the affect-oriented theorist of aesthetic experience may attempt to water down the notion of release from the everyday to the point where it amounts to nothing more than that the percipient, while experiencing an object aesthetically, is not distracted by everyday concerns like the mortgage payments or ecological disaster. But in such cases, it does not seem apposite to describe the percipient's focus in terms of an emotional liberation or emancipation from everyday concerns. This is not a special process of release; it is a matter of simply paying attention on a par with the way in which we bracket thoughts about our mortgage payments from our minds when we carefully attend to the steps in a recipe while carrying out the practical task of preparing a meal.

Though I have not canvassed every candidate an affect-oriented aesthetic theorist might put forward, my review of some of the most recurrent ones provisionally indicates that aesthetic experience does not necessarily possess unique experiential qualia that set it off from other sorts of experience. If there is such a quale, then the burden of proof falls to the affect-oriented theorist to produce it, though let us not hold our breath while waiting, since the diversity of the objects of aesthetic experience and the wide variety of the responses they are designed to elicit would seem to be so heterogeneous as to resist summary in terms of a single affect; surely the odds are stacked precipitously against the likelihood of there being a common perturbation, tickle, or feeling tone that runs through every aesthetic experience. And if it is improbable that aesthetic experience can be identified in terms of a distinctive affective property, then such experiences must be identified either in terms of the way they are known, or in terms of the distinctive form of value they embody, or in terms of their content.

The Epistemic Approach

Like the affect-oriented approach to characterizing aesthetic experience, the epistemic approach[5] is also connected to the original idea that the realm of the aesthetic is that of sensitive knowledge or apprehension by the senses or perception. For the epistemic approach to aesthetic experience presupposes that an aesthetic experience involves coming to know its object in a specific way, namely directly. To encounter an object aesthetically is to perceive it – to hear it or to see it – or, if it is a work of literature, one must nevertheless inspect it directly. One does not have an aesthetic experience of an object, on this view, unless one peruses the particular object in question for oneself. You cannot have an aesthetic experience on the basis of a report about the object by some second party. The particular object at issue must be the immediate source of an aesthetic experience, properly so called. This approach to aesthetic experience can be called epistemic insofar as it requires that what qualifies an experience as aesthetic is the manner in which one is required to come to know or otherwise cognitively engage the relevant objects of said experience: one's experiences must be object-directed; one must experience the particular object of that experience directly. This is a necessary condition of aesthetic experience.

The deep association of the aesthetic with the perceptual shows the influence of this tradition. This sometimes surfaces in talk that links the aesthetic exclusively with appearances. Also, the notion that the aesthetic is tied to the particular rather than to the general or the conceptual belies the link between thinking about the aesthetic and the perceptual, since the object of perception is most naturally thought of as a particular. But, of course, the putative correlation of the aesthetic with the perceptual is inadequate as long as one wishes to grant that there are aesthetic experiences of literature and especially poetry, since one does not encounter the objects of these representations by looking (that is, *perceptually* in the requisite sense) but by reading. So in order to sustain some link to perception, the requirement needs to be weakened to no more than that for an experience to be aesthetic, the percipient must examine the pertinent object directly for himself or herself. One does not have an aesthetic experience based on the second-hand testimony of others. An experience is aesthetic only if it is governed by a close encounter of the third kind with the pertinent object.

Sometimes this epistemic requirement may be stated in terms of the idea that the experience is being pursued for its *own sake* or that it is directed at *intrinsic properties of the object*. This language can be confusing, since very similar locutions also figure in axiological characterizations of aesthetic experience. However, when these locutions appear in epistemic accounts, they boil down to the notion that aesthetic experiences are restricted to the direct experience of something – the experience of the intrinsic properties of the object (those available by direct inspection)[6] pursued for the sake of encountering or perceiving those properties "in the flesh," so to speak, rather than as an optional pretext for daydreaming or free-floating fantasies.[7] The aesthetic experience, properly so called, must be directed by an object that is literally present to the aesthete and its literal presence mandates the way in which it is to be negotiated by the percipient.

The notion of object-directedness is central to the epistemic approach to aesthetic experience. This appears to have two ideas built into it: that one must directly encounter the object of such an experience and that one's response be governed by the object. In all likelihood, there is also the assumption that in order to guarantee that one's response to the object is governed by it, one must be experiencing the object directly. However, that does not seem to me to be the case. One's response to the object may be governed by the object in a normatively appropriate way – that is, one's cognitions with respect to the object can be precisely those mandated by the object – without requiring one's direct inspection of the object. But if this is the case, then the crux of the epistemic approach to aesthetic experience – the claim that something is an aesthetic experience only if it involves the direct inspection of its objects – is false, and, in consequence, aesthetic experience does not necessarily demand a specific type of knowledge, namely knowledge by personal acquaintance.

Evidence for the claim that one can have normatively appropriate, aesthetic experiences of objects such as artworks without directly encountering the works in question abound in the arena of artmaking often referred to as *conceptual art*. One of the most famous examples of this kind of art is *Fountain* by Marcel Duchamp. This work, in its various manifestations, has been widely discussed by artists, philosophers, critics, art historians, and innumerable members of the lay audience who follow the art world. But one wonders whether all those who speak of it have seen it or even a photograph of it. Of course, that they speak of it shows nothing. Yet I conjecture that quite often commentators who have not directly encountered *Fountain* have nevertheless made insightful remarks about it or, at least, have thought them to themselves when they have heard or read about *Fountain* second hand – that is, they have, so to say, "gotten it," but without eyeballing it. Have they not then had an aesthetic experience?

At this point, the proponent of the epistemic account is apt to cry "foul!" The kind of responses to *Fountain* to which I have just adverted, it may be charged, cannot be called aesthetic experiences, save by begging the question against the epistemic theorist of aesthetic experience. For on this view, an experience cannot be aesthetic, unless it is "face-to-face." Moreover, the epistemic theorist of aesthetic experience may also claim further support in this matter from the conceptual artists themselves, including Duchamp. For those artists maintain that their work is antiaesthetic (Duchamp intended to undermine the retinal or *perceptual* claims of painting); and their understanding of the way in which their work is "antiaesthetic" is that it does not support aesthetic experience either in terms of yielding visual pleasure or, crucially in the present case, in terms of requiring a direct encounter with the artwork (thereby supposedly undermining the alleged commodity value of the artwork). So if the theorists of aesthetic experience and the conceptual artists themselves agree that the experiences to which I am alluding are not aesthetic experiences, on what grounds can I use responses to conceptual art, or, at least some of them, as counterexamples to the epistemic approach?

My argument is this: the identification and/or appreciation of the form of an artwork is perhaps the paradigmatic example of an aesthetic experience. This view finds voice in the work of Bell and can arguably be traced back to Kant. I take it that every participant in the discussion accepts this premise, even if he or she does not limit aesthetic experience to the experience of form. Nevertheless, it is not the case that one must inspect an artwork directly in order to identify and/or appreciate the form of an artwork.

The form of an artwork is the ensemble of choices intended to realize the point or purpose of an artwork.[8] Furthermore, one may be able to grasp the pertinent choice or ensemble of the choices and the corresponding interrelationships that enable an artwork to secure its point or purpose without inspecting the work directly. From a

Noël Carroll

photograph, or, even more importantly for my argument, from a reliable description of *Fountain*, someone informed about art history can glean the subversive purpose of the piece and see how the choice of a urinal and its inversion ingeniously challenges various presuppositions about art; one can, again simply from a reliable description of the work, savor how suitable – how diabolically apposite – Duchamp's choices and minimal artisanship advance the point of the work: that anything, even something remote from the imprint of the artist, can be an artwork.

Calling the work *Fountain*, for example, connects it with the sort of Renaissance marvels that decorate Rome and which no one would deny are artworks. Duchamp's found object explores the same territory as more ornate fountains, trading, as it does, in running water. Likewise, as is the case of other recognized artworks, Duchamp's *Fountain* has a subject, namely the nature of art, and it may even afford for some either the aesthetic pleasure of a witty jest, a Hobbesian chuckle of superiority at the apoplexy of the outraged philistine, or a sense of satisfaction at the elegance with which Duchamp has combined his materials so economically to make his points.

That is, one can contemplate the form of *Fountain* from afar, from a photograph, but, again more significantly, from a reliable description as well. One need not see *Fountain* to grasp and/or to appreciate the form of the work – that is, the way its elements interact cleverly to carry its purpose. A reliable description will do.

At this point, it may be alleged that one cannot have a full aesthetic experience of the work without seeing it. But apart from the question of what would constitute a *full* aesthetic experience, all that is required to show that the epistemic approach to aesthetic experience is false is that some quantum of aesthetic experience is possible without directly confronting the relevant object. And clearly one can derive an accurate sense of the form of many conceptual artworks – for example, of their structures of rhetorical address – and perhaps even come to admire them on the basis of a reliable description.[9] Moreover, if this is true of the experience of the formal structures of conceptual artworks, might not it also be true of other kinds of art?[10]

Similar stories can be told of further works by Duchamp, such as *In Advance of a Broken Arm*, and of works by his followers, including Language Artists, performance artists, and conceptual artists in general. One of the animating ideas of much conceptual art is that, even if it exists as a performance or a specific object, it is primarily as a concept that it is to be approached; one may cogitate about the design of such objects – their point, their subtending rhetorical construction, and the interrelation of the two – without being in their presence. Photographs, other forms of documentation, and, in the most pertinent case for our purposes, reliable descriptions, suffice. In many instances, this very feature of the conceptual artwork is of central importance, since it is putatively intended to subvert the alleged commodity fetishism of the artworld. But, be that as it may, one can experience the formal design of many conceptual artworks as it is relayed to us by a reliable description. So, insofar as an experience of the formal design of an artwork is an aesthetic experience, it is not necessary to inspect such an object directly in order to have an aesthetic experience of it.

Often it is said that one cannot have an aesthetic experience of an artwork on the basis of a description because features of the artwork – like the precise thickness of a line – may be omitted from the best imaginable description, and yet, inasmuch as that feature may influence our perception of the object subtly, any experience based on such a description will be defective. Here, of course, one wonders whether we are talking about aesthetic experiences of objects or aesthetic judgments of objects. The real anxiety seems to be that if we are judging the object aesthetically, we cannot judge (in the sense of evaluate) its perceptual effects fairly unless we see it. But even if one disagrees with my contention that aesthetic experiences are distinct from aesthetic judgments, considerations like this will not deflect the conceptual art case, since the conceptual artworks we have in mind, like Duchamp's readymades, are designed and/or selected in such a way that such perceptible variations are irrelevant to the formal structure of the work. When one thinks of form in terms of features like symmetry and balance, fine differences in line and shading can be decisive to one's experience. But the formal design of many conceptual works does not require the eye to descry it; it can be retrieved through a description. Therefore, direct inspection is not necessarily a condition for aesthetic experience.

One objection to the preceding argument might be that the "close encounter" requirement is just built into the notion of an experience of X of any sort, including an aesthetic experience. If that were true, it would, of course, undermine any attempt to use the epistemic account as a sufficient condition for aesthetic experience.[11] But, in any event, it does not seem convincing to regard every experience as necessarily direct; if they were, why would we speak of "direct experience" as if it contrasted with some other kind of experience? Furthermore, it does not seem to be the case that even the aesthetic experiences the epistemic theorist countenances must be direct in all instances. For surely an epistemic theorist will regard as an aesthetic experience a reflection on the form of a poem once read (once experienced directly) in memory.

A second response to my denial that direct experience of the relevant object is necessary for aesthetic experience may involve a reconstrual of the requirement on the part of the epistemic theorist. Instead of demanding that the aesthete must inspect the object directly in order to experience it aesthetically, it might be proposed that in order to verify that the object has the property upon which the aesthetic experience is putatively focused, one must engage in the activity of direct inspection; thus, in order to have a flawless aesthetic experience, direct inspection of the object of said experience is requisite.

But, again, the identification of the formal design of certain conceptual artworks and their associated formal properties need not require direct inspection in order to verify that the works in question possess the imputed properties, so long as one has access to a reliable description of the work; indeed, some conceptual works may be designed in such a way that one cannot directly inspect them. Needless to say, the epistemic theorist may maintain that one cannot know that one is relying on a reliable account of the work, unless one has directly experienced the work. But why should that be true of accounts of artworks when it is not true of accounts of other sorts of things? This is something the epistemic theorist would have to establish in a way that does not beg the question. After all, scientists do not have to run every experiment themselves in order to presume that the findings reported by respected authorities in reputable journals are reliable.[12]

Noël Carroll

The Axiological Approach

The axiological approach to characterizing aesthetic experience identifies it in terms of the kind of value it is thought to secure, typically intrinsic value or value for its own sake. This is perhaps the most common way of regarding aesthetic experience today. It probably is a descendant of the view that aesthetic experience is essentially pleasurable. For if one regards pleasure as its own reward, as many philosophers do, then aesthetic pleasure is consequently valuable for its own sake. That is, it is a short step from the belief that pleasure is valued for its own sake to the view that aesthetic experience, conceived as essentially pleasure, is something valued for its own sake.

The concept of disinterested pleasure, beloved of the tradition since at least Kant, moreover, intensifies the association of aesthetic experience with intrinsic value, since the very idea of "disinterestedness" tends to be defined as "not instrumentally valuable." Thus the view that aesthetic experience is valuable for its own sake emerges from two converging lines of thought: that it is essentially pleasurable *and* disinterested.

Of course, we have already seen that the correlation of aesthetic experience with pleasure is inadequate. But the axiological approach, though probably a mutation of the affect-oriented approach, does not connect aesthetic experience to pleasure essentially. It requires rather that the aesthetic experience be valued for its own sake. Perhaps in some cases, the alleged intrinsic value of the experience in question is rooted in the pleasure it imparts. But inasmuch as the axiologists maintain that an experience can be valued for its own sake without being pleasurable, they can agree that there are aesthetic experiences that are not pleasurable. Thus the axiological approach is not vulnerable to certain of the counterexamples that were raised against the affect-oriented approach, such as the experience of paintings predicated on eliciting revulsion toward the delights of the flesh. For if such experiences of mortification are valued by percipients for their own sake, they are aesthetic experiences, albeit unpleasant ones.[13]

By the same token, however, valuation for its own sake cannot be a sufficient condition for aesthetic experience, since if one believes in intrinsic value, one is likely to countenance other sorts of purportedly autotelic activities,[14] such as playing chess, as equally valuable for their own sake. Consequently, the safest version of the axiological approach claims no more than that being valued for its own sake is at most a necessary condition for aesthetic experience.

When speaking of the aesthetic experience of artworks, it is important to locate in the right place that which is being valued for its own sake. One must be careful not to confuse the artwork with the experience of the artwork. For if one values the artwork because it affords an experience valued for its own sake then, without further qualification, the artwork would not appear to be valued for its own sake, but rather to be valued instrumentally as something that makes an intrinsically valuable experience available to the percipient.

Furthermore, a great many of the artworks of the past, especially the premodern past, are religious – religious in content and religious in virtue of the sorts of experiences they are supposed to engender. One wonders whether the reverence for the artwork – that experience said to be valued for its own sake – as putatively evinced by modern aestheticians is not merely a displacement of the religious reception of previous art. Has the experience of the numinous, putatively valuable for its own sake, been confused with the response to the artwork as the vehicle that makes the holy manifest? Is that why museums are sometimes called our contemporary cathedrals?

Though the axiological approach does not have all the liabilities of the affect-oriented approach, it does share some of them. It too appears to conflate having an aesthetic experience with rendering an aesthetic judgment. For surely to assign intrinsic value to an experience is to evaluate it positively. But this then raises the problems of unrewarding experiences of bad art, on the one hand, and indifferent experiences of routine artworks, on the other hand.

One may follow the formal permutations of a musical theme as it moves from one section of the orchestra to another and yet judge the experience as without value, either intrinsic or otherwise, because the artwork itself is unintentionally grating. Or perhaps the formal structure is respectable enough, but uninspired in a way that gives rise to indifference. In such cases, where one's attention is directed in the right way at the formal design of the work, it seems appropriate to call the aforesaid responses aesthetic experiences (how else should we categorize them), but they are not valued for their own sake, since they are not valued at all.

It may be true that an aesthetic judgment qua evaluation must contain a positive value element (intrinsic or instrumental) or maybe just some value element (positive or negative). But undoubtedly there are aesthetic experiences that are negative or indifferent. One cannot deny this, save by confusing aesthetic judgments with aesthetic experiences – that is, by conflating a form of commendation and/or evaluation with experiencing the object aesthetically.

It might be said in response to the case of the unrewarding experience elicited by bad artworks that the relevant aesthetic experiences are not necessarily valuable for their own sake, but only that they must be intended to be so. Yet this seems false: the experience of terror that certain tribal masks are supposed to provoke in the enemy is not intended by the artificers of such designs to be valued by foreign onlookers for their own sake. The experience promoted by such masks is intended to elicit flight, something that the makers of the images value not for its own sake, but for the security of their tribe.

Another problem with the axiological approach is that it is stupendously uninformative. It provides no guidance about how to go about having an aesthetic experience. Probably the reason for this amazing absence of specificity has to do with the fact that the axiologist, in effect, defines aesthetic experience almost exclusively in negative terms. Aesthetic experience is valuable intrinsically – that is, it supposedly has no instrumental value of any sort. It is an experience *not* valued for its service to morality, politics, religion, and so on. It is something one values for its own sake. But how precisely does one go about doing that?

The axiologist's concept of aesthetic experience is woefully empty in terms of informational content; it leaves someone interested in having such experiences with no directions about how to proceed. Perhaps a corollary of this problem is that if one wishes to do empirical research on the subject of aesthetic experience, one would have no idea, on the basis of the axiological account, of what features of our interactions

Noël Carroll

with artworks to scrutinize; the pertinent variables of aesthetic experience that the psychologist might interrogate are left completely blank and undefined by the axiologist.

Nevertheless, despite the axiological theory, we do know how to teach children ways in which to have aesthetic experiences – we know to tell them to look at certain aspects of artworks and in certain ways. Having an aesthetic experience can be specified in terms of certain concrete operations, like listening for recurring themes and echoes in music, which can be taught explicitly and also observed by psychologists. But this would hardly seem feasible, if aesthetic experience is to be simply defined as that sort of experience which is valued for its own sake. Who could instruct anyone else in how to have such an experience or to find one on the basis of the exceedingly thin account the axiologist offers?

There is also an important ambiguity that lies at the heart of many axiological characterizations of aesthetic experience; it pertains to the way in which we are to understand the qualification "for its own sake." Is the aesthetic experience one that is said to be necessarily valuable for its own sake from an objective point of view (the view from nowhere) or from the subjective point of view (from the perspective of the percipient's own belief system). That is, is aesthetic experience, on the axiologist's conception, good in a noninstrumental way, an aspect of human flourishing rather than a cause or means to flourishing, *or* is aesthetic experience merely such that those who have it believe it to be noninstrumentally valuable (where so believing is compatible with the said experiences really being instrumentally valuable)? In other words, when it is claimed that aesthetic experience is valuable for its own sake, is the axiologist saying the experience actually is, in some sense, valuable for its own sake, or only that this is what the people who undergo such experiences necessarily, typically believe of them.

The contention that aesthetic experience is objectively valuable for its own sake – that it possesses no instrumental value whatsoever – is difficult to fathom. Cultures, both literate and tribal, have spent large resources, sometimes on a grandiose scale, in order to secure the conditions for aesthetic experience, such as artworks. But this would be a mystery were it true that aesthetic experience yields no instrumental value whatsoever. It confounds the naturalistic perspective to imagine that so many sacrifices, both individual and social, have been made in order to facilitate experiences that have no beneficial or adaptive consequences. The view that aesthetic experiences are objectively valuable for their own sake does not fit with what secularists generally presume about human nature. Typically, where humans make great efforts, those endeavors are rewarded with advantages, even if they are not initially obvious ones (but only "known" by our naturally selected hard-wiring). That, at least, is certainly our best framework for explaining long-standing human (and animal and vegetable) regularities.

But this makes the notion that aesthetic experience is objectively valuable for its own sake anomalous. Why would natural selection tolerate such an expensive evolutionary attribute without some sort of instrumental advantage?

Moreover, this query is not merely methodological, since there are numerous and even attractive hypotheses that connect what are uncontroversial examples of aesthetic experience to beneficial or adaptive consequences. Surely these hypotheses are

Aesthetic Experience: A Question of Content | 83

extremely plausible rivals to the naturalistically deficient view that aesthetic experiences are simply intrinsically valuable objectively.

For example, aesthetic experiences are generally shared amongst audiences – theatergoers, filmgoers, concertgoers, dance aficionados, and the like – who find themselves in congruent emotive states. This is clearly an advantage from an evolutionary point of view, since it nurtures a feeling of group cohesion.[15] This suggests one way in which aesthetic experience is objectively valuable instrumentally and explains, at least in part, why societies cultivate it – why it appears to be a focus of important activity universally or nearly universally.

In a related vein, aesthetic experience involves the detection of expressive properties in the actions and products of conspecifics, sometimes by, as already mentioned, arousing parallel emotional states in us or by means of triggering our other capacities for recognizing the emotive states of others. Aesthetic experiences in this way make possible the transmission of a common culture of feeling – with obvious benefits for both the group and the individual. Inasmuch as aesthetic experience involves the detection of expressive properties, having such experiences exercises our powers for determining the emotive states of conspecifics as well as for expressing our own, while contemplating the form of artworks also refines our abilities to comprehend the purposes and intentions of others. These powers are clearly advantageous to social beings such as ourselves.[16]

Aesthetic experience, it is generally conceded, also enhances our perceptual powers of discrimination, thereby facilitating our capacities for recognizing, cataloguing, and reidentifying objects, capabilities whose sophistication can make one better able to navigate the world.[17] Furthermore, by engaging audiences in the play of their emotive, sensuous, and intellective potential, typically simultaneously, aesthetic experiences of art redundantly encode useful cultural knowledge about conspecifics and the environment across several faculties, thereby rendering it both more entrenched in memory and easier to access than it might otherwise be.[18]

Admittedly, these hypotheses require much more substantiation than one has space for in an essay of this sort. Nevertheless, even in their abbreviated form they or comparable biologically oriented accounts would appear to command more initial plausibility from the naturalistic point of view than what the axiologist can muster by way of explaining why aesthetic experiences of art have been sought by every known culture in every period of history. For what kind of explanation is it to say that these experiences just are objectively valuable for themselves? That seems virtually tantamount to saying that one simply does not know why they are valuable.

Impressed by the sort of evolutionary accounts suggested above, the axiologist, of course, might try to accommodate them by means of a compromise: namely, by saying that aesthetic experiences are valuable *both* for their own sake and for the sake of the instrumental benefits various evolutionary hypotheses suggest that they afford. But this solution raises certain questions. First, if aesthetic experience is to be defined in this manner, how will the axiologist differentiate aesthetic experience from other types of experience? Isn't this how the axiologist understands most other sorts of experience? So, even if this were, in some sense, a convincing resolution, wouldn't it signal the uselessness of the axiological approach for characterizing aesthetic experience?

Yet one wonders if this gambit can be persuasive in the least, since once the axiologist agrees that aesthetic experience is valued both instrumentally and intrinsically, one wants to ask what additional explanatory work the notion of intrinsic valuation contributes to our understanding of the persistence of the aesthetic experience of art. The instrumental value of aesthetic experience alone, it would appear, gives us what we need – our simplest explanation. Adding to the story that aesthetic experience is also intrinsically valuable brings no further insight into why human societies systematically pursue aesthetic experience. From an explanatory viewpoint, the notion that aesthetic experience is valuable for its own sake appears to be a gear that is extraneous to turning any other part of the mechanism. That is, it is not needed to explain why humans have the capacity for aesthetic experience, once the evolutionary advantages of that capacity are adumbrated.[19]

So challenged, the axiologists may modify their thesis: instead of contending that aesthetic experiences are objectively valuable for their own sake, they may only claim that they are subjectively valued for their own sake. That is, the subject who has such an experience regards it as valuable for its own sake. This belief may either be the cause or motivation that leads the subject to pursue aesthetic experiences or it may be how he or she assesses the experience retrospectively. In either case, what is being claimed is not that aesthetic experience *is* intrinsically valuable, but only that those who have these experiences think they are valuable for their own sake.[20]

Perhaps needless to say, that subjects believe aesthetic experiences to be intrinsically valuable cannot provide a sufficient condition for aesthetic experience, since subjects prone to believe in intrinsic value will declare other sorts of experience as well to be valuable for their own sake, as will the axiologists themselves. Thus the cautious axiologist will claim nothing more than that an experience is aesthetic only if it is believed to be valuable for its own sake by the person who has it. That is, a belief in the intrinsic value of the experience by the person who undergoes it is a necessary condition for aesthetic experience.

Undeniably there are people like this – people who would sincerely report that they read poetry for the intrinsic value of the experience it affords. Nor is there any reason to suspect that they are self-deceiving or incoherent in this matter. But even if there are some, or even a great many, who hold such convictions, it is not the case that a belief in the intrinsic value of an experience is essential to having an aesthetic experience.

In order to see why, consider the following case: a believer in the intrinsic value of aesthetic experience (whom we shall call "an aesthete") and an evolutionary psychologist both attend to the same piece of music. The evolutionary psychologist believes that this sort of aesthetic experience is instrumentally valuable objectively, perhaps for the kinds of reasons sketched above. Nevertheless, the evolutionary psychologist is alert to the same features of the music that the aesthete contemplates: the evolutionary psychologist tracks the same developments, recognizes the same expressive and aesthetic properties in the work, and discerns the same formal relationships that the aesthete does. Everything the aesthete surmises about the way in which the music modulates his attention, the evolutionary psychologist surmises; everything the aesthete feels, the evolutionary psychologist feels; both are cognitively and affectively tuned to the music in the same way; they both notice the same things about the structure of the music and its impact on their cognitive-perceptual-emotive system.

In short, we are imagining the possibility that the succession of computational states in these two individuals are type-identical with each other. They attend to the same artistic stimulus in the same ways, ways furthermore that are canonical within the traditions of reception within the relevant culture. Nor is there anything self-contradictory about imagining this sort of parallel.

Both percipients, then, are processing the artwork in the same ways, correctly noticing the same formal articulations and the same expressive and aesthetic properties. The only difference is that the aesthete believes this experience is valuable for its own sake, whereas the evolutionary psychologist believes it is instrumentally valuable.

According to the axiologist, this difference in belief is enough to discount the evolutionary psychologist's experience as aesthetic. But isn't this simply arbitrary? If the evolutionary psychologist is following the formal and expressive evolution of the music correctly and perceptively – indeed, precisely as the aesthete does – why should her beliefs about the value of the experience compromise the aesthetic standing of her experience? After all, there is no reason to suppose that the evolutionary psychologist's beliefs in the instrumental value of the experience would lead her to misidentify a formal pattern or to ignore an expressive property, or to deviate in any way from the same pathways of thought and attention mobilized by the aesthete. Surely the evolutionary psychologist is processing her experience aesthetically, if the aesthete is, since the two processes are step-by-step identical. Moreover, how else, other than as aesthetic experience, would we describe searching for formal designs with understanding or detecting expressive properties? Thus, inasmuch as those activities can be discharged successfully, irrespective of one's beliefs about the nature of the value of such experiences, there is no reason to regard the evolutionary psychologist's experience as any less aesthetic than the aesthete's. If anything is an aesthetic experience, grasping with comprehension the formal design of an artwork is. But one can do that effectively whether one's beliefs correspond to our aesthete's or our evolutionary psychologist's. Thus, both are having aesthetic experiences. Therefore, a belief in the intrinsic value of the experience in question is not a necessary condition for having an aesthetic experience.

Some axiologists have gone so far as to claim that critics cannot have aesthetic experiences insofar as they attend to artworks with an avowed, self-acknowledged instrumental interest in finding material for their next article. But good critics are paradigms of the way in which we should respond to and experience artworks. Thus the axiologist's position has the paradoxical consequence that the critic whose experience of an artwork serves as a model for the aesthete is not having an aesthetic experience, whereas the aesthete whose receptive behavior strictly parallels the critic's, but who believes his or her experience is intrinsically valuable, is having an aesthetic experience. As in the case of the comparison of the evolutionary psychologist and the aesthete, this conclusion seems arbitrary and unacceptable.

Though our thought experiment involved an evolutionary psychologist, it is not necessary to the argument for the believer in the instrumental value of aesthetic experience to be a scientist. Like Ralph Waldo Emerson, the instrumentalist might believe that the aesthetic experience of art is instrumentally valuable as a propaedeutic exercise that prepares or trains us for seeing the wonders that surround us in the natural world.[21] Or the instrumentalist might be: a Hindu who regards aesthetic experience as an avenue to or foretaste of the bliss of emancipation;[22] a Sufi who thinks of the experience of outward beauty as a gateway to spiritual beauty;[23] a Daoist who pursues aesthetic sophistication as a means of self-improvement, a way of cultivating in oneself the harmonious patterns immanent in the natural order;[24] and so on. Holding any of these beliefs or comparable ones about the instrumental value of experiencing the form and expressive properties should be no impediment to having aesthetic experiences of artworks so long as the percipient is attending to the appropriate features of the object in terms of proper strategies, patterns, and techniques of reception.

Indeed, it is not even required that the instrumentalist's beliefs about the value of the experience be true in order for the experience to be aesthetic, so long as it focuses on the right things in the right ways for the right reasons. Daoists may be wrong in believing that attending to artistic harmony instrumentally promotes personal harmony, and yet be experiencing the relevant artwork aesthetically, so long as they are noticing the formal equilibrium in it and intuiting its serenity. There is no reason to think experiences like these are aesthetically foreclosed if the agent holds beliefs, whether true or false, in the instrumental value of undergoing such experiences.[25] Thus it cannot be the case that a belief in the intrinsic value of the sort of experience under discussion is a necessary requirement in order for said experience to be classified as aesthetic.

Moreover, in order to motivate this objection it is not even necessary to postulate subjects who have doctrinal or theoretical commitments, like the evolutionary psychologist, about the nature of all aesthetic experience. Without any general views about the relation of aesthetic experience to instrumental value, someone may pick up a novel in order to satisfy the very instrumental end of getting a handle on recent social developments. One might read Jay Cantor's *Great Neck* to get a clearer understanding of the politically tumultuous 1960s and 1970s; Jane Smiley's *Good Faith* for insight into the realty boom of the 1980s; or Don DeLillo's *Cosmopolis* for his take on the financial bubble of the 1990s. In all these cases, readers may carefully attend to formal structures – such as the contrasts between various character types – in order to see how the relations and tensions between these incarnated abstractions illuminate the interplay of concrete social forces. But if readers track formal relations, even if they do so in pursuit of instrumentally valuable knowledge about the lay of society, I see no reason to deny that their experience is aesthetic, since, once again, we would not deny that title to the aesthetes who spend their time and energy doing exactly the same thing – contemplating the same structures and their relations.

A frequent axiological riposte to cases like the preceding ones is to ask us to imagine what would happen if the kinds of subjects we've described came to believe their conjectures about the instrumental value of aesthetic experience were not viable. Would they still pursue aesthetic experience? The axiologist asserts that, of course, they will. Moreover, the axiologist then goes on to explain this putative response by hypothesizing that subconsciously these so-called instrumentalists really believe in the intrinsic value of aesthetic experience. Why else would they continue to pursue aesthetic experience, once their beliefs about the extrinsic value of aesthetic experience have fallen by the wayside.[26]

I, however, am not so sure that the imagined experiment will turn out as the axiologist presumes. If someone pursues aesthetic experience as part of a spiritual regime, but then comes to suspect its transcendental efficacy, I see little cause to predict that the true believer will continue to say "yes" to aesthetic experience. Religionists can be quite stern about what they come to regard as irrelevant or frivolous. Remember Puritanism?

Furthermore, even if our instrumentalists continue to pursue aesthetic experience in the face of the defeat of their pet theories and beliefs, that does not entail that they have a subconscious belief in the value of aesthetic experience for its own sake. It might equally support the hypothesis that they continue to believe that aesthetic experience is instrumentally valuable – that it is good for them – despite the embarrassing fact that their best account of why this is so has just been refuted. That is, instrumentalists may concede that their best account of why aesthetic experience is beneficial has been problematized, but remain convinced in their hearts that such experiences are (instrumentally) good for them in a way that future research will eventually reveal and clarify. Such a response could, for example, be sustained by an evolutionary psychologist, who, on theoretical grounds, maintains the reasonable expectation that it is only a matter of time before the adaptive advantages of aesthetic experience are finally pinpointed. Alternatively, such a view could be held by someone who experiences the hankering for aesthetic experience as satisfying a drive – perhaps a subsidiary of the curiosity drive – and speculates, quite rationally, that where there is drive, there is an ulterior purpose.[27] Or it may be that the subject holds to the common notion that having aesthetic experience improves one – a tenet of many cultures and classes – even if one cannot articulate exactly how; for that reason he or she continues to pursue aesthetic experience, even while the philosophical jurists are out (betting, all the while, that sooner or later they will figure out why what is good for us is good for us).

Moreover, since the subjective variation of the axiological approach trades essentially in beliefs, a perhaps ignominious counterexample to the theory would be the case of the subject who irrationally believes that aesthetic experience is instrumentally rather than intrinsically valuable. For certainly we can consistently entertain the possibility of an art lover who believes some truly insane theory about the instrumental value of the aesthetic experience of art (that it builds strong bodies 12 ways) but who is, at the same time, astoundingly adept at detecting the formal patterns and expressive qualities of artworks. If, immersed in an experience of an artwork, this person is preoccupied with unraveling its intricate relationships and resonating with its expressive effects, then there is certainly more reason to categorize his or her experience as aesthetic rather than as any other sort. This is not the sort of counterexample that someone, like myself, who is sympathetic to instrumentalism, reaches for with relish, but logically it is another nail in the coffin of the axiological approach to aesthetic experience.

Noël Carroll

The Content-Oriented Approach

We have so far examined the claims that all aesthetic experiences involve affective arousal, or direct engagement, or valuation for their own sake (at least subjectively). But though there may be a great many cases that exemplify each of these claims, we have seen that none of these theories obtains universally.

Nevertheless, there appears to be one aspect of the aesthetic experience of artworks that does hold across the board, namely: all such experiences take objects. All aesthetic experiences of art have content. This, in turn, suggests that this particular experiential state may be definable, at least partially, in terms of its content – that is, in terms of the kinds of objects toward which it is directed. For obvious reasons, we call this research program the content-oriented approach to characterizing the aesthetic experience of art.

But what comprises the content of aesthetic experience? When speaking of art, the most commonly mentioned candidates include the form of the work of art and its aesthetic properties, of which expressive properties comprise a very large and especially noteworthy subclass. The form and the aesthetic and expressive properties of the artwork also interact in various ways. Sometimes form gives rise to aesthetic properties, such as unity, while the succession, evolution, or juxtaposition of expressive properties can constitute the form of the artwork. Form, expressive and aesthetic properties, and the interaction between these elements, are the most commonly indicated objects of aesthetic experience, as well as being the ones about which there is the least controversy.

In addition, aesthetic experience is also often directed at the way in which these elements engage and mold our attention to and awareness of them. So, to observe aperceptively the way in which the perspective draws our eye to the narrative center of the picture is an aesthetic experience. Consequently, another object of aesthetic experience is the relation of the form, expressive properties, aesthetic properties, and/or the interaction thereof to our response to them – to the way in which they shape and guide our reactions. Thus the content-oriented theorist of aesthetic experience conjectures that if attention is directed with understanding to the form of the artwork, and/or to its expressive or aesthetic properties, and/or to the interaction between these features, and/or to the way in which the aforesaid factors modulate our response to the artwork, then the experience is aesthetic.

This account of aesthetic experience, in other words, provides us with a disjunctive set of sufficient conditions for categorizing aesthetic experiences of artworks. That is, a specimen of experience is aesthetic if it involves the apprehension/comprehension by an informed subject in the ways mandated (by the tradition, the object, and/or the artist) of the formal structures, aesthetic and/or expressive properties of the object, and/or the emergence of those features from the base properties of the work and/or of the manner in which those features interact with each other and/or address the cognitive, perceptual, emotive, and/or imaginative powers of the subject.[28]

Admittedly, there may be further objects of aesthetic experience that could be added to this list. However, given the tradition, these are the most recurrent, noncontroversial ones. So, on the basis of the tradition, we can say that at least the satisfaction of one or more of these conditions is the most straightforward way of determining whether or not an experience of an artwork or a feature thereof is aesthetic.[29] This list has the virtue of excluding some of the more controversial candidates for aesthetic experience. For example, the simple recognition of what a representation, such as a picture, is of does not traditionally count as an aesthetic experience; seeing-in, as it is called, is not an aesthetic experience. So it is not on the list.

The list was assembled by thinking about the features of art works, attention to which are most likely to elicit consensus and least likely to spur controversy among people who talk about aesthetic experience. The consideration of the moral consequences as such of an artwork for the commonweal is typically said not to be germane to aesthetic experience, so it is not on the list. This makes the content-oriented approach superior to the axiological approach, inasmuch as someone might intrinsically value reflecting on the moral consequences of an artwork; but that would make such contemplation an aesthetic experience, thereby contradicting the tradition. On the other hand, form is taken to be a prima facie object of aesthetic experience by everyone, even if they do not believe that it is the only object of aesthetic experience. Therefore, it is high on the content-oriented theorist's list.

Moreover, though form is being treated as a prima facie object of aesthetic experience, this should not be rejected as what is often referred to as formalism. Those who criticize formalism do so because they reject the attempt to solve the demarcation problem by defining art in terms of significant form. However, by invoking form to define aesthetic experience partially, nothing is being said about whether or not form is any sort of criterion for art status. Moreover, those who object to the notion that attention to form is a necessary condition for aesthetic experience have no quarrel with me, since I have only advanced it as one of a disjunctive set of sufficient conditions.

If attention with understanding is directed at the form of an artwork, then it is an aesthetic experience. As mentioned earlier, by the form of an artwork is meant the ensemble of choices intended to realize the point or the purpose of the artwork. To consider an organism biologically is to consider the features of the organism that are relevant to its biological operation; to consider an artwork formally is to consider the features of the work relevant to its formal operation – that is, to consider the features of the work (and their coordination) that realize the point or purpose of the work. Attention to the form of a work is attention to its design – to the way the work is intended to work. Noticing how the spacing of the last line of A. R. Ammons's poem "Beautiful Woman" visually reinforces the puns he means to wring out of the word "fall" is an example of attention to the form or design of a work.[30]

Aesthetic properties are another source of aesthetic experience. Some examples include: detecting the sadness in the music, the apparent massiveness of the building, the balance in the sculpture, and the lightness of the dancer's step. These are all aesthetic experiences. Furthermore, as this brief, incomplete inventory suggests, there are various different kinds of aesthetic experience, insofar as aesthetic experiences may take a variety of objects. Some are sensuous properties like massiveness and lightness; others – like balance – could be called Gestalt properties. Sadness, on the other hand, is an expressive or anthropomorphic property. Moreover, one might discern or detect expressive properties by at least two different, though not mutually preclusive, routes: either by having a comparable feeling aroused

Noël Carroll

in one or by recognizing certain emotive configurations (that is, one can take note of the sadness of the drooping weeping willow tree without feeling sad oneself).

There are, of course, even more types of aesthetic and expressive properties than enumerated so far. What they have in common is that they are response-dependent insofar as their existence depends on creatures like us with our sensibilities and imaginative powers. These properties supervene on the primary and secondary properties of the relevant objects of attention, as well as upon certain relational properties, including art-historical ones, such as genre or category membership. Aesthetic properties emerge from these lower order properties; they are dispositions to promote impressions or effects on appropriately backgrounded creatures with our perceptual and imaginative capabilities.[31]

Because aesthetic properties are response-dependent, some may argue that defining aesthetic experience in light of them is circular. But one does not need to use the concept of aesthetic experience to define such things as form or aesthetic properties. These can be defined without explicit or implicit reliance on the notion of aesthetic experience. We have already defined form in this way; the aesthetic properties of artworks, then, are dispositions to promote impressions or effects, notably of expressivity, mood, figuration (metaphoricity), synesthesia or cross-modal correspondence, perceptual salience, Gestalt organization, and/or qualitative intensity, which emerge from the base properties of the works at hand in relation to suitably informed percipients with standard-issue human sensibilities and imaginative powers. It is true that this account makes reference to human capacities for experience, but inasmuch as no appeal is made to *aesthetic* experience, there is no circularity here.

In visual and sonic artworks, aesthetic properties are predominantly involved in promoting the ways in which the work appears phenomenally, over and above the operation of its primary and secondary properties. In literary works, aesthetic properties are typically less a matter of direct address and primarily emerge from the descriptions in the text in relation to the imagination. Though scarcely an exhaustive accounting of aesthetic properties, these brief remarks should nevertheless suggest that an aesthetic experience can be identified in terms of its content, without reference to affective states like pleasure, disinterested or otherwise, or to evaluative postures, such as finding the experience of such properties to be valuable for their own sake.

Whereas the axiological approach to aesthetic experience is remarkably uninformative, the content-oriented approach can begin to tell aspiring aesthetes about what they should do in order to have an aesthetic experience – to wit: attend to the form, to the aesthetic properties, and so forth of artworks. Of course, this must be done with understanding – that is, in terms of certain strategies and techniques of reception. But these strategies and techniques, though they may vary from artform to artform and from genre to genre, can also be described with a high degree of specificity and without circular appeal to aesthetic experience. For example, if one is reading poetry, one is well advised to attend to where the line breaks – to invest it with a special pause and then to listen for its expressive reverberations.

Likewise, anyone who wishes to study aesthetic experience rigorously should be drawn to the content-oriented approach, since it zooms in with some precision on the leading variables – the properties and techniques of reception – that give rise to it.

Friends of the epistemological approach may think that, by including understanding in the content-oriented approach to aesthetic experience, we have encroached on their territory. For it is clear that the content-oriented theorist does not countenance just any encounter with the form and/or aesthetic properties of the artwork as aesthetic experiences, but only epistemically appropriate ones. This is true, but I think that this is not the distinctive domain of the epistemic approach. Rather, I think it is shared by every approach to aesthetic experience. All require that the subject engage the artwork with understanding. What is distinctive about the epistemological approach is that it demands a close encounter of the third kind with the artwork. But since this is not necessary – one can apprehend the form of a ready-made without seeing it – and since the content-oriented approach is not committed to it, the content-oriented approach seems superior to the epistemological approach as the latter is distinguishable from other approaches to aesthetic experience.

Some will charge that, by limiting the aesthetic experience of artworks to attention with understanding to the work's formal and aesthetic properties and their interaction with each other and with our sensibilities and imagination, I have made the range of aesthetic experience unduly restrictive. For, they will say, there are other legitimate responses to artworks than these, such as deriving moral insight from them. However, the presupposition underlying this criticism is that the concept of aesthetic experience should be large enough to incorporate every legitimate response to an art work, whereas I maintain, on the basis of traditional usage, that aesthetic experiences constitute only one family of responses, albeit an important one, that we may appropriately mobilize with respect to artworks.

Call the larger category of legitimate responses to artworks "art responses." Aesthetic experience is one kind of art response; moral learning is another. This way of treating the matter, I think, accords better with how the concept is commonly applied. It certainly fits better with the tradition than versions of the axiological approach that would count as an aesthetic experience any occasion where a reader, viewer, or listener subjectively valued for its own sake his or her experience of acquiring moral insight from an artwork.

It is frequently noted that aesthetic experiences are not only characteristically derived from artworks, but also from nature. In fact, some might contend that an adequate account of aesthetic experience must have something to say about responses to both art and nature. Though the content-oriented account defended above has concentrated on the aesthetic experience of art, it also has suggestive ramifications for the analysis of the aesthetic experience of nature. Clearly, nature lacks form in the way that we apply that concept to artworks. Nevertheless, inasmuch as form is to be understood functionally, we can note an analogous way of engaging nature to apprehending the formal design of artworks. Specifically, one can attend to nature functionally, sizing up the ways in which the contours of an ecological system have evolved from natural processes, pressures, and constraints. Allen Carlson has called this mode of attending to nature "the natural environmental model."[32] Attention to

Noël Carroll

form in works of art, then, has an analogue in the aesthetic experience of nature in the naturalistically informed attention to the apparent teleology of natural processes and prospects.

Similarly, attention to aesthetic and expressive properties in artworks has close analogues to the aesthetic experience of nature, insofar as nature often moves us feelingly or arouses us in ways that engage our sensibilities and imagination so that, in consequence, we attribute aesthetic and expressive properties to it.[33] Thus, if it is a requirement of a satisfying account of the aesthetic experience of art that it have some connection to the aesthetic experience of nature, then the content-oriented approach can meet this desideratum in that attention to the formal and expressive properties of artworks has strong analogues in the prominently acknowledged varieties of the aesthetic experience of nature.

If it is a virtue of affect-oriented, epistemic, and axiological approaches to the aesthetic experience of art that they can also say something comparable about the aesthetic experience of nature, then this too is a virtue of the content-oriented approach.

Summary and Conclusion

The affect-oriented, epistemic, axiological, and content-oriented approaches appear to offer our most promising accounts of aesthetic experience. In favor of the affect-oriented approach, it is indisputable that many aesthetic experiences of art engender pleasure (or displeasure). However, the experiential qualia of aesthetic experiences are quite diverse, too diverse in fact to be assimilated to a single formulaic, phenomenological characterization, such as pleasure, and, in fact, to make matters worse, some aesthetic experiences may have no accompanying affect, feeling tone, or quality.

Likewise, aesthetic experiences may or may not issue in any evaluation of their own worth, including taking it to be something that is valuable for its own sake. For example, I note that a poem has a unifying A/B/A/B rhyme scheme, but this does not lead me or other appropriately informed readers to find it valuable, either intrinsically or instrumentally. Nor, in such a case, need one assess such an experience negatively. I may regard some aesthetic experiences indifferently, as neither good nor bad, intrinsically or instrumentally, just as I may be indifferent affectively to such an experience.

Finally, *pace* the epistemic account of aesthetic experience, I may have a response to the form of certain artworks – such as some examples of conceptual art – without directly encountering the work in question. Thus the distinctive claim of epistemic accounts – that direct acquaintance with the relevant stimulus is a necessary condition of aesthetic experience – is false.

Therefore, insofar as the content-oriented account of the aesthetic experience of artworks shares none of these liabilities with its competitors, has no evident liabilities of its own, and even possesses certain strengths, notably in terms of its informativeness, the content-oriented account is at present our best bet – the odds-on favorite in this particular horse race.

Notes

1 For the record, I do not believe that art can be defined in terms of aesthetic experience or that artistic value is reducible to the promotion of aesthetic experience.

2 That is, inasmuch as literature addresses the imagination, it could be regarded by eighteenth-century theorists as functioning rather like painting with regard to the senses. For the senses and the imagination were thought to be very much alike. Kant writes "sense is the power of intuiting when the object is present; imagination, that of intuiting even when the object is not present." Both faculties, that is, *intuit* images. See Kant (1978: Ak. Vii, p. 153). Similarly, Aquinas regards the imagination as something like the counterpart of the senses; images passively apprehended by perception are actively created by the imagination. Perhaps the poet's imaginative suggestions are then grist for the reader's imaginative construction. See Thomas Aquinas (1945), *Summa Theologica*, I, 85, ad. 3.

3 I have also attempted to defend this position in Carroll (2000, 2001a, 2002).

4 For a discussion of this sense of appreciation, see Carroll (2001b).

5 The notion of an epistemic approach to aesthetic experience is derived from Gary Iseminger (2003).

6 See, for example, Marcia Muelder Eaton (2001), chapter 1.

7 Iseminger (2003: 110).

8 This conception of artistic form is defended in Carroll (1999), chapter 3.

9 Though I would not require admiration for the experience to count as aesthetic, since, as I argued earlier, I take the concept to be descriptive and not essentially commendatory.

10 Perhaps one could apprehend the basic structures of dramatic conflict in a literary work from a reliable description of its plot and even, though this would not be necessary for the encounter to count as aesthetic, be pleased by its ingenuity.

11 Marcia Eaton seems to me to hold an epistemic view of aesthetic experience. She maintains that "An aesthetic response is a response to the aesthetic properties of an object or event, that is to intrinsic properties considered worthy of attention within a particular culture." Here "intrinsic properties," those verified by direct inspection, mark her commitment to the epistemic approach. The added stipulation – that the properties in question be considered worthy within a particular culture – I speculate is her way of securing sufficiency for her definition. I challenge her intrinsic-properties requirement above. But, in addition, I do not see how she hopes the "worthy of attention" clause will succeed, since a culture might consider the patriotism of a work that wears it on its sleeve to be worthy of attention (perception or reflection) but an experience of patriotism, however appropriate given the function of the work, is not what is typically thought of as an aesthetic experience. See Eaton (2001), p. 10.

12 Paisley Livingston has offered a series of arguments against what he tags as the "apparent truism" that an aesthetic judgment requires a close encounter of the third kind with the pertinent artwork. Inasmuch as this truism is closely related to the epistemic approach to aesthetic experience, some of Livingston's objections are germane to the present discussion. At the same time, I wonder whether counterexamples from the realm of conceptual art won't undermine the successor that Livingston proposes to the "apparent truism." See Livingston (2003).

13 Of course, this feature of the axiological approach may also have a downside. For percipients may subjectively value for their own sake experiences that would not be characteristically regarded as aesthetic. If one values for its own sake the absorption of what one takes to be the spiritual insight of an artwork, then that will count as an aesthetic experience for the axiologist; but this is precisely the sort of experience that the tradition typ-

ically refuses to regard as aesthetic. Can the axiologist claim to be capturing the prevailing concept of aesthetic experience, or do cases like this indicate that the axiologist has actually changed the subject?

14   See Mihaly Csikszentmihalyi (1975).

15   Ellen Dissanayake (1992, 2000).

16   Though we have been emphasizing the instrumental value for social existence of the pursuit of aesthetic experience, it should also be noted that aesthetic experience may afford significant benefits for the individual as well. By exercising certain of our powers of perception, association, comparison, contrast, and so on, having aesthetic experiences enhances mental fitness by tuning our cognitive organizational powers. Aesthetic experience helps develop the mind's capacities for organization and discrimination, while also sharpening and refining them. See John Tooby and Leda Cosmides (2001).

17   Many early artworks and the structures they employ, such as rhyme, were mnemonic devices that facilitated the recall of information, especially culturally significant information. The aesthetic experience involved in response to these structures undoubtedly served an instrumental purpose in keeping the relevant information alive for the relevant peoples. Moreover, the information was not only exclusively cultural; songs can encode geographical information. In such cases, the aesthetic experience of the song may serve the practical purpose of making important information more accessible than it would otherwise be. See, for example: Bruce Chatwin's fact-based fiction, *The Songlines* (1987); similarly, the African-American song "The Drinking Gourd" encoded information about traveling on the underground railroad.

18   Evolutionary hypotheses like those just canvassed always raise the worry that they are "just-so" stories, unconstrained by any canons of proof. Some have suggested that, in order to insure that one has not simply concocted a just-so story, for any case where one claims that such and such an attribute is adaptive for a group, one should be able to point to a contrasting group that lacks the attribute in question and that did not survive. I am not sure that we always need to find such a contrasting group in order for an evolutionary hypothesis to be satisfactory. Isn't common sense enough to assure us that an organism's speed relative to slower predators is a naturally selected adaptation? Might we say the same about the way in which aesthetic experience fosters social cohesion? But if skeptics reject this appeal, we may nevertheless be able to satisfy them by producing the contrast they desire. Cro-Magnon peoples possessed art; the Neanderthals, it appears, did not. Neanderthal social units were small whereas Cro-Magnon social units were much larger, enabling Cro-Magnons to engage in more ambitious economic activities and a greater scale of warmaking. Whether by more effectively exploiting the environment or by conflict, the Cro-Magnons bested the Neanderthals in the competition for survival. Cro-Magnon social organization was undoubtedly an important ingredient in how this came about. Insofar as aesthetic experience contributes to social cohesion, as proposed above, it is probably an evolutionary asset. The anxiety that this is merely a just-so story may be somewhat allayed by pointing to the contrasting case of the Neanderthals, who do not appear to have had the advantage of the aesthetic experience of artworks. On the need for contrast cases in evolutionary reasoning, see Elliott Sober (2002). On prehistory, see Steven Mithen (1996). The information about Neanderthal and Cro-Magnon social organization and art is derived from Mithen. Marshaling that information so as to claim that aesthetic experience can be seen, through the preceding contrast, to be an evolutionary bonus is my own invention.

19   At this point, the axiologist may say that here aesthetic pleasure has a role to play. People pursue the aesthetic experience because of the pleasure it yields. Pleasure is the device that natural selection has elected to insure that humans pursue the benefits that aesthetic experience has to offer. Moreover, pleasure is valuable for its own sake. So adverting to

something in aesthetic experience that is valued for its own sake does have explanatory value. One problem with this response is that, as we have seen, pleasure is not a feature of every aesthetic experience. However, a deeper problem here is that on the preceding story, pleasure is not objectively valuable for its own sake. It is objectively valuable for the evolutionary job it facilitates. Thomas Aquinas speaks of delight or pleasure that is conducive to the operation of an end – as carnal pleasure is conducive to the end of procreation. But this sort of pleasure is not objectively valuable for its own sake; it is valuable for what it brings about. Thus the evolutionary psychologist may argue that aesthetic pleasure, where it obtains, does not force her to make room for intrinsic value in her account. See Thomas Aquinas, "The End of Man," *Summa Contra Gentiles*, Book III, in *Basic Writings of St. Thomas Aquinas* (1945).

20   This belief is, of course, compatible with it really being the case that aesthetic experience is instrumentally valuable, objectively speaking.

21   Ralph Waldo Emerson (1936), p. 246. Similarly, Russian Formalists thought of their paradigmatic aesthetic experience of art – what they called *ostranenie* (defamiliarization) – as being valuable for reinvigorating our powers of perceiving the world.

22   Edwin Gerow (1997), p. 317.

23   Seyyed Hossein Nasr (1997). p. 455.

24   Stephen J. Goldberg (1997), p. 228.

25   Moreover, since the subjective version of the axiological approach is framed in virtue of *beliefs*, it is irrelevant to having an aesthetic experience, on this view, if the percipient's conviction that aesthetic experience is intrinsically valuable is false.

26   Perhaps the axiologist will try to bolster this conjecture by claiming that the alleged instrumentalists will continue to pursue aesthetic experience in this case because they believe it will yield pleasure where pleasure, it will be maintained, is something that everyone values for its own sake. On the other hand, perhaps like Aristotle, they believe that pleasure is a sign that the pertinent faculties – in this case, the cognitive, emotive, and perceptual faculties engaged in aesthetic experience – are functioning well. They seek pleasure, if they do, as a means of ascertaining that the system is running optimally. Surely such a perspective is coherent.

27   Richard Miller regards aesthetic experience as a learning-like response. For him, it is only learning-*like* because it supposedly is divorced from a concern with truth. Nevertheless, the characteristic behaviors associated with the aesthetic experience of art do mirror those of learning acquisition. They include inspecting, comparing, contrasting, grouping, discriminating, and so on. Having an aesthetic experience of an artwork is not a matter of staring at it vacantly; it involves an active investigatory or exploratory stance. Thus it is not amiss to regard it as connected to what some psychologists see as our curiosity drive, something of the utmost instrumental value in the human appropriation of nature. Perhaps, in this light, aesthetic experience is fitness-enhancing in that it hones both the mind's appetite for curiosity along with its abilities to develop talents for satisfying it.

Furthermore, if aesthetic satisfaction is related to the satisfaction of a drive, one wonders whether we should say that it is valuable for its own sake? Consider the following: humans and some animals possess the curiosity drive. Animals without the capacity to form conscious beliefs explore under its pressure. We do not explain their behavior as a result of their belief in the intrinsic value of such activity. If humans are behaving as a result of the same kind of instinctual mechanism, why should we say that they are doing so because they believe in the intrinsic value of the experience? Even if they have such a belief (and they may not), it does not seem to be what is causing their behavior. The curiosity drive is. Thus if the imputation of a belief in the intrinsic value of something is ultimately meant to isolate a proximate cause of a person's behavior, then it is not clear that the alleged belief in the intrinsic value of aesthetic experience is doing any explanatory work here. Moreover, since we would not attribute an intrinsic valuation of exploration to a nonbelief-forming animal responding to the pressure of the curiosity drive, maybe for consistency's sake, it would be advisable to withhold it from the human case as well. This is not to deny that people may have such beliefs about aesthetic experience, but only that, inasmuch they have no explanatory value with respect to the agent's behavior, they are not beliefs in the value of the experience for its own sake in the most robust sense.

Indeed, what these beliefs come down to seems to be the subject's admission of having no idea of why he or she really values the aesthetic experience of art. But if the notion of valuing the aesthetic experience of art for its own sake actually amounts to no more than a confession of ignorance, then the idea is much less exalted than it is usually imagined to be. It is at least questionable as to whether or not someone should proudly advertise holding such a belief.

See Richard Miller (1998). On the curiosity drive, see: Jaak Panksepp (1985), pp. 273–4.

28   As the emphasis on apprehension/comprehension in this formulation might suggest, I regard the cognitive dimension of aesthetic experience as its primary locus of value.

29   Some commentators have asked what makes this list hang together? Is there some essence, like valuation for its own sake, that groups these objects together? Why is it that the tradition treats the apprehension of formal, aesthetic, and expressive properties as of a piece? My own suspicion is that this is best explained genealogically. When the notion of the aesthetic was first introduced, people thought of form in terms of something that could be seen or heard – something manifest – like the geometric alignment of figures in a painting or the echo of a theme in music. Similarly they thought of aesthetic and expressive properties as things that could been seen or heard (either outwardly by the senses or as some sort of internal representation intuited by the imagination). Strictly speaking, as we have seen, this does not provide us with adequate conceptions of either form or of aesthetic and expressive properties. Nevertheless, it is this mistaken prejudice that led the tradition to lump these things together under the rubric of objects of aesthetic experience. The content-oriented theorist deals with this by preferring to treat each type of experience (such as the experience of form) specifically on its own term and to continue to regard them as a package only in the deflationary sense that they are a disjunctive enumeration of sufficient conditions for what has been nominally bequeathed to us under the title of aesthetic experience.

30   "Beautiful Woman" by A. R. Ammons:

> The spring
> in
> her step
> has
> turned to
> fall.

31   Jerrold Levinson (2001).

32   Allen Carlson (2000), Part I.

33   Noël Carroll (2001c).

CHAPTER
S I X

The Aesthetic State of Mind

Gary Iseminger

Reflating the Aesthetic State of Mind

The term "aesthetics" in its current use, roughly synonymous with "philosophy of art," is traceable to Alexander Baumgarten's 1750 work *Aesthetica*. A plausible consequence of this designation is the thought that there is something, "the aesthetic," that is what aesthetics is about. So there has been a proliferation of terms for what Noël Carroll has called "aesthetic what-not" – aesthetic objects, aesthetic properties, aesthetic terms, aesthetic judgments, aesthetic value, aesthetic experience, aesthetic distance, aesthetic detachment, aesthetic contemplation, aesthetic appreciation, aesthetic pleasure. If these terms could be explained in terms of one of them, and that one understood without appeal to some prior idea of the aesthetic or to the concept of art, one could reasonably hope to invoke the concept of the aesthetic in the philosophical understanding of art.

Notably predominant on this list are terms that refer, broadly speaking, to *psychological* states, and Baumgarten's idea of the aesthetic seems to fit this description, for, according to Paul Guyer, aesthetics as he conceived it is "a study of the perfection of and pleasure in the exercise of sensibility for its own sake, as manifested in the production of works of artistic beauty" (Guyer 1998: 227). Accordingly, the philosophical project I have described has often begun with an attempt to characterize either phenomenologically or structurally an *aesthetic state of mind*.

This attempt has for some time been out of favor. In the 1960s, George Dickie famously went through most of the usual suspects and found them guilty one by one (see, e.g., Dickie 1964, 1965, 1973). There are, however, symptoms of a revival of interest in the idea of an aesthetic state of mind among philosophers (see Iseminger 2003). In response, Carroll has assumed something like Dickie's role, vigorously objecting in several recent publications (see especially Carroll 2000, 2001e, and 2002) to various defenses of this idea.

In the process Carroll advances his own account of the aesthetic experience, which he characterizes as "deflationary, content-oriented, [and] enumerative" (Carroll 2000: 207): "An aesthetic experience is one that involves design appreciation and/or the detection of aesthetic and expressive properties . . ." (Carroll 2000: 207). He "enumerates" a third disjunct as well: ". . . and/or attention to the ways in which the formal, aesthetic, and expressive properties of the artwork are contrived." I omit this disjunct from consideration in order to abstract from the fact that at this point he is officially talking only about the aesthetic experience *of art*, while I have in mind no such limitation.

This account is "enumerative" in that it does not pretend to offer a set of jointly necessary and sufficient conditions for an experience's being aesthetic but only an admittedly incomplete disjunctive list of kinds of examples. It is "content-oriented" in that, furthermore, the members of the list are characterized not in terms of anything that might be called the nature of the experience itself, either as a state of mind with a distinctive phenomenology or as a state of mind with a distinctive structure, but rather in terms of what sorts of states of affairs the experience is an experience *of*. I think it is fair to say that these two features together are what make the account "deflationary," in that it is presented as the best account on offer, given that *there is no such thing as the "aesthetic state of mind" conceived of as a state of mind whose essence is a distinctive phenomenology and/or structure.*

My aim in this chapter is to reflate the concept of the aesthetic state of mind by defending a nondeflationary account of it against Carroll's objections.

Appreciation as the Aesthetic State of Mind

I shall call the aesthetic state of mind appreciation, and I propose the following structural (as distinct from phenomenological) account of its essence:

> Someone is *appreciating* a state of affairs just in case she or he is *valuing for its own sake the experiencing of that state of affairs*. (See Iseminger 1981 for an earlier version.)

Here are some examples, reflection on which will help to explain what this amounts to:

> Someone hearing and following the intricate contrapuntal interplay in the coda of the last movement of Mozart's *Symphony No. 41* values this experience for its own sake.
>
> Someone noticing a piece of driftwood on a beach and observing the striking pattern that its jagged and bleached branches make values this experience for its own sake.
>
> Someone reading or watching Shakespeare's *Much Ado About Nothing* and understanding the humorous bathos of Benedick's reply to Beatrice's request that he come with her to hear the news of Hero's vindication –

Beatrice: Will you go hear this news, signior?

Benedick: I will live in thy heart, die in thy lap, and be buried in thy eyes; and moreover I will go with thee to thy uncle's.

– values this experience for its own sake.

Someone watching the end of Berg's opera *Wozzeck* and understanding the devastation of innocence in prospect for Marie's son values this experience for its own sake.

Someone savoring the finish of a wine values this experience for its own sake.

Someone noticing the elegance of a new proof of a familiar mathematical theorem values this experience for its own sake.

Someone watching Leni Riefenstahl's *Triumph of the Will*, noticing the way in which its formal features help to express its message, values this experience for its own sake.

A few clarifications and observations are in order. First, it is important to note that appreciation is not here defined in terms of any prior notion of the aesthetic. It is not the aesthetic species of the genus appreciation; it is rather appreciation *sans phrase*, and my proposal is to identify it as the aesthetic state of mind. (Note that an experiencing – a seeing, hearing, tasting, grasping, and so forth – that is valued in itself is not thereby *itself* transformed into an aesthetic experience; rather, the complexly structured state of mind consisting of valuing-some-experience-in-itself constitutes the aesthetic state of mind.)

Further, the notion of experiencing invoked here is to be construed as a *cognitive* notion. It is the idea of *noticing* something, and, as a way of knowing, it is *noninferential* (though not necessarily nonconceptual).

Next, instances of sensing are instances of experiencing in this sense, but so too are many instances of understanding. Of course there are cases of merely *seeming* to see, hear, and understand, so the immediacy of these experiences is no guarantee that they are *accurate*. But in each of these cases, there is a sense in which it can be said that at a time or for a time someone's experience consisted, at least in part, of seeing, hearing, or otherwise grasping that some state of affairs obtained, and this distinguishes experiencing a state of affairs from other possible ways of knowing that it obtains. For example, someone might be in a position to justifiably assert that the contrapuntal interplay in Mozart's symphony is intricate by means other than hearing that it is, or that the passage in *Much Ado* is humorously bathetic by means other than currently recognizing that it is – for example, on the basis of memory or the testimony of a reliable authority.

Someone who appreciates something in this sense may, but need not, become a "spellbound spectator," lost in contemplation. Appreciation may sometimes be all-consuming and drive out all other thoughts, but, as I have described it, it seems possible that it may be relatively fleeting and casual. The rapt attention that features in some accounts of the aesthetic state of mind undoubtedly characterizes some instances of appreciation, but it is by no means a necessary condition of appreciation as I conceive it.

By the same token, though it may be that an appreciator has no thought that the experience will serve some ulterior purpose, this does not seem necessary. Certainly

Gary Iseminger

valuing an experience for its own sake is *different* from valuing it for some other reason, and in particular cases there might be reasons for valuing something that effectively *preclude* valuing it for its own sake, but that someone values an experience for some other reason and that he or she values it for its own sake are not necessarily incompatible with one another. A critic who attends a concert may value the experience because it is necessary in order to do his or her job, but may also find it valuable for its own sake. Indeed, to the extent that he or she does so, the review of the concert will probably be that much more enthusiastic.

Again, an appreciator may sometimes restrict his or her attention to a limited set of states of affairs, such as those Carroll enumerates, and it may well be that his set includes those the experience of which is most likely to be valued for its own sake, but nothing in this account of appreciation restricts an appreciator in principle to such qualities. The only restriction is to qualities that are in the relevant sense hearable, seeable, graspable; the aesthetic state of mind need not have as its object only formal features or features of design. A movie critic who finds Nazi ideology despicable but who recognizes the way in which the characteristics of design and expression in *Triumph of the Will* are suited to express that ideology may not only appreciate those characteristics but even this particular message as embodied in them. (And, of course, someone's hatred of Nazi ideology may be such as to prevent his or her appreciation of this message in any embodiment, or even this embodiment abstracted from that message.)

Again, it is not surprising to find someone who values the experience of a state of affairs *enjoying* or taking *pleasure* in that experience, but enjoying or taking pleasure in experiencing a state of affairs does not seem to be a necessary condition of appreciation. (Who *enjoys* the concluding bars of *Wozzeck?*)

Finally, though one is not surprised to find someone appreciating works of art, it seems clear that both natural objects – pieces of driftwood – and artifacts that are evidently not works of art – glasses of wine – can be appreciated in the current sense as well. In any case, it is important to note that the idea of appreciation is as conceptually independent of the idea of art as it is of any prior concept of the aesthetic. Though my main aim here is to reflate the idea of the aesthetic state of mind, this can hardly be worth doing unless there is in view some payoff in the form of a plausibly explained and defended connection between it and art. I shall have something to say about this at the end of this chapter.

A Subjective Version of the Traditional or Axiological Approach to the Aesthetic State of Mind

The account just given is an example of what Carroll calls the *subjective* version of what in some places he refers to as the *traditional* account (Carroll 2001e: 44) and in this volume and elsewhere as the *axiological* approach (Carroll 2002: 159). The account is *traditional* in that it is the upshot of a line of argument that runs from Hutcheson through Clive Bell and has been recently and most systematically worked out by Monroe Beardsley; it is *axiological* in that the concept of value is essential to it; it is *subjective* in that it is in the form of some person's subjectively *valuing or finding value* in an experience rather than the experience's objectively *having value or being valuable* that that concept figures in the account.

On Carroll's telling, something like this view is the last one left standing if one pursues in a reflective way the idea that the aesthetic can be explicated in terms of the notion of a state of mind. If one starts, as have many in the tradition in question, with the idea of some kind of pleasure, one quickly sees that what seem to be aesthetic states of mind need not include pleasure or enjoyment. The thought then is that the notion of being *valuable in itself*, in some sense that might include pleasure as an instance but not be limited to it, might help us out. But the notion that aesthetic experience is experience that is valuable in itself, where this is construed objectively, strikes Carroll as a nonstarter, given the current state of evolutionary thinking about human beings, in which the objective value of a human organ or capacity is constituted by its conferring some reproductive advantage, manifestly not an instance of value in itself but rather of instrumental value. "The hypothesis that aesthetic experience is valuable for its own sake leaves us literally speechless, since it appears divorced from our best frameworks for understanding human nature. . . . [It] makes the phenomenon essentially mysterious, an orphan from the natural world as we think we know it" (Carroll 2002: 158–9). The fall-back position, according to Carroll, is to adopt a subjective reading of value: "At this point in the debate, it is open to the axiologist to propose that valuation for its own sake be construed subjectively not objectively. That is, the objective facts of the matter are not relevant, so long as the percipient *believes* [my emphasis] that the relevant experience is valuable for its own sake" (Carroll 2002: 159).

At this point, something like my account of appreciation clearly comes into play, and Carroll's main argument against it, which appears in this volume and several other places, goes essentially as follows: suppose that two people experience a painting and notice exactly the same formal and expressive features. One of them values his or her experience for its own sake; the other values it only for its contribution to some other good; for instance, he or she believes that "tracking" these formal and expressive features promotes "an instrumentally valuable mobility and alertness of mind." The subjective axiological account is committed to saying that the first but not the second is having an aesthetic experience. But this is an "unacceptable result." Given that both are "mentally processing" the work in the same way and are engaged in the same "paradigmatic sorts of aesthetic behaviors," it is "perfectly arbitrary and completely unsatisfactory to maintain that . . . [the first person] is undergoing an aesthetic experience, but . . . [the second] is not" (See Carroll 2000: 204–6, 2001e: 48–9, and 2002: 159–60 for the argument. Carroll 2001a defends it against objections in Stecker 2001 related to mine below.)

Carroll's argument can be interpreted as an attempted *reductio ad absurdum*: the subjective axiological account entails that one of the people described is having an aesthetic experience and the other is not. However, the experience of the two people is, by hypothesis, identical, and, moreover, identical in ways that are paradigmatically aesthetic. Therefore, if one person is having an aesthetic experience so is the other. It follows that the subjective axiological account, entailing as it does the denial of this truth, is false.

The key to avoiding this *reductio* is to make the distinction between the experience the people are having and what might be called the total state of mind that they are in. (Carroll 2002: 160 n. 29 recognizes this distinction but does not draw from it the consequences I do.) The aesthetic state of mind, in my view, is not merely the experience of tracking formal and expressive features but it is the state of mind in which, while tracking such features (among others, I would say), one finds this tracking valuable for its own sake. So it is at least misleading if not just wrong to say that on the current view the aesthetic experience is to be *identified* as "an experience essentially valued for its own sake." Rather, the aesthetic state of mind – appreciation – is to be identified as essentially valuing an experience for its own sake. That I am valuing an experience for its own sake does not make *the experience thus valued* aesthetic. Rather the aesthetic state of mind I have called appreciation is one essentially *consisting* in valuing an experience for its own sake. There is an essential experiential component to this state, but the experiential part is not essentially aesthetic. So perhaps I am committed to the view that there is no such thing as a distinctively aesthetic *experience*, in the sense in which I am using the term "experience," but the point of this denial is to clear the way for the idea that there is a more complex aesthetic state of mind of which experience is a component.

How, then, does the purported *reductio* fare once this distinction is made? The main point is that it is no longer obviously false to say that one of the people mentioned is in an aesthetic state of mind while the other is not, for the present version of the subjective axiological account entails not that one is having a different kind of experience than the other (in the relevant sense of "experience") but rather that they are in different states of mind even though the same experience is a component of both those states of mind. The fact that they are, as we suppose, having the same *experience* is consistent with one of them being in the aesthetic state of mind while the other is not; in a word, one is *appreciating* the work of art while the other is not.

Although this reply allows us to say without flatly contradicting ourselves that, even though so far as their *experience* goes two people are in the same state, one of them is in the aesthetic state of mind while the other is not, one could still imagine Carroll insisting that it remains "arbitrary" and "unsatisfactory" to distinguish them in this way. The reply to this ultimately would have to involve showing how distinguishing them in this way – in particular, distinguishing appreciating in my sense from what we might call tracking without appreciating – did some philosophical work. I will have a little more to say about this at the end of this chapter.

Recognizing what I have called the structural point about the aesthetic state of mind also provides a response to Carroll's remark that the (subjective version of the) axiological approach cannot plausibly be advanced as a sufficient-condition claim about the aesthetic state of mind. Immediately after describing the axiological approach in general in terms appropriate to its subjective version as one that identifies the aesthetic experience as "an experience essentially valued for its own sake," he goes on to say that "this cannot serve as a sufficient condition for aesthetic experience, since, if one believes in intrinsic value, then presumably consistency would appear to require that one acknowledge that there are experiences other than aesthetic ones that are also valued for their own sake" (Carroll 2002: 153–4). In another place Carroll suggests an example of such an experience, the experience of "genuine sociability – a pleasant conversation about nothing in particular" (Carroll 2000: 204 n.17).

In view of the structural point, however, adopting the axiological approach as providing a sufficient condition of the aesthetic state of mind would not entail that the experience of a pleasant conversation was *itself* sufficient for being in the aesthetic state of mind. At most it would suggest that valuing such a conversation for its own sake was. But even this would not follow if, as appears to be the case, the "experience" of a pleasant conversation is not an experience *in the relevant sense*, namely, a case of knowing something immediately. And if there are *components* of a conversation that *do* involve experience in the relevant sense – say, getting a joke that a participant in the conversation has just told – and if *that* experience is valued for its own sake, then it seems to me that it is no longer implausible to think of this as a case of being in the aesthetic state of mind.

Valuing Something for Its Own Sake and Believing Something to be Intrinsically Valuable

So far I have taken the notion of valuing something for its own sake pretty much for granted, insisting only that, as Carroll officially admits (2001a: 81) but sometimes appears to argue as if he denies (2000: 197, 198), it is perfectly possible for someone to value something *both* for its own sake *and* as a means to some further end. In an earlier attempt to formulate this idea of appreciation (Iseminger 1981), I appealed to the notion of *believing . . . to be intrinsically valuable* rather than that of *valuing . . . for its own sake* (see also Anderson 2000). Carroll seems to take the notions of intrinsic value and value for its own sake as equivalent, for example, in describing the axiological approach as aiming at "defining aesthetic experience in terms of the kind of value it is meant to secure. Here the usual suspect is intrinsic value or value for its own sake" (Carroll 2002: 147).

Consideration of another objection, due to Aaron Meskin, suggests that it will be useful to distinguish them. His objection is that if it were true that "to aesthetically appreciate a work of art we must believe that our experience of the art is intrinsically valuable," then "possessing the concept of intrinsic value would be necessary to aesthetic appreciation and aesthetic experience" (Meskin 2001: 219–20). Perhaps on the assumption that the concept of intrinsic value is a "philosopher's concept," Meskin evidently supposes that any such necessary condition would make such heavy demands on the conceptual capacities of appreciators as to limit appreciation to the philosophically educated, a view that would surely disqualify the notion of appreciation from doing any serious philosophical work, as well as exemplifying a kind of elitism that would not only be offensive as such but would surely identify the wrong "elite."

Carroll offers a variant. In one version of his main argument against something like the current account of appreciation, one of the people described, Charles, is an evolutionary psychologist who holds the general belief that contemplating artworks in terms of their forms, and so forth, is worthwhile only because it enhances one's discriminatory powers (Carroll 2000: 204–5). But then, "it would be logically impossible for people who hold theories like Charles's to have aesthetic experiences" (Carroll 2000: 205–6), given that, consistent with their theory, they could not hold *any* belief to the effect that some experience is intrinsically valuable.

What is at stake here is just what kind of beliefs and what kind of concepts we must attribute to those who appreciate something in the present sense, and the claim in effect is that requiring that they so much as have a concept of intrinsic value, let alone that they believe that concept to be instantiated, leads to clearly counterintuitive judgments to the effect that certain people cannot appreciate states of affairs.

How might distinguishing between intrinsic value and value for its own sake help to meet these objections? This distinction, or something like it, is made by Korsgaard (1983). In a way that is reminiscent of Kripke's (1970) argument that the necessary should not be directly opposed to the *a posteriori* (necessity being a *metaphysical* status which cannot without begging important questions be assumed to resist *a posteriori epistemic* access), she objects to the tendency in value theorists to oppose the *intrinsic* to the *instrumental*. Her claim is that, somewhat in the way that the opposite of necessary is contingent and the opposite of *a posteriori* is *a priori*, the opposite of intrinsic is extrinsic and the opposite of instrumental is *in itself*. Even more specifically, just as, when one recognizes the difference between the metaphysical and epistemic, it becomes clear that "necessary" and "contingent" qualify truth, while "a posteriori" and "a priori" qualify knowledge, so, too, it now appears that "intrinsic" and "extrinsic" qualify *values,* while "instrumentally" and "for its own sake" qualify *valuings.*

However, even though intrinsic value may be a metaphysical concept and *valuing* for its own sake an epistemic one, *believing* that something has intrinsic value and *valuing* something for its own sake are both epistemic, and the question arises what the difference between them may be.

First, is valuing believing? The alternative, I suppose, is that valuing something might be having some kind of feeling, such as taking pleasure in it or enjoying it, but, though this may be characteristically associated with experiences we value for their own sake and one of the things which disposes us to value them, it seems not to be a necessary condition of such valuing (remember the conclusion of *Wozzeck*), nor, where it *is* present, does it *constitute* such valuing. Accordingly, it seems plausible to regard valuing as consisting in having a certain belief.

But what is the content of that belief, if it is not the belief that that experience has intrinsic value? Partly, of course, it is the belief that the experience is *good*, and the concept of *good* is surely not a concept peculiarly available only to philosophers. But what distinguishes believing that it is good for its own sake and believing that it is good instrumentally? Is not, for example, "instrumentally good" (and, hence, its opposite, "good for its own sake") as much a philosopher's concept as "intrinsically valuable"?

Believing that an experience is good for its own sake is not, I think, believing that it has a kind of goodness, goodness for its own sake, in the way that believing that an experience is intrinsically good is believing that it has a kind of goodness, intrinsic goodness. Rather, it is believing *not merely for reasons that describe something as a means to other ends* that it is good. What distinguishes the belief that something is good for its own sake from the belief that something is (only) instrumentally good is not a distinctive content but a distinctive kind of reason that the holder of the first belief but not the second has or perhaps would have for it. (Under pressure and upon reflection, where what is being valued is an experience, this reason might turn out to be something like "a human life is better all else being equal just for having included this experience.")

So one need not be a philosopher to appreciate some state of affairs some way; one need not have a concept of intrinsic value. Nor is an evolutionary psychologist of Charles's stripe prevented from appreciating on pain of contradicting himself; he need not think that the concept of intrinsic value is instantiated. (This latter point is reinforced by the reflection that the evaluative belief that partly constitutes appreciation is not a belief about the value in general of certain kinds of experiences, such as an evolutionary psychologist might hold, nor is that belief the motive for which those experiences are sought out, as Carroll typically takes the axiologist to hold (Carroll 2000: 204). It is rather a belief about a particular experience one is engaged in or has had, and the motive for seeking out such an experience might better be seen as the *hope* that the belief will turn out to be true – that one *will* find the experience valuable in itself, that is, that one *will* appreciate the state of affairs experienced.) Moreover, no theory that Charles might hold about the evolutionary value of scanning pictures would seem to be in logical conflict with the thought that his life is better all things being equal for his scanning or having scanned this picture at this time.

Certainly on this view of appreciation one must be able to make certain kinds of moves in the "space of reasons," one must have beliefs that one has not considered and expressed, and one must be said to have or not to have certain reasons in situations where one has not in fact articulated them. So although on the current view we need not attribute philosophical training nor deny a belief in evolutionary theory to the appreciator, we certainly do need to attribute to him or her a rich, sophisticated, and by no means self-transparent mental life (let alone a mental life easily accessible to others). Carroll (2002: 161–2) makes much of the difficulties inherent in thus attributing unconscious and unformulated beliefs to people, and to this we may add the difficulty of attributing to them *reasons* for those beliefs on the basis of guesses at counterfactuals about what they would say if they were asked.

To a considerable extent, however, these difficulties seem to me to mirror the difficulties of attributing knowledge to someone given any of the many versions of a justified-true-belief (or perhaps rather nowadays a justified-true-belief-plus) account of knowledge. On the one hand, there is the question whether it is plausible to attribute to knowers (or appreciators) the equipment they must have if they are to fulfill the putative conditions of knowledge (or appreciation). Here we must be careful not to require them to be philosophers, even philosophers who, cleverer than G. E. Moore, know the analysis of the concepts that they use, but it seems to me that the equipment required to believe that an experience is good without requiring a certain kind of reason for that belief is far from excessive.

On the other hand, there is the difficulty of telling in a particular situation whether the equipment is so deployed as to make it the case that someone knows something or appreciates a state of affairs, even leaving aside the fact that, in both cases, the world has to cooperate with the equipment, given that what is known must be true, and what is appreciated as being some way must be that way. (But doesn't someone who steps confidently forward typically *believe* that the ground ahead is solid? Doesn't that person typically even *know* this?) I have nothing profound to offer here, but we do the best we can with our folk psychology, observations of behavior, conversations – whatever helps. We are, I think, at least no worse off in this regard in the case of appreciation as I have conceived it than we are in the case of knowledge as traditionally conceived.

Changing the Subject?

I have emphasized ways in which the concept of appreciation as I understand it provides an account of the aesthetic state of mind that differs significantly from accounts that emphasize disinterested attention to and rapt contemplation of qualities of form and design. Carroll suggests that, though this retreat from formalism is admirable in itself, promoting it under the banner of the concept of an aesthetic state of mind may amount to false advertising, since "it casts the net of aesthetic experience far wider than the tradition standardly permits. Thus the axiological approach runs the danger of introducing a neologism into the discussion. And, all things being equal, an account of aesthetic experience that better approximates traditional usage should be preferred, lest we run the danger of changing the subject altogether" (Carroll 2002: 163). Whether I have "changed the subject altogether" will, I think, depend on whether the concept of appreciation, as I understand it, can ultimately do anything like the work that, for example, Beardsley tried to do with his concept of aesthetic experience, most notably help us to an understanding of what art is and of what makes works of art better or worse as works of art. Again, I will have something to say about this – but only a little – at the end of this chapter.

In the meantime, I would like to try to connect my account of appreciation to the aestheticist tradition with which, on Carroll's view, it is in danger of losing contact. My suggestion will be that the tradition of the aesthetic state of mind as consisting in disinterested attention and rapt contemplation of formal qualities represents only one possible development of what is arguably its source, namely Baumgarten's *Aesthetica*.

On Guyer's view, as we have seen, Baumgarten conceives of aesthetics as "the study of the perfection of and pleasure in the exercise of sensibility for its own sake, as manifested in the production of works of artistic beauty." If we allow ourselves the supposition that aesthetics is the study of the aesthetic then we can, as it were, construct an account of the aesthetic state of mind on his behalf by concentrating on the notion of perfection of and pleasure in the exercise of sensibility for its own sake. It will be instructive, I think, to see how the description of appreciation that I have given can be arrived at in a fairly straightforward way by tweaking this much of Baumgarten's account in a couple of ways.

First, *sensibility*. Whatever exactly Baumgarten may have had in mind, what I have called appreciation includes but is not limited to sense perception. Where it involves sense perception – seeing, hearing, tasting, and so on – it also typically involves sophisticated conceptual capacities, knowledge of counterpoint, for instance, or of human needs, values, and capacities. In such cases, as well as in our appreciation of literature (from which, interestingly enough in view of his emphasis on sense perception, Baumgarten takes most of his examples) what makes the seeing, the hearing, *and the understanding* "exercises of sensibility" is that they are all *experiences* at least in the sense that they are "lived through." One can imagine not only merely remembering having done these things – listening to the contrapuntal interplay of the voices, looking at the pattern of branches, grasping the humor of Benedick's response – but going back and doing them again.

Next, *pleasure for its own sake*. As we have seen (and Carroll 2001a emphasizes), pleasure seems not to be a necessary condition of the aesthetic state of mind. But, as Carroll, as we have also seen, suggested, it is also natural in the face of this realization to modify the condition to one of valuing an experience for its own sake. For it seems clear that very many "exercises of sensibility" that we value for their own sake *are* experiences in which we take pleasure, so that the lead from pleasure to value is a natural one, even if it is a mistake to suppose that experiences that we value for their own sake *must* be experiences in which we take pleasure.

Finally, *perfection*. Experiences can be better or worse. An important way in which this is true of experiences such as seeing, hearing, and understanding is that they are not characterized merely (if at all) by their manifestation of certain *qualia* but, as I have argued, by their *cognitive* ambitions. They are experiences not only in the sense that they are lived though but also in the sense that they are direct (noninferential, but not thereby necessarily nonconceptual) ways of *knowing*. Aiming to *perfect* the exercise of our sensibility can be construed as aiming to see what is, in some sense, really there to be seen, hear what is really there to be heard, and understand what is really there to be understood – experiencing *correctly*.

Appreciation in my sense – valuing an experience (in the cognitive sense exemplified by experiences of seeing, hearing, understanding, etc.) for its own sake – seems, then, to be readily interpretable as a variation on one way of taking Baumgarten's idea of taking pleasure in the perfected exercise of sensibility for its own sake. Another variation, indeed a more familiar one and one that is closer to Carroll's reading of the aestheticist tradition, might be something like "valuing for its own sake, while not valuing instrumentally, the rapt contemplation of the formal qualities of an immediately given appearance." But my account of appreciation seems to have an equally legitimate claim to aestheticist ancestry, besides having the advantage of being less susceptible to antiformalist objections. The subject has not been much changed.

Art and the Aesthetic State of Mind

It remains to say something about art and the aesthetic. For one thing, in explaining why I can in good conscience march under Baumgarten's banner, I have not yet taken

account of that part of his notion of the aesthetic which connects it with "the production of works of artistic beauty." In addition, I have alluded several times to the
question of how the notion of appreciation might fare if it were to be enlisted in the
service of an aesthetic theory of art.

On the first point, it is worth noting that by now we have mostly come to
think of beauty as just one of many qualities, from the sublime and the picturesque
on to the gritty, the dainty (if not the dumpy), the shocking, and so on, that may
be appreciated. This seems to me to be of a piece with the move beyond pleasure
to valuing in itself as a constituent of appreciation. Furthermore, though the
aesthetic state of mind may be frequently and even preeminently *manifested* in
connection with art, there seems no reason to suppose that it is restricted to art on
Baumgarten's account. So far, then, there seems to be nothing in his idea of the
aesthetic state of mind regarding its connections with art and beauty that seriously
challenges the claim that my idea of appreciation is a legitimate descendant
of it.

What is striking, however, is that Baumgarten concerns himself specifically with
the *artist's production* of artworks rather than, as might be expected from someone
talking about a mode of sensory cognition, and as I have done, with the *spectator's
appreciation* of them. Mary J. Gregor, having remarked that "Baumgarten has little
to say about the appreciation of art as distinguished from its production" (Gregor
1983: 368), nonetheless feels justified in generalizing his ideas about production to
apply to appreciation as well. For example, she attributes to him the claim that sensory
cognition is "the kind of cognition achieved in the production (and appreciation)
of art" (Gregor 1983: 364), as well as the claim that this mode of cognition, in
combination with "the 'aesthetic temperament,' whose desires tend toward the
production (and appreciation) of beauty," helps to "define the *felix aestheticus,
the artist (and the man of taste)" (Gregor 1983: 373). If she is right in this,
then there is here no challenge to my claim of ancestry either, but there is a salutary
reminder that any account of art that starts from the notion of appreciation must show how the artist is more than merely adventitious, along with a
hint that invoking the possibility that something like *the very same state of
mind* may occur in both the artist and the appreciator may be one step in this
direction.

Finally, Carroll, quite independently of his animadversions concerning the notion
of an aesthetic state of mind with an essential structure, is convinced that aesthetic
accounts of the nature and value of art are fundamentally misconceived (see, especially, Carroll 2001d: 35–41). How might the notion of appreciation be deployed in
some such account?

Here in briefest outline is one way. Recall first that, as is well-known from the
work of Kristeller ([1951] 1980), the concept of the fine arts, as distinguished from
earlier groupings of the liberal arts, only clearly emerged in Western Europe in the
middle of the eighteenth century. On this basis it can be argued that the practice of
(fine)-art-in-general – as distinct from but encompassing the already existing practices of painting, music, poetry, and so on – and the *informal institution* of the (fine)-
artworld-in-general – as distinct from but encompassing the worlds of music, of

painting, of poetry, and so on – depending, as they do, on people *recognizing* one another as engaged in this practice and as members of this world, cannot have existed prior to this time and did in fact come into existence at about this time. (It is not, I think, a coincidence that Baumgarten's work was roughly contemporaneous.) Furthermore, it is possible to regard this practice with its associated informal institution as a *human artifact*; something that, as such, has a *function* – what it was made to do and does preeminently well. Finally, it can be argued that this function was and is, as a matter of contingent historical fact, the promotion of what I call *aesthetic communication*, where aesthetic communication paradigmatically takes place when someone makes something with the aim and effect that someone else appreciates it, in the sense of appreciation I have discussed. (This argument is adumbrated in Iseminger 1999 and presented in detail in Iseminger 2004.)

On the basis of this understanding of the nature of art and its connection with the aesthetic, I do *not* claim that the *essence* of the practice of art is to promote aesthetic communication; my claim is rather about its actual history and present state. Nor do I claim that the essence or function of *works* of art is necessarily to afford appreciation. Insofar as I make any claim about the essence of works of art it is that that essence is fundamentally institutional, and I recognize that when works of art are conceived in this way, it is obvious that many do not and are not intended to afford appreciation. I do claim, however, that one may evaluate what voluntary participants in a practice do while acting in their roles in that practice, as well as the products of what they thus do, in terms of the contribution those actions and their products make to that practice's function, and on this basis I argue that the value of works of art as works of art consists in their capacity to afford appreciation in the present sense.

Surely this deserves to be called an aesthetic theory of art. (But see Anderson 2000 for an aesthetic theory of art, based on a version of the present concept of appreciation, which aims to fulfill even more of the ambitions generally associated with such theories.) To try to show that this view can meet Carroll's objections to aesthetic theories of art is, however, a task for another day.

Gary Iseminger

References for Chapters 5 and 6

Anderson, J. C. (2000). "Aesthetic Concepts of Art." In Noël Carroll (ed.), *Theories of Art Today* (pp. 65–92). Madison: University of Wisconsin Press.

Aquinas, T. (1945). *Basic Writings of St. Thomas Aquinas*, ed. A. C. Pegis. New York: Random House.

Carlson, A. (2000). *Aesthetics and the Environment: the Appreciation of Nature.* London: Routledge.

Carroll, N. (1999). *Philosophy of Art: a Contemporary Introduction.* London: Routledge.

Carroll, N. (2000). "Art and the Domain of the Aesthetic." *British Journal of Aesthetics*, 40(2): 191–208.

Carroll, N. (2001a). "Enjoyment, Indifference, and Aesthetic Experience." *British Journal of Aesthetics.* 41(1): 81–3.

Carroll, N. (2001b)."Emotion, Appreciation, and Nature." In Noël Carroll, *Beyond Aesthetics* (pp. 384–94). New York: Cambridge University Press.

Carroll, N. (2001c). "On Being Moved by Nature." In N. Carroll, *Beyond Aesthetics* (pp. 368–84). New York: Cambridge University Press.

Carroll, N. (2001d). "Beauty and the Genealogy of Art Theory." In N. Carroll, *Beyond Aesthetics* (pp. 20–41). New York: Cambridge University Press.

Carroll, N. (2001e). "Four Concepts of Aesthetic Experience." In N. Carroll, *Beyond Aesthetics* (pp. 41–62). New York: Cambridge University Press.

Carroll, N. (2002). "Aesthetic Experience Revisited." *British Journal of Aesthetics*, 42(2): 145–68.

Chatwin, B. (1987). *The Songlines.* New York: Viking.

Csikszentmihalyi, M. (1975). *Beyond Boredom and Anxiety.* San Francisco: Jossey-Bass.

Dickie, G. (1964). "The Myth of the Aesthetic Attitude." *American Philosophical Quarterly,* 1: 56–65.

Dickie, G. (1965). "Beardsley's Phantom Aesthetic Experience." *Journal of Philosophy,* 62: 129–36.

Dickie. G. (1973). "Psychical Distance: In a Fog at Sea." *British Journal of Aesthetics,* 13: 17–29.

Dissanayake, E. (1992). *Homo Aestheticus.* Seattle: University of Washington Press.

Dissanayake, E. (2000). *Art and Intimacy.* Seattle: University of Washington Press.

Eaton, M. M. (2001). *Merit: Aesthetic and Ethical.* New York: Oxford University Press.

Emerson, R. W. (1936). "Art." In R. W. Emerson, *Essays* (pp. 239–50). Reading, PA: Spencer Press.

Gerow, T. (1997). "Indian Aesthetics: a Philosophical Survey." In E. Deutsch and R. Bontekoe (eds.), *A Companion to World Philosophies* (pp. 315–25). Oxford: Blackwell.

Goldberg, S. J. (1997). "Chinese Aesthetics." In E. Deutsch and R. Bontekoe (eds.), *A Companion to World Philosophies* (pp. 225–36). Oxford: Blackwell.

Gregor, M. J. (1983). "Baumgarten's *Aesthetica.*" *Review of Metaphysics,* 37: 357–85.

Guyer, P. (1998). "Baumgarten, Alexander Gottlieb." In M. Kelly (ed.), *Encyclopedia of Aesthetics,* vol. 1 (pp. 227–8). Oxford: Oxford University Press.

Iseminger, G. (1981). "Aesthetic Appreciation." *Journal of Aesthetics and Art Criticism,* 39: 389–97.

Iseminger, G. (1999). "The Aesthetic Function of Art." In Kevin L. Stoehr (ed.), *Proceedings of the Twentieth World Congress of Philosophy, Volume 4, Philosophies of Religion, Art, and Creativity* (pp. 169–76). Bowling Green, OH: Philosophy Documentation Center.

Iseminger, G. (2003). "Aesthetic Experience." In J. Levinson (ed.), *The Oxford Handbook of Aesthetics* (pp. 99–116). Oxford: Oxford University Press.

Iseminger, G. (2004). *The Aesthetic Function of Art.* Ithaca, NY and London: Cornell University Press.

Kant, I. ([1798] 1978). *Anthropology from a Pragmatic Point of View*, trans. V. L. Dowell. Carbondale: University of Illinois Press.

Korsgaard, C. M. (1983). "Two Distinctions in Goodness." *Philosophical Review*, 92: 169–95.

Kripke, S. (1970). *Naming and Necessity*. Oxford: Blackwell.

Kristeller, P. O. ([1951] 1980), "The Modern System of the Arts." In *Renaissance Thought and the Arts* (pp. 163–227). Princeton: Princeton University Press.

Levinson, J. (2001). "Aesthetic Properties, Evaluative Force, and Differences in Sensibility." In E. Brady and J. Levinson (eds.), *Aesthetic Concepts: Essays After Sibley* (pp. 61–80). Oxford: Oxford University Press.

Livingston, P. (2003). "On an Apparent Truism in Aesthetics." *British Journal of Aesthetics*, 43(3): 60–278.

Meskin, A. (2001). "Review of *Theories of Art Today*, ed. Noël Carroll." *Journal of Aesthetics and Art Criticism*, 59: 219–20.

Miller, R. (1998). "Three Versions of Objectivity: Aesthetic, Moral and Scientific." In J. Levinson (ed.), *Aesthetics and Ethics* (pp. 26–58). Cambridge, UK: Cambridge University Press.

Mithen, S. (1996). *The Prehistory of the Mind: The Cognitive Origins of Art and Science*. London: Thames and Hudson.

Nasr, H. S. (1997). "Islamic Aesthetics." In E. Deutsch and R. Bontekoe (eds.), *A Companion to World Philosophies* (pp. 448–59). Oxford: Blackwell.

Panksepp, J. (1985). "Mood Changes." In P. Vinken, C. Bruyn, and H. Klawans (eds.), *Handbook of Clinical Neurology*, vol. 1 (45, pp. 271–85). Amsterdam: Elsevier.

Sober, E. (2002). "Intelligent Design and Probability Reasoning." *International Journal for the Philosophy of Religion*, 52: 65–80.

Stecker, R. (2001). "Only Jerome: a Reply to Noël Carroll." *British Journal of Aesthetics*, 41: 76–80.

Tooby, J. and Cosmides, L. (2001). "Does Beauty Build Adapted Minds? Toward an Evolutionary Theory of Aesthetics, Fiction and the Arts." *SubStance*, 30 (1 & 2): 6–27.

Further Reading for Chapters 5 and 6

Beardsley, M. (1958). *Aesthetics: Problems in the Philosophy of Criticism*. New York: Harcourt Brace and Company.

Beardsley, M. (1969). "Aesthetic Experience Regained." *Journal of Aesthetics and Art Criticism*, 28: 3–11.

Beardsley, M. (1982). *The Aesthetic Point of View*. Ithaca, NY and London: Cornell University Press.

Budd, M. (1995). *Values of Art*. London: Penguin Books

Dickie, G. (1974). *Art and the Aesthetic: an Institutional Analysis*. Ithaca, NY and London, Cornell University Press.

Fenner, D. W. (1996). *The Aesthetic Attitude*. Atlantic Highlands, NJ: Humanities Press International.

Levinson, J. (1996). *The Pleasures of Aesthetics*. Ithaca, NY and London: Cornell University Press.

Mitias, M. (1988). *The Possibility of Aesthetic Experience*. Dordrecht: Martinus Nijhoff.

Scruton, R. (1974). *Art and Imagination*. London: Methuen.

Shusterman, R. "The End of Aesthetic Experience." *Journal of Aesthetics and Art Criticism*, 55: 29–41,

Walton, K. (1993). "How Marvelous! Towards a Theory of Aesthetic Value." *Journal of Aesthetics and Art Criticism*, 51: 499–510.

SHOULD WE VALUE WORKS AS ART FOR WHAT WE CAN LEARN FROM THEM?

Art and Cognition

Berys Gaut

I am going to argue for a cognitivist view of the value of art; more precisely, I will argue that art can nontrivially teach us and that this (partly) determines its artistic value. This view, aesthetic cognitivism, need not hold that the *only* value of art is cognitive; indeed, the sensible cognitivist holds that there is a plurality of artistic values, of which cognitive ones are just one kind. Beauty, expressive qualities, various affective properties, and so on, have a role to play in constituting the value of art on a pluralist version of cognitivism. Moreover, most cognitivists correctly hold that there is a wide variety of different kinds of knowledge that art can impart to its appreciators: propositional knowledge, know-how (skills), phenomenal knowledge (knowledge of what it is like to experience something), conceptual knowledge, knowledge of values and of significance, for example. Cognitivism also differs in the scope of its application to the arts. It has been argued by some that abstract arts such as purely instrumental music are valuable partly because of their cognitive value (Young 1999). I will not address the issue of scope here, but will instead focus on the representational arts, particularly literature, where the debate about cognitivism has been at its most intense. The scope of aesthetic cognitivism as defended here should be understood as appropriately restricted.

Aesthetic cognitivism is the conjunction of two claims. The first, an epistemic claim, holds that art can nontrivially teach us; the second, an aesthetic claim, holds that this capacity to teach partly determines art's aesthetic value. (I employ "aesthetic value" here in a broad sense, in which it is equivalent to "artistic value" in its application to art.) Since aesthetic cognitivism is stated as a conjunction, aesthetic noncognitivism (or anticognitivism) is the denial of either or both of the epistemic and aesthetic claims; so the noncognitivist can attack cognitivism on either epistemic or aesthetic grounds.

Aesthetic cognitivism has been intensely debated in recent years, particularly in relation to the claim of whether literature can impart knowledge of values.

Cognitivists include Beardsmore (1973), Carroll (2002), Currie (1997, 1998), Goodman (1976), Graham (1995), Kivy (1997), Novitz (1987), Nussbaum (1990), Putnam (1978), and Young (2001). Noncognitivists include Beardsley (1981), Diffey (1997), Gass (1987), Lamarque (1997), Lamarque and Olsen (1994), and Stolnitz (1992).

Arguing for cognitivism may seem easy. Consider the vocabulary of literary appraisal: we celebrate some works for their profundity, their insights into the human condition, for how they make us see the world anew; we criticize other works for their shallowness and their escapist pandering to people's illusions. The vocabulary of literary evaluation is laden, overtly and covertly, with cognitivist freight. This, and the fact that we confidently apply the vocabulary to literary works, is surely all the cognitivists need to establish their case? But appearances can deceive: consider the use of "profundity" as a term of evaluation of music. To claim that a work is profound appears to require that it conveys some true proposition about matters of central importance to human beings. But how can purely instrumental music convey any propositions at all? So, the noncognitivist may claim, "profundity" is not being employed in its normal sense here; why assume, then, that it is being employed in this normal sense when used of literature and the other representational arts?

So cognitivists need to do more than simply appeal to the vocabulary and practices of literary appraisal. But this opening sally establishes the proper dialectic of the debate: anticognitivists should seek to undermine the cognitivist appearances of literary appraisal, and if they fail in so doing, cognitivism should carry the day.

The Epistemic Claim

Art on the cognitivist view teaches us nontrivially about the world; but this has been denied on a variety of grounds, including that any truth-claims advanced by fictional works cannot be confirmed by them (Stolnitz 1992). I have argued elsewhere that these criticisms can be met, and that fiction's claims can be confirmed both by experience and testimony (Gaut 2003). One can also learn from imagination, and this has particular importance in the way that art can teach us, in guiding our imaginings (see also Currie 1997, 1998). Consider some examples: I can correctly determine that I ought to become a philosopher, not a medical doctor, by imagining both careers, and seeing how I imaginatively fare in them; I can learn something about how courageous I am by imagining myself being tortured and contemplating how I react; I can learn what it is like to be a bereaved woman whose husband has died after 60 years of marriage by imagining myself in her position; I can meditate on whether there ought to be free universal healthcare by imagining myself to be poor and ill in a society without such a system, and seeing whether I can endorse what would happen to me. Knowledge about what one should choose, self-knowledge, knowledge about others, and knowledge about what is morally right are all it seems achievable by imagination. If this is so, then it is no surprise that literature can aid in our imaginative pursuit of knowledge: novels can describe the lives of philosophers and doctors, scenes of torture, the loneliness of the bereaved, and the plight of the poor and ill.

It may be objected that one cannot learn about the world from imagination, for only experience or testimony can fulfill this role, while imagination can only teach

Berys Gaut

one about what is possible; so the claims just advanced must be false. However, the objection presupposes an oversimple distinction between the world and mere possibilities (counterfactual states of affairs). Statements about the features of the world, such as psychological states and what is valuable, often entail or otherwise ground statements about counterfactuals. Consider dispositional psychological states: if I am truly courageous, I would withstand certain sorts of hardship (such as torture), and this claim concerns counterfactuals; and I may never have been subject to such hardships. So it is relevant to determining whether I am courageous to establish what I would do under these merely possible circumstances. Likewise, choices concern whether to actualize counterfactual states of affairs: saying that it would be best for me to be a doctor makes a claim about a counterfactual situation, and how I respond to this imagined situation is relevant in determining its value for me. Further, since moral judgments are universalizable, they commit one to a claim about what ought to be done in all counterfactual situations that possess the universal properties referred to in the judgment. So, if I hold that sickness is not a sufficient ground for a right to free healthcare, I must also hold that were I sick, I would have no right to free healthcare, even were I too poor to afford it. (See Carroll 2002 for a similar point about literature's capacity to teach us about morality; however, such knowledge is not merely, as he seems to hold, conceptual: if I learn something from the healthcare thought-experiment, it is not about the concept of a right, but something substantive about what rights we have.) And, finally, in considering how others, such as a bereaved woman, react to adversity, then, given a suitably fine-grained description of psychological character, it follows that anyone with that character would react similarly. So it is relevant to imagine how I, had I that character, would react. Hence many kinds of statements about the world involve or imply claims about counterfactual conditions, about whose features we can learn through imagination.

This cognitivist view fits smoothly with one influential conception of literature, as the exploration of kinds of possibilities. Aristotle, the first aesthetic cognitivist known to us, talks in the *Poetics* of possibility when he describes the goal of the poet: "the poet's function is to describe, not the thing that has happened, but a kind of thing that might happen, i.e. what is possible as being probable or necessary" (Aristotle 1984: 1451a 37–9). And reporting his own literary practice, Milan Kundera makes a similar point more eloquently: "characters are not born like people, of woman; they are born of a situation, a sentence, a metaphor containing in a nutshell a basic human possibility that the author thinks no one else has discovered or said something essential about" (Kundera 1984: 221).

Such a view can itself seem puzzling: for whereas one might concede that one can discover logical or conceptual possibilities through imagination, how could one discover through it, say, a "basic human possibility"? That clearly is more substantive than what is merely logically possible; indeed, the kind of cases discussed above might be described as those where we explore what is morally possible or psychologically possible, given certain conditions. Yet there is a confirmation problem here, for one could imagine that something would occur, or be permissible, yet one's imaginings could be mistaken; and if one can be mistaken, one needs confirmation that one has imagined correctly. Yet surely confirmation requires appeal to some kind of testimony or experience.

Art and Cognition

There is a way in which imagination can provide a degree of confirmation in such cases; for the objection presupposes another oversimple contrast, this time between experience and imagination. Certainly, sensory experience is an important source of knowledge about the world. But experience is a broader category, covering conscious states that have a phenomenology, which include affective experiences (emotions and feelings) as well as sense experience. Part of the explanation of how we can learn from imagination is that we can affectively respond to imagined states of affairs. I know how I would react to torture partly because on vividly imagining the instruments of torture laid out before me, I come to feel apprehension, disquiet, even fear. I may well not know in advance how I would react – I may even be happily self-deceived, and suppose that I would nobly resist the torturer's ministrations. My affective reactions to the imagined states of affairs show that, sadly, I am no hero. Secondly, what we imagine is itself revealing of who we are. The fact that I go on to imagine myself screaming and confessing everything when I vividly imagine being tortured itself reveals something about how I am likely to respond in the real situation. It is tempting to think of imagination as an entirely free-wheeling faculty, for it seems one can imagine anything that is logically possible (and arguably also some things that are not logically possible). And that is true; but the fact that one *can* imagine (almost) anything doesn't mean that one *will* imagine (almost) anything. What we actually do imagine can be symptomatic of the kind of people we are (Walton 1997: especially 49, n. 15). Thirdly, there is the role of extrapolation from one's everyday experience: if, I might wonder, I get nervous when going to the dentist, how might I respond to the prospect of far worse pain? And, as we shall see shortly, normative constraints on imagination are also crucial in grounding its role in learning.

These examples involve simple imaginative projection: imagining a case where you are confronted with a particular situation. A more complex kind of imaginative projection involves imagining being another person confronting a particular situation. Here one has to imagine being relevantly different from the way one actually is – say, being an aged woman confronting a bereavement. Though the imaginative task is more complex, it is not in principle different; imagining being another person is, I believe, actually a matter of imagining possessing the relevant properties of that person (Gaut 1999). So both simple and complex imaginative projection involve imagining properties of oneself. Complex projection presupposes in addition enough basic commonality between people to secure a reasonable degree of accuracy in one's imaginings, despite the relevant differences between oneself and others. Its use is common in normal life, in coming to understand someone else through "putting oneself in the other person's shoes," and in role-playing, whether in children's games or in various therapeutic contexts.

How does complex imaginative projection work in literature? In the opening scene of *King Lear* Shakespeare asks us to imagine an aged king, who through receiving years of unquestioned obedience has come to think of those around him, even his daughters, as mere subjects, owing him public and humble obedience. He has come to think of love as a kind of tribute, to be publicly proclaimed and handed over by the supplicant to the king. Lear's conception of love is shallow and distorted, but entirely explicable, given the life of undisputed power and privilege that he has enjoyed. From his (mis)conceptions about love and the nature of human relationships

Berys Gaut

springs much of the tragic action of the play. When we imagine events as Shakespeare asks us to do, we have a sense that this is indeed how a king with Lear's history and personality would react, and that his subsequent actions make sense in the light of his personality as revealed in that first scene. And we do not just concur that this is how things might go; we also have a sense of being shown things that might not have occurred to us had we imagined a similar scenario ourselves. For instance, Lear's infantilism is initially striking and odd, yet on reflection it makes perfect sense, given his great age, and the fact that he has spent his life being treated like a pampered child by his subjects and children.

Imagine, in contrast, a rewritten version of the play, in which in the second scene a reconciliation is staged between Lear and Cordelia: Lear, having reflected on his harsh public denunciation of his daughter, abjectly apologizes to her, proclaims that he ought not to let his temper get out of control, and that he is an egoistic and foolish old man. Apart from ruining the play, we would quite properly think that things couldn't possibly turn out like that. We would imaginatively resist this outcome; we might exclaim "I can't imagine him doing that!"

Now whatever is going on with this remark? Taken one way it is necessarily self-refuting, for when one asks what "that" denotes, the answer is that it is the situation in which Lear, with the features ascribed to him in the first scene of the play, apologizes to Cordelia immediately after that scene. And in stating that, I have in a certain sense imagined the event just described as occurring. But I have asserted that I can't imagine that. Clearly, we have two rather distinct uses of the term "imagining" here: in one sense, I can imagine the described scene, for I can entertain the propositions which describe it. But in another sense, I can't imagine it, and that is the sense of complex imaginative projection involving role-playing to which I have drawn attention. When I project myself imaginatively into Lear's situation, with his ascribed characteristics, I find I can't imagine myself doing what the mangled version of the play describes him as doing. I can entertain the propositions that he does that, but I can't imagine it "from the inside" (compare Moran 1994).

The real *Lear*, then, deploys our capacities for complex imaginative projection, and we concur with the described scenario. We may well discover things that we would not have imagined ourselves, such as Lear's infantilism, and we know that is how things might well be, because when we imagine him having those features, in addition to the others ascribed to him, we find our projection goes through smoothly. In contrast, we imaginatively resist the mangled version because our deployment of imaginative abilities spurns the ascription of these actions to him. Literature thus can deploy our imaginative capacities. And we can in turn test out its claims in imagination, by discovering whether or not the called-for imaginative projection is one with which we concur or is one which we resist. The claims of literature can be tested out in imagination.

We can learn through imagination about psychology and character by the means sketched earlier. The same mechanisms also explain how we can learn about what we prudentially or morally ought to do. In prudential choices, such as that of choosing a career, one considers how one affectively responds to oneself in the imagined career: responding with pleasure to the thought of one's life as a doctor is a (defeasible) reason for thinking that it may be a good career. One also needs to know how one would change in the imagined scenario, so here again extrapolation and discovering what one goes on to imagine are relevant. Likewise, in determining whether it is permissible not to have a free healthcare system, it is relevant to determine how one affectively responds to the prospects of being poor, sick, and unable to afford medical care; and here again one needs to know what it would be like to be in that imagined scenario. And in choosing for other people (what would be best for them), one must bring complex imaginative projection to bear on the question of value. So the fundamental means of learning from imagination are the same both for psychology and for values.

It is worth considering a general objection to the view defended here: imagination, it may be claimed, can never deliver knowledge, because it is not subject to any constraints. If I can imagine anything, I cannot learn from imagination; for learning requires some independent testing of one's hypotheses. And this also applies to cases where one's imaginings are guided by something outside oneself, rather than being spontaneously generated. Literature can be a matter of pure fantasy, of imagining things for the sake of pure pleasure, however wildly implausible those imaginings might be. Ian Fleming's James Bond novels, for instance, are not noted for their robust realism. Since literature, like imagination, can engage in this free-wheeling mode, serving no more than fantasy, how can it be a source of knowledge?

The objection is important, since it brings out a subtlety not yet fully explored. Imagination has many uses, fixed by one's aims in imagining. I can aim, for instance, to imagine whatever is required to make me feel good about myself and to give me pleasure. That is the central aim of personal fantasy. However, even in this case my imagination does not operate in a normatively unconstrained fashion: for what I should imagine is determined by the goal of maximizing my pleasure. If I find myself imagining scenes of personal misery and humiliation, I have failed in my project of fantasizing. The constraints on what and how one should imagine are fixed, then, by one's goal in imagining. Some literary works feed and foster personal fantasy in just this way; Bond novels, at least for their target audience, successfully obey the norms of fantasizing.

A different aim of imagining is to learn about the world. The examples of imagining being tortured, and of imagining being a bereaved woman are of this kind. This kind of imaginative project too has normative constraints, likewise laid down by one's goal in imagining. Imaginers should try, for instance, to be as faithful to the facts as they can, to avoid heroic self-delusion in the case of torture, and shallowness and sentimentality in the case of bereavement. They have to ask themselves, honestly, about how they would respond were they in these situations, and in the case of imagining being someone else the scope for getting it wrong is especially large, since they are trying to imagine themselves in a situation radically different from their actual one.

Literature can share these goals in prescribing imaginings, and it too can be subject to the same norms of imagining comprehensively, vividly, unsentimentally, and with fidelity to how things might be. Douglas Dunn's *Elegies* (1985) asks us to imagine the situation of a poet (Dunn himself) who has suffered a bereavement, and the poems do so in a way that evinces a commitment to honesty and an avoidance of sentimentality which tells us much about the nature of loss of a loved one. Likewise, Jane

Austen's *Emma* shares the goal of a truthful exploration of human psychology and social relationships, and, unlike the Fleming novels, eschews the pursuit of fantasy – is indeed about the destruction of Emma's fantasy about her having insight into her own and others' romantic needs. Literature, like imagination, can have the goal of learning about the world and in such cases shares the normative disciplines on imagination which promote successful pursuit of that goal.

Note that I have defended the cognitive power of imagination without adverting to simulation theory, which holds that imagination is a kind of "offline" running of cognitive processes, and that this is a source of knowledge of psychological states. Some have defended this theory and its application to aesthetics (Currie 1995a: chapter 5). Nothing that I have said commits me to this theory. The idea of imagination as centrally involved in *verstehen*, in understanding oneself and others, is at least as old as Vico, and finds important expression in the work of the sociologist Max Weber. It is this older story that I have in mind.

The Aesthetic Claim

Suppose that we have shown that literature can nontrivially teach us about the world. This does not yet establish cognitivism, because cognitivists also hold that the fact that an artwork teaches us something is under certain conditions an aspect of its artistic value. Yet even when we learn from literary works, this may have nothing to do with their literary value: the *Iliad* and *Odyssey* are amongst our prime sources for the ways of life and values of the rulers of archaic Greece, but the epics' (presumably accurate) portrayal of these things does not make them better as works of literature, even though it makes them important historical evidence. The cognitivist must establish the relevance of cognitive values, when present, to the artistic value of a work.

As we have just seen, cognitivists should not hold that every cognitive merit in an artwork is aesthetically relevant; but if they simply leave it like that, as an unsupported claim, the noncognitivist can embrace relevance skepticism, and hold that here we have a merely adventitious coincidence of values: in some cases cognitive values are possessed by works which also have artistic value, but it isn't ever the case that these works have artistic value *because* of their cognitive value.

One might reply that the pleasure we take from works is partly to be explained by our enjoyment of the exercise of our imaginative powers in their cognitive employment. And that seems right: but the skeptic will respond that this doesn't show that the pleasure is aesthetic: we can enjoy learning about ancient Greece from reading Homer, but that does not yet show that we are taking aesthetic pleasure in his works. The cognitivist might instead reply by looking for a general criterion such that, if some set of descriptive conditions $C_1 \ldots C_n$ hold, then the cognitive value of a literary work is an artistic value of it. But, given the sheer complexity and variety of artworks and their appreciation, finding a completely general and precise reductive criterion for this looks like an implausible endeavor.

Fortunately, there is an easier way to show that cognitive values really do sometimes confer artistic value on a work, rather than just being adventitious coincidents of such value. Recall the opening sally in the debate between cognitivism and noncognitivism. We noted there that much of the vocabulary of literary appraisal and its application appears to show that the practice of literary evaluation is cognitivist: we praise works for their profundity, for opening our eyes to something, for giving a radically different perspective on the world, and decry them for being shallow and full of worn clichés. And the cognitive component of literary evaluations extends in less obvious ways. When we talk of a work as being sentimental, we are also making a cognitive claim, for sentimental emotions are ones which involve false or idealizing thoughts about their objects (Savile 1982: 237–45). In fact, emotion-terms in general have a cognitive component: we talk about the emotions which works ask us to feel as being appropriate, just, or true: that is, the evaluative thoughts which partly constitute the emotions are correctly applied to the objects of the emotions (Roberts 1988). For example, the anger a work asks us to feel about the murder of a character is appropriate because anger involves the thought of something wrong having been done, and this is indeed (fictionally) so. In asking us to feel that anger, the work may implicitly claim that things of that kind are wrong; so the work is through its particular prescriptions making a more general claim. And many traditions of literary criticism, particularly strands of political criticism, are explicit in their negative evaluations of works because they misrepresent kinds of people, whether they be workers, women, or racial minorities (Rowe 1997, Carroll 2002).

Our usage of cognitivist evaluative terms shows not only that we hold works to have these epistemic virtues, but also that these cognitive merits are relevant to their artistic merit. Consider someone who said "This novel is a profound and insightful exploration of death without a trace of sentimentality, but this of course has nothing to do with its artistic merit." That is as bizarre as someone who said "This novel is well-written, elegant, and witty, but this of course has nothing to do with its artistic merit." Clearly, our usage shows that cognitive merits of works are, in the evaluations mentioned, artistic merits too. It is partly *because* a work is profound that it is a good work of literature.

The noncognitivist may try to sever the link by denying that these apparent cognitive merits are really cognitive at all: but we argued above that concepts, such as profundity, really are used in literary evaluations in a *bona fide* cognitive way, since their epistemic claims can be vindicated by appealing to the cognitive role of imagination. So the reply to the relevance skeptic is simple: our application of key terms of literary appraisal shows that cognitive and artistic merits do not simply happen to coincide in a work, but rather when those cognitive merits are of certain kinds, and are conveyed by works in a certain way, as captured in our literary appraisals (of being profound, opening up new perspectives, etc.), then these cognitive merits constitute artistic merits. Our evaluative practices embody cognitivist commitments and those practices do not succumb to epistemic objections advanced against them, so those practices should stand. And that means that cognitivism about at least representational art is correct.

While eschewing a precise reductive account of relevance-conditions for cognitive merits, we can briefly note some conditions which *tend* to favor their relevance. It is the *way* that a work conveys its cognitive merits – the mode by which it conveys its insights – that makes them of aesthetic relevance. General statements explicitly made in the work, even if true, original, and germane to the work's themes, do not usually

Berys Gaut

enhance artistic merit if disconnected from the work's details. Cognitive merits tend to be aesthetically relevant when they are displayed in the particular descriptions of characters, the narrative details, and the feelings prescribed by works. The claims are general, but they are made implicitly in the description of particulars. In creating a character, a novelist creates in effect a new concept, which bundles together a set of characteristics; and we can learn to see a real person in terms of that character, as, say, an Anna Karenina or a Madame Bovary. If the novelist has some genuine insight into human personality – if he or she discovers, in Kundera's words, "a basic human possibility" – then we can come to learn more about a real person by application of the concept. And it is by displaying that insight through the description of particularities that it tends to gain aesthetic relevance. The mechanism of seeing-as here, as elsewhere in aesthetics, is crucial: it allows us to apply the imaginative world of the fiction to the real world, and thereby to discover truths about the world. In this, the application of fictional characters and situations to the real world is akin to the use of metaphor: when I say "man is a wolf" I invite you to see men as wolves, and to use this bit of imagining to seek out similarities between the two creatures that should lead to an open-ended cognitive exploration. Thus not only is the fictional world a product of imagination, its application to the external world also involves imagination. In both ways we learn from imagination.

The aesthetic role of cognitive values has encountered various objections, of which I will consider two. The first is due to William Gass, who holds that great works differ considerably in their cognitive claims, including moral claims, and may even contradict each other. This being so, it cannot matter to their aesthetic value whether the works' claims are correct or not: "Balzac sees the world quite differently than Butor does; Goethe and Milton cannot both be right; so if being right mattered, we should be in a mess indeed, and most of our classics headed for the midden" (Gass 1987: 43). We can add that great works disagree not just amongst themselves, but also with many of our current views of the world – not many lovers of Milton's verse would sign up to his full-fledged theodicy.

In reply, the cognitivist should first embrace pluralism, holding that there are several values besides cognitive ones; so a work might have a cognitive defect, but still overall be judged a great work because of its other aesthetic merits, such as its beauty, expressive power, accomplished style, and so on. Second, a work can have many cognitive merits, while being wrong about many things. A work may introduce interesting new concepts and exhibit important imaginative skills, while being wrong in its claims – for advancing true propositions is only one aspect of cognition. (Indeed, this is why, on purely cognitive grounds, one can think that both Hume's and Kant's philosophical works are great achievements, even though they cannot both be right, since they contradict each other in their central claims.) And a work can be wrong about what its author would have thought of as its most important claims, but its other claims be insightful and to seem to us, who do not share the author's basic views, to be more important. Even if we reject Milton's theology, we can still celebrate *Paradise Lost* for its acuity about the psychological dynamics of pride and its insights into how a kind of heroic courage can subsist with evil. Third, if an author presents a view as true of the actual world, he or she must logically implicitly hold that the view is true of a possible world (since the actual world is a possible world).

And this allows authors to be correct about features of this possible world, while being wrong about the actual world: they can be right in thinking what would happen, if such and such were the case, but nevertheless be wrong in thinking that such-and-such is in fact the case (they can, of course, also be wrong about the conditional claim, as was the author of the mangled Lear). Given Milton's theological premises, his views about what would happen in such a world, and the way that people ought to behave in it, have considerable conviction. So one can hold that the poet is right in what he says of this possible world, and so his work has this cognitive merit, but that he was wrong in holding that this is true of the actual world, so his work has in that respect a cognitive defect. This leads to the surprising, but I think correct, conclusion that Milton's work would have been artistically even better than it is in one respect, had his religious views been correct. And it also follows that religious believers and atheists may legitimately differ in their assessment of the artistic value of religious works; for the believer may hold that there are in such works deep spiritual insights, subtly and skillfully conveyed, whereas the atheist may see them merely as the expression (however subtly and skillfully done) of a tired, discredited, and irrelevant view. It is simply a formalist dogma to insist that, despite their differing views of the world, two people must in principle always be able to agree on the exact artistic value of a work that expresses the views on which they differ.

A second important objection is due to Peter Lamarque (1997, Lamarque and Olsen 1994). Lamarque holds that literature (as well as fiction) can offer distinctive opportunities to learn, and so he supports a version of the epistemic claim. But nevertheless he holds that these opportunities are not *essential* to the practices of literature (or fiction), for it is not true that the constitutive end of these practices is truth (a constitutive end of a practice is an end that at least partly defines the practice). Here one should contrast literature with a genuinely cognitive practice, such as philosophy, where the constitutive aim of philosophical writing is truth and works are evaluated in terms of the achievement of this aim. Literary values, in contrast, concern the exploration and development of themes as they are manifest in the details of a work (Lamarque 1997: 16–17). Though we may learn from fiction and literature, we should not confuse "the contingent by-products" of these practices with "the very nature of the practices themselves" (Lamarque 1997: 21).

Let us agree that it is not a constitutive end of the practice of literature that it aims at truth; this supports the claim that it is not *essential* to literature that truth is a literary value. So the argument would undermine what we might call cognitivist *essentialism* – that it is essential to any literary practice that it takes truth as a value. But this doctrine is stronger than the cognitivism defended here (or indeed by the general run of cognitivists), which does not make an essentialist claim. Values can be *genuine* literary values without being *essential* literary values. (A property is an essential literary value just in case it is a necessary condition for any practice of writing to count as literary that it acknowledge that property as a value.) Complexity and expressive properties are uncontentiously literary values when possessed by literary works, but one can imagine literary practices that did not acknowledge them as values – such practices might aim for the purest simplicity or abjure all expressive properties, aspiring to be the literary equivalent of some kinds of conceptual art. One can even imagine practices of literature in which the exploration and development of themes-as-manifested-in-details would not be counted as a literary value. Such practices might consist entirely in the writing of pithy epigrams (themes without their development through details) or in the subtle and evocative description of experiences (details without the themes). So given his implicit move from what is an essential literary value to what is a genuine one, Lamarque would have to reject his own candidate for literary value on the same grounds that he rejects truth as a literary value. Values can be genuinely literary or artistic without being essential to the practices concerned; and this is just as well, since one should have serious doubts as to whether there is an essence in the ordinary sense of the term or constitutive end of art in general (Gaut 2000).

Lamarque also makes a stronger claim than the anticonstitutive point; for he maintains that learning is neither an "integral [i.e., essential] *or even important* feature" of our response to literature (Lamarque 1997: 18; my italics). The critic J. Hillis Miller praises Dickens's novel *Our Mutual Friend* because "The novel is a brilliant revelation of the results of this false worship of money" (Miller 1964: 903). Lamarque objects that this is not a reason to value the novel artistically, for such a theme is "thin and banal," endlessly treated in literature (compare Stolnitz 1992). So the truth of the proposition expressing this theme does not contribute to the literary value of the novel; what matters is how the theme organizes and makes sense of the particularities of the novel (Lamarque 1997: 17–18).

Yet this is a false dichotomy. The cognitivist should admit that the theme as stated is thin and banal; but as we saw, the object of our aesthetic interest lies in a cognitive claim as expressed in the particularities of the work – through the details of characterization and narrative, and implied in the feelings prescribed by the work. That is very similar to Lamarque's view that the object of our literary interest is the theme as manifested in the details. So the value of detail and its relation to theme is not under dispute between the cognitivist and the noncognitivist. What is in contention is whether the *truth* (amongst other cognitive features) of the propositions expressing the theme matters aesthetically or not. If the noncognitivist is right, the theme's truth matters aesthetically not at all. But if that were so, one could imagine an equally successful novel as *Our Mutual Friend*, which had as its theme the contrary of that novel's theme. This novel – call it *Our Common Enemy* – has as its theme that the worship of money is the greatest of human goods, and other values such as love, companionship, and human achievement are mere glittering illusions, baubles to be cast aside for the enduring value of wealth. The hero of this novel is a miser, and the novel shows us how by giving up all of the chimerical opportunities for friendship, love, achievement, and understanding in his life, he discovers that the only deep, true value is amassing huge wealth. In its closing scene, *Our Common Enemy* celebrates the miser lovingly fingering his gold, having achieved true satisfaction, while all the other characters in the novel, who pursued other values, are revealed as shallow, trivial creatures, blind to what really matters in life. Clearly, this novel is not going to be an artistic success, for as we try to develop the theme through the details of characterization, narrative, and how the reader is invited to respond to events, we end up with absurdities. How could one write that last scene so as not to make it simply ludicrous? (Of course one could write a novel like this as a spoof or parody, but that is a case where the theme is handled tongue-in-cheek, not seriously meant.) It is precisely *in* developing a theme through the details of a work, then, that its truth becomes of artistic relevance, in part because it allows a depth and correctness of characterization that the false theme resists. (See Rowe 1997 for a similar objection directed at Lamarque and Olsen's treatment of a theme in *Middlemarch*, and see also Currie 1995b).

Though his noncognitivism should be rejected, Lamarque's discussion brings out an important point. Truth and cognitive values in general are of more central importance to practices such as philosophy (or indeed to science, history, psychology, and so on) than they are to art; for the ultimate aim of these disciplines is explanatory truth. But to acknowledge that the same is not true of art is quite consistent with holding that truth, and cognitive values more generally, feature among the many aesthetic values that are possessed by artworks.

Conclusion

I have argued that our practices of literary evaluation are cognitivist, in holding both that artworks can nontrivially teach us and that this is under certain conditions an artistic merit in them. My defense of these practices has shown that crucial to the cognitive value of art is the way we can learn from imagination, and that these cognitive values tend to be artistically relevant when they are embodied not in explicit universal statements, but in particular descriptions of the characters and events in terms of which we can fruitfully see real people and events. Aristotle was right when he wrote that poetry is more philosophical than history because it deals with universals (Aristotle 1984: 1451b 5–7). But he should have added that it tends to work better as poetry when those universals are implicit in the rich, detailed descriptions of particulars.

Cognitive Values in the Arts: Marking the Boundaries

Peter Lamarque

The position I will defend is this: that to value a work of art as *a work of art* is not to value it for its truth or the knowledge it imparts or its capacity to teach. In short, truth is not an artistic value.

To clarify the position, let me state some theses I am *not* defending and which are not entailed by the above. First, I am not defending any kind of aestheticism or formalism or doctrine of "art for art's sake." I do not believe that art is in any sense "cut off from the world" – a view virtually unintelligible – or that the content of representational works is of no concern or not subject to judgments of artistic value. Second, I do not believe that artistic values are restricted to narrowly "aesthetic" values, in the sense of being grounded only in aesthetic properties such as beauty, unity, coherence, gracefulness, or elegance. Third, I do not hold that art is in any sense nonserious or mere play or entertainment or diversion. I believe there is a central place for art, including literature, in education: indeed, education without involvement of the arts is impoverished. Fourth, I do not deny that truth crops up quite legitimately in critical discourse about the arts. It might be important for critics to notice what truths are presupposed in, or what beliefs underlie, a work, and many literary works will contain propositions at least amenable to truth assessment. Also, of course, critical discourse itself aims at truth. Fifth, I do not deny that works of art can convey truths, impart knowledge, and be vehicles for learning. What is being denied is only that these are part of a work's value as art. Finally, I am not even denying that works of art can be valued for their truth or conveying of knowledge; only that when they are valued in those terms it is not their artistic value that is under consideration. All of these points will be further elaborated as we proceed.

Cognitivism Across the Arts

The cognitivist thesis that artistic value does partially reside in truth or knowledge or learning does not seem to be universally applicable across the arts. It is not easy to make the case – in fact few have tried to make the case – that the value of a Schubert string quartet, a Brancusi sculpture, a Zen rock garden, a Frank Lloyd Wright house, a Merce Cunningham dance, or a Bridget Riley painting, lies even partially in what truths these works can teach. Cognitive concepts like learning, truth, or knowledge seem out of place in the critical vocabulary applied to such works (indeed to music in general, as well as sculpture, gardens, architecture, nonnarrative dance, and abstract painting). The modes of appreciation they invite are of a quite different dimension. This observation is important as it reminds us right at the outset that there is nothing about art per se that demands appreciation in terms of truth and learning. The battleground over artistic cognitivism does not focus on the arts just mentioned but on a more restricted class of artworks, broadly those that have a representational or narrative element. In particular, of course, this means the literary arts but might also include film and some painting. It is on this ground – the most promising for cognitivism – that I will primarily engage the debate.

It might be thought a bit hasty, though, to set aside so many of the major art forms so early on. Not all cognitivists will accept such a concession. Gordon Graham, for example, does not. He offers a subtle defense of cognitivism in the arts right across the board (Graham 1997). While Graham does not hold that cognitive values are essential to art (not all works of art need exhibit such values to count as art) he does argue that all of the major forms of art do have the potential for cognitive assessment. Crucially, however, Graham does not defend cognitivism in terms of "truth" but in terms of "understanding" (Graham 1997: 45). His thesis is that "art is most valuable when it serves as a source of understanding" (Graham 1997: 62) and he goes on to apply the thesis to different art forms. Thus the cognitive value of music, Graham argues, lies in the fact that through music "we explore the dimensions of aural experience," and "by enlarging and exploring that aspect of experience, music assists us in understanding better what it is to be a human being" (Graham 1997: 85). On the visual arts, he writes: "by providing us with visual images of emotion and character, painting and sculpture may heighten our awareness ... of those states in ourselves and in others ... [and] ... broaden the horizons of our understanding by imagining possibilities and giving form to things whose substance is in doubt" (Graham 1997: 98). Even architecture can have cognitive value: "it is plausible to interpret some of the very finest buildings as being vehicles for the exploration and elaboration of certain human ideals, religious devotion being an obvious example" (Graham 1997: 147).

Is cognitivism, then, more deeply entrenched across the arts than might first appear? Possibly. But what really emerges from Graham's treatment is how slippery a topic artistic cognitivism is. Clearly Graham's detailed defense deserves careful consideration (for further comments, see Lamarque 1999), but the fact that he does not defend artistic value in terms of truth, that he emphasizes the difference between art and other cognitive enterprises like science, history, and philosophy (Graham 1997: ch.3), and that he often qualifies the understanding art can yield with metaphors like "enriched," "heightened," or "enhanced," suggests that the purported cognitive benefits of art are not as straightforward as might be hoped. In fact there is much in Graham's picture of the arts that strikes me as entirely right and important, yet also entirely consistent with the view I am defending. Who would deny that art is often

Peter Lamarque

involved with "exploring aspects of experience," "providing visual images," "broadening horizons," "imagining possibilities," "exploring and elaborating human ideals"? If this is cognitivism, then I too am a cognitivist. But I don't think this has anything essentially to do with truth or knowledge or learning. In fact Graham's cognitivism might seem half-hearted even to the anticognitivist on his treatment of music. That music's highest achievement is to offer a better understanding of aural experience (i.e., hearing) seems a paltry reward. Does music not explore human emotion and stir human feeling? Graham does not deny this, of course, but he does not think it is the source of music's deepest (i.e., cognitive) value.

The slipperiness of cognitivism comes out in other ways as well. We have seen the reluctance, as evidenced in Graham but also in Gaut (ch. 7, this volume), to rest the case on the relevance of truth in art. It might be thought that any defense of the view that art can teach or impart knowledge must appeal to truths learnt or imparted. But for Graham understanding can be "enriched" without truths being acquired, and Gaut readily accepts that cognitive values might not be restricted to propositional knowledge. Art might teach by imparting skills, intellectual and practical, or by showing what it is like to be such-and-such or to have experiences of a certain kind, or by showing what is possible or what significance or value something has (Gaut 2003: 437–8). My own focus is on truth and knowledge but the arguments I will advance against the artistic value of imparting knowledge will encompass these more diffuse achievements as well, again not by denying their occurrence or even their intrinsic value but only their contribution to *artistic* value, properly so-called.

The shift away from propositional knowledge marks a difficulty cognitivists have with truth per se. The truth of art is an elusive creature and, in the hands of the artistic truth-theorist, can come to look like something less than the notion familiar to philosophers, scientists, and historians. I. A. Richards, for example, held that the "scientific sense" of "truth" is "little involved by any of the arts" and that within criticism "truth" most often means "acceptability" and "sincerity" (Richards 1926: 212–13). Colin Falck describes artistic truth as "ontological truth" (Falck 1989: 74) without saying exactly what that is. Other conceptions include "truth to" (Hospers 1946), or "a kind of transcendence" (Murdoch 1992: 86), or "poetic truth . . . unverifiable . . . but operative" (Day Lewis 1947: ch.1), or "authenticity" (Walsh 1969), or the "concrete universal" (Wimsatt 1954), or "depth meaning" (Weitz 1943, 1955). This motley of conceptions shows the uneasiness of artistic cognitivists with ordinary notions of truth. But if artistic truth is just truthfulness or sincerity or a kind of symbolic meaning then the discussion shifts. Truthfulness and integrity might well be artistic values, in which case the controversy withers away.

Truth, though, is the high ground for cognitivists and they tread a difficult line between, on the one hand, wanting to keep a conception of truth sufficiently like that employed by philosophers or scientists to give weight to the idea of cognitive value and, on the other, seeking to secure something special about the truth achievement of the arts. The question artistic cognitivists dread most is what (nontrivial) truths they have learnt from works of art. In propositional terms the best they can come up with are usually generalities about human nature of a numbingly banal kind (Stolnitz 1992, Lamarque 1997). That is why cognitivists quickly revert to nonpropositional knowledge – knowing how, knowing what it is like, and so forth – or to more exotic kinds of truth, like those listed, to bolster the cognitive claim and to establish the peculiarity of art's contribution.

It is also common to appeal to critical vocabulary – "profound," "shallow," "sentimental" – to show the implicit reference to truth in literary criticism (Miller 1979, Gaut, this volume). But while it is indisputable, as Gaut shows, that these are value terms it is far from clear, in the literary critical context, that they bear directly on truth. It is usually a work's treatment of a theme which is judged profound or sentimental and that is a mark of originality, lack of cliché, attention to detail, and so forth, rather than truth. Milton's treatment of the Fall is profound just as is Descartes's appeal to God to refute skepticism but neither need be accepted as true. Much that is true, or that actually happened, can be deemed sentimental so sentimentality cannot literally (i.e., in a nonexotic sense) contrast with truth.

Representation and Truth

As stated earlier, the case for artistic cognitivism is at its strongest in relation to the representational arts. The reason is obvious: these arts purport to be about something or stand for something in a way that nonrepresentational arts, from architecture to music, do not. Paradigmatic of the representational arts is the painted portrait or landscape. We might expect the cognitivist to argue as follows: that the artistic value of a portrait or landscape rests, even if only in part, on its accuracy of representation, thus, in an only slightly extended sense, on its truth (as correspondence to fact). We can learn about people or landscapes – what they look like – from an accurate painting and that is partly why we value the painting. All the required cognitivist elements are here: truth, learning, value. But of course things are not as simple as that. Certainly there has been a tradition in painting where mimesis or the "imitation of nature" has been highly valued, but writers like E. H. Gombrich (1962) and Nelson Goodman ([1968] 1976) have shown not only how problematic is the very concept of "resemblance" but also that it is neither essential to representation nor inseparable from artistic value. What counts as a "good" representation relies as much on artistic convention and the aims of the artist as on simple matching. A caricature sketch with highly exaggerated features might give a far more accurate impression of a subject than a laboriously faithful but uninspired portrait.

R. G. Collingwood makes a penetrating observation about portraiture, which, to say the least, complicates matters for the simple cognitivist position. Speaking about portraits by Raphael, Titian, Velasquez, and Rembrandt, he writes: "The sitters are dead and gone, and we cannot check the likeness for ourselves. If, therefore, the only kind of merit a portrait could have were its likeness to the sitter, we could not possibly distinguish, except where the sitter is still alive and unchanged, between a good portrait and a bad" (Collingwood 1938: 44, quoted in Graham 1997: 55). The implication is that we can know whether a portrait is good or bad without matching it to the sitter so a faithful match is not what gives a portrait its artistic value. The cognitivist might of course respond by challenging Collingwood's assumption that the "only" merit in a portrait is its likeness. Could this not be just part of what is valued? That seems right, but what the cognitivist must show is that the artistic value rests

Peter Lamarque

on the likeness. There are other values than artistic ones: for example, value as a public record. It would seem bizarre to conclude that we can be less certain of our artistic judgments of Titian's portraits of Pope Paul III than of his mythological scenes, like *Diana and Actaeon*, because the artistic value of the former but not that of the latter rests (partially) on a likeness to an actual person, something in this case we are not able to confirm for ourselves. What makes portraits works of art that endure long after their subjects are no longer known has little to do with fidelity to fact but rests on other features: skills of composition, handling of subject matter, use of materials to maximum effect, the "exploration of visual experience," as Graham puts it (Graham 1997: 96), but perhaps above all something that transcends the immediate occasion and touches on the universally or timelessly human, be it character, aspiration, or state of mind.

It is here surely that we find a more promising line for the cognitivist about portraiture. It hints at an all-important distinction in the representational arts – one I will pursue in the case of literature – between subject and theme. A portrait might well teach us what a subject looked like at the time of the portrait and that is a kind of learning but it is not yet an artistic value. Holiday snaps tell us what someone looked like but few have value as art. The artistic achievement is to move beyond subject to something more universal, to reveal, as one might say, the universal in the particular. The great artistic portraits explore themes of love or despair or hope or longing or old age or power. Rembrandt's self-portraits are not just studies of an individual at a time but explorations of mood and character. Landscape paintings engage our artistic interest not just for the faithful rendering of place – many landscapes (Poussin, Tassi, Claude Lorraine) are idealized – but because they convey an atmosphere or a conception of nature and natural beauty. For the artistic cognitivist it might seem that the thematic level offers the best possibilities of truth or learning. By being invited to reflect on something universal or timeless we increase our knowledge. This, though, is where I depart from the cognitivists. The move from the subject level to the thematic level is crucial to an understanding of great art – on that I do agree – but it does not need to be linked to the acquisition of truths or knowledge. So let us examine the matter by turning to the area where it is most pressing and also most controversial: literature.

Literature and Cognition

There is a huge weight of tradition supporting the cognitive benefits of literature (or "poetry" in an earlier designation). (For a general outline of this tradition, see Lamarque and Olsen 1998, 2004.) The main staging posts are all too familiar: Aristotle's assertion that "poetry is something more philosophic and of graver import than history" (Aristotle 1984: 1451b 5–7); Horace's distinction, in *Ars poetica*, between the *utile* and the *dulce* in poetry; Dr Johnson's observation that "The end of writing is to instruct, the end of poetry is to instruct by pleasing" (Johnson, 1969, ll. 280–2); interspersed with "defenses of poetry" from Sidney to Shelley and contributions from realist novelists such as Emile Zola – "the novelist is equally an observer and an experimentalist" (Zola [1880] 1893: 8) – to Marxists like Georg Lukács – "The goal for all great art is to provide a picture of reality" (Lukács 1970: 34). It would be fool-hardy to challenge such a weight of authority and only a wit or an aesthete would agree with Oscar Wilde that "All art is quite useless" (Preface, *The Picture of Dorian Gray*). But on closer inspection the cognitivist tradition is not of one mind. Those who hold that poetry is useful or instructive do so on different grounds employing different terminology.

My own position is far from a dogged resistance to the entire tradition. Indeed I believe it is possible to harness many of the intuitions of the cognitivists, including those of Aristotle, without invoking the terminology of truth and knowledge (Lamarque 1996: ch.1). Bear in mind that the reason why defenses of poetry have been needed through the ages is that poetry (especially fiction) has so often been under attack (from Platonists or Puritans), either for its triviality or for its dangers in promoting immorality or illusion. In a culture where knowledge and learning are highly prized, defenders of poetry have felt the need to emphasize the value of their art in these terms. The cognitivist's case, more often than not, has been a plea for poetry to be taken seriously, as an engagement of the mind, not just a plaything of the passions. In my view, the seriousness of poetry can be defended without tying it to the coattails of philosophy or the sciences. Literary value does not need the extra ballast of the pursuit of truth.

Let us take it one step at a time. First, the distinction between fiction and literature. The debate about literary cognitivism usually focuses on fictional or "imaginative" literature, that is, literature at least partly based on imaginary or made-up characters and incidents. Not all literary works are fictional in this sense and "literature" can encompass works of philosophy and history (see Lamarque 2001). No one disputes the cognitive aims and achievements of the latter so it might seem that they deliver an easy victory for the cognitivist. But things are not quite so straightforward. To read Hume's *Dialogues on Natural Religion* "as philosophy" is indeed to give concern to truth and argument. But to read it "as literature" or "from a literary point of view" is not so obviously to highlight the truth of its central claims. Could not the bishop as well as the atheist admire its literary qualities? Arguably the literary value of such a work is not vested in its philosophical soundness but in its structure and tone, its use of dialogue as rhetorical device, its wit, its irony, or the consonance of ends and means. A similar consideration would apply to those literary works, like some lyric poetry, which are not obviously fictional but do not fall into any other extraliterary genre, such as philosophy or history. They might well express some real response of a real person (e.g., the poet). The question now is whether the literary value of such poetry resides in the literal truth of what is expressed. Again, arguably, it does not. A literary interest, as against a biographical one, has its focus elsewhere. The literary value of Shakespeare's sonnets does not hang on the identity of the "dark lady" or the autobiographical accuracy of the poems' sentiments. From a literary point of view the sonnets are recognized as highly conventionalized.

Our principal concern, though, is with the values of literary fiction. It might be thought that the cognitivist's problem is that of finding connections between imaginary content and the real world. In fact this is not a serious problem. Fiction has all kinds of connections with fact. Works of fiction can make reference to people and objects in the real world; they often have a real world setting (place and historical

Peter Lamarque

period); in realist genres they are constrained by principles of verisimilitude, portraying characters as having habits, modes of speech, appearance, motivation, desires, and human competences familiar in actual people; works of fiction can offer generalizations about human nature; fiction requires knowledge of the real world to be understood and appreciated. All this makes learning from fiction itself unproblematic. No one could dispute that readers can learn about the real world from works of fiction: they pick up facts about history, geography, points of etiquette, clothing and fashions, idiomatic usage, as well as how to perform practical tasks, how people behave in certain situations, what it is like to be in an earthquake, a storm at sea, or a blazing house. Fiction is often a vehicle for teaching even outside the normal literary context. Parables, moral tales told to children, philosophers' thought-experiments, sermons, and police profiles, all employ fiction (i.e., imaginary examples) to convey ideas or lessons. The question is not whether we can learn from fiction – indeed it can be shown that fiction is an especially apt vehicle for certain kinds of learning (Lamarque 1997, John 1998, Carroll 2002) – but what value to attach to this learning.

For the cognitivist learning is a literary value. My own view is that learning is a value, but not a literary one. Clearly at the heart of the issue is a conception of literature. Literature – even limited to the sense of imaginative literature – is not easy to define, not least because it takes many forms and the term is often loosely applied. It seems unlikely, though, that any adequate definition will rest on formal or linguistic properties alone (Lamarque 2001). More promising is to try to identify and characterize an "institution" or "practice" associated with literature, which underpins the activities of writers, critics, and all who read and appreciate literary works (Olsen 1978, Lamarque and Olsen 1994: ch.10). On this view it is not intrinsic properties of texts that determine their literariness but the "stance" they invite, conventionally adopted by those engaged in the practice. What needs further attention is a notion already introduced, of reading "from a literary point of view" (Lamarque 1996: ch.12). A literary work might be defined as a work that invites, or is especially amenable to, literary appreciation or interest from a literary point of view. Of course as it stands the definition is circular and largely uninformative but it puts the emphasis in the right place.

Literary Appreciation and the Bounds of Critical Practice

So what is literary appreciation (see Olsen 1987b, Lamarque 2002)? It is partly an expectation of value, an expectation that a work will reward a certain kind of interest. First of all, this is an interest that foregrounds the design or structure of the work, how its parts cohere into a satisfying aesthetic whole. Even a work that deliberately eschews overt unity or "closure" can invite literary interest in the interrelation of its parts. Second, it is an interest that goes beyond the immediate subject matter of the work – narrative, plot, character, poetic image – and seeks a broader thematic characterization that both unites discrete elements of the subject matter and offers a filter through which to reflect on it. Here again is the distinction between subject and theme, common to so many, if not all, of the arts. We will need to return to it as the argument over cognitivism largely hinges on the status of thematic content. A third feature of literary interest relates to the second: susceptibility to a certain kind of interpretation. Literary works are those to which interpretation – involving the relating of theme to subject – is particularly rewarding. The great works of literature seem to invite different perspectives on their content, different ways in which the subject matter can be conceived. This is partly why readers return to them. Literary interpretation is the seeking out of thematic perspectives, finding different unifying visions which give interest to the whole. Finally, then, the value of a work, as a literary work, arises from these three features. Literary value resides in works that, through the coherence of their formal properties, subject matter, and thematic vision, reward literary appreciation.

This bare outline does scant justice to the complexities of literary appreciation but it already marks a distinct difference from modes of attention characteristic of other reading practices, notably that associated with philosophy. If literary reading is reading for significance, philosophical reading is reading for truth. The practice of writing, studying, and valuing philosophy is essentially connected with cognition (Lamarque 1997: 10). To attend to a philosophical work, as such, is to attend to its reasoning, its persuasiveness, its arguments, and its goal of truth. A work of philosophy is judged, qua philosophy, by its ability to cast light on an issue of interest and to do so with rational support. That the practice of philosophy is cognitivist through and through is evidenced by the central role of debate as an appropriate response to philosophy. A work of philosophy is valued for prompting other philosophers to pursue its ideas, test its logical consequences, seek out counterexamples or intellectual difficulties, and restate or develop the ideas in other terms. It's not just that we look for rational argument in the presentation of philosophy but we expect it also in the response to philosophy.

The differences with literary attention couldn't be more striking. It is often thought to be a flaw in a work of imaginative literature that it pursues intellectual ideas in too explicit or philosophical a manner. Certainly readers do not expect novels to argue for points of view (even though individual characters might do so – a fact that can help understand the characters better). But crucially it is not part of literary appreciation to pursue debates about the extraliterary truth of literary themes (Olsen 1978: ch 3). While no competent discussion of a philosophical work will fail to engage a debate about whether the views it advances are true, we find that literary criticism, of the highest order, by the most authoritative critics, only on the rarest occasions and then only superficially debates truth in a comparable fashion. What better opportunity, one might think, to debate the truth of profound moral issues than in a critical reading of Dostoevsky's *Crime and Punishment*. Yet when one looks at the critical tradition about this novel – as against its appropriation by moral philosophers – one finds a different kind of attention. Consider this snippet of critical discussion:

> Raskolnikov never repented of his crime because he did not hold himself responsible for the murder. He had fancied that he could plan and carry out the deed, but when the time came to act, it were as if he were impelled by forces over which he had no control, by "some decree of blind fate." Man must suffer, he decides, because man, his intellect a delusion and its power demonic, trapped by his instinctive brutality and the conspiracy

of his victims, does not will his destiny. "Not on earth, but up yonder," Marmeladov has cried out, "they grieve over men, they weep, but they don't blame them, they don't blame them! But it hurts more when they don't blame!" (I:2). The aloneness of man is offended by the gods' refusal to blame what they cannot blame, but once suffering, man's bondage, is accepted, man feels a part of something beyond aloneness, feels no longer that he can be a god but that he is a part of the God that is "everything." The revelation that comes to Raskolnikov through love and humility "in prison, in freedom," is inevitable because it is the obverse side, the pro, of the will-to-suffering, the contra, that has been throughout the entire novel his primary motivation. (Beebe 1975: 596)

The critic's concerns are to make sense of the motivation of the central character and thus identify important themes in the novel. He is not concerned to connect the themes he identifies to a debate in moral philosophy about free will. Nor does he debate the truth of thematic propositions like "The aloneness of man is offended by the gods' refusal to blame what they cannot blame, ..." To do so would be to switch practices, to move from literary criticism to philosophy (or theology).

The claim that literary criticism is not a practice in which philosophical or moral issues are debated for their own sake might appear to be, if true, simply a matter of fact, testable by observation. Indeed a survey of critical practice would undoubtedly bear it out as an empirical generalization. But the claim is more than that. It is also a normative claim, bearing on the very nature of critical practice. Not any mode of attention to a text counts as literary attention, and literary critical discourse is necessarily circumscribed within the more or less flexible limits earlier characterized. Is this a kind of essentialism about literature (Gaut, this volume)? Yes, in the sense that it draws boundaries round practices, but no, if what is meant is that literary works can be defined by a special kind of "literary" property.

M. W. Rowe seeks to refute the claim that critical discourse does not debate the truth of literary themes by pointing to counterexamples (Rowe 1997). His principal case is that of the line "Beauty is truth, truth beauty" in Keats's ode "On a Grecian Urn." Rowe supposes that a great deal of critical discussion centers on whether the line is true and he quotes Lionel Trilling:

To say, as many do, that "truth is beauty" is a false statement is to ignore our experience of tragic art. Keats' statement is an accurate description of the response to evil or ugliness which tragedy makes: the matter of tragedy is ugly or painful truth seen as beauty. To see life in this way, Keats believes, is to see life truly. (Rowe 1997: 325–6, quoting Trilling 1980: 32)

Trilling's apparent endorsement of the truth of Keats's line in the word "accurate" shows, Rowe believes, that critics are concerned not just with identifying general themes but with weighing their truth.

The example, though, is unfortunate in many respects. For one thing, Trilling is commenting not directly on Keats's ode but on some remarks by Keats on Beauty and Truth in a letter. Also, as Rowe himself points out, the main problem that critics have with the line is what exactly it means (in the context of the poem). Now it is widely agreed that one way of determining the meaning of a sentence is to ask under what conditions the sentence might be true. Trilling's remarks can be seen as offering an interpretation of Keats's line through suggesting one possible set of truth-conditions. This is an entirely legitimate part of the literary critical enterprise. If Trilling were engaged in philosophy he would then go on to debate the alleged truth independently and in much more detail than his casual endorsement of its "accuracy," the latter merely supporting the plausibility of his own interpretation. On the face of it, debating the literal truth of Keats's line seems a drearily philistine – not to say futile – response to the poem. Any sophisticated reader would notice the deep embeddedness of the line in the structure of the poem – attributed by the implied speaker to the urn itself – and the layers of irony in which it is couched (see Brooks 1968: 124–35, Olsen 1978: 132–4). Its tone and status within the ode and the way it illuminates the underlying themes are of far more interest than the focus proposed by the plodding literalist. Finally, the example offers little support for the cognitivist case. A simple knockdown argument shows why:

1 There is near universal agreement that the ode "On a Grecian Urn" is one of the finest poems in the English language.
2 There is no general agreement about the truth of the line "Beauty is truth, truth beauty," indeed little agreement even on how to interpret it; therefore:
3 The literary value of the poem cannot reside, even in part, in the literal truth of its most famous line.

Literary Themes

What is a theme in literary criticism? It is an organizing principle that seeks coherence both among diffuse elements of a work's subject and in the imaginative interest aroused by the work. Themes are characterized in different ways. Sometimes they are simply abstract concepts, such as evil or goodness or damnation, as in this passage: "in order to present a convincing image of damnation, Shakespeare had to describe and create the good which Macbeth had sacrificed; so that although there is no play in which evil is presented so forcibly, it may also be said that there is no play which puts so persuasively the contrasting good" (Muir 1962: xlix). Sometimes themes are presented through noun phrases, for example: "The first section of 'The Burial of the Dead' develops the theme of *the attractiveness of death*, or of *the difficulty in rousing oneself from the death in life* in which people of the waste land live" (Brooks 1967: 138, my italics). In neither of these cases are themes – characterized by abstract concepts or noun phrases – even candidates for truth assessment. A work can be about pride or prejudice or love or desire or the yearning for youth or the futility of war without making any statement about these conceptions.

Sometimes, however, themes are characterized in sentential or propositional form. Such formulations might appear explicitly in a literary work itself, as in Lear's anguished cry, "As flies to wanton boys, are we to th'gods; / They kill us for their sport" (*King Lear*, IV, I, 36–7), or they might arise as a reader's reflection on a work, as, for example, in this summary of the theme of Hawthorne's *The Scarlet Letter*: "Unacknowledged guilt leads to perdition, whereas expiated guilt leads to salvation" (Sirridge 1974–5: 455). Themes formulated propositionally are inevitably the focus for the cognitivist's attention (Rowe 1997). That they can be assessed for truth is beyond doubt. But it is important to distinguish their truth about the work, as part of a thematic interpretation, and their truth about the world at large. These need by no means coincide, as surely Martha Nussbaum's interpretation of Euripides's *Hecuba* illustrates well: "In this sense nothing human is ever worthy of trust: there are no guarantees at all, short of revenge or death" (Nussbaum 1986: 419). Only an extreme pessimist would endorse that as a worldly truth yet it is plausibly a theme of this most dark tragedy. In the literary context what matters pre-eminently is whether a purported theme (as concept or proposition) helps give significance and coherence to the details of a work and thereby becomes a focus for reflecting on the work as a whole. A bare thematic statement on its own is of little intrinsic interest even from a literary point of view for what matters is not the summary itself but how the theme is elicited and supported through an imaginative reconstruction (Olsen's term: 1987a: 16) of the work in detailed interpretation.

To dwell on the worldly truth of a thematic proposition can seem a remote and pedestrian preoccupation. For one thing, such very general propositions are rarely demonstrably true or false; they represent perspectives on the world which can be adopted, qualified, or rejected without much impact elsewhere. Further evidence that truth is largely a red herring in relation to themes lies in the fact that themes characterized propositionally can usually be reduced to nonpropositional form, as noun phrases, without loss of content: for example, being about "the path from unacknowledged guilt to perdition" or about "the lack of trustworthiness in humans." These now cease to be candidates for truth. Nor are themes, so characterized, unique to individual works. Many novels and plays are about unacknowledged guilt or untrustworthiness or the consequences of infidelity or the false lure of money. It is not the theme itself that gives the interest but the way the particularities of the subject give life to the theme. Themes provide a filter through which to reflect on the characters and events (in narrative) or the images and sentiments (in poetry). The cognitivist is right, as against the formalist, in supposing that a proper literary response involves reflecting on and engaging imaginatively with the content of literary works – again, through the coherence of themes and subjects – rather than merely concentrating on diction, style, structure, or figure (Kivy's notion of an "afterlife" of reflection is apt: Kivy 1997: ch.5). But the cognitivist is wrong in giving prominence to truth and knowledge as a locus of literary value in this reflective process.

The Problem of Falsehood

Even if cognitivists fail to make their case for truth as a literary value they often suppose that they can fall back on the obvious disvalue of falsehood, either at a factual level of detail or at a grander thematic level. Let us take factual mistakes first. Christopher Ricks (1996) and Rowe (1997) marshal some nice examples where authors make unintended slips. In Golding's *Lord of the Flies* Piggy is short-sighted. This means that the lenses in his glasses are concave, but concave lenses cannot be used to light fires, which is the reason why his glasses are stolen. Without his glasses he is unable to see the attack which kills him, so the glasses have double importance in the plot.

As Rowe points out, it would be unsatisfactory simply to make Piggy long-sighted, as that would not be an obvious disadvantage to him. There are many comparable mistakes in fiction. Some authors on having mistakes pointed out try to remedy them in later editions (Rowe 1997: 333–4). Do such examples show that truth and falsity are after all literary values? No, not in any significant way. The literary interest in *Lord of the Flies* is diminished not at all in this revelation. Most readers would be amused to find it out (Golding himself might be irritated) but quite able to brush it aside. It is like noticing that one's favorite teacher at school is wearing different colored socks: a nice diversion but having no impact on the quality of the lesson. What makes the novel powerful is its chilling and vivid exploration of such themes as the innocence of youth, the vulnerability of civilized values, and the underlying savagery of human nature. Facts about lenses have little to do with any of that. For Rowe, the examples show that "truth is always a virtue and falsehood always a vice" (Rowe 1997: 335). But even that's not right. It is false that there is a number 221B in Baker Street but that is irrelevant to the value of the Sherlock Holmes stories.

Perhaps, though, we should not be too dismissive of the role (and importance) of fidelity to fact in imaginative fiction. As Rowe points out this is largely related to genre (Rowe 1997: 339). In a genre – like realist fiction, the historical novel – where factual accuracy in the background setting is an established convention and thus an expectation of readers, then inaccuracies (of a certain kind) are a fault and can affect appreciation. But the fault is a literary fault only to the extent that it involves a breach of convention, much as on Aristotle's account a tragedy is flawed (it breaches convention) if the tragic hero is not of the requisite moral standing or the plot lacks unity or probability. It is not falsity as such that renders a work flawed – falsity is never a sufficient condition for a negative literary judgment – for even in the strictest realist genres there can be deliberate and effective departures from fact. But if a work invites a reader's interest in terms of well-known genre conventions and then, unintention-ally and to no literary purpose, breaches those conventions, then to that extent the work has failed, if only to a small degree.

What about falsehood at the level of thematic statement (Currie 1995a, Rowe 1997: 338, Gaut in this volume)? Could a work be of any literary value if it sustained a theme to the effect that the worship of money is the greatest human good (Gaut) or that human hopes are never thwarted (Rowe 1997)? The question is spurious on many counts. First, to start with a statement and ask what kind of work it might charac-terize and what value such a work might have distorts the whole process of literary interpretation, which always begins with a specific work and reaches a judgment of value, if at all, on a plurality of measures. Second, we have seen that the proposi-tional form (amenable to truth assessment) is only a contingent and reducible feature of thematic characterization. Third, it is common for different works to develop dia-metrically opposed thematic visions. Love destroys, love liberates; hope springs eternal, hopelessness prevails. Or take free will. A work with an existentialist theme (we create our own nature and shape our own destiny) apparently conflicts with a deterministic work (we are subject to, perhaps tragically destroyed by, forces, social or personal, over which we have no control). The position of the truth theorist is espe-cially dire in these familiar circumstances for one of "Humans have free will" and "Humans do not have free will" must be false. But which is false is perennially disputed so the truth theorist, it seems, in urging that truth matters, must hold that no final literary judgment is possible on any novels that take sides on the free will debate. That is patently absurd. Fourth, the themes explored in the great literary works (of all cultures) are drawn from a relatively small pool of concerns that are of perennial interest to reflective human beings: about love, death, hope, failure, choice, chance, duty, desire, conflict, despair, and so on (these are the universals of which Aristotle speaks). Literary works seldom add to this pool, though they can provide fresh perspectives on each item. The literary exploration – through imaginative detail, narrative and imagery – parallels the philosophical exploration but complements rather than competes with it. Thematic visions in literary works can be more or less engaging, plausible, and serious. The postulated works by Rowe and Gaut, as described, seem none of these things, but the least of their failings is literal falsehood (any more than *Hecuba* fails for this reason). And, as noted, no literary judgment is possible without a work to judge.

In the end what matters in the literary tradition is not the themes themselves – these being familiar and constantly revisited – but their relation to the particularities on display. There are other qualities than truth by which to assess a literary vision: its coherence, its complexity or simple-mindedness, the fruitfulness of its imaginative development. The ideas explored might be, using a list from Beardsley (1981: 429), "charming, monumental, powerful, pedantic, fussy, imposing, crude, dramatic, [or] magnificent." These are far more salient qualities in literary judgments than truth.

References for Chapters 7 and 8

Aristotle (1984). *Poetics*. In *The Complete Works of Aristotle, Vol. II: the Revised Oxford Translation* (pp. 2316–41), ed. J. Barnes. Princeton, NJ: Princeton University Press.

Beardsley, M. C. (1981). *Aesthetics: Problems in the Philosophy of Criticism*, 2nd edn. Indianapolis, IN: Hackett.

Beardsmore, R. (1973). "Learning from a Novel." In G. Vesey (ed.), *Philosophy and the Arts: Royal Institute Of Philosophy Lectures* (vol. VI, pp. 23–46). London: Macmillan.

Beebe, M. (1975). "The Three Motives of Rasknolnikov: a Reinterpretation of *Crime and Punishment*." In F. Dostoevsky, *Crime and Punishment* (pp. 585–96), ed. George Gibian. New York: W W Norton.

Brooks, C. (1967). *Modern Poetry and the Tradition*. Chapel Hill, NC: University of North Carolina Press.

Brooks, C. (1968). *The Well Wrought Urn*, rev. edn. London: Methuen.

Carroll, N. (2002). "The Wheel of Virtue: Art, Literature, and Moral Knowledge." *Journal of Aesthetics and Art Criticism*, 60: 3–26.

Collingwood, R. G. (1938). *The Principles of Art*. Oxford: Clarendon Press.

Currie, G. (1995a). *Image and Mind: Film, Philosophy and Cognitive Science*. Cambridge, UK: Cambridge University Press.

Currie, Gregory (1995b). "Review of *Truth, Fiction, and Literature*." *Mind*, 104: 911–13.

Currie, G. (1997). "The Moral Psychology of Fiction." In S. Davies (ed.), *Art and its Messages: Meaning, Morality and Society* (pp. 49–58). University Park: Pennsylvania State University Press.

Currie, G. (1998). "Realism of Character and the Value of Fiction." In J. Levinson (ed.), *Aesthetics and Ethics: Essays at the Intersection* (pp. 161–81). Cambridge, UK: Cambridge University Press.

Day Lewis, C. (1947). *The Poetic Image*. New York: Oxford University Press.

Diffey, T. (1997). "What Can we Learn from Art?". In S. Davies (ed.), *Art and its Messages: Meaning, Morality and Society* (pp. 26–33). University Park: Pennsylvania State University Press.

Dunn, D. (1985). *Elegies*. London: Faber and Faber.

Falck, C. (1989). *Myth, Truth and Literature*. Cambridge, UK: Cambridge University Press.

Gass, W. (1987). "Beauty Knows Nothing of Beauty: on the Distance between Morality and Art." *Harper's Magazine*, 274: 37–44.

Gaut, B. (1999). "Identification and Emotion in Narrative Film." In C. Plantinga and G. Smith (eds.), *Passionate Views: Film, Cognition, and Emotion* (pp. 200–16). Baltimore: Johns Hopkins University Press.

Gaut (2000). "Art' as a Cluster Concept." In N. Carroll (ed.), *Theories of Art Today* (pp. 25–44). Madison: University of Wisconsin Press.

Gaut, B. (2003). "Art and Knowledge". In J. Levinson (ed.), *The Oxford Handbook of Aesthetics* (pp. 436–50). New York: Oxford University Press.

Gombrich, E. H. (1962). *Art and Illusion: a Study in the Psychology of Pictorial Representation*, 2nd edn. London: Phaidon Press.

Goodman, N. ([1968] 1976). *Languages of Art: an Approach to the Theory of Symbols*, 2nd edn. Indianapolis, IN: Hackett.

Graham, G. (1995). "Learning from Art." *British Journal of Aesthetics*, 35: 26–37.

Graham, G. (1997). *Philosophy of the Arts: an Introduction to Aesthetics*. London & New York: Routledge.

Hospers, J. (1946). *Meaning and Truth in the Arts*. Chapel Hill, NC: University of North Carolina Press.

John, E. (1998). "Reading Fiction and Conceptual Knowledge: Philosophical Thought in Literary Context." *Journal of Aesthetics and Art Criticism*, 56: 331–48.

Johnson, S. (1969). *Preface to Shakespeare's Plays*. London: Scholar Press.

Kivy, P. (1997). *Philosophies of Arts: an Essay in Differences*. Cambridge, UK: Cambridge University Press.

Kundera, M. (1984). *The Unbearable Lightness of Being*, trans. M. Heim. New York: Harper & Row.

Lamarque, P. (1996). *Fictional Points of View*. Ithaca, N.: Cornell University Press.

Lamarque, P. (1997). "Learning from Literature." *Dalhousie Review*, 77: 7–21.

Lamarque, P. (1999). "Arguing about Art." *European Journal of Philosophy*, 7: 89–100.

Lamarque, P. (2001). "Literature." In B. Gaut and D. Lopes (eds.), *The Routledge Companion to Aesthetics* (pp. 449–61). London: Routledge.

Lamarque, P. (2002). "Appreciation and Literary Interpretation." In Michael Krausz (ed.), *Is There a Single Right Interpretation?* (pp. 285–306). University Park: Pennsylvania State University Press.

Lamarque, P. and Olsen, S. H. (1994). *Truth, Fiction, and Literature: a Philosophical Perspective*. Oxford: Clarendon Press.

Lamarque, P. and Olsen, S. H. (1998). "Truth." In Michael Kelly (ed.), *Encyclopedia of Aesthetics* (vol. 4, pp. 406–15). New York: Oxford University Press.

Lamarque, P. and Olsen, S. H. (2004). "The Philosophy of Literature: Pleasure Restored." In Peter Kivy (ed.), *Blackwell Guide to Aesthetics* (pp. 195–214). Oxford: Blackwell.

Lukács, G. (1970). "Art and Objective Truth." In *Writer and Critic and Other Essays*, ed. and trans. Arthur Kahn. London: Merlin Press.

Miller, R. H. (1964). "Afterword" to Charles Dickens, *Our Mutual Friend*. New York: Signet.

Miller, R. M. (1979). "Truth in Beauty." *American Philosophical Quarterly*, 16: 317–26.

Moran, R. (1994). "The Expression of Feeling in Imagination." *Philosophical Review*, 103: 75–106.

Muir, K. (1962). "Introduction" to the New Arden Shakespeare, *Macbeth*. London: Methuen.

Murdoch, I. (1992). *Metaphysics as a Guide to Morals*. Harmondsworth, UK: Penguin Books.

Novitz, D. (1987). *Knowledge, Fiction and Imagination*. Philadelphia, PA: Temple University Press.

Nussbaum, M. (1986). *The Fragility of Goodness: Luck and Ethics in Greek Tragedy and Philosophy*. Cambridge, UK: Cambridge University Press.

Nussbaum, M. (1990). *Love's Knowledge: Essays on Philosophy and Literature*. New York: Oxford University Press.

Olsen, S. H. (1978). *The Structure of Literary Understanding*. Cambridge, UK: Cambridge University Press.

Olsen, S. H. (1987a). *The End of Literary Theory*. Cambridge, UK: Cambridge University Press.

Olsen, S. H. (1987b). "Criticism and Appreciation." In *The End of Literary Theory* (pp. 121–37). Cambridge, UK: Cambridge University Press.

Putnam, H. (1978). *Meaning and the Moral Sciences*. London: Routledge & Kegan Paul.

Richards, I. A. (1926). *Principles of Literary Criticism*, 2nd edn. London: Routledge & Kegan Paul.

Ricks, C. (1996). "Literature and the Matter of Fact." In *Essays in Appreciation* (pp. 280–310). Oxford: Clarendon Press.

Roberts, R. C. (1988). "What an Emotion is: a Sketch." *Philosophical Review*, 97: 183–209.

Rowe, M. (1997). "Lamarque and Olsen on Literature and Truth." *Philosophical Quarterly*, 47: 322–41.

Savile, A. (1982). *The Test of Time: an Essay in Philosophical Aesthetics*. Oxford: Oxford University Press.

Sirridge, M. (1974–5). "Truth from Fiction?" *Philosophy and Phenomenological Research*, 35: 453–71.

Stolnitz, J. (1992). "On the Cognitive Triviality of Art." *British Journal of Aesthetics*, 32: 191–200.

Trilling, L. (1980). *The Opposing Self*. Oxford: Oxford University Press.

Walsh, D. (1969). *Literature and Knowledge*. Middletown: University of Connecticut Press.

Walton, K. (1997). "Spelunking, Simulation, and Slime: on being Moved by Fiction." In M. Hjort and S. Laver (eds.), *Emotion and the Arts* (pp. 37–49). Oxford: Oxford University Press.

Weitz, M. (1943). "Does Art Tell the Truth?" *Philosophy and Phenomenological Research*, III: 338–48.

Weitz, M. (1955). "Truth in Literature." *Revue Internationale de Philosophie*, IX: 1–14

Wimsatt, W. (1954). *The Verbal Icon*. Lexington: University of Kentucky Press.

Young, J. (1999). "The Cognitive Value of Music." *Journal of Aesthetics and Art Criticism*, 57: 41–54.

Young, J. (2001). *Art and Knowledge*. London: Routledge.

Zola, E. ([1880] 1893). "The Experimental Novel." In *The Experimental Novel and other Essays*, trans. Belle M. Sherman. New York: Cassell.

References

HOW DO PICTURES REPRESENT?

The Speaking Image: Visual Communication and the Nature of Depiction

Robert Hopkins

Some First Moves

Communication is one of the most pervasive features of human life. It lies at the center of many of our activities, from engaging with art to describing one's day. Many other activities, although not centered on communication, would be impossible without it. To do all this communicating, we use a wide range of tools. We gesticulate, impersonate, act out a train of events, and use objects at hand to stand in for those which are absent. Two forms of communication, however, dominate. The most important is language. Second by some distance, but far ahead of its nearest rival, is representation by pictures. What is this representation, and how does it differ from representation in language, or the representation our other tools allow us to achieve?

A natural first thought is that pictorial representation (or depiction, as I will sometimes call it) is specially visual. This is not the obvious claim that we get the point of pictures by looking at them. That is true of written language too. The idea is that pictures are visual as words are not. This is why pictures are often described as *showing* what they represent, rather than *saying* anything about it. However, as it stands the idea is hardly clear. To help, here are six claims about pictorial representation. As well as clarifying the idea that it is visual, they are of independent importance.

First, as the cliché has it, a picture paints a thousand words. It is possible to refer to a particular thing using a word (e.g., the name "Osama Bin Laden") without saying anything about it. Likewise, one can talk about a kind of thing using a phrase (e.g., "a small blackbird") which does not tell us anything else about things of that kind. In contrast, a picture of Bin Laden, or of a small blackbird, however schematic, must depict more than that. It must, for instance, depict a man with certain features, or a small bird of some shape, in some posture. Second, all depiction is from a point of view. The blackbird will be shown from the side, or the front, or above, or even (in some cubist work) from all three positions at once; but not from no position at all.

The words, in contrast, need not describe the bird from any angle. Third, only what can be seen can be depicted, and everything is depicted as having a certain (visual) appearance. So I can depict blackbirds, and depict them as black; but I can't depict an electron (though I can use a picture of something else to represent one nondepictively), and I can't depict Bin Laden as completely invisible (though I can depict the Bin Laden-shaped bulge in the carpet where he is hiding). Fourth, although the picture need not ascribe to its object the visual appearance it really has, there is only so much room for misrepresentation. I can depict a blackbird as much larger and more aggressive than blackbirds really are, but I can't depict it as having only the looks of an eagle. For then, while I may have depicted an eagle, I have not depicted a blackbird at all. Fifth, to understand a picture one needs to know what the thing depicted looks like. I can't tell that it's a picture of Bin Laden unless I know how he looks. Can't I learn this from a picture? Of course, but when I do, I only understand the picture in the first place, say as of a bearded man with sensitive eyes, because I know what *that* looks like. Being able to tell that the picture depicts *a bearded man* requires me to know what a bearded man looks like, and I don't gain the ability to tell that it depicts *Bin Laden* without simultaneously learning what Bin Laden looks like. Sixth, and finally, I do not need much more than knowledge of appearance to understand pictures. Perhaps I must have some general familiarity with pictorial representation. (So perhaps the stories of tribes who are simply perplexed by pictures are true.) But I do not need anything more than this general ability, coupled to knowledge of appearance. Once I can understand some pictures, I can understand all – provided I know the appearance of the things depicted.

Now you might doubt any of these six claims. For any of them, it is possible to think of cases which provide prima facie counterexamples. But the six features listed are certainly true for the vast majority of pictures. Moreover, they cohere, in a way which makes them more plausible *en masse* than individually. They suggest that pictorial representation works by capturing the appearance of things. That is why anything represented must have an appearance, and be represented as having one; why the discrepancies between these two can only be so great; why, since something's appearance is relative to the point from which it is seen, all depiction is from a point of view; why depicted content is always relatively rich (the "thousand words") – since otherwise, not enough of the appearance would be captured for the representation to be of *that thing*; and why, to understand a picture of something, you need to know what that thing looks like, and not much more. In cohering in this way around the idea that depiction is representation which captures (visual) appearance, the six features provide a way to make more precise the idea that depiction is specially visual. But this coherence also reinforces the claims. Since they hang together in this way, and since they are undeniably true of the vast majority of pictures, there is good reason to think that they trace the boundaries of a genuine phenomenon, pictorial representation. The apparent counterexamples are not really so. Whatever they involve, it cannot be pictorial representation, properly understood.

Can we then *define* pictorial representation by the six features? I doubt it. It seems likely that the same features will hold for representation by three-dimensional models, such as sculpture. Perhaps sculpture represents in just the same way as pictures, but it is natural to think it does not. If we are not to rule this out from the first, it seems

Robert Hopkins

there must be more to pictorial representation than the above. What we need is a deeper account of its nature, one that will provide a more profound explanation for the six features.

Moving Towards an Answer

What would such an account look like? An idea that has been very influential in recent years is that pictorial representation works by bringing about a distinctive visual experience. Suppose we said – falsely – that whenever we see a picture, we are in the grip of the illusion of seeing its object face-to-face. We could then understand pictorial representation as the generation of such experiences. Each picture gives us an experience just like that of seeing some object in the flesh, and what the marks depict is whatever object we then seem to see. Now, as noted, this description of our experience of pictures is false. When we see a marked surface, what our experience presents us with is just a set of marks. Perhaps we see them as organized in a special way, but we do not seem to see the picture's object. Nonetheless, even if the specific claims of the illusion view are wrong, the basic approach it exemplifies is attractive. The most powerful advocate of that approach has been Richard Wollheim (1980, 1987). Wollheim calls our experience of pictures "seeing-in." While I don't accept Wollheim's own account of the experience either (see the final section below), I agree with him that this is the right general line to take, and I like the terminology. What I need, then, is a plausible way to characterize seeing-in. What is it to see something in a picture?

The problems with illusion show that we need from the first to give a prominent role, in our account of seeing-in, to our awareness of the marks *as marks*. But we also need to give a prominent role to the thought of the picture's object. Otherwise, the experience can't do the work intended: securing what the picture represents. Both needs can be met if we take seeing-in to be an experience *of resemblance*. To see something, O, in a picture P, is to experience P as resembling O. We see the marks, but see them as resembling something else – say, a blackbird. However, in what way are the marks seen as resembling a blackbird? After all, since the marks are seen as just that, marks on a flat surface, and since a blackbird is a plump, feathery rounded object, full of life, there are plenty of respects in which the picture is *not* seen as resembling its object. In what respect is resemblance experienced?

Outline Shape

An answer can be found in the work of the great eighteenth-century Scottish philosopher, Thomas Reid ([1764] 1997, especially ch.VI, 7). He describes a property he calls "visible figure," but which I prefer to call "outline shape." This is to be distinguished from two-dimensional or three-dimensional shape, which, says Reid, is a matter of the positions of an object's parts in relation to each other. A sphere, say, is just an object every part of the surface of which is an equal distance from the object's center. Outline shape, in contrast, is a matter of the direction of the parts of an object

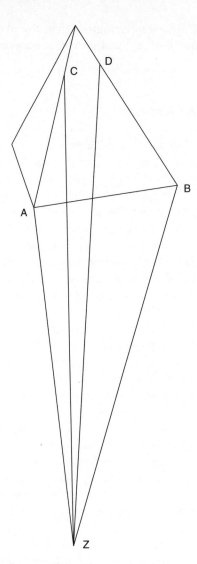

Figure 9.1 The outline shape of a pyramid.

from a point in its surroundings. I will explain what this means with the help of a diagram.

Figure 9.1 illustrates the directions of parts of a pyramid from a point Z. From that point, one of the corners of the base, A, lies in a certain direction (downwards, and to the left, we might say, if we were at Z). Another corner, B, lies in a different direction, traced by the line ZB (downwards, but more to the right). Points further up that face of the pyramid, C and D, lie in their own directions from Z. And in fact every visible part of the pyramid will lie in a distinct direction from the point. The pyramid's outline shape, at the point Z, is just a matter of the combined directions from Z in which its various parts lie.

Robert Hopkins

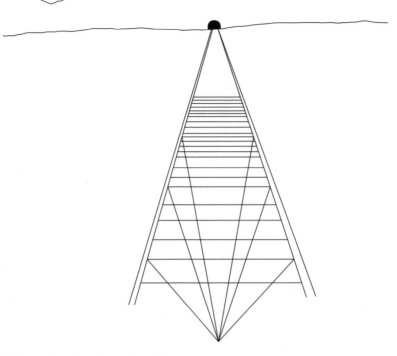

Figure 9.2 The outline shape of receding rails.

This makes outline shape sound rather recherché, but it is perfectly familiar. Suppose you are looking down receding railway lines. They present a distinctive appearance. As we are tempted to say, they seem to converge. But is this really how things seem? This is, surely, just how receding parallel lines present themselves to our vision. If they did not look that way, your experience would not present them as parallel, but as diverging. Their being parallel is a matter of their three-dimensional shape, the relations of their various parts to each other, as Reid would say. It is not misrepresented in experience. So in what sense do the lines look converging? Reid's answer, and mine, is that what we are seeing is the outline shape of the receding rails. From the point from which we view them, opposing points on the two lines lie in directions which get ever closer together, as our glance passes down the tracks (see figure 9.2). And we can offer related accounts of other familiar visual phenomena, such as the increasingly "elliptical" appearance of a round dinner plate, as it is tilted away.

So outline shape is a property of things, albeit a property they have only in relation to some point. And it is a property we see. But what has it to do with pictures?

The beauty of outline shape is that it ignores the third dimension. Go back to figure 9.1. Anything lying on the line ZA lies in the same direction from Z as does A. The same is true for anything lying on ZB, ZC, or ZD. Since outline shape is just a matter of the combined directions in which parts of a thing lie, it is possible for something with a quite different three-dimensional shape to share the pyramid's outline shape.

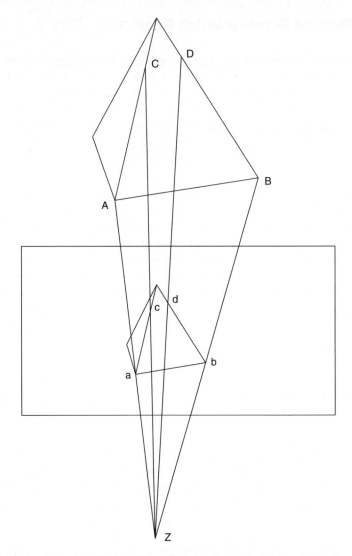

Figure 9.3 A tracing reproduces the pyramid's outline shape.

One such thing might be a flat surface, with marks in the right places so that, for each part of the pyramid, there is a mark lying in the same direction from Z. If we were to mark a surface in this way, the result would be a picture of the pyramid (see figure 9.3). Outline shape, it seems, is independent of three-dimensional shape in just the right way for it to be a property that pictures and their objects share.

Reid knew this. He said that the artist's job was to capture outline shape ([1764] 1997: ch.VI, 3, 7). However, Reid and I do not quite agree on how outline shape is relevant to pictorial representation. For my idea is not that artists produce pictures which share the outline shape of the things they depict. That does not tell us anything about our experience of pictures, seeing-in. My claim is instead that pictures are *seen as resembling* their objects in outline shape.

What Pictorial Representation Really Is

We now know what seeing-in is: experienced resemblance in outline shape. But is this enough to tell us what pictorial representation is? It is not. The problem is that, given the right circumstances or a little luck, many things might, at least on occasion, lead us to have that experience. As Wollheim notes (1987: 46–50) we sometimes see things in the frosty patterns on window panes, although they do not depict at all; or see something in a picture, even though it depicts something else. So there is a gap between someone's seeing something in a surface, and that surface depicting that thing. How can we close that gap?

The answer is obvious, especially when we remember that pictures are tools in communication. We should appeal to the intentions of the artist. Pictures depict what they do because (1) we see those things in them; and (2) we are supposed to see them there – someone made those marks *intending* us to see that thing in them. In fact, the appeal to the artist's intentions only gets us so far. For some pictures, there need be no such intentions. The most obvious examples are photographs. Although a photograph usually represents what the photographer intended, it need not. The photographer might not have noticed the grinning face in the corner of the scene. Or the photo might have been taken by accident, the shutter opening by chance when the camera was dropped. In either case, the resulting photo may depict some thing, even though no one intended it to. So, to close the gap between seeing-in and pictorial representation, we need to appeal both to intention, and to the sort of causal connection involved in photography.

If we put all this together, this is what our theory of depiction looks like:

A picture P depicts something O if, and only if,
(1) O can be seen in P
and either
(2a) The explanation for (1) is that someone intended that O be seen in P.
or
(2b) The explanation for (1) is that P is causally related in the right way to O.

This does not tell us much unless we know what it is to see something in a set of marks, but of course we do:

O is seen in a surface P if and only if P is experienced as resembling O in outline shape.

So much for what my view is. Why should you believe it? I will try and persuade you in two steps. First, I defend the view against what is perhaps the most serious objection to it. Second, I compare its advantages with those of its rivals.

Defending the View

There is a natural, and serious, worry about the experienced resemblance view – that it applies to only some pictorial representation. Consider pictures in classical perspective, those pictures meeting the rules laid down by the theorists of the Renaissance. For instance, Leon Battista Alberti suggested that artists should think of themselves as tracing the contours of the object on a transparent glass plane, or "window," lying between their viewpoint and the thing ([1435-6] 1966: 51). The rules were enormously influential over the following centuries. But there would be no need for such rules if all depiction met them. So it seems the very idea of these rules presupposes that much depiction is not in perspective. This is surely right: examples include much medieval and primitive art, children's drawings, some cartoons, and a good deal else besides. Yet – and here's the worry – the experienced resemblance view seems especially well suited to pictures in perspective. For, by and large, the rules of perspective are rules for capturing the outline shape of things. That is why Alberti's advice seems so reminiscent of my exposition of outline shape, and in particular my figure 9.3. Of course, it's a good thing that my view covers these pictures, since it should cover all. The challenge is to show that it can cover *more than* perspectival depiction.

Although there is some unclarity to this challenge, it has enough intuitive appeal to be worth answering at some length. I make six points.

First, at least some perspectival systems, such as Alberti's, tell us how to project objects onto planes. It is very natural to think of such systems as providing recipes for depicting real objects. At least if this is what is meant by perspective, the experienced resemblance view is in no way committed to this being the only depiction there is. The view tells us nothing about how to make pictures. (That is not the point of figure 9.3, which instead illustrates how two objects of very different three-dimensional shape might resemble each other in outline shape.) All the view does is to put a condition on the result of any picture-making process: if the marks are to depict 0, they must be experienced as resembling 0 in outline shape.

The second point is really a consequence of the first: the view not only allows for the idea that marks depicting something might not resemble it in outline shape; in certain important cases it predicts it. Remember what the view is trying to do. It states what it is for a picture to depict whatever it is that it depicts. When the picture depicts something, such as Tony Blair, as it really is, then the view says the picture will be experienced as resembling in outline shape Blair *as he really is*. But if the picture depicts Blair with distorted features, as a caricature might, then the view claims that the marks will be experienced as resembling just that – Tony Blair *with distorted features*. This is how the view makes room for the possibility of pictorial misrepresentation, the fourth of the six features in the first section above.

Misrepresentation is about inaccuracy. My third point concerns imprecision. No picture represents every property its object actually has, and some pictures represent relatively few of their objects' properties, and those only vaguely. An example is a simple silhouette of a face. It shows the rough shape of the nose, but no more; and does not depict any of the details, such as eyebrows. (This is not to depict the face as *lacking* eyebrows – the picture is simply silent on the matter.) What will the experienced resemblance view say about relatively imprecise pictorial content? Again, it will say that the marks are experienced as resembling whatever the picture depicts. If it depicts a face full of detail, they are experienced as resembling just that. If it depicts only a vaguely defined face, that is what they are experienced as resembling. In the latter case, the precise shape of the marks on the page may not matter. What matters is that what is

Robert Hopkins

before the viewer is a set of marks of this rough shape, in virtue of which they can be experienced as resembling in outline shape a face the features of which are relatively unspecified. Thus in the case of imprecise depiction, the view can allow for a good deal of variation in marks which, because they all share the relevant rough outline shape, are equally well suited to depicting O. There is no reason to think that those variations stay within the bounds set by some system of perspective.

Fourth, the view does not anyway place any stress on P's resembling O in outline shape. What matters is that P be *experienced as* resembling O in that respect. No doubt in general these two requirements will stand or fall together: what meets one will meet the other. But this need not always be so. Resemblance in outline shape is a (second order) property of the resembling objects, but in general the presence of a property is neither necessary nor sufficient for experience of it. Take an example. A half-submerged stick, although straight, looks bent. The outline shape we see it as having is that of a kinked stick, not a straight one. How should we mark a piece of paper, if we want to capture how the stick looks? If we produce marks which really resemble the stick's outline shape, by drawing a straight line, we will fail. We need to draw a kinked line. So we depict the stick by producing marks which, although they do not resemble the stick in outline shape, are seen as doing so. And this, of course, is just what the experienced resemblance view says we should do. Now, the rules of perspective, in so far as they tell us how to capture outline shape at all, tell us how to produce marks which actually resemble objects in outline shape. But the view tells us that what matters to depiction is experienced resemblance. Since the view does not even agree with the rules of perspective, it can hardly limit depiction to items produced according to those rules.

Fifth, and relatedly, many factors affect what we experience a picture as resembling in outline shape. Some of these factors are a matter of our biology, or of our physical environment. But others may be cultural. Outline shape is often hard to see. Reid called it "this fugitive form" ([1764] 1997: ch.VI, 7). It is difficult to isolate from three-dimensional shape and other properties, especially in objects of some complexity. Thus it is quite possible that people differ in their sensitivity to outline shape. And, if I am right that pictures work by exploiting that sensitivity, it is surely possible that cultural factors, including the styles of depiction people are familiar with, affect how sensitive to outline shape those people are. If that's right, what we experience a picture as resembling in outline shape may differ from what its original viewers saw it as resembling. For example, at first glance many medieval pictures of cities show the various buildings stacked up one behind another, higher and higher in the picture plane. We, being familiar with painting in linear perspective, cannot help but see in these canvases a certain spatial disorderliness. But there is no reason to think that the original viewers did. Perhaps they, because unfamiliar with painting in perspective, were simply less sensitive to the discrepancy between the outline shape a city presents and the outline shape of the marks. If so, we need not claim that the picture is in any sense a failure. If its intended audience saw in it what the artist intended, that is what it depicts. The existence now of a visually more sophisticated set of viewers is by the by.

Sixth, and finally, although my view places experienced resemblance in outline shape at the heart of depiction, it does allow for some slippage between the two.

Nothing depicts unless it is seen as resembling something else in outline shape. But the picture need not depict precisely that thing. For pictorial representation is essentially a tool for communicating. If the point is got across, the job has been done. As a result, it is possible for the depictive content of a picture to differ slightly from what is seen in it. In particular, certain details of the object seen in the marks may be discounted, by the viewer, as irrelevant to the point the picture is intended to convey. (I make this point for intentional depiction, but related claims apply to accidental photographs and the like.) For instance, it may be that I experience a stick-figure picture as resembling a very thin man, with a balloon-like head. But even if I do, I will not take this as what it represents. I know that you have chosen this method of drawing for its speed and ease. You want to convey something – perhaps what the man is up to – but you are not, in all probability, interested in representing a strangely deformed person. So I set aside certain aspects of what I see in the picture. Seeing-in still governs depiction, since I don't take the marks to depict some feature unless I see that feature in them. But not every feature seen-in is taken as part of what is depicted. Since depiction is about communication, what is reasonably set aside as irrelevant to your representational intention is not part of what is depicted at all. This is how today's viewers treat the disorderliness of the buildings we see in the medieval depiction of the city. Perhaps it is also (contrary to the suggestion above) how the original viewers of this picture reacted. Certainly that is a possibility for other non-perspectival images. Thus once again what is not in perspective need not be treated by the experienced resemblance view as not depictive.

In short, perspective may preserve outline shape, but the view does not see depiction as being about such preservation. Now, these six points may not satisfy the critic. They all exploit either nonveridical pictorial content (points one and two), or imprecise content (this is explicit for three, but in effect also underlies five and six), or the slightly arcane possibility that experienced resemblance comes apart from resemblance (four). And one might wonder whether there could be depiction which, though not in classical perspective, is of highly precise and accurate pictorial contents and which does not rely on the arcane possibility. Indeed, Dominic Lopes has suggested that so-called inverse perspective provides just such a counterexample to my view (Lopes 2003). Now, I deny that pictures in inverse perspective depict what Lopes says they do. They do depict, but only somewhat imprecisely; and they do represent precise contents, but only nondepictively. Moreover, I do not merely assert this, but offer an argument (Hopkins 2003a). If that argument works (and its premises are ones Lopes himself seems to accept), it shows, not just that the experienced resemblance view should deny that these pictures depict precise contents, but that Lopes's own recognitional theory (see below) should also do so. The only remaining counterexample thus seems to be one that its proponent cannot use.

Comparing the View with the Alternatives

To defend the view against criticism is one thing, to make a positive case for it is quite another. I will do this last by comparing the position with its main rivals. First, then, let me say what these are. I begin with a view which, like mine, adopts the experiential approach to depiction.

Richard Wollheim has not only been the most forceful advocate of the experiential approach in general, he has also offered his own characterization of seeing-in (1987). The distinguishing feature of Wollheim's view is its modesty. He says that seeing-in is an experience with two "folds" or "aspects." One fold is somehow analogous to seeing the marks without making any sense of them. The other is somehow analogous to seeing the depicted object in the flesh. But Wollheim refuses to say how these two aspects are related to those independent experiences. He thinks that to do so would be a mistake. All we can say is that there are these two folds to seeing-in, that both occur at once, and that attention can nevertheless shift between them (provided neither is entirely extinguished).

There are two other positions I want to discuss. Neither is a form of experiential view, although they differ in their distance from such accounts. The *recognition theory* (Schier 1986, Lopes 1996) agrees with experiential accounts that pictures are importantly visual representations. But instead of trying to understand their visual nature in terms of an experience which pictures provoke, the theory appeals to the processing involved in understanding them. The claim is that pictures engage the very same abilities that are involved in recognizing the depicted object in the flesh. In fact, there are two claims here. The first is that I can understand a picture as representing a blackbird if, and only if, I can recognize blackbirds when I see them. There is "co-variance" (Schier 1986) between the ability to interpret pictures and the ability to recognize their objects in the flesh. The second claim is that whatever subpersonal processing is involved in recognizing the object in the flesh, significantly overlapping processing is involved in understanding a depiction of that object. The second claim, concerning overlap, is inferred as the best explanation of the first, concerning covariance. The inference is to some overlap, no more, because we do not in general confuse pictures with their objects. Given this, there must be some stage at which the two processing chains differ. Otherwise, they would yield the same output, and we would misidentify the picture as the blackbird (or vice versa).

Finally, there is the view brilliantly advocated by Nelson Goodman (1976, Goodman and Elgin 1988). He argues that pictures form a symbol system in just the sense in which words do. What distinguishes pictures is formal features of the symbol system to which they belong. In particular, Goodman suggests that pictorial symbol systems are *relatively replete*, and *syntactically and semantically dense*. The details here are very interesting, but need not concern us. The gist is that pictorial systems allow for an infinite number of possible symbols, and possible referents of those symbols, and that, for a wide range of properties of the marks on the surface, the smallest difference in one of those properties affects what the symbol represents. In written language, in contrast, variations in many properties of the marks (their color, size, and even many aspects of their shape) are unimportant. They simply do not affect which word is inscribed, and hence what is represented.

How, then, do these various positions and mine compare? I will make three points.

1   Pictures are tools for communication, or representations. But they are particularly visual representations. I think it clear that some of the positions emphasize one of these features at the cost of the other.

Goodman's view puts all the stress on the first. Pictures are just symbols, like words, differing from them only in formal respects. In effect, Goodman denies that pictures are, in any interesting sense, visual. This seems implausible. For instance, it leaves Goodman unable to explain how at one extreme depiction shades into illusion, as clever *trompe l'œil* demonstrates; or how it could be possible to produce pictures mechanically, using only the geometrically regular movement of light, as do photographs. Both these aspects of depiction should be as puzzling for Goodman as the thought that at the limit linguistic description might aim to delude readers into thinking that they are looking at the thing described, or that we might produce descriptions using only mirrors and photosensitive film.

The recognition theory, in contrast, puts all the weight on the visual, and none on the communication. It gives very pure expression to the idea that pictures are visual representations, in its claim that they engage the same visual processing as their objects. In fact, the view need not privilege the *visual* over other perceptual modes. It could see pictorial representation as encompassing various types of symbol, all of which work by engaging the same processing, in *some* modality, as their objects. This clearly appeals to Lopes, who has drawn our attention to some fascinating psychological evidence concerning the ability of blind people to draw and understand raised-line pictures (Lopes 1997, and see Hopkins 2000). But, whether pictures are specially visual, or specially perceptual, their communicative aspect needs accommodating. And it is not clear how the recognition theory can do this. True, it concedes that we can tell pictures and their objects apart, and so supposes that the processing story in the two cases diverges at some point. But the concession is rather grudging. The view has nothing concrete to say about the difference between the processing a picture demands, and that triggered by its object. All its ingenuity is expended in trying to understand the link between our looking at a flat surface and our looking at the robustly three-dimensional world. This does not strictly make it impossible to accommodate the communicative aspect of pictures. (Indeed Schier spends considerable energy making room for it; 1986: chs. 6–8.) But it does doom this accommodation to the role of afterthought. In contrast, I claim, when we encounter pictures we encounter objects which are patently communicative episodes. They are the messages in a bottle of the visual world.

Both aspects of pictures are given their proper place by the experienced resemblance view. An experience of resemblance makes no sense without both a resembler experienced and a resembled in the light of which it is experienced. Thus the view gives equal weight, in describing our experience of pictures, to the marks (the resembler) and the object the thought of which organizes them (the resembled). So one encounters a communication, in the form of a deliberately marked surface; but one that is particularly visual, a grasp of its meaning requiring one to see it in a particular way. However, the view is not the only position to attain a proper balance between the two aspects. Wollheim's view certainly does so, since it in effect makes the two features definitive of seeing-in.

156   **Robert Hopkins**

2   However, there is a related issue where even this rival falls away. One consequence of the imbalance in the recognitional account and Goodman's view is that they are unable to distinguish pictorial representation from representation by sculpture. Goodman can find no difference between pictorial and sculptural representation because any formal features of the former, such as density and repleteness, will also be found in the latter. And the recognitional view, since it puts all the weight on the link between picture and object, has no resources for distinguishing the rather different link between sculpture and object. In so far as it is plausible that pictures engage the same processing as their objects, it is just as much so for sculpture. Schier, indeed, acknowledges this point, and takes himself to be defining a far wider category, "iconic" representation in general (1986: ch. 4).

Lopes, however, is more optimistic (see his chapter in this volume). He might try to capture the distinction in two ways. One would be to supplement the claims of the recognition theory. For instance, it might be stipulated that, while pictures and sculptures both engage our abilities to recognize O, the former are two-dimensional, the latter three-dimensional. Any such move looks like an unsatisfactory afterthought. It is not the recognition view which is doing the work here, but these other claims, and they could be attached to almost any position. So it is as well that Lopes explores an alternative. This is to adjust one of the centerpieces of the recognition theory, the overlap claim. What pictures engage is not merely our ability to recognize O in the flesh, but our ability to recognize O "seen two-dimensionally." Sculptures, in contrast, engage our ability to recognize O when presented in three dimensions.

I doubt that this second option is genuine. It is simply unclear what it means to say that we recognize O presented in two dimensions. Suppose I said that, in understanding a passage describing O, we recognize O presented linguistically. This is just a misleading way of saying that a bit of language represents O, and we can understand it as doing so. How does Lopes's claim fare any better? We no more see O when seeing a picture of it, than when reading the description. So in neither case do we recognize O, if that means correctly identifying what we see as O. And in both cases what we can do is identify the thing as a *representation of O*. Now, this does not show that the adjusted recognition theory fails to distinguish pictorial from linguistic representation. The covariance claim blocks this unwelcome consequence: linguistic understanding fails to covary with the ability to recognize O in the flesh. However, what the example does show is that our options for interpreting talk of "recognizing O seen two-dimensionally" are very limited. Either it means (1) that we identify a representation as of O, and that representation is two-dimensional; or it means (2) that what we are seeing is O in two-dimensional form, and we recognize it as such. The problem with (1) is twofold. First, it turns the overlap claim from an interesting assertion about the cognitive processing involved in understanding pictures into the wholly uncontroversial claim that we are able to understand them. Second, it allows us to distinguish picturing from sculpture only by an appeal, quite independent of the rest of the view, to the fact that one is in two-dimensions, the other in three. We are back at the original way to handle the distinction, as a mere afterthought. The problem with (2), on the other hand, is that it is, if not nonsense, then certainly false.

Difficulties in differentiating picturing from sculpture are not restricted to the unbalanced accounts. Wollheim's rather minimal description of seeing-in surely applies just as readily to our experience of sculpture. There too, there is an aspect which is somewhat analogous to seeing the sculpted object in the flesh, and an aspect somewhat analogous to seeing the sculpture without making sense of it, seeing it, for instance, as nothing more than a lump of stone.

In sharp contrast, the experienced resemblance view distinguishes the two with ease. To see something in a picture is to see it as resembling its object in one respect, outline shape. Our experience of sculpture is of a quite distinct resemblance – resemblance in three-dimensional shape. Perhaps we should finish the job by adding a negative claim to our account of pictures: we do not see them as resembling their objects in three-dimensional shape. But this is both easily done, and independently plausible.

3   Finally, let me return to the six features of depiction with which I began. I said we should aim for an account of pictorial representation which explained these six features. Does the view I have suggested do this? And do any of its rivals do as well?

Here is the experienced resemblance view's explanation for the six features. If a set of marks is to depict something, it must be experienced as resembling it in outline shape – this is just the view. But you can't experience resemblance in outline shape to something unless you think of that thing as having certain properties – at least outline shape itself, and any other properties that entails. Hence feature one. But outline shape is relative to a point. Nothing has an outline shape *tout court*. It has different outline shapes at different points in its surroundings. Since resemblance can only be experienced to something with an outline shape, and since outline shape is relative to a point, resemblance is experienced to something considered *from a certain point*. Hence feature two. Now, outline shape is not a visual notion. But our grasp of it is visual: we only perceive outline shapes, at least to any very determinate degree, in vision. So the only things to which we can experience resemblance in outline shape will be visible ones. Hence feature three. There is no need for the resemblance to be experienced to the thing as it actually is – misrepresentation is possible. But it cannot be to the thing transformed beyond all recognition, on pain of the experience of resemblance breaking down. Hence feature four. Since to interpret a picture is, more or less, just to see the right thing in it, the resources necessary for understanding pictures are just those necessary for experiencing resemblance in outline shape. The latter amount to little more than knowledge of a thing's appearance. Hence features five and six.

What of the other candidates? How do they fare? It would be laborious to run through each of the six features for each of the rivals, so I will confine myself, in closing, to some brief observations.

Goodman is at sea with almost all of the features. His refusal to allow depiction to be visual, coupled to the fact that most of the features concern visual aspects of what can be depicted, block explanations at the first. Wollheim simply says too little about seeing-in for his view to explain much. Until we are told in what way each

Robert Hopkins

"fold" of the experience is analogous to the experience of seeing the object, or seeing the marks as marks, we cannot tell what properties seeing-in, and hence depiction, will have. For instance, all seeing is from a point of view. But will this feature of seeing a blackbird transfer to seeing one in a picture? Wollheim's blank formula that the one experience is "somewhat analogous" to the other prevents us from knowing. The recognition theory in effect takes features five and six as basic. It translates their talk of knowing the object's appearance into talk of being able to recognize it, but this difference, though not trivial, is not enormous. It then treats those two claims combined as its first, and most elemental, claim (the covariance thesis). Of course, it also infers overlap as the best explanation for covariance. But since the overlap claim is just that there is as much overlap in processing as is required to explain covariance, this hardly constitutes a genuine explanation of the latter (compare soporific virtue). However, it might try to explain some of the other features. Schier himself has a go at features one and two (1986: 164), and Lopes has buttressed those moves against an attack from me (Hopkins 1998, Lopes 2003). For my part, I cannot see how the explanations appeal to more than contingent facts about our processing system. Since I think the features are *necessary* features of depiction, I don't think any explanation the view offers will ever be strong enough (Hopkins 2003b).

Well, so what? After all, none of the six features are unassailable. This is true. However, I think that those who reject them ought to find substitutes. They ought to propose other features of depiction which have some claim to trace a unified phenomenon for us all to study, and which are both sufficiently interesting to merit explanation, and sufficiently superficial to leave room for it. It would help if those features also cohered, in the way I suggested my six did. Perhaps the proponents of these other views will come up with a rival set. At the moment, no one has even seriously tried. Until they do, I contend that the fact that my six features are plausible, and that the experienced resemblance view is the only plausible position to offer explanations of them, is reason enough to believe it.

The Domain of Depiction

Dominic McIver Lopes

Depiction, or pictorial representation, is a type of representation – this is one of the few bedrock truths approved by all philosophers who have worked up opinions on the matter. Another is that depiction has *something* to do with resemblance – nobody denies that either. But little effort is needed to locate a philosopher or art theorist who has given a respectable reason to deny any additional claim about depiction, however obvious, that does not follow directly from one of the two bedrock truths. Thus it is tempting to put the two bedrock truths in relation to one another by taking resemblance to explain the kind of representation found in pictures (e.g., Hopkins in the previous chapter). Yet some philosophers object to this move: they accept both bedrock truths but refuse to use the second to understand the first (e.g., the recognition theory defended in this chapter). The point of contention is not whether pictures have to do with resemblance but whether this truth helps us to understand the kind of representation found in pictures.

Goodman's Challenge

Nelson Goodman's *Languages of Art* (1976) disputes a cluster of ideas about resemblance in pictures that enjoy strong intuitive appeal. "Goodman's challenge" is inspired by *Languages of Art* though it is by no means a reading of that book.

Nicolas Poussin described pictures as "imitations in line and color." There is something right about this and something wrong with it. If "imitation" just means "representation," then Poussin's statement is hardly informative, since it fails to distinguish pictures from other representations made up of lines – the text you are reading is a representation in line and color. So it is natural to read Poussin as holding that the lines and colors that make up a picture's surface resemble visible features of the depicted scene. Comparable statements are sprinkled throughout writing on depiction from Plato onwards.

At this point you might think that the trouble with Poussin's statement is that, as a general rule, pictures obviously do not resemble the scenes they depict. Poussin's *Dance to the Music of Time* is small, flat, and inanimate when compared to four dancing figures, and no dancing figures look like dabs of paint. But this is not Goodman's challenge. In truth, there are many similarities between Poussin's *Dance* and dancing figures: if the similarity between two objects lies in their sharing a property in common, then every two objects are similar because every two objects share some property in common. Moreover, we do experience the configurations of lines and colors on the surfaces of pictures as visually resembling the scenes they depict. Pictures are *seen* to share properties in common with the objects they depict. We have every reason to believe the second bedrock truth.

Goodman's challenge comprises two points. The first is that resemblances are too easy to find, not too hard. Picture–scene similarity explains the depiction of a scene only if the picture is more similar to the scene than to all things that it does not depict. But if a picture is at all similar to the scene it depicts, sharing properties in common with it, then it is also equally or more similar to many other objects – other pictures, for instance. The proper response to this problem is to privilege resemblances that obtain between pictures and depicted scenes over those that obtain between pictures and other objects, ruling out the latter as irrelevant to depiction. Identifying the relevant resemblances is no easy task. It will not do to say that only visual similarities are relevant, because most pictures share more visible properties with other pictures than with the scenes they depict. A better idea is that the relevant similarities are not objective but subjective: they are not similarities between object and scene but *experienced* similarities between object and scene.

It is here that Goodman's challenge has maximal purchase. Experienced similarities, like objective similarities, are also too easy to find. It is true that pictures are experienced as similar in some respects to the scenes they depict. But what things we experience as similar to each other is a function of our psychological make-up, and our psychological make-up is shaped in turn by the imaging practices in which we are immersed. As Goodman observes, "resemblance and deceptiveness, far from being constant and independent sources and criteria of representational practice, are in some degree products of it" (1976: 39). A picture may look like nature simply because it looks the way nature is usually painted. The history of depiction confirms this (Gombrich 1961). Although the medievals, the cubists, the painters of the Italian quattrocento, and the artists of the Qing dynasty made pictures that look remarkably different, contemporary audiences seem to have experienced the pictures as similar to their subjects. The best explanation of this fact is that experiences of picture–object similarity are artifacts of imaging practices.

The second point comprising Goodman's challenge is that it targets resemblance-based explanations of depiction, not resemblance-based definitions of pictures. Suppose that all and only pictures are experienced as similar to nonpictures in certain respects. This fact would provide individually necessary and jointly sufficient conditions which fix the extension of the class of pictures, as any good definition should. Perhaps Poussin's statement stands when interpreted as a definition. However, an explanation of depiction is something more than a definition. Explanations, when successful, help us to understand a phenomenon and not just to demarcate its boundaries. They link some superficial facts about the phenomenon to be explained to some deeper, less obvious facts.

The particular target of Goodman's challenge is appeals to resemblance in explaining pictorial content determination. Every depiction has a content and we may wonder what sorts of facts determine what content it has. One answer is that the mappings of pictures onto contents are determined by the resemblances or experienced resemblances between picture surfaces and depicted scenes. The challenge warns that facts about what we experience a picture's surface as resembling cannot explain what the picture represents as long as what the picture represents determines what we experience its surface as resembling. Experienced similarity cannot explain depiction if it is a product of depiction.

We should be wary about drawing connections between the two bedrock truths about depiction. That pictures have something to do with resemblance may help to define depiction but Goodman's challenge warns that picture–object resemblances may not determine what pictures represent. An explanation of pictorial content determination may explain the second as well as the first bedrock truth about pictures.

EROS

Hopkins, in the previous chapter, proposes an explanation of depiction in terms of experienced resemblance in outline shape (EROS for short). But he is also explicit about what EROS is designed to explain, providing a list of six explananda. This is a major advance on earlier resemblance theories of depiction, for it replaces one question with two – (1) what should the theory explain? and (2) does the theory explain it? – and earlier resemblance theories tried to answer (2) explicitly while making unexamined assumptions about the answer to (1). Moreover, Hopkins's answer to (1) appears to sidestep Goodman's challenge entirely: Hopkins claims that his theory of depiction need not explain pictorial content determination.

There are six cardinal facts about depiction that EROS is intended to explain. First, there is no bare depiction: no picture depicts an O unless it depicts O as having some property F. Second, all depiction is from a point of view, so that objects are always depicted from some (sometimes indeterminate) point or points in the space around them. Third, only what can be seen can be depicted. An electron is invisible and so cannot be depicted. Fourth, objects can be pictorially misrepresented only to some partial degree. A blackbird cannot be depicted as having exactly the looks of an eagle. Fifth, understanding a picture entails knowledge of what the depicted object looks like. This knowledge need not precede understanding the picture: understanding the picture may confer knowledge of the depicted object's appearance. Finally, little more than knowledge of the depicted object's appearance (and perhaps general familiarity with depiction) is needed in order to understand a depiction of the object.

These six facts are not, as Hopkins concedes, definitive of pictorial representation – analogous statements may be made about other forms of representation, notably sculpture. No matter. What is wanted is not a definition but an explanation: a small number of deeper facts about depiction that determine the six explananda and make sense of their appearing to hang together as a unit.

Hopkins's proposal is that a picture depicts an object only if the object can be seen in the picture. An object is seen in a picture if and only if some part of the picture's surface is experienced as resembling the object in outline shape. The outline shape of an object is a set of directions from a point to parts of the object. An object's outline shape from a point is a property of the object and two objects sharing the property objectively resemble each other in outline shape. Hence, since outline shape is specified two-dimensionally, a flat picture can share an outline shape with a three-dimensional object. But the proposal is not that *objective* resemblance in outline shape is necessary or sufficient for seeing an object in a picture; it is rather that seeing-in is constituted by an *experience* of resemblance in outline shape (this is subjective resemblance). To see an object in a picture is to experience a certain resemblance between picture and object. Seeing-in is an experience with a certain type of content and since seeing-in is required for depiction, depiction is a type of representation that involves an experience with that type of content.

There is more to depiction than seeing-in, however. Hopkins adds that a picture depicts an object only if the picture is either causally related in the right way to the object or else is made with the intention that the object be seen in the picture. In fact, the second, intentional disjunct may be folded into the first, causal disjunct – provided intentional making is a causal relation of the right kind. This is not controversial, for any reasonable alternative to EROS includes a causal/intentional condition, disputes only concern what counts as the right kind of causal relation (e.g., Lopes 1996), and the causal relation plays no role in explaining the six explananda.

The argument for EROS is that it explains the six cardinal facts about depiction whereas alternative views do not. There is no bare depiction of particular objects because a picture depicts an object only by showing, at the very least, its outline shape. Depiction is from a point of view because outline shape is viewpoint-relative. Only what can be seen can be depicted because we grasp outline shapes only via vision. Misrepresentation is possible but limited lest the experience of resemblance in outline shape dissolve. Knowledge of an object's appearance suffices for and is entailed by grasping a picture of it because grasping a picture of it is a matter of experiencing the picture's outline shape resemblance to the object.

The Limits of EROS

Goodman's challenge threatens to block appeals to resemblance in explaining pictorial content determination and Hopkins's proposal appears to sidestep the challenge by excluding pictorial content determination from the six cardinal explananda. But a series of tough cases present the proposal with a dilemma. One response to the tough cases transforms EROS into a content determiner; the other is vulnerable to Goodman's challenge. Neither response is acceptable.

The first case is The Box, a cube drawn in a type of projection (parallel oblique perspective) that is often used by architects and technical draftsmen (figure 10.1). Consider the following three propositions:

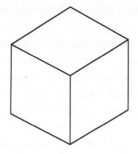

Figure 10.1 Cube rendered in parallel oblique perspective.

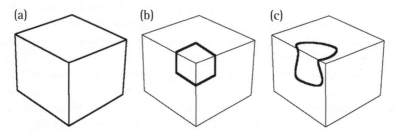

Figure 10.2 Three outline shapes of parts of a cube. The thick line on each figure is the outline shape for part of a cube, shown by a thin line. Only figure 2a shows the outline shape normally chosen to depict the cube.

1. Figure 10.1 depicts an object as cubical;
2. We see a cube in figure 10.1;
3. We do not experience figure 10.1 as matching a cube in outline shape.

If (1) to (3) are true then EROS does not provide a necessary condition for either seeing-in or depiction. Are all three claims true? It is possible to deny (1) and accept (2) only on the dubious assumption that the figure could not have been made with the intention that a box be seen in it, but the fact that the figure is offered as a counterexample to EROS is ample evidence of an intention that a cubical box be seen in it. (2) is meant to be intuitively obvious. The reason for (3) is that the picture does not in fact match a cubical box in outline shape, and experiences of outline shape, like experiences in general, presumably track actual properties of the world.

The Box is generated by violating the rules of vanishing point perspective projection laid down for artists during the Renaissance (cf. fig. 10.2a). However, the above objection does not derive its force from this fact. Hopkins's account does not entail that depictions must be created according to the rules of any system of perspective. Nevertheless, experienced resemblance in outline shape is most likely in cases where there is objective resemblance in outline shape and the use of vanishing point perspective ensures objective resemblance in outline shape. Thus depictions like figure 10.1 that violate the rules of vanishing point perspective supply counterexamples to EROS (see Lopes 2003). The objection is not that depictions need not conform to some

Dominic McIver Lopes

standard of perspective to which EROS is committed. It is that EROS wrongly makes (1) to (3) inconsistent.

Hopkins's chapter suggests two replies to the objection. The first reply denies (2) but accepts (3). There are in turn two ways to implement the reply. One is to claim that the figure misrepresents a cubical box. We do not experience the picture as resembling a cubic box in outline shape and so we see no such box in it. If the picture depicts a cubic box, it does not depict it as cubic – it misrepresents it as being non-cubic. Thus (1) is false as well as (2).

The second implementation of the first reply accepts (1) as well as (3) and denies (2) by claiming that the content of the experience of seeing the box in the picture is imprecise. While it is true that we do not experience figure 10.1 as resembling a cubic box in outline shape, this only shows that what we see in the figure is not a cube but an irregular hexahedron. What, then, does the figure depict if we see an irregular hexahedron in it? One option is that the figure depicts an irregular hexahedron. Another is that it does not depict that determinate hexahedron but rather a generic one. After all, what we see in a picture is sometimes representationally irrelevant – we do not take a stick figure to depict a stick-shaped person though this is what we see in it.

In both its implementations, the first reply accepts (3) and denies (2). They grant that figure 10.1 is not experienced as resembling a cubic box in outline shape but insist, for different reasons, that neither is a cubic box seen in the figure. Since the only reason given for (2) appealed to intuitions, we should accept the replies and revise our intuitions if the explanatory benefits of EROS are substantial. You may think you see a cube in figure 10.1 but in fact you see only a cube caricature or an irregular hexahedron; and we can better understand seeing-in if we revise intuitions in this way.

The second reply denies the assumption that experiences track properties of the world. It grants that figure 10.1 does not objectively resemble a cube in outline shape but insists we experience it as resembling a cube in outline shape. The situation is comparable to that of perceptual illusion: a straight stick may look bent in water. The gap between objective and subjective resemblance also makes room for subjective resemblance to vary across visual cultures. Medievals may have experienced pictures in which we see buildings piled up one on top of the other as resembling actual sky-lines in outline shape. By denying (3), this reply makes it possible to accept (1) and (2). It takes intuitions about what we see in figure 10.1 to govern what resemblances in outline shape we experience: if you see a cube in figure 10.1 then you nonveridically experience the figure as resembling one in outline shape.

The two replies are in tension with one another. The first reassigns many cases of intuitively straightforward depiction to misdepiction or imprecision whereas the second accommodates intuitions about the domain of accurate, precise depiction by allowing experienced resemblance in outline shape such flexibility that it detaches from objective resemblance in outline shape.

The same tension arises in The Shadow. Any object has indeterminately many outline shapes from one point since it has indeterminately many parts. For example, the thicker lines in figures 10.2a–c show three different outline shapes of the same cube viewed from the same point. What matters, of course, are certain salient outline

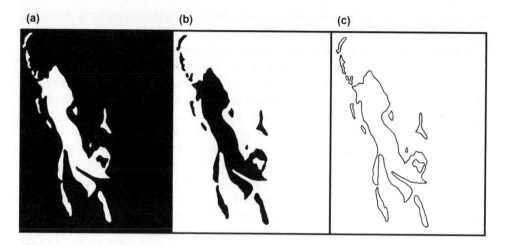

Figure 10.3 The outline of shading on a face, shown in positive, negative, and outline. Figures 3a and 3b are recognized as a face; figure 3c is not. From Kennedy (1993: 29).

shapes of an object – those that correspond to significant contours or boundaries. But it is no trivial task to say which contours or boundaries matter. Seeing a face in figures 10.3a and 3b consists in experiencing an outline shape resemblance at an illumination boundary. Now consider figure 10.3c. Very few people see a face in this figure, even when they see either that its outline shape is identical to that of figure 10.3a or even that its outline shape resembles that of the face at the illumination boundary. Whereas figure 10.1 suggests that experienced resemblance in outline shape is not necessary for seeing-in. The Shadow suggests that it is not sufficient for seeing-in.

Again, two replies are available. One is to insist that since figure 10.3c objectively resembles a face in outline shape just as much as 10.3a, we experience it, once the resemblance is drawn to our attention, as resembling a face in outline shape, hence we see a face in it. So much the worse for our intuitions, which must give way to the explanatory virtues of EROS. The alternative is to take our not seeing a face in figure 10.3c as showing that we do not experience it as resembling a face in outline shape. Since figure 10.3c objectively resembles a face in outline shape just as much as 10.3a, experienced resemblance in outline shape detaches from objective resemblance in outline shape.

Similar replies have been given to The Box and The Shadow and both lead to trouble. The first construes EROS as a theory of depictive content determination. Figure 10.1 is said (counterintuitively) to misdepict a cube as an irregular hexahedron or else to depict a generic hexahedron. Only this is what it is experienced as resembling in outline shape for only this is what it actually resembles in outline shape. Likewise, figure 10.3c depicts a face, intuitions aside. True, one may consider figure 10.3c an exotic case that need hardly be taken seriously. Intuitions often go wrong in exotic cases. But figure 10.3c is only the tip of the iceberg. Its rarity is a consequence of its straddling a fine line at the boundary of depiction. Any object has an indeterminate number of outline shapes from one viewpoint (fig. 10.3) and there is no reason pictures cannot be fashioned that match each one of those outline shapes.

Dominic McIver Lopes

But these resemblances do not determine what the pictures depict. In many cases, the pictures depict nothing. Our intuitions have been pushed too far.

A rejoinder is that only experienced resemblance in respect of certain salient outline shapes determines the content of seeing-in and hence depictive content. The outline shapes in figure 10.3c, like those in figures 10.2b and 2c, are not salient. At this point Goodman's challenge has purchase. Perhaps the salient experienced resemblances are those that pictures make salient.

This rejoinder takes us to the second reply, namely that experienced resemblance in outline shape need not track objective resemblance in outline shape. On this reply, EROS has no aspiration to fill the shoes of a theory of depictive content determination. Any attempt to do so would have to contend with the difficulties that face any subjectivist theory of property determination, such as the proposal that red is the property that objects have when we experience them as causing a sensation of red. Moreover, suppose that pictures consisting of spirals were experienced as similar in outline shape to Henry VIII when viewed under the influence of a certain drug. Do they depict King Henry (if made with the intention that he be seen in them)? These difficulties might prove surmountable – much ink has been spilled in attempting to surmount them in the case of colors – but the prospects do not look good. A more promising strategy claims that we see in pictures what they depict, that seeing-in consists in experienced resemblance in outline shape, but that experienced resemblance in outline shape does not determine, but is determined by, what pictures depict.

Consider The Invisible Dalmatian. It is quite plausible that seeing the dog in figure 10.4 amounts to experiencing an outline shape on the picture as resembling the outline shape of a dog. But the outline shape on the picture is what psychologists call a "sub-jective contour" – seeing it depends on seeing the dog in the picture. Most perceivers are able to switch between seeing a dog in the figure and seeing nothing but a smat-tering of black blots. What is interesting is that the outline shape on the picture surface that is experienced as resembling that of a dog is not seen as an outline shape at all unless the dog is seen in the figure. If seeing a resemblance between two outline shapes depends on seeing a depicted object, then the former does not explain the latter, since, in general, a phenomenon F cannot be explained as a matter of G if G depends on F. Experiences of resemblance in outline shape between a picture and some object may proceed from rather than undergird the picture's depicting the object.

Figure 10.4 is a striking instance of a common phenomenon. When we look at a picture we typically see both the picture's surface features and a depicted scene. Richard Wollheim (1987) contends that this twofoldness is essential to our experience and aesthetic appreciation of pictures, and it is certainly an important element of both (see Lopes 2005). But one way of understanding twofoldness is mistaken: one might think that the first fold of the experience – the experience of the picture surface – is always an experience of the picture as having just the features it would be seen to have if we saw no depicted scene in it. On the contrary, the features we see a picture surface as having may depend in part on what we see in the picture. Thus seeing a dog in figure 10.4 causes one to see part of the picture surface as having a bounded subjective contour, which is invisible when no dog is seen in the picture.

Figure 10.4 R. C. James "Photograph of a Dalmatian." Seeing the outline shape on the image surface as matching that of a dog is a consequence of seeing the dog in the picture.

This phenomenon is widespread in pictures and affects the perceived relative size, shape, color, and contrast of parts of picture surfaces. Those unfamiliar with analytical cubism often fail to see anything *in* their first cubist picture – they simply see the picture surface. But once they see the depicted scene in the picture, that scene shapes their experience of the picture surface. Seeing-in does not always leave surface seeing unchanged.

Hopkins proposes that a picture P depicts something O only if O can be seen in P. O is seen in P if and only if P is experienced as resembling O in outline shape. However, if the experienced resemblance between P and O is detached from an actual resemblance between P and O, then there is the danger that it is a function of P's depicting O. Experienced resemblance cannot explain depiction if it is beholden to depiction. Hopkins's theory fails to sidestep Goodman's challenge.

The Domain of Depiction

According to EROS, nothing is a depiction unless it is experienced as resembling its depictum in outline shape. This is true, argues Hopkins, because it explains the six cardinal facts about depiction. The trouble is that EROS requires an account of depictive content determination according to which a representation has depictive content only if its having that content entails its being experienced as resembling its subject

Dominic McIver Lopes

in respect of outline shape. The objective resemblance theory meets this condition by stating that a picture depicts an object in virtue of having an outline shape actually resembling that of the object. The problem with this theory is that it far too narrowly restricts the domain of depiction. Some pictures depict objects that they actually do not resemble in outline shape.

Suppose, then, that we accept that depiction has a broader domain. Suppose we accept that figure 10.1 depicts a cube (and not merely a generic hexahedron) even when it is not experienced as resembling a cube in outline shape and that figure 10.3c does not depict a face even when it is experienced (by someone who has been shown fig. 10.3a) as resembling one in outline shape. Can we give an account of depictive content determination that explains this?

The Recognition Theory

According to the recognition theory,

> A picture P depicts something O if and only if (1) P is able to trigger the capacity of a suitable perceiver in suitable viewing conditions to recognize an O by its appearance, and (2) the satisfaction of (1) is a consequence of a causal relation of the right kind between O and P.

Several elements of this proposal require elucidation.

Condition (2) acknowledges that triggering an ability to recognize an object is not sufficient for depiction. Stains on a wall may trigger an ability to recognize butterflies and fail to depict butterflies. What is also required is that butterflies have caused, in the right way, the representation's having a surface so marked that it be able to trigger a butterfly-recognition capacity. Many causal processes may be involved: mechanical ones, such as photography; computational ones, such as digital imaging; and intentional ones, as when one draws on a surface with the aim of making it satisfy condition (1). At any rate, condition (2) is not at issue: if intentional making is a causal process, it has been given a formulation equivalent to that given by Hopkins.

The main burden of the theory is borne by condition (1), which requires that depictions be able to trigger a recognition ability. A representation need not always trigger a recognition ability, though. The conditions of viewing must be appropriate – the lighting must be adequate, nothing may obstruct perception of the representation's surface organization, and that surface organization must have remained perceivable (and not have degenerated, as happens with some old pictures). In addition, the perceiver must be suitable, possessing general capacities (a) to understand pictures or pictures of the kind in question and (b) to recognize objects by their appearance. Neither (a) nor (b) may be read too narrowly: it will not do to take "pictures of the kind in question" to mean "only the very picture interpreted" or to take "the ability to recognize objects by their appearance" to mean "only as they appear in the very picture interpreted." So both capacities must be general; but they need not be perfectly general: a suitable perceiver need not be able to understand all pictures or recognize objects no matter how they look. Finally, recognition is a perceptual capacity. The recognition theory relies on the distinction between perceptual processes and other cognitive processes, notably believing. The perceptual process in question is usually visual but need not be – blind people can understand raised line drawings by touch (Kennedy 1993, Lopes 1997).

Perceptual recognition is a crucial skill for sophisticated cognizers, especially those who must accomplish complex social interchanges requiring them to identify places, objects, and other creatures as ones previously encountered. But objects change over time and one function of recognition is to identify objects despite these changes. Psychologists typically assume that recognition requires constancy, so that objects are recognized in virtue of some features that do not change. But a second office of recognition is the identification of objects as changed. Of course, recognition has limits and not everything remains recognizable in the face of any change. Moreover, recognition has a structure. The ability to recognize an object is relative to different kinds of change. Thus faces can be recognized as they age and objects can be recognized from different distances and viewing angles.

The recognition theory proposes that depiction depends on the exercise of the same kinds of abilities as are involved in the recognition of objects in the flesh. To put the point in psychological terms, pictorial recognition involves some of the same processing as implements recognizing objects face-to-face. Of course, something needs to be said about which processes overlap pictorial and face-to-face recognition. The processes do not overlap entirely because we do not normally recognize figure 10.4 as a dog (we see that it is only a picture); and yet there is more overlap than their involving the same sense organs and basic perceptual processing.

The ability to work out what pictures depict covaries with the ability to recognize their depicta in the flesh. There are two points here. The first is that being able to recognize an object O in the flesh is necessary and sufficient (assuming general competence with pictures of the same kind) for understanding a picture of an O. More importantly, if Lauren Bacall's face can be recognized when aged, or the Statue of Liberty when seen from above, then a picture can be understood as depicting Bacall's aged face or the Statue of Liberty from above. Competence in understanding pictures tracks the structure of recognitional competence.

The difference between pictorial and face-to-face recognition is that the former is typically triggered by a flat, marked surface. This is crucial: when a picture triggers the ability to recognize the Statue of Liberty, that recognition ability has been stretched to include recognizing the statue as it appears in two dimensions. Thus a massive failure to understand depictions (as seen in some mammals) is a failure to recognize objects when they appear in two dimensions.

The overlap in processing that underlies pictorial and face-to-face recognition is just that needed to explain these three facts about pictorial competence: that understanding a picture of an O tracks a recognitional capacity for Os, that understanding a picture of an O in different guises tracks the ability to recognize Os in those guises, and that understanding a picture of an O entails the ability to recognize Os appearing, as it were, two-dimensionally. Exactly what commonalities and differences in processing explain these facts is a matter for psychologists and brain scientists to seek out.

170   **Dominic McIver Lopes**

Nothing in the recognition theory entails that the two-dimensional properties of a picture surface correspond to three-dimensional properties of the depicted scene by any relation that preserves outline shape. Since it is contingent what marked surfaces trigger what recognition abilities, many differently marked picture surfaces could trigger the same recognition ability. Figure 10.1 depicts a cube if it triggers an ability to recognize a cube seen as a cube (and was made with an intention to trigger such an ability). There is no need to say either that it really depicts a generic hexahedron or that it is really experienced as resembling a cube in outline shape. It depicts a cube looking one of the ways a cube looks when it is depicted.

Defending the Recognition Theory

One may object off the bat that the theory is not an account of *depictive* content determination. After all, why not say that figure 10.1 represents a cube and does not depict one? Granted, it represents a cube because it can trigger the capacity of a certain kind of perceiver to recognize cubes, but it may be that there is more than this to depicting a cube – perhaps experienced resemblance in outline shape is also required. The recognition theory is not a theory of depiction unless it explains what pictures depict and not merely what they represent.

An adequate reply to this objection must establish a conceptual connection between recognition and depiction; it must show how the content of pictures that is grasped via recognition is depictive content. A good place to look for the resources to construct such a reply is in the nature of pictures. Pictures are essentially two-dimensional representations of three-dimensional scenes and it is this fact that must be connected to pictorial recognition. Note, by way of comparison, that EROS is a viable theory of depiction partly because it requires that a two-dimensional surface be experienced as resembling the three-dimensional object that is depicted. Likewise, pictorial recognition (unlike face-to-face recognition) is always the triggering by a two-dimensional surface of an ability to recognize a three-dimensional object. A flat surface triggers such a capacity only when the capacity to recognize the object has been extended so as to enable recognizing the object when it appears two-dimensionally. Thus pictorial recognition never occurs except by the mediation of a two-dimensional surface: such a surface must be perceived. But we can say more. Since there are many ways to transform three-dimensional spatial information into two dimensions, the recognition theory explains why there are many ways to depict a three-dimensional object. It thereby forges an essential link between depictive representation and pictorial flatness.

It follows that pictures do not depict two-dimensional objects when they represent them as two-dimensional. Thus there are three ways a picture may fail to depict. It may not represent anything at all (e.g., Jackson Pollock's drips). Alternatively, it may represent something that it does not depict (e.g., the bits of text in some of Barbara Kruger's images represent linguistically, not depictively). Finally, a picture may fail to depict because it *is* its subject. Jasper Johns's target, flag, and map paintings do not represent targets, flags, or maps because they *are* targets, flags, and maps. The art historian Saul Steinberg writes that,

Under the enormous literal representation of an unmistakable pipe Magritte wrote *Ceci n'est pas une pipe*. And to the puzzled spectator who mistakes image for reality, he would have said – "Try to smoke it." Johns's images do not seek this immunity of the unreal. You can't smoke Magritte's painted pipe, but you could throw a dart at a Johns target, or use his painted alphabets for testing myopia (Steinberg 1972: 41–2).

A picture does not depict O if it is an O (see Danto 1981).

A second consequence for the recognition theory of the essential link between depictive representation and pictorial flatness is that the theory endorses a form of twofoldness. The reason some experiences of pictures are twofold is that the experiences are generated by simultaneous perception of the flat picture surface and the triggering of a perceptual ability to recognize a three-dimensional object. Indeed, the three-dimensional object is recognized in a two-dimensional guise. But the theory does not entail that encounters with pictures are *invariably* twofold. As a result, the domain of pictures encompasses *trompe-l'œil* representation, whose surfaces are sometimes not objects of awareness. (*Trompe-l'œil* representation is not depictive, according to EROS, since it involves no experienced picture–object similarity.)

It is easy to see that the recognition theory accommodates the distinction between depiction and sculptural representation. Whereas sculptural recognition only requires the triggering of an ability to recognize the represented object in three dimensions, pictorial recognition involves the triggering of an ability to recognize the represented object seen two-dimensionally. We can also distinguish still from moving pictures, for an ability to recognize an object represented in a still format is not identical to an ability to recognize it in motion.

While the principal aim of the recognition theory is to say what determines depictive content – or to explain what pictures depict what objects – it would be helpful were the recognition theory also to explain Hopkins's six cardinal facts about pictures. First, there is no bare depiction of particulars and this is because objects are recognized on the basis of their appearance (see Hopkins 2003b, Lopes 2003). Second, all depiction is from a point of view because objects are recognized only relative to a viewpoint. Having said that, "point of view" should be interpreted loosely, for an object may be recognizable even when so rendered in two dimensions that the point of view is indeterminate or multiple, as in East Asian "roving eye" painting or analytic cubism. The third fact is that only what can be perceived (Hopkins says "seen") can be depicted and this is because depiction depends on recognition, which is a component of perception. Fourth, there are limits to misrepresentation. The reason is that there are limits to recognition (though they are less restrictive than EROS implies). Misrecognition entails misrepresentation – a picture triggering a recognition ability for a raven can only misrepresent a dove. Finally, the recognition theory explicitly sets out to explain the final two cardinal facts about pictorial competence, namely that understanding a picture entails knowledge of what the depicted object looks like, and little more than this knowledge (plus familiarity with depiction in general) is needed to understand a picture. The knowledge in question consists in possessing a recognitional capacity for the depicted object.

Dominic McIver Lopes

Suppose that the recognition theory survives the main objections to it and that it explains the six cardinal facts about pictures. In that case, we are warranted in judging the recognition theory on a par with EROS. Have we any reason to prefer it?

The recognition theory makes sense of depiction occupying a larger domain than is envisaged on the conception of depiction embodied in EROS. Many pictures that according to EROS either misdepict or are imprecise are allowed on the recognition theory to be perfectly accurate, precise depictions. On EROS, central cases of depiction comprise only pictures that are experienced as matching their depicta in outline shape; all others are marginal. By contrast, the recognition theory counts among central cases of depiction many pictures in nonstandard projection systems, cubist pictures, and otherwise stylized pictures. The margin continues to be occupied by pictures that misrepresent or are imprecise but whole modes of representation are not consigned to the realm of misrepresentation and imprecision. The recognition theory welcomes this variety because recognition is a capacity for seeing sameness in difference: the same object is generally recognized in different guises.

How does this give the recognition theory an advantage over its competition? Answering this question, we revisit the two replies to the cases of The Box and The Shadow (figs. 10.1 and 10.3). One reply accepts the conception of depiction as occupying the larger domain but insists that all pictures within that domain are experienced as resembling their depicta in outline shape – even, perhaps, a Japanese scroll painting, Cézanne's fruit, and Picasso's cubist paintings. We saw that the trouble with this is that it begs the question of depictive content determination. Now a remedy to this trouble comes into sight. Why not conjoin EROS as an explanation of the six cardinal facts with the recognition theory as an explanation of depictive content determination? Why not allow the mechanism of recognition to explain what pictures depict and allow EROS to explain what it is for the contents determined by recognition to be depictive? Unfortunately this remedy has unacceptable side effects, for it implies that we do not have privileged access to the contents of our experience. It implies, for example, that you experience figure 10.1 as resembling a cube in outline shape despite your avowals that this is not how you experience it (especially after you compare it to fig. 10.2a). The only reason to swallow this bitter pill is that it is necessary to explain the six cardinal facts about pictures; but so, we have supposed, does the recognition theory.

The second reply to The Box and The Shadow has defenders of EROS stick to their guns, insisting that the conception of depiction as occupying a narrow domain is the correct one. That it is counterintuitive shows only that our intuitions need revision. This is to take a stand fundamentally at odds with the recognition theory. Perhaps the best way to decide what side to take is to consider what purposes a conception of depiction is meant to serve, so as to identify which conception of depiction, as occupying a narrow or a broad domain, serves us better. We should then prefer the theory that is twinned with the better conception of depiction given our needs. Hopkins rightly observes that pictures are communicative tools. "Depiction" is a concept picking out a mode of communication and if depictive communication requires experiencing picture–object outline shape resemblance, then EROS is preferable. But depiction in the absence of this experienced resemblance serves the needs of communication at least as well and probably better. Figure 10.1, for example, if it

The Domain of Depiction

depicts a cube, also communicates in a clear manner that its sides are parallel, and this can be useful in some contexts, especially technical ones (see Lopes 2004).

The concept of depiction also does service in other domains. One is critical judgment, for pictures are valued objects. It is a rule of critical judgment that to value an artwork as an artwork is to value it for the kind of thing that it is (Walton 1970). Thus the proper evaluation of depictive pictures must acknowledge the value that accrues to them in so far as they depict. The concept of depiction that is relevant here may favor EROS or the recognition theory, or neither. Philosophers interested in depiction should start to think about pictures as objects valued as depictions (see Schier 1993, Hopkins 1997, Lopes 2005).

Dominic McIver Lopes

References for Chapters 9 and 10

Alberti, L. B. ([1435–6] 1966). *On Painting*, trans. John R. Spencer. New Haven, CT: Yale University Press.

Danto, A. C. (1981). *Transfiguration of the Commonplace*. Cambridge, MA: Harvard University Press.

Gombrich, E. H. (1961). *Art and Illusion*, 2nd edn. Princeton, NJ: Princeton University Press.

Goodman, N. (1976). *Languages of Art*, 2nd edn. Indianapolis: Hackett.

Goodman, N. and Elgin, C. (1988). *Reconceptions in Philosophy and Other Arts and Sciences*. London: Routledge

Hopkins, R. (1997). "Pictures and Beauty." *Proceedings of the Aristotelian Society*, 42: 177–94.

Hopkins, R. (1998). *Picture, Image and Experience*. Cambridge, UK: Cambridge University Press.

Hopkins, R. (2000). "Touching Pictures." *British Journal of Aesthetics*, 40: 149–67.

Hopkins, R. (2003a). "Perspective, Convention and Compromise." In M. Atherton, R. Schwartz, and H. Hecht (eds.), *Reconceiving Pictorial Space* (pp. 145–65). Cambridge, MA: MIT Press.

Hopkins, R. (2003b). "Pictures, Phenomenology and Cognitive Science." *Monist*, 86: 653–75.

Kennedy, J. M. (1993). *Drawing and the Blind: Pictures to Touch*. New Haven, CT: Yale University Press.

Lopes, D. M. (1996). *Understanding Pictures*. Oxford: Oxford University Press.

Lopes, D. M. (1997). "Art Media and the Sense Modalities: Tactile Pictures." *Philosophical Quarterly*, 47: 425–40.

Lopes, D. M. (2003). "Pictures and the Representational Mind." *Monist*, 86: 35–52.

Lopes, D. M. (2004). "Directive Pictures," *Journal of Aesthetics and Art Criticism*, 63: 189–96.

Lopes, D. M. (2005). *Sight and Sensibility: Evaluating Pictures*. Oxford: Oxford University Press.

Reid, T. ([1764] 1997). *Inquiry into the Human Mind*, ed. Derek R. Brookes. Edinburgh and University Park: Edinburgh University Press and Pennsylvania State University Press.

Schier, F. (1986). *Deeper Into Pictures*. Cambridge, UK: Cambridge University Press.

Schier, F. (1993). "Van Gogh's Boots: The Claims of Representation." In D. Knowles and J. Skorupski (eds.), *Virtue and Taste* (pp. 176–99). Oxford: Blackwell.

Steinberg, L. (1972). *Other Criteria*. Oxford: Oxford University Press.

Walton, K. (1970). "Categories of Art." *Philosophical Review*, 79: 334–67.

Wollheim, R. (1980). *Art and Its Objects*, 2nd edn. Cambridge, UK: Cambridge University Press.

Wollheim, R. (1987). *Painting as an Art*. London and New York: Thames and Hudson.

Further Reading for Chapters 9 and 10

Budd, M. (1992). "On Looking at a Picture." In J. Hopkins and A. Savile (eds.), *Psychoanalysis, Mind and Art* (pp. 259–80). Oxford: Blackwell.

Budd, M. (1993). "How Pictures Look." In D. Knowles and J. Skorupski (eds.), *Virtues and Taste: Essays on Politics, Ethics and Aesthetics* (pp. 154–75). Oxford: Blackwell.

Gombrich, E. (1977). *Art and Illusion*, 5th edn. Oxford: Phaidon.

Hopkins, R. (1997). "El Greco's Eyesight: Interpreting Pictures and the Psychology of Vision." *Philosophical Quarterly*, 47 (189): 441–58.

Peacocke, C. (1983). *Sense and Content*. Oxford: Clarendon Press.

Peacocke, C. (1987). "Depiction." *Philosophical Review* 96: 383–410.

Walton, K. (1990). *Mimesis as Make-Believe*. Cambridge, MA: Harvard University Press.

Willats, D. (2000). *Art and Representation*. Cambridge, MA: Harvard University Press.

WHAT CONSTITUTES
ARTISTIC EXPRESSION?

Artistic Expression and the Hard Case of Pure Music

Stephen Davies

In its narrative, dramatic, and representational genres, art regularly depicts contexts for human emotions and their expressions. It is not surprising, then, that these art-forms are often about emotional experiences and displays, and that they are also concerned with the expression of emotion. What is more interesting is that abstract art genres may also include examples that are highly expressive of human emotion. Pure music – that is, stand-alone music played on musical instruments excluding the human voice, and without words, literary titles, or associated texts connected to it by its composer – is often characterized as the expressive art *par excellence*. Yet how could that be possible, given that such music lacks semantic or representational content? Pure music presents the hardest and most vivid philosophical challenge to any account of expressiveness in the arts, which is why it is crucial to consider the musical case for the light it sheds on the underlying principles and issues.

In this chapter I consider two accounts of expressiveness in pure music. Both regard expressiveness as an objective property of such music. I argue for the position I call *appearance emotionalism* and against the alternative, which I label *hypothetical emotionalism*. But before I get to that, there is a different mode of musical expression to be acknowledged.

Even instrumental music comes charged with associations. Some of these are private to the listener, but many are widely shared. The latter may be included in a piece by accident but are, more often, deliberately placed for their effects. For instance, when a song is quoted in an instrumental work, its title or words may be brought to mind. Certain melodies (e.g., "Ode to Joy"), styles (e.g., tarantella), idioms (e.g., fanfares), forms (e.g., minuet), modalities (e.g., church modes), and instruments (e.g., fifes and snare drums) recall particular social events, geocultural regions, historical periods, ideas, and sensibilities, and in this way can hook up with affective life-experiences.

Though it is music's associative ties that are likely to be referred to when most people are asked about music's significance, philosophers say little about them. The reason for this neglect is straightforward: the mechanisms and results of association are not philosophically puzzling. There is a form of musical expressiveness, however, that is so. After taking into account the contribution to the expressiveness of pure instrumental music made by association, a significant residue remains. I observed before that the expressiveness of such music is not semantic or representational; now we can add that nor is it all associative. The crucial question remains: how can music express emotion when it is abstract and insentient?

Appearance Emotionalism

Appearance emotionalism maintains that the expressiveness of a piece of music is an objective and literally possessed but response-dependent property of that piece.

By calling it response-*dependent* I mean it is the concept it is in virtue of its ability to produce a certain characteristic response in creatures of an appropriate kind under suitable conditions. We might think of response-dependent properties as powers things have to produce certain kinds of responses, including experiences. Green, as a color, is available only to those creatures that experience light-reflecting objects as colored and that are motivated to respond to color discriminations. And to turn to a typical musical example, the pitch of a note is a response-dependent property of that note; it is its causal power to generate an experience of pitchness. More generally, the relevant response in the case of musical concepts, such as ones of expressiveness or sadness in music, is a kind of experience of auditory phenomena.

Cats can hear sounds falling within the same range as humans, but they show no signs of hearing music as such; they do not hear the music in the noise it makes. So, what is the difference between experiencing music as sound and as music? People who hear music as such hear it as organized. They can recognize where a melody begins and ends and when it is repeated or varied; they can experience the difference between the music's coming to a close and its being halted or interrupted before its end; they can often predict how a phrase will continue or a chord resolve; they can frequently tell accidental mistakes from unexpected but correct continuations; and so on. These are ways they *experience* the music. Whether or not they can describe these differences in technical terms is another matter. The majority of listeners are ignorant of the technical vocabulary familiar to musicians, composers, and theorists.

Even if the acoustic properties of sounds are governed by natural laws, the ways music can be organized vary from time to time and place to place, so the experience of music includes an inescapable cultural component. Most musics are based on pitch scales and all pitch scales may treat octaves as equivalents, but after that, many ways of dividing up the available scale space have been adopted. (For a list of 2,900 scales, see <http://www.xs4all.nl/~huygensf/scala/downloads.html>.) The same goes for all of music's dimensions. Musics can differ so markedly from society to society that they are transparent only to the culturally initiated, but I see no reason to think it impossible for outsiders to learn and adjust to the music of another culture.

When we move to the more specific case in which the listener recognizes the music's expressive qualities, another dimension of cultural difference can come into play. For many cognitively rich emotions, differences in the prevailing beliefs, desires, and attitudes affect when and how often they are elicited and how they might be displayed. And even with the most basic emotions, cultures vary as regards both the situations in which they might be engendered and the propriety of giving expression to them. If death is viewed as a time of loss and extinction, it will be an occasion for sadness, but if it marks a passage from the pain of earthly life to a more enjoyable spiritual existence, it may be greeted with happiness. So the capacities on which the appropriate response to expressiveness in music depend include ones concerned with recognizing contexts and behaviors appropriate to various emotional experiences and displays for the culture and period in which the music finds its home.

So much for the dependence, what of the response? What form does it take when what is experienced is music's expressiveness? I believe it is an experience of resemblance between the music and the realm of human emotion.

Several elements within the human sphere are candidates for that side of the resemblance relation: the phenomenological profile of inner experiences of emotion, expressive qualities of the voice, emotion-relevant facial expressions, and other bodily behaviors through which emotions are given outward expression. As examples of the first view, Langer (1942) argues that the forms of music are iconic maps of the structure of feelings, and Budd (1995) suggests that music mimics the sensational pattern of emotions. I doubt, however, that emotions can be individuated in terms of their structural or phenomenological profiles. A single emotion can present different mixes or orderings of sensation and feeling on different occasions, and contrasting emotions can often share a similar outline. Meanwhile, while we are prone to recognize human faces bearing emotionally suggestive expressions in many nonhuman objects, such as the facades of houses, the fronts of cars, and the faces of basset hounds, I do not think we experience music as wearing a smiling or frowning face. A crucial aspect of our experience of music is that of its temporal unfolding, whereas the expression worn on a face comes as an atemporally structured gestalt.

As for the voice, if the similarity is supposed to lie in timbre and inflection, I am skeptical. The saxophone can sound similar, and toing and froing between duetting instruments can be very like a dialogue, but in general, the whoops, whines, bawls, wails, groans, cries, shrieks, moans, grunts, screeches, and whimpers with which emotions are vocalized strike me as very unlike the sound of expressive music. More suggestive, though, are studies showing that the distinctive prosodic contours of specific emotions can be recreated musically (Juslin 2001). The voice and music are more alike in dynamic structure, articulation, pitch, intensity, and periodicity of phrase lengths and shapes than in timbre or inflection as such. It is also instructive to recall that European composers in the eighteenth century went to considerable lengths to pattern their music according to the rules and figures of vocal rhetoric (Neubauer 1986), though I suspect this process depends more on conventional stipulations than iconic similarity.

The resemblance that counts most for musical expressiveness, I believe, is that between music's temporally unfolding dynamic structure and configurations of human behavior associated with the expression of emotion (Davies 1994). We experience movement in music – in terms of progress from high to low or fast to slow, say, but as well in the multistranded waxing and waning of tensions generated variously within the harmony, the mode of articulation and phrasing, subtle nuances of timing, the delay or defeat of expected continuations, and so on. Moreover, this movement is like human behavior in that it seems purposeful and goal-directed. There are expositions, developments, and recapitulations, not merely succession; there is closure, not merely stopping. As a result, we expect to be able to account for what happens subsequently in terms of what went before, even where what will happen later is not easily predicted. To put the point as pithily as possible, the course of music usually makes sense, as is also the case typically with the activities of human agents.

More particularly, I think music is expressive in recalling the gait, attitude, air, carriage, posture, and comportment of the human body. Just as someone who is stooped over, dragging, faltering, subdued, and slow in his or her movements cuts a sad figure, so music that is slow, quiet, with heavy or thick harmonic bass textures, with underlying patterns of unresolved tension, with dark timbres, and a recurrently downward impetus sounds sad. Just as someone who skips and leaps quickly and lightly, makes expansive gestures, and so on, has a happy bearing, so music with a similar vivacity and exuberance is happy sounding.

Critics of appearance emotionalism deny that the movement of music exactly resembles human behavior. The claim of appearance emotionalism is that they are similar in only one crucial respect, however, not that they are indistinguishable. And to the person who points out that movement within music resembles the movements of clouds as closely as it resembles human expressive behavior, so that the similarity cannot *explain* why we hear the music as expressive (Matravers 1998), there is this reply: the connection is given in the *experience* of similarity, not in some absolute measure of verisimilitude. Resemblance is a symmetrical relation, but we do not find all resemblances salient or reversible. We are likely to be struck more by the way weeping willows resemble downcast people than by the way they resemble frozen waterfalls, even if the latter similarity is closer in many elements than is the former. And we are less inclined to see people as tree-like than to see trees as presenting a human aspect, though the resemblance is equal and symmetrical between these possibilities. Our interests shape how we see the world, thereby making some resemblances more salient than others and giving them the direction they take. For our social species, openness to the minds and hearts of others is vital, so that it becomes an attitude we adopt unthinkingly toward the world at large. Accordingly, we experience many things, events, and processes as similar to aspects of human experience, thought, and behavior. So it is with music, I claim. It is expressive because we experience it as possessing a dynamic character relating it to humanly expressive behavior.

Given the emphasis on the way the music is experienced, where is the warrant for claiming that expressiveness is an *objective* property of the music? In answering this question, it is important not to mistake the subjective/objective distinction for the independent-of-human-experience/dependent-on-human-experience one. Musical expressiveness is response-dependent, I have allowed, but this does not mean it is subjective in the sense of being personal, idiosyncratic, and nonobjective. To hold that expressiveness is an objective property of music is to assume that, among qualified listeners who attend to it under appropriate conditions, there is considerable agreement in the emotion-terms with which they describe the music's expressive character.

Stephen Davies

This last is an empirical claim. Is it true? How one answers may depend on the degree of expressive specificity one expects to find. At the level of fine-grained discriminations between emotions, according to which grief, sadness, despair, depression, misery, sorrow, and despondency are distinct, there appears to be only a low level of agreement, but if these are classed as falling under a single generic emotion, the level of interpersonal agreement is high (Gabrielsson 2002). My claim is that music is capable of expressing a fairly limited number of emotional types, but that it can express these objectively, so that suitable skilled and situated listeners agree highly in attributing them to the music.

Which emotional types are these and why is their number restricted? Only a limited range of emotional types can be individuated solely on the basis of observed bodily comportment (where the face cannot be seen and nothing is known about the context of action). Music is expressive because it is experienced as resembling such behaviors, and it can express only the emotion types that they do. Sadness and happiness are the leading candidates, along with timidity and anger. Swaggering arrogance, the mechanical rigidity that goes with repression and alienation from the physicality of existence, ethereal dreaminess, and sassy sexuality are further possibilities.

Still, since music is nonsentient and only sentient creatures can be literally sad or happy, in what sense does music *literally* possess its expressive properties? Human bodily attitudes have an expressive character even in those cases where the owners of those bodies do not feel as they look. When we say someone "cuts a sad figure," we are referring to the look of the person, not to how he or she feels. Admittedly, this secondary use of the word "sad" is a natural extension from the primary one, because behavior that in one context produces an expressive appearance, without regard to how the person feels, in another gives direct, primary expression to the person's felt emotion. Though connected, these uses are distinct. The same secondary use applies to music when it is experienced as generating appearances of expressiveness like those presented by the carriage and deportment of the human body.

Though I have just described the predication of terms such as "sad" to attitudes of the human body and to music as involving a secondary use, this does not entail the further claim that such attributions are metaphoric. Secondary uses can be literal. Live metaphors are not listed in dictionaries, but I note that the *Concise Oxford Dictionary* gives among the meanings of "expression," "a person's facial appearance or intonation of voice, esp. as indicating feeling; depiction of feeling, movement, etc., in art; conveying of feeling in the performance of music." To say of a face or body that it looks sad, independently of what its "owner" may feel, is to use the word "sad" literally. The same applies when we call the sound of music sad.

Let me outline some advantages of appearance emotionalism. It does not lose the connection between music's expressive character and the human world of emotional expression, whereas this is a crucial fault in theories analyzing music's expressiveness reductively in terms of technically described musical events and processes, or that characterize music's expressiveness as belonging to a distinctive genus unconnected from the realm of human experience. And it explains how music can be objectively and literally expressive, which is preferable to theories (as in Goodman 1968, Scruton 1997) purportedly analyzing musical expressiveness as metaphoric and then not explaining what this means. Given that metaphor is a figure of speech, what is to be understood by the claim that the *music* is metaphorically sad? Declining to take the analysis further amounts to a refusal to engage with the philosophical problem that is the subject of the debate.

Appearance emotionalism has the advantage also over theories that account for music's expressiveness as involving a mediated process of abstract symbolization or indirect representation; namely, it provides, as such accounts do not, for the phenomenal vivacity with which we experience expressiveness in music. We encounter music's expressiveness fully frontally. The listener's awareness of the music's expressiveness is more like a direct confrontation with, say, a sad-looking person than like an experience of reading or hearing a description of such a person. Appearance emotionalism, because it is grounded in perceptually revealed experiences of similarity, has the quality of immediate access that is so phenomenologically distinctive of the outward show of emotions in humans, other animals, and music.

Appearance Emotionalism: Criticisms and Replies

Despite the advantages just listed, appearance emotionalism has its critics. In this section I elaborate and develop the theory by considering some objections it faces.

If an emotion is expressed only if it is shown by someone who *feels* it, then appearance emotionalism does not involve the expression of emotion (Stecker 1999) since, by its own account, the appearance stands to no feeling as its direct expression. There is the *presentation* of the *appearance* of an emotion but not the *expression* of an *occurrent* emotion. And this is embarrassing since the theory is offered as explaining the expression of emotion in music.

What is needed by way of answer is clarification of the relation between the music's expressive character and the composer's or performer's intentions and emotions. This much must be conceded at the outset: it is possible for the music to present an expressive aspect without this being intended by its composer or performer. The music's expressive appearance depends on other of its objective qualities and need not be consciously contrived or depend on the composer's or performer's feelings. Nevertheless, the music's expressive character is usually intended by its creator, and the performer aims to deliver and refine that expressive character. Where this is so, it is appropriate to talk about the expression of emotion in the music. We commonly mean by "expression" that a given content has been intentionally created and communicated. Moreover, this first kind of expression or communication does often connect to emotional experiences undergone by the composer or performer. For instance, composers who feel sad and who wish to express this may intentionally write music with an expressiveness that matches their own feeling. The resulting composition is not a direct or primary expression of the composer's sadness; it is unlike the tears to which composers give way under the force of their feelings. Instead, composers intentionally appropriate the music's expressive potential (which it has independently of how they feel) in order to have it correspond to their emotions. The composer is like those who show how they feel not in the usual fashion but by pointing to the mask of tragedy, or, more dramatically, by taking it up and wearing it. This manner of dis-

Stephen Davies

playing emotion is more sophisticated than primary, direct ventings. Nevertheless, it falls easily and naturally under the notion of expression.

In brief: while appearance emotionalism is not automatically associated with acts of expression, in the musical case this connection is frequent because musical works and performances are designed to have most of their salient properties, including their emotion-resembling ones. So long as it is deliberately created, the appearance of emotion presented in the music is the result of an act of expression (in the sense of "expression" that is synonymous with "communication"). Moreover, when the composer or performer does match the music's expressive tone to his or her own feelings in order to display those feelings indirectly, the feelings are expressed in the music. Appearance emotionalism does not sever the presentation of emotional appearances from genuine expression via the acts of the composer and performer.

Another possible criticism observes that music can express only a severely restricted palette of emotions according to appearance emotionalism, whereas it is often praised for the richness and ineffable subtlety of the expressive appearances it can present.

The replies to this objection come in a number of forms. The first ones try to duck the bullet. Even if pure instrumental music is limited with respect to the range of emotions it can present, music with words and the rest can express the full gamut by linking complex contexts for feeling with the cognitive and attitudinal states of the characters represented within it. Moreover, in the case of pure instrumental music there is the possibility of ordering successive emotional appearances in ways suggestive of subtler or more complex states. Where deep sadness gives way gradually to joy and abandonment, it may be reasonable to regard the transition as consistent with acceptance and resolution. As well, it is important to recall the variety that can be imposed on the more general frame of the work's expressive profile via the performer's interpretation of the piece. Performers control many fine shades of phrasing, timing, dynamics, and articulation, and these features play a highly important expressive role within the performance. There is no inconsistency in maintaining both that the expressive scope of musical works is limited and that there is huge diversity and plasticity in the manner in which this expressive schema can be elaborated (or contradicted, or undermined) in the course of its realization in performance.

Other replies seek to bite the bullet by acknowledging music's limited expressive powers and by rejecting claims for its ineffable subtlety. As was observed at the outset, if expressiveness is to be predicable of the music, there must be a wide coincidence in judgments of expressiveness by suitably qualified listeners under appropriate conditions. It is only with respect to broad categories of emotion – happiness versus sadness, for instance – that this consensus is achieved. This is not to deny the importance and interest of the idiosyncratic responses of the individual (Koopman and Davies 2001), but it is to suggest that these are more revealing of the person who has them than of the music itself.

A further observation might help clarify what is at issue. Appearance emotionalists do not deny that there is an astonishing subtlety and multiplicity in the expressiveness of musical works. They claim, however, that this nuanced variety applies to the manner of musical expression, not to the identities of the emotions thereby presented (Davies 1999). It is fallacious to reason from the fact that differing musical works are each expressive to the conclusion that each work therefore must express a different emotion; and it compounds the fallacy to infer that the differences between these emotions are ineffable simply because we cannot agree on the emotion terms that would capture their distinctness. Of course it is true that the expression of sadness in the funeral march in Beethoven's Third Symphony is not the same as that in the slow movement of Mahler's Fifth, but this is not because each expresses some emotion other than sadness in general. And if we find it hard to think of qualifying terms that capture how the two movements differ, this may be because it is the wrong type of description that is being sought. These works differ in the musical specifics by which each expresses the same general emotion. To capture the difference, it is not necessary to qualify *what* is expressed but, instead, to describe *how* the musical means for bringing about this result diverge in their detail. The difference, to put it bluntly, lies in the notes and how they work together, not in the identity of the emotion that gets presented.

The last of the objections I consider argues that appearance emotionalism cannot account adequately for the emotional responses music's expressiveness elicits from the listener. The objection can be presented as a dilemma: given the tenets of appearance emotionalism, either the listener has no basis for an emotional response to the music's expressiveness or the response is an inappropriate one. The first horn of the dilemma can be developed this way: while we have every reason to respond to others' emotions and feelings, mere appearances of emotion, recognized as such, give us no basis for an emotional response. We are not deeply moved by the sight of weeping willows, even if their bearing strikes us as sad looking, precisely because their appearance does not signal that any sentient being is suffering. And the second horn notes that, even if listeners do respond, for instance by mirroring what the music expresses, the music is not the object of their response, since they do not believe (or imagine) that it has the emotion-relevant qualities that are required. If sad music makes us feel sad, we are not sad *about* the music because we do not believe that it suffers or that its expressiveness is somehow unfortunate or regrettable. But in that case, our response is not of the standard, cognitively informed and directed kind, and it is thereby not a response about the music as such (Kivy 1999).

Kivy (1990) would take on the dilemma's first horn. He denies that sad music makes listeners feel sad, or that happy music can cheer them, unless they are pathological. When listeners report such things, their self-reports are mistaken. Kivy does not deny, however, that listeners can be intensely moved by music. They experience emotions for which the music is an appropriate object. They are moved to awe and delight by the music's beauty, to admiration by the composer's skill and ingenuity, to disappointment by the performer's ineptitude.

Kivy is correct, of course, in holding that music is a source of many responses for which it becomes a proper object by satisfying beliefs relevant to those responses. I am reluctant, however, to follow him in his assertion that listeners are never moved to respond to music's expressiveness with echoing emotions. It would be very surprising if their self-reports were systematically mistaken. As well as personal and anecdotal evidence for the kind of emotional osmosis the existence of which Kivy denies, there is experimental data in support of it, both as regards catching the mood of other people (Hatfield, Cacioppo, and Rapson 1994) and of music's producing mirroring reactions (Gabrielsson 2002). Some emotional responses can be generated through a kind of contagion, even in the absence of the cognitive and attitudinal elements that accompany them in the default or normal situation. I contend that music provides a case in point. It is far from inevitable that sad music calls forth a sad response, or happy music a happy one, but this happens frequently. It is not pathological for someone to choose a joyous musical work in the hope of sloughing off a depressed or sad mood.

This now leaves us facing the dilemma's second horn. Its first challenge, recall, is that the mirroring response to music's expressiveness is unacceptably aberrant. If the sadness we feel on hearing sad music is not about something we believe to be unfortunate and regrettable, it lacks the cognitive component essential to genuine sadness. A reply could suggest emotions lie on a continuum, rather than forming a unified, invariant class. At one end are emotions in which the cognitive elements are necessary, even dominant; examples would be envy and patriotism. Without the appropriate beliefs – for instance, that someone else has something I lack and desire, or that the action or quality I take to be admirable is attributable to my country – it cannot be envy or patriotism I feel. But at the other end are emotions in which the cognitive aspects are less important or sometimes are circumvented. They are likely to include emotions we share with nonhuman animals that lack our cognitive capacities. These emotions may be adaptively helpful precisely because of their "fast and frugal" nature. Given the power of emotions as triggers for action, when it is best to shoot first and ask questions later there may be an advantage to emotions that do not require cognitive appraisal of the situation and of the options it presents as a prerequisite to their motivating a response. Sadness, happiness, fear, and anger seem to be regarded as falling into this category by psychologists (such as Ekman 1992) who write of emotions as "affect programs" operating independently of cognition. But the claim need not be that sadness and happiness are always independent of the cognitive states of the person who experiences them, but merely that they may be so sometimes. In short: the mirroring response to music is aberrant only if one assumes inappropriately that cognition always plays a central or necessary role in emotional experience. Mirroring responses to music's expressiveness are clearly consistent with a broader view that rightly acknowledges the centrality of cognition for only some emotions or for only some contexts.

So far so good, but another problem seems to remain. If the sadness one feels on listening to sad music does not take the music or some other thing as its emotional object, then it is not about anything (Madell 2002). In that case, the response must be an objectless mood; it must be vague and undirected. As such, it might always be produced in some other way. It is only contingently related to the music and is bound to detract from concentration on it. The reply: it is true that the mirroring response does not take the music as its intentional or emotional object. The response is not *about* the music, and it does not involve believing (or make-believing) that there is something about the music's expressiveness that is unfortunate and regrettable. But this does not entail that the response is objectless, vague, and without any target. The music is the perceptual object and cause of the response. The response develops and unfolds as the music, which is its focus, does. What is important is not that the listener's response of sadness is *about* the music but that it is *to* the music and tracks the music's elaboration through time. A sad response that mirrors a sadness presented in the music's dynamic profile is locked on to the music in the way just described, even if that response is not also tied to the music via the usual kinds of sadness-relevant beliefs.

Hypothetical Emotionalism

The alternative to appearance emotionalism on which I concentrate here, hypothetical emotionalism, holds that what makes it true that the music expresses an emotion, E, is that a qualified listener imagines of the music that it presents a narrative or drama about a persona who experiences E. We hear music as presenting the life or experiences of a persona who is subject to various emotional events or episodes; and the music expresses these emotions because it has the power to lead us to imagine such things.

As a theory of musical expressiveness, hypothetical emotionalism is offered not merely as a heuristic that will facilitate the listener's perception of the music's expressiveness. More is claimed than that listeners might better recognize and appreciate the expressiveness of the work if they think of it as strings controlling the inner life of some human puppet. The hypothetical emotionalist is committed to this stronger position: it is a necessary condition for hearing the music's expressiveness that listeners imaginatively project into it a persona whose situation or inner life it then portrays. Levinson's formulation of hypothetical emotionalism makes this strong commitment explicit: "A passage of music P is expressive of an emotion or other psychic condition E *iff* [i.e., if and only if] P, in context, is readily and aptly heard by an appropriately backgrounded listener as the expression of E, in a sui generis, 'musical,' manner, by an indefinite agent, the music's persona" (Levinson 1996: 107).

Hypothetical emotionalism differs from appearance emotionalism about the conditions under which claims about music's expressiveness are true. In particular, these rival accounts disagree about the kind and content of the response that is called forth from "an appropriately backgrounded listener." In the one view, the listener is said to imagine a persona undergoing appropriate emotional vicissitudes; in the other, the listener is said to experience a similarity between music's dynamic pattern and human experiences that are expressive without regard to felt-emotions. At a more general level, the two theories are alike in that both regard musical expressiveness as an objective, response-dependent property possessed literally by the music. In consequence, hypothetical emotionalism can also claim the advantages I listed earlier as accruing to appearance emotionalism; namely, it preserves a connection between musical expressiveness and (imagined) human feeling; it does not characterize expressiveness as irreducibly and mysteriously metaphorical; and it explains how expressiveness is immediately present in the music. But are there any further advantages it claims over appearance emotionalism? There are two.

Hypothetical emotionalism is better suited to admit to the sphere of musical expression the full range of human emotions and experiences, including ones that normally presuppose a complex cognitive aspect. This is because the persona that is to be imagined is a human being, who has desires, beliefs, attitudes, and the rest. It should not be surprising, then, that hypothetical emotionalist have been keen to argue that music

Stephen Davies

is sometimes capable of expressing "higher," cognitively subtle and complex emotions, such as hope (Levinson 1990, Karl and Robinson 1997) and cheerful confidence turning to despair (Robinson 1998).

Second, hypothetical emotionalism might seem better situated to explain why the listener is sometimes moved to an emotional response, since the listener is confronted not merely with appearances displaying the characteristics of emotions but with a person who undergoes psychological states and experiences expressed via the music. Admittedly, hypothetical emotionalism is not yet clear of the woods, because the person to whom the listener reacts is a figment of the listener's imagination, and there are many well-known problems in trying to account for our reacting emotionally to stories about people we know not to exist. Still, whatever difficulties remain, it might be thought that fictional people inhabiting worlds spun from the material of musical works are closer to the human realm of feeling than are appearances of emotion transposed to an inanimate universe of pure sound.

The proponent of appearance emotionalism could dispute these claims for the greater plausibility or desirability of hypothetical emotionalism. In its fully developed form, appearance emotionalism allows rich and subtle expressive powers to extended, complex musical pieces. And it is highly questionable that the cognitively complex setting required by the hypothetical emotionalist in accounting for the listener's reaction to music comes closer to the psychological reality of that familiar experience than does the theory of emotional contagion or osmosis put forward by the appearance emotionalist. But let us bypass these debates in order to focus on the important one, which concerns the overall plausibility of hypothetical emotionalism as an account of music's expressiveness. I argue that it fails in its most central assumptions.

The most direct objection to hypothetical emotionalism asks how listeners know what to imagine when it comes to putting the persona they have envisaged through the relevant emotional hoops. If the music guides this process, then surely this means that the music is already successful in expressing the emotions that are to be grafted onto the persona's life? If I am to imagine that the persona is sad, won't this be only because I have already recognized expressions of sadness in the music? In that case, hypothetical emotionalism is both circular and redundant (Scruton 1997). Or on the other hand, if the music provides no guide to what is to be imagined, how can the content of that imagining be truly ascribed to the music as a property it possesses?

The hypothetical emotionalist can make this reply: the music does prompt and constrain what is to be imagined, but not by anticipating the expressive content that belongs to the music through the listener's imaginative engagement with it. Robinson (1998) develops the response: the music's dynamic tension causes in the listener sensations or feelings of being pushed, prodded, pulled, dragged, and stirred. These primitive responses are largely noncognitive. They fuel and direct the narrative that listeners construct about the experience of the persona they hypothesize as residing in the music. So it is true that listeners know what to imagine only on the basis of responses they have to the music, but it is not true that these responses are the emotions they go on to attribute to the imagined persona.

Though hypothetical emotionalism can dodge the charge of question-begging circularity, it faces two further major objections. The first simply doubts the empirical claim that all those who are qualified to predicate expressiveness to music do so on the basis of imagining a persona as subject to a narrative directed by the course of the music. The second denies that what is supplied by the music sufficiently controls what the listener may imagine, with the result that the process described by the theory should lead to an idiosyncratic medley of experiences, not to general agreement on the basis of which expressiveness could be attributed to the music. Of course, the hypothetical emotionalist is not committed to the implausible suggestion that everyone will independently imagine exactly the same when they give fictional life to a persona as they listen to the music. It is sufficient that they agree in their judgments about what the music expresses as a result of pursuing this imaginative process, even if each conjures up a distinctive scenario. Allowing this, the present criticism doubts that agreement in listeners' judgments about musical expressiveness could be explained by appeal to the control exercised by the music over what can be concluded on the basis of what is imagined.

The first objection is empirical. What goes on in people's heads as they listen attentively to music and correctly recognize its expressive character is very varied (DeNora 2000). Some may allow the music to direct their imaginings about the psychological experiences of a persona, but many who arrive at informed judgments about the music's expressiveness apparently do not imagine the things required by hypothetical emotionalism.

The second objection can be developed as follows: there is no constraint on the number of personas imagined as inhabiting a musical work. And there are innumerable coherent narratives about them that would coincide with and reflect the progress of the music. So long as these different narratives all license the same judgment about what the music expresses there need be no difficulty for hypothetical emotionalism, but there is no reason to suppose this will be the case. Where one persona bursts with joy, another might be imagined blowing his or her top; where one persona is pictured as growing increasingly despondent, a series of others might be envisioned as independently sad; where one persona overcomes fear to show courageous defiance, another moves from uncertainty to conviction, a third puts aside troubles and turns to something more positive, a fourth is gripped by a strange passion, a fifth first questions and then reaffirms his or her faith, a sixth reflects on the contrasting personalities of his or her children, and so on. These various stories do not fall under a single archetype and there is no basis for supposing that they will lead "readily and aptly," to use Levinson's words, to agreement concerning the music's expressive character. Music is too indefinite to dictate the content and form of such narratives so that they might issue in the sorts of intersubjectively congruent judgments that justify the view that music is objectively expressive of emotion (Davies 1997).

Conclusion

The assumption driving many theories of musical expressiveness is that there can be expressiveness only where there is an agent – the composer, the listener, or a persona imagined in the music – who feels emotion and displays this. I accept that composers sometimes express their emotions in the music they write, but they do so not by discharging their feelings through the act of composition but by appropriating and shaping an expressive potential already inherent in the musical materials on which they work. I allow also that listeners sometimes are moved to experience what they hear expressed in the music, but the music has its expressiveness independently of this reaction. As well, a listener might sometimes entertain the thought of a persona in the music, but I deny that the apprehension of musical expressiveness depends on such imaginings. For myself, the experience is one of hearing the music as possessing appearances of emotion, while regarding it as neither alive nor as haunted by a persona. The virtue of the account for which I have argued is that it makes sense of this experience, which I hope and believe is a common one. There is a familiar kind of expressiveness that pays no regard to experienced emotion, as when we find a face mask, or bodily bearing, or willow tree, or house front presenting an expressive appearance. Music is expressive in that way, and it is powerfully so because it is deliberately created to have the relevant properties.

What does this analysis contribute to our understanding of expressiveness in art more generally? First, it provides a basic model for understanding expressiveness in abstract genres of painting and image-making, sculpture, and dance. Also, it should draw attention to the fact that many works of art have an expressiveness of their own; they present an expressive point of view that cannot be predicated of the work's characters, narrator, creator, or performer. This is an easily overlooked but important fact about narrative and other representational artistic forms.

Musical Expressiveness as Hearability-as-expression

Jerrold Levinson

Expression and Expressiveness

As a number of philosophers have rightly underlined, expression is essentially a matter of something outward giving evidence of something inward. (See Tormey 1971, Vermazen 1986, Ridley 2003.) Otherwise put, expression is essentially the manifesting or externalizing of mind or psychology. The scope of expression is thus not, *pace* Goodman and others, properties in general, or properties metaphorically possessed, but rather psychological properties, those pertaining to the mental states of sentient creatures. For only those can be intelligibly expressed, whoever or whatever is doing the expressing. And this holds as well for expressiveness, which we can initially understand as the sort of expression that some objects, and perhaps most notably, musical works, manage to achieve, despite their not literally having inner lives. Exactly what sort of expression expressiveness amounts to will emerge as the argument proceeds. My discussion will focus on the case of musical expressiveness, but at a later point I also offer some reflections on artistic expressiveness in general.

Musical Expressiveness

I here defend an account of musical expressiveness elaborated in earlier papers (Levinson 1990, 1996, 2002), replying to certain objections it has elicited, and underlining its superiority to the most plausible competing accounts on offer. Crucial to the account is the idea that the expressiveness of music resides in the invitation that music extends to the listener to hear it as expression in the primary sense – that is, expression, by persons, of inner states through outer signs. Thus to hear music as expressive is to hear it as an instance of personal expression. Expressive music is music we are disposed to hear *as* expressing; that is what its expressiveness fundamentally consists in.

Since the primary vehicle of the expressing of states of mind – as opposed to articulate thoughts – is gesture, broadly understood, and since music is naturally assimilated to that kind of expressing, that means that we hear expressive music as gesturing of some sort, that we hear a sort of gesture in expressive music. Call this *musical gesture*. It is important to stress that though musical gesture is related to both the ordinary behavioral gestures connected to expression of states of mind and the specific performing gestures involved in the sounding of music, it is not equivalent to either of those. It is a matter, at base, of what we hear the music to be *doing*, in virtue, most importantly, of the *movement* we hear in music. (See Davies 1994 and Scruton 1997 for discussion of musical movement, and Scruton 1997 and Levinson 2002 for discussion of gesture in music.)

Summon up in your mind the opening of Brahms's First Symphony. You are ineluctably presented, in listening, with the image of someone in the throes of emotion, which emotion is being manifested to you, through what one might call musical gestures. You may perhaps not know, or be able to articulate, what emotion the agent heard in the music is in the grip of, but in the grip of it he is, and this is something you directly hear. It is as if an emotion is being expressed, in the most literal sense, though it is somehow happening through music.

The musical expression of states of mind – including emotions, feelings, attitudes, desires, and beliefs – must thus be modeled on the primary expression of such states by persons or human beings, whereby such states are revealed or evinced through behavior or other outward manifestation. In the case of emotions, the usual focus of musical expression, such manifestations include countenance, posture, bearing, demeanor, actions, gestures, and modifications of voice.

Naturally there are differences between human expression and musical expression. For one, music is not literally behavior, and musical gesture is not literal gesture. For another, expression in music is not the result of emotion experienced by the music, since music is not sentient, nor is it invariably the upshot of emotion experienced by the composer, since lived emotion and musically imagined emotion can readily diverge. But despite those evident differences between musical expression of emotion and human expression of emotion, we should not consider a piece of music to be strictly *expressive* of an emotion – rather than standing in some *other*, weaker, relation to it, such as possessing a perceptual quality associated with the emotion – unless we regard it as analogous to a being endowed with sentiments capable of announcing themselves in an external manner. In short, music expresses an emotion only to the extent that we are disposed to hear it as the expression of an emotion, albeit in a nonstandard manner, by a person or person-like entity.

More formally, what I propose as an analysis of expression in music goes something like this: a passage of music P is expressive of an emotion E if and only if P, in context, is readily heard, by a listener experienced in the genre in question, as an expression of E. Since expressing requires an expresser, this means that in so hearing the music the listener is in effect committed to hearing an agent in the music – what we can call the music's *persona* – or to at least imagining such an agent in a backgrounded manner. But this agent or persona, it must be stressed, is almost entirely

Musical Expressiveness as Hearability

indefinite, a sort of minimal person, characterized only by the emotion we hear it to be expressing and the musical gesture through which it does so. It is important to keep that in mind when reviewing skepticism as to whether understanding listeners normally hear or imagine personas when they apprehend expressiveness in music.

My basic analysis of musical expressiveness, again, is that music expressive of E is music heard as, or as if, someone expressing E. Of course one could fairly expand this as "music heard as, or as if, someone experiencing, and as a result expressing, E," since "A expresses E" presupposes "A experiences E." But it is presumably the expressing part alone that enters into what the music can intelligibly be heard as, since we can, it seems, have no idea what it would be to hear music or musical process, as if it, the music or musical process, were an experiencing of something.

It has been suggested, incidentally, that not all *expressions* are such that we think of their possessors or bearers as engaged in acts of *expressing*, in the sense of intentionally trying to communicate a state of mind (Vermazen 1986: 198–9). Since I analyze expressiveness in terms of as-if-expression, not as-if-expressing, then even if that suggestion is valid, it is immaterial for my account. The suggestion can, in any event, be challenged. For it can be argued, *pace* Vermazen, that all expressions ascribable to an agent in fact are cases of expressings by the agent. It is just that not all such expressions are cases of *intentional, self-conscious* expressing.

Earlier formulations of my proposal made appeal to the idea of a *sui generis* mode of expression of emotion, suggesting that music, when heard as expressing, was such a mode. But that idea may be an unfortunate one, and has attracted its share of criticism. Some commentators, for instance, have charged that there is something incoherent in the suggestion that one hears a passage of music as a *sui generis* expression of some emotion, on the grounds that we can form no conception of a mode of expression declared to be *sui generis* (Matravers 1998: 131, Eiholzer, quoted in Levinson 1996: 120); others have charged that the appeal to a *sui generis* mode of expression in connection with music implies that we experience music as a novel bodily means of sound production (Walton 1994: 56, Budd 1995: 132) or else as an odd creature that somehow behaves musically (Walton 1999: 435).

In light of these charges, it is probably a mistake to insist that the expression that music is heard as when its expressiveness is being perceived is *sui generis* expression, rather than just expression *tout court*. Little appears to be gained, and only confusion sowed, by that insistence. And yet the notion of a *sui generis* mode of expression, which the singularity of our experience of music as expressive suggests to us, may still have a role to play in the full explanation of musical expressiveness.

What should be avoided, it seems, is making the idea of a *sui generis* mode of expression part of the *content* of the hearing-as experience involved in registering music's expressiveness. After all, one might add, and not entirely unseriously, thinking in Latin can hardly be a prerequisite for the grasping of expression in music! The *sui generis*-ness, so to speak, if a valid intuition, will have to come in elsewhere.

Compare hearing the sound of train's wheels as a baby whining (but in an unusual, because regular and rhythmic, way), and hearing a stretch of music as an expression of sadness (but of an unusual, because noncorporeal and extraordinarily fluid, sort). Now, do the parentheticals in those cases give part of the content of the hearing-as experiences in question? Perhaps yes, if we view such contents as highly back-

Jerrold Levinson

grounded ones. But we might with more justice answer no, viewing those parenthet- icals not as giving part of the contents of those *experiences*, but rather part of the contents of subsequent *reflections* on those experiences. Thus perhaps the qualifica- tion *sui generis* that attaches to the expressing that we hear music as doing when we register its expressiveness does not enter into the hearing-as experience *itself*, but only into our spontaneous further thoughts *about* that experience. The modifier, "in *sui generis* fashion," plausibly belongs to the content of a subsidiary thought on the expressing we hear in expressive music, not part of the content of the core experi- ence of hearing the music as, or as if it were, an expression of some sort.

The notion of *hearing-as*, it will not have escaped notice, has been relied on heavily in the preceding. So what is it to hear a stretch of music *as* something else – or alter- natively, to hear that something else *in* that stretch of music? (On the effective equiv- alence of hearing-in and hearing-as in regard to music, see Levinson 1996.) This remains a difficult matter, but for present purposes it suffices to locate hearing-as and hearing-in among perceptual acts that partake freely of, or that substantially enlist, the *imagination*. The agents one hears in music when one hears it as an expression of emotion, *sui generis* or not, are thus inescapably *imaginary* ones, ones displaying the indefiniteness characteristic of all imaginary objects. To hear music as such and such is, perhaps, to imagine *that* the music is such and such, and more specifically, to imagine *of* the music, *as* you are hearing it, that it is such and such.

The worry is sometimes voiced, concerning the appeal to imagination in the analy- sis of musical expressiveness, that imagination is too unconstrained to secure the degree of objectivity musical expressiveness appears to enjoy. But this worry can be allayed by recalling that the appeal is not to what a passage *just might* be imagined to be the expression of, but rather to what a passage is *most readily and sponta- neously* imagined to be the expression of, in which case there is often a fairly unequiv- ocal upshot of the exercise.

Resemblance-based Views of Musical Expressiveness

Malcolm Budd's account

Malcolm Budd, in his most recent discussion of our topic, distinguishes a minimal, or basic, concept of musical expressiveness, and then identifies three accretions to that minimal concept, resulting in three more elaborate conceptions of musical expres- siveness, the third of which is more or less the conception defended here (Budd 1995). The minimal conception goes like this: a stretch of music is expressive of E if one hears the music as sounding like the way E feels, or perceives a likeness between the music and the experience of E, and it is correct to do so.

My main objection to Budd's minimal conception, which is a resemblance-based one, is that it is simply too minimal. What it defines isn't yet musical expressiveness, but at most a rough precondition or typical upshot of it. Perceiving a likeness between two things A and B – and especially where, as in the present instance of musical pas- sages and emotional states, it is a matter of cross-categorial perception – is not suf- ficient for hearing A as B; the latter is a distinct occurrence that neither entails nor presupposes the former. Resemblance in various respects between the sound and shape of a passage of music and the inner experience or outer expression of an emotion is undoubtedly one of the chief grounds or *bases* of musical expressiveness, but neither the resemblance as such, nor the capacity to make listeners aware of that resemblance, *constitutes* the expressiveness in question.

I can perceive that, or acquire the perceptual belief that, a leafy tree resembles a bushy beard, for instance, and not have the experience of seeing the tree as a beard. I can notice the likeness between the two and yet not see the one *in* the other. But surely we cannot speak of a musical passage being *expressive* of an emotion unless listeners are induced to hear the emotion, or more precisely, an expressing of the emotion, in the passage, whatever degree of resemblance they might note, in whatever respects, between the passage and the emotion.

Note further that even if a resemblance-based account of musical expressiveness could deliver the right verdicts in individual cases – that is, even if the degree of resemblance that an ensemble of musical features needs to have to some emotion for a passage possessing such an ensemble to be expressive of the emotion in question could be specified in some general manner – that would not constitute an acceptable *analysis* of musical expressiveness. For it would not elucidate what musical expressiveness *was*, but only what ensembles of musical features were coextensive with and underlay such expressiveness.

Stephen Davies's account

Stephen Davies, the most prominent defender of a resemblance-based view of musical expressiveness, maintains that emotion words used to describe appearances, whether in persons, natural objects, or works of art, are parasitic on the use of such words to refer to felt emotions; they thus represent a secondary, though literal, use of such words. In this secondary use, says Davies, emotion words describe *emotion-charac-teristics-in-appearance*, and it is in such that musical expressiveness lies. According to Davies, "... the expressiveness of music consists in its presenting emotion characteristics in its appearance ... These expressive appearances ... are not occurrent emotions at all. They are emergent properties of the things to which they are attributed" (Davies 1994: 228). Davies goes on to explain that such musical expressiveness "... depends mainly on a resemblance we perceive between the dynamic character of music and human movement, gait, bearing, or carriage" (Davies 1994: 229). In conclusion, Davies affirms that emotions "... are heard in music as belonging to it, just as appearances of emotion are present in the bearing, gait, or deportment of our fellow humans and other creatures" (Davies 1994: 239).

Davies's view might, I think, be stated as follows: P is expressive of E if and only if P exhibits an emotion-characteristic-in-sound associated with E, that is, exhibits a sound-appearance analogous to the human emotion-characteristic-in-appearance of E.

Though not unsympathetic to the basic thrust of this account of musical expressiveness, I have major qualms about the central notion in terms of which it is framed, namely that of *musical* emotion-characteristics-in-appearance. The problem is that the appearance of a passage of music is not *precisely* that of a person, or a person's face or body in any condition, or a person's behavior at any moment. It is instead a matter, when a passage displays an emotion characteristic in its medium of sound sequences, of an appearance *similar* to that presented by a person in some state. But since everything is similar to everything else to some degree, the issue then becomes one of *how* similar such an appearance must be to one presented by human behavior in order to constitute an emotion-characteristic-in-sound of the emotion in question, or else, as Davies sometimes puts it, of how similar the *experience* of musical movement and of expressive behavior must be, in order for the appearance generated by such movement to constitute an emotion-characteristic-in-sound of the emotion in question.

I think it is plain that there is no answer to this except by appeal to our disposition to *hear* that emotion – rather than another, or none at all – in the music, that is, by appeal to our disposition to aurally construe the music as an instance of personal expression, perceiving the human appearances in the musical ones, in effect animating the sounds in a certain manner, to use a phrase given currency by Peter Kivy (Kivy 1989). Only if this occurs does the music have the expressiveness in question, regardless of the degree of similarity between the music's appearances and the human appearances by relation to which it ends up being expressive, or alternatively, the degree of similarity between the experiences of those appearances.

There is simply no independent conception of and no access to what Davies calls musical emotion-characteristics-in-appearance *apart from* satisfaction of the hearability-in-the-music-of-an-expressing-of-emotion condition vis-à-vis attuned listeners; the latter is what gives content, ultimately, to the former, however familiar the appearances in question might be. What the musical emotion-characteristic-in-appearance of sadness is, in general, cannot be derived from the behavioral emotion-characteristic-in-appearance of sadness in persons. There is no translation rule from behavioral appearance-characteristics to musical appearance-characteristics; only the act of perceiving in music the outlines of the former gives rise, so to speak, to the latter.

Though Davies does not want to be committed to the view that musical expressiveness consists in analogy or resemblance to literally expressive behavior, his invocation of emotion-characteristics-in-sound as something founded in and emerging out of such analogy or resemblance in any event suggests that such characteristics are specifiable independently of experiences of hearing emotional expression in music, as are the behavioral emotion-characteristics-in-appearance associated directly with felt emotion. But that is to overlook the real differences between human emotion-characteristics-in-appearance and the putative musical emotion-characteristics-in-appearance being appealed to; the former can to some extent be catalogued independently of individual judgments of expressive import on the part of perceivers, whereas the latter cannot. Let me elaborate on this.

We can give content to "sad human appearance" by glossing it as "the appearance or kind of appearance sad humans typically display." But we can't analogously give content to "sad musical appearance." There is no such thing as the appearance or kind of appearance that sad music typically displays. There is no extractable profile of "sad musical appearance," as there is of "sad human face" or "sad human posture"; "sad musical appearance," unlike "sad human face" and "sad human posture," is not, as it were, paraphrasable. The only way to anchor "sad musical appearance," I submit, is in terms of our disposition to hear such music as sad. The analysis of music's expressiveness must thus foreground that perceptual-imaginative experience, and not the resemblances that, no doubt, underlie it. Musical "emotion-characteristics-in-appearance," if supposed to be something identifiable apart from experiences of hearing such and such emotion or expression of emotion in music, and as parallel to human emotion-characteristics-in-appearance, are an illusion.

Take *sadness*. Sadness is an emotion, that is, a mental condition with various cognitive, conative, affective, evaluative, behavioral, and possibly physiological aspects. Next we have *sad look*, which is more or less the look – in face and body – that sad people typically wear, or wear when they are not trying to conceal or suppress their sadness. And then we have *sad sound*, which is more or less the sound – vocal, for the most part – that sad people typically make, at least when not trying to conceal or suppress their sadness. So characterized, sad look and sad sound are *human* emotion-characteristics-in-appearance, as is their conjunction, which we might label *sad appearance*.

But now we come to the alleged corresponding musical emotion-characteristic-in appearance, or *sad musical sound*. How is that to be cashed out, in light of the characterizations of *sad look* and *sad sound* just given? One possibility would be: as the musical sound that sad people typically make. But that can't be right, since sad people don't typically make musical sounds of any sort, and the sounds they do make – weeping, sighing – are clearly distinguishable from music of an ordinary sort. A second possibility would be: as the sound that sad pieces of music have in common. But that is an even worse proposal, since presupposing the prior identification of pieces of music as sad. A third possibility would be to appeal to purely technical or structural features of music, such as those of melody, harmony, tempo, and texture. But that would be of no use, since even if there is a complex disjunction of technical or structural features coextensive with sadness in music, such a disjunction would not serve to explicate the concept of sad musical sound, nor would such a disjunction appear to play a role in our identifying passages as sad.

The only proposal with any chance of success, then, must be that *sad musical sound* is sound resembling *sad sound* (the standard aural appearance of sadness) and/or, cross-modally, *sad look* (the standard visual appearance of sadness). But to what *degree*? There's the rub, for as we all know, everything resembles everything else, yet the degree of resemblance to an emotion required to make a musical appearance a musical emotion characteristic in appearance of that emotion cannot be specified in terms of some fixable degree of resemblance between the two. It can only be specified, it seems, as whatever resemblance is sufficient to induce appropriately backgrounded listeners to *hear* the music as sad, or as expressing sadness. But that, surely, is to give up the idea that there is a recognizable musical emotion-characteristic-in-appearance of sadness, somehow analogous to the human emotion-characteristic-in-appearance of sadness, on which the analysis of musical expressiveness can rest.

In sum, if there really are musical emotion-characteristics-in-appearance, to which the explication of musical expressiveness must advert, we should be able to identify them other than simply as being appearances in which the corresponding emotion can be heard. Thus for *sad musical sound*, there should be some possible specification or profile, however schematic, of what sort of sound that is, other than "sound that invites hearing-as-sad." But there isn't.

Inference-based Views of Musical Expressiveness

Bruce Vermazen, Jenefer Robinson, and Robert Stecker are philosophers who subscribe to inference-based views of musical expressiveness (see Vermazen 1986, Robinson 1998, and Stecker 2001). In the view of each of them, the expressiveness a passage of music possesses is something like the upshot of an inference to the best explanation. In Vermazen's case it is an ascription of a state of mind to the imagined utterer of the passage that best explains its distinctive features; in Robinson's case it is an ascription of a state of mind to the imaginary protagonist of the passage that figures in the best interpretation of the musical work taken as a whole; in Stecker's case it is a best hypothesis on the part of an ideal listener as to what state of mind the composer of the music intended such a listener to hear in the passage.

Though I share with Vermazen and Robinson the commitment to personae in the analysis of musical expressiveness, and with Stecker the notion that certain dimensions of artistic meaning are amenable to analysis in hypotheticalist terms, I disagree with all three that *basic* musical expressiveness – that is, the expressiveness of individual passages – can be constitutively tied to the sustaining of inferences about the music. That is because of my conviction that basic musical expressiveness – though perhaps not all sorts of expressiveness, such as that more typical of literature, involving articulate states of mind, nor that perhaps attaching to works of music as wholes – is something directly heard, not inferred, by attuned or properly back-grounded listeners. Otherwise put, inferentialist views of expressiveness fail to capture the immediacy with which we register basic musical expressiveness.

I thus continue to think, *pace* Stecker, that immediacy is a proper desideratum for an account of musical expressiveness, and that my ready-hearability-as-expression account acknowledges that better than the hypotheticalist account that Stecker proposes instead. It is true, as Stecker points out, that *hearing emotion* in music and *judging of the expressiveness* of music are not the same things. But there is a third thing, *perceiving the music's expressiveness*, and that is not the same as judging its expressiveness to be such and such. The expressiveness of music, I claim, and not just the emotion in music, is standardly something directly registered, not just conjectured about. My account can accommodate this fact, as can also a resemblance-based account, but an inferentialist account, obviously, cannot.

Now Stecker, seeking to hoist me with my own petard, argues that my ready-hearability-as-expression proposal is ultimately as inferentialist as his own, since in order to determine that a work was expressive of E on the basis of hearing an expression of E in it, even properly backgrounded listeners would have to engage in inference, taking the fact of their so responding as a premise together with the premise that they were in fact properly backgrounded listeners listening properly (Stecker 2001: 92). But I anticipated and replied to that line of criticism in my previous paper on this topic (Levinson 1996: 118–19). I there emphasized that a qualified listener who hears the expression of some emotion in music normally acquires, without reflection, the conviction that the music is expressive of that emotion, that is, would be readily hearable as such by other qualified listeners. And that, I suggest, counts as *perceiving* the music's expressiveness, or as much as anything could. Whether the listener in addition thereby *knows* that the music is thus so expressive is another matter, one that may indeed involve further reflection or investigation.

Here is a variant of that reply. Qualified listeners arguably tacitly assume, while listening to music, that they are qualified listeners, and are listening appropriately. Thus on the view I favor, hearing an expression of E in a stretch of music becomes, for such listeners, tantamount to hearing the music's expressiveness of E. All qualified listeners need do to hear the expressiveness of the music is to readily hear expression of emotion in it. Since they are, and unreflectingly assume they are, qualified listeners, listening appropriately, their readily hearing such and such an expression in the music directly manifests its being readily so hearable by such listeners! Note, however, that this line would not work to secure the immediacy of musical expressiveness on a hypothetical-intentionalist view of it; even were we to grant a parallel tacit assumption on the listener's part, to the effect that he or she was an ideal listener. For arriving at a best hypothesis of what the historically rooted composer intended for one to hear in a given passage remains an ineliminably inferential affair.

There is still another reason to resist a hypothetical-intentionalist account of musical expressiveness. Expressive content in music and expressive content in poetry seem of quite different sorts, hence it would not be surprising if they lent themselves to different sorts of analyses. The latter is largely propositional, and thus reasonably assimilated to the kind of meaning – basic literary meaning – that a view like hypothetical intentionalism is designed to account for, whereas the former is largely non-propositional, hence not reasonably assimilable to basic literary meaning.

I am inclined to think that a perceivability-as-if-expression account is apt not only for music, but for nonrepresentational art generally. But where we have to do with representational, and perhaps especially, literary art – including lyric poetry, epic poetry, history painting, theatre, cinema, novel – emphasis on the immediacy of expressiveness seems less apt, and the merit of a more inferentialist account of expressiveness seems correspondingly greater. The reason may simply be that immediacy of expression is an appropriate demand for affective states or attitudes, the core expressive content of nonliterary arts such as music or abstract painting, but not for propositional beliefs or thoughts, the core expressive content of literary arts such as cinema or the novel.

We can now offer an observation about expressiveness in art applicable across the arts, whether representational or nonrepresentational, literary or nonliterary. Remember that expression in general can be characterized roughly as the evidencing of a state of mind through some sort of external manifestation. In the case of art, the external manifestation is not behavior, but rather the artwork itself, in all its perceivable particularity. But just as we grasp literally expressed states in and through the behavior, verbal and otherwise, that expresses them, so with expressive art we grasp the as-if-expressed states in and through the concrete vehicle of the work, its metaphorical body. With expressive art, expressiveness is grasped through perceiving the work in its specific detail – whether of word, paint, sound, or stone – and the states expressed are ones that perceivers are thus aided to enter into in imagination precisely in virtue of perceiving the work, through which, either immediately or inferentially, they grasp what states those are.

Some Objections to the Hearability-as-expression View of Musical Expressiveness

The first and most common objection is this. A number of writers charge that competent listeners do not in fact – or at least do not all of them, all of the time – hear or imagine personae in music whose expressiveness they are registering, and thus that such imaginative hearing cannot be constitutive of hearing music as expressive and the disposition to induce such hearing as constitutive of the music's being so expressive (Davies 1997, Walton 1999, Stecker 2001).

Well, that may be how it sometimes seems, or seems on the surface, but if expressive music is, as I maintain, music readily heard as, or as if, expression, and if, in addition, expression requires an expresser, then personae or agents, however minimal, just *are* presupposed in the standard experience of such music. But of course, one may not always notice or acknowledge what is presupposed in one's imaginative hearing of music. The claim is not that listeners are always explicitly aware that personae are involved in their hearing music as expressive. For people are often not entirely aware of what is implicated in a perception or experience they are having.

A point noted in Levinson (1996) is worth recalling here. It may indeed be true that listeners who recognize the expressiveness of a passage of music do not invariably hear it, then and there, as the expression of an emotion. But all that the theory requires is that they *recognize* the music as readily hearable as the expression of an emotion, even if, for one reason or another, they do not themselves give in to that inducement on a given occasion. Moreover, quite possibly all such cases are ones in which listeners are recognizing passages they have *previously* heard as the expression of given emotions, or else as ones highly *similar* to such passages, thus presupposing occasions on which the expressiveness in question was in fact grasped through an experience of hearing-as-the-expression-of.

Furthermore, some of the discrepancy with the avowals of listeners on this subject, I suggest, is that a passage of music may more loosely have an emotional *quality*, in virtue of suggesting an emotion through its appearance, without being strictly speaking emotionally *expressive*, understood as being such as to induce hearing-as-expression of that emotion. The finale of Beethoven's Fifth Symphony, to take a stock example, is expressive of something like triumphant joy, and I think it is hard not to hear that finale as if there is someone, or some agent, there who is expressing his, her, or its triumphant joy in those familiar musical gestures, the character of which is rendered especially vivid in virtue of the movement in which they occur being the successor and culmination of the three that precede it. By contrast, the opening Prelude of Bach's *Well-tempered Clavier* has an emotional *quality* one might describe as contentment or equanimity, and yet perhaps one is not induced to hear it as, or as if, the expression of that state of mind; but then it is probably also right to deny that it is *expressive* of contentment or equanimity, in addition to just possessing the corresponding emotional quality.

The second objection is as follows. It has been suggested that the appeal to *apt* hearability-as-expression as a benchmark of real, as opposed to merely apparent, expressiveness, a feature of my original formula, will either not do the work that is required of it or else is called upon to do too much work (Stecker 2001: 91–4).

I am at this point inclined to agree. The qualification of "apt" in my original formula was an unwarranted hedge. What I now think is that the burden of securing the objectivity of expressiveness, or equivalently, the normativity of judgments of expressiveness, must simply rest on the properly backgrounded listener and his or her hearing of a passage in its proper intrawork and extrawork context. Where there is ready hearability-as-expression under such conditions – evidenced most clearly by convergence in experiences among such listeners – then objectivity and normativity are present. Where not, then not. Exactly how large is the domain of objective expressiveness in music, which depends on such convergence, thus remains an open question.

The third objection is centered on a related worry about my original formula, voiced by Roger Scruton, to the effect that appeal to a reference class of qualified listeners whose ready hearing of a passage as expression of E serves as the mark of the passage's being truly expressive of E is doomed to vacuity, because the reference class can only be characterized as the class of listeners who in fact discern the passage's expressiveness (Scruton 1997: 353).

But that is not true. It is like suggesting that the only way to characterize the class of appropriate, objectivity-anchoring perceivers for the color of a given patch of greenish paint is as perceivers who correctly perceive that the patch in question is greenish. The reference class of listeners anchoring the objectivity of expressiveness in a given musical genre – what I mean by "properly backgrounded listeners" – is roughly that of listeners demonstrably competent at understanding such music, such competence being manifested through various recognitional, continuational, and descriptive abilities, and whose other judgments of expressiveness are in line with established ones in uncontroversial cases. There is perhaps a certain amount of bootstrapping involved in this picture of the qualified listener for a given musical genre vis-à-vis the expressive and other qualities of works in that genre of whose objectivity he or she is to serve as a benchmark, but there is nothing, I think, fatally circular in it. At any rate, it seems the sort of difficulty that affects all attempts to analyze perceivable properties in terms of appearances or dispositions to appear relative to a class of perceivers of a certain sort.

Paul Boghossian has recently seconded Scruton's worry in a more general form (Boghossian forthcoming). Boghossian charges that the appeal to qualified listeners in the analysis is vacuous because there is no way to characterize what makes for a qualified listener without presupposing an understanding of musical expressiveness that does not invoke such listeners or the ways such listeners are disposed to hear or otherwise respond to music.

Again, qualified listeners for a given piece of music are naturally not to be characterized, stultifyingly, as ones who correctly hear the expressiveness of the given piece. How, then, are they to be characterized? As suggested earlier, perhaps as musically competent listeners whose judgments of expressiveness in the tradition in question accord with accepted ones in *paradigm* cases. But what are paradigm cases of musical expressiveness? Well, one conception of them would be as pieces in a given

Jerrold Levinson

tradition on whose expressiveness *almost all* at least minimally musically competent listeners agree.

Boghossian retorts that even on this suggestion, paradigm cases having the expressiveness they do remains unanalyzed, thus presupposing some ultimately nonexperiential, nonresponse-dependent notion of such expressiveness. But I am not so sure. For the expressiveness of paradigm cases, we may suggest, comes to precisely the same thing as it does for nonparadigm cases, namely, the music's being most readily hearable as the expression of such and such emotion by qualified listeners, the only difference being that, those being paradigm cases of expressiveness, they will be so heard by virtually all listeners who are at least minimally musically competent.

The fourth objection is another difficulty about my proposal that has been articulated by Scruton, and is worth addressing here. It is a particular elaboration of the skepticism acknowledged earlier as to whether we can form an idea of the singular way of expressing emotions that expressive music on my proposal is made out to be, at least in imagination, and whether or not in so doing we characterize it to ourselves as *sui generis*. I quote the objection in full:

> When we hear expression in music, Levinson suggests, this is like hearing another person express his feelings. But in what way like? We have no prior conception of what it would be to express feelings in *music*: if we can think of someone doing this, it is because we have an idea of the expressive character of music, and therefore can imagine someone choosing just *this* piece of music, to convey just *this* state of mind. Our ability to imagine a subject expressing his feelings in just *this* way is predicated upon our ability to recognize the expressive content of music. Only if we can independently recognize the emotional content of music, therefore, can we embark on the thought-experiment required by Levinson's definition. (Scruton 1997: 352)

Scruton claims that my account is committed to listeners being able to conceive what it would be to express an emotion, in the literal sense, in or through music. He then suggests that their only way of doing so would be by imagining someone choosing suitable music to convey the emotion in question, which obviously presupposes an antecedent grasp of the music's expressiveness, thus rendering the putative account of such expressiveness otiose. But both points in this objection are misplaced. First, my account does not imply that listeners who register expressiveness in music possess a concrete *conception* of what literally expressing emotions through music instead of behavior would amount to, or how such expressing would work. The account requires only that listeners are able to *imagine* music to be such a literal expression. Second, listeners who do that are not constrained to think of the music's persona as somehow *choosing* from available musical items ones suitable to convey his or her changing moods, like a sound editor selecting tracks to go with the successive scenes of a film.

Scruton has simply misunderstood the nature of the thought-experiment that, if my account of musical expressiveness is correct, one is effectively called upon to perform in order to grasp the expressiveness of music. It is not "imagine someone choosing from among preexisting music to convey a given state of mind; now, what state of mind would that be if he or she chose the music you are hearing?" It is, rather, "imagine the music you are hearing to be the literal expressing of a state of mind; now, what state of mind does that appear to be?," or perhaps, "imagine that the musical gesture you hear in the music was your own; now, what state of mind do you appear to be in?" That thought-experiment, which my proposal is committed to, *grounds* identification of the music's expressiveness, but does not, like the one Scruton saddles me with, *presuppose* such identification. If I am right, one grasps what a musical passage expresses precisely in virtue of imagining, or being disposed to imagine, a mental state that it is as if the literal expression of. That there is no algorithm or procedure for this thought-experiment, unlike the one Scruton would substitute for it, does not entail that it cannot be carried out. We carry it out, in fact, every time we attend to music's expressive dimension.

Personae in Music

In closing I briefly comment on the concerns aired by many writers, including those sympathetic to imagined expressions and their personae, regarding the indeterminacy of musical personae and the indefiniteness of the principles governing their postulation. (See Maus 1988, Walton 1994, Karl and Robinson 1997, Davies 1997.) When is the persona of one passage the same as the persona of another passage? When is there continuity of persona and when discontinuity, as a work progresses from beginning to end? Might there be multiple personae present in a single passage? Might personae be related to one another through recognition, sympathy, or antagonism?

I cannot address these questions here, which go beyond the scope of this chapter. What I wish to underline is just that the sustainability of the thesis of a minimal persona we are induced to hear in expressive music, and typically do hear in it when listening attentively, is not affected by worries of this sort, even if ultimately unresolvable. The persona implicated in the ready-hearability-as-expression account of musical expressiveness is merely the agent of the expression we hear in expressive music, or the owner of the musical gesture that is the vehicle of that expression. Whether that persona persists as the music proceeds, whether a given persona is accompanied by others, whether persona enter into relation with one another, and so on, are matters on which the account of basic musical expressiveness here defended can remain agnostic.

Note

Thanks to Paul Boghossian, David Davies, Derek Matravers, and Robert Stecker for helpful suggestions and spirited discussion.

Jerrold Levinson

References for Chapters 11 and 12

Boghossian, P. (forthcoming). "Musical Experience and Musical Meaning." In Kathleen Stock (ed.), *Philosophers on Music*. Oxford: Oxford University Press.

Budd, M. (1995). *The Values of Art: Pictures, Poetry, and Music*. London: Allen Lane, The Penguin Press.

Davies, S. (1994). *Musical Meaning and Expression*. Ithaca, NY: Cornell University Press.

Davies, S. (1997). "Contra the Hypothetical Persona in Music." In M. Hjort and S. Laver (eds.), *Emotion and the Arts* (pp. 95–109). Oxford: Oxford University Press.

Davies, S. (1999). "Response to Robert Stecker." *British Journal of Aesthetics*, 39: 282–7.

DeNora, T. (2000). *Music in Everyday Life*. Cambridge, UK: Cambridge University Press.

Ekman, P. (1992). "An Argument for Basic Emotions." *Cognition and Emotion*, 6: 169–200.

Gabrielsson, A. (2002). "Emotion Perceived and Emotion Felt: Same or Different?" *Musicae Scientiae*, Special issue 2001–2002: 123–47.

Goodman, N. (1968). *Languages of Art*. New York: Bobbs-Merrill.

Hatfield, E., Cacioppo, J. T., and Rapson, R. L. (1994). *Emotional Contagion*. New York: Cambridge University Press.

Juslin, P. N. (2001). "Communicating Emotion in Music Performance: A Review and Theoretical Framework." In P. N. Juslin and J. A. Sloboda (eds.), *Music and Emotion: Theory and Research* (pp. 309–37). Oxford: Oxford University Press.

Karl, G. and Robinson, J. (1995). "Shostakovitch's Tenth Symphony and the Musical Expression of Cognitively Complex Emotions." *Journal of Aesthetics and Art Criticism*, 53: 401–15.

Karl, G. and Robinson, J. (1997). "Shostakovitch's Tenth Symphony and the Musical Expression of Cognitively Complex Emotions." In J. Robinson (ed.), *Music and Meaning* (pp. 154–78). Ithaca, NY: Cornell University Press,

Kivy, P. (1989). *Sound Sentiment*. Philadelphia, PA: Temple University Press.

Kivy, P. (1990). *Music Alone: Philosophical Reflection on the Purely Musical Experience*. Ithaca, NY: Cornell University Press.

Kivy, P. (1999). "Feeling the Musical Emotions." *British Journal of Aesthetics*, 39: 1–13.

Koopman, C. and Davies, S. (2001). "Musical Meaning in a Broader Perspective." *Journal of Aesthetics and Art Criticism*, 59: 261–73.

Langer, S. (1942). *Philosophy in a New Key*. Cambridge, MA: Harvard University Press.

Levinson, J. (1990). "Hope in 'The Hebrides'." In *Music, Art, and Metaphysics* (pp. 336–75). Ithaca, NY: Cornell University Press.

Levinson, J. (1996). "Musical Expressiveness." In *The Pleasures of Aesthetics* (pp. 90–125). Ithaca, NY: Cornell University Press.

Levinson, J. (2002). "Sound, Gesture, Spatial Imagination, and the Expression of Emotion in Music." *European Review of Philosophy*, 5: 137–150.

Madell, G. (2002). *Philosophy, Music and Emotion*. Edinburgh: Edinburgh University Press.

Matravers, D. (1998). *Art and Emotion*. Oxford: Clarendon Press.

Maus, F. (1988). "Music as Drama." *Music Theory Spectrum*, 10: 56–73.

Neubauer, J. (1986). *The Emancipation of Music from Language: Departure from Mimesis in Eighteenth-century Aesthetics*. New Haven, CT: Yale University Press.

Ridley, A. (2003). "Expression in Art." In J. Levinson (ed.), *Oxford Handbook of Aesthetics* (pp. 211–27). Oxford: Oxford University Press.

Robinson, J. (1998). "The Expression and Arousal of Emotion in Music." In P. Alperson (ed.), *Musical Worlds: New Directions in the Philosophy of Music* (pp. 13–22). University Park: Pennsylvania State University Press.

Scruton, R. (1997). *The Aesthetics of Music*. Oxford: Clarendon Press.

Stecker, R. (1999). "Davies on the Musical Expression of Emotion." *British Journal of Aesthetics*, 39: 273–81.

Stecker, R. (2001). "Expressiveness and Expression in Music and Poetry." *Journal of Aesthetics and Art Criticism*, 59: 85–96.

Tormey, A. (1971). *The Concept of Expression*. Princeton, NJ: Princeton University Press.

Vermazen, B. (1986). "Expression as Expression." *Pacific Philosophical Quarterly*, 67: 196–224.

Walton, K. (1994). "Listening with Imagination: Is Music Representational?" *Journal of Aesthetics and Art Criticism*, 52: 47–61.

Walton, K. (1999). "Projectivism, Empathy, and Musical Tension." *Philosophical Topics*, 26: 407–40.

Further Reading for Chapters 11 and 12

Addis, L. (1999). *Of Mind and Music*. Ithaca, NY: Cornell University Press.

Boghossian, P. (2002). "On Hearing the Music in the Sound: Scruton on Musical Expression." *Journal of Aesthetics and Art Criticism*, 60: 49–55.

Budd, M. (1985). *Music and the Emotions: The Philosophical Theories*. London: Routledge & Kegan Paul.

Higgins, K. (1991). *The Music of Our Lives*. Philadelphia, PA: Temple University Press.

Kivy, P. (2001). *New Essays on Musical Understanding*. Oxford: Oxford University Press.

Levinson, J. (1997). "Emotion in Response to Art: A Survey of the Terrain." In M. Hjort and S. Laver (eds.), *Emotion and the Arts* (pp. 20–34). Oxford: Oxford University Press.

Levinson, J. (2000). "Review of Scruton *The Aesthetics of Music*." *Philosophical Review*, 109: 608–14.

Matravers, D. (2003). "The Experience of Expression in Music." *Journal of Aesthetics and Art Criticism*, 61(4): 353–63.

Ridley, A. (1995). *Music, Value, and the Passions*. Ithaca, NY: Cornell University Press.

Sharpe, R. A. (2000). *Music and Humanism*. Oxford: Oxford University Press.

IN WHAT WAYS IS THE IMAGINATION INVOLVED IN ENGAGING WITH ARTWORKS?

CHAPTER THIRTEEN

Anne Brontë and the Uses of Imagination

Gregory Currie

Giving an account of the relations between art and imagination is an ambitious project. Apart from its intrinsic difficulty, history bears down hard on the writer, who is obliged to make sense of an army of theorists, among whom Kant, Hegel, and Nietzsche are perhaps the most intimidating. But the problem transcends national boundaries. Collingwood's remark that "the aesthetic experience . . . is the total imaginative activity called indifferently language or art" (Collingwood 1938: 275) is bad news for anyone seeking clarification on this issue. It is unsurprising that recent, analytically framed, discussions of the concept of art rarely mention imagination as one of its constituents.

While general formulations may not be helpful in this area, we should not abandon the idea that art and imagination are related. Particular works of art encourage and reward imagination, and some do so in complex ways. "Imagination" has an adverbial sense, where we say that this or that is done imaginatively (Scruton 1974); it is also the name of a particular activity: we imagine flying, or that Napoleon won at Waterloo. I shall call this content-imagining. Can we say that content-imagining is done more or less imaginatively? If we specify in advance precisely the content of the imagining, we leave no room for more or less imaginative ways of doing it, but that is true of other activities. If my guitar teacher somehow organizes every detail of my performance I can't be said to perform imaginatively, however pleasing the sound. But for a less fully specified imaginative project there are different, and differently imaginative, ways to carry it out. Such a project might be to engage imaginatively with a novel. In part the project involves following detailed instructions, for the novel specifies a good deal of what is to be imagined. But we will imagine many things the author does not explicitly mention, and which the work does not mandate. And where there is something uniquely appropriate to imagine, it may take an imaginative performance to see what it is.

How are content-imagining and doing something imaginatively related? Again, in complex ways. Adverbial imagining is a matter of style, and style is predicable of some things and not of others. Take belief-formation. I may come to believe P through an act of judgment, but not all beliefs are formed that way; I see your car and simply come to believe it is red, without judging that it is. In this latter case we cannot talk about imaginative thinking, or of thinking with any kind of style; that comes with the judgment. And much judgment requires a capacity for content-imagining. We judge when we hold an assumption in thought, consider its consequences and its relations to what else we think is true, and convert the assumption into a belief. Holding the assumption is an act of content-imagining (or so I claim; see Currie 2002), the capacity for which is required for judgment of a certain sort, and hence for one kind of imaginative thinking.

Does judgment always involve the prior assumption of the proposition to be judged? There are cases where this is not obviously so: I set myself to carefully examine the evidence, and conclude that Smith was the murderer; at no stage prior to concluding this did I think the thought "Smith is guilty," yet it may be appropriate to say that this was judgment on my part. For this kind of case we can formulate a weaker version of my position: judgment requires the exercise of our capacity for assumption, even though it may not require the assumption of the very proposition in question. The belief that P, arrived at in the course of a controlled inquiry, may count as a judgment, not because it involves the assumption of P, but because it is part of a process of thought that involves assumption at some stage. Still, not all judgment is assumption-involving even in the weak sense. The concept of judgment is wider than that, signifying belief-formation that in some way or other is an activity, rather than mere passive registration. We talk of judging the vase to be ugly, without implying that I assumed this (or anything else) prior to believing it. This is judgment because I deployed a special capacity – taste might be a good name for it – in the process of forming the belief. And thinking which deploys that special capacity is another sort of thinking apt to be described as imaginative. Assumption-making (that is, content-imagining) is one way to make thought imaginative; there are others.

The capacity for content-imagining creates, or at least draws attention to, other opportunities for imaginative performance. I've already said that imagining can itself be done imaginatively; indeed, an act of content-imagining is particularly apt to be the focus of a judgment about how (adverbially) imaginative we are being. Acts of content-imagining stack up with acts of pretense or imitation, and pretending to do something tends to display opportunities for imaginative behavior not displayed by the thing which is pretended. In real action, much that is done is given over to processes that are habitual, which may be subpersonally driven, or are at least not much the subject of reflection. Pretense tends to bring these aspects of performance under greater personal control. An extreme case is the pretense of sleep, which requires conscious regulation even of breathing. And pretense is usually less constrained than the real activity it targets; compare driving/pretending to drive at high speed. With more control and less constraint comes more opportunity for imaginative performance. There are imaginative opportunities available in the real act that are sometimes not available in its pretense; you can paint a picture in imaginative ways that are not available if you pretend to paint. So the traffic is not always one way. But pretense, by virtue of being a performance, has a greater tendency to focus us on the available opportunities.

As we shall see, content-imagining is often undertaken with the aim of reproducing, in pretend-mode, the mental processes of another. This is said to be a way to understand and predict the other's decisions without our having a theory about how decisions are made. We simply use our own natural capacity to decide, and this no more requires of us a theory of decision making than walking requires of us a theory of walking. But we should not conclude from the fact that such simulations can be done uncomprehendingly that they are done unimaginatively; impersonations of voice, with subtle and telling exaggeration, are done by people who have no theory of speech production. So exploring other people's mental lives through acts of content-imagining can be done imaginatively. Later I will give an example of a work that encourages imaginative imaginings of this kind. I start by examining content-imagination itself, and then turn to a special case.

Imagination and Simulation

We have a serviceable theory – simulation theory (ST) – able to extend the idea of content-imagining: it tells us what is going on when I imagine some fact or occurrence, or imagine doing something (Gordon 1986, Heal 1986). Here is one statement of this view:

> Every normal agent has a set of mental mechanisms for generating new mental states from initial ones – for example, a decision-making system that takes desires and beliefs as inputs and churns out decisions as outputs. Such mechanisms or systems might be employed in a derivative fashion to simulate and ascribe mental states to oneself and others. To use the simulation heuristic, one would feed pretend initial states into such a mechanism – the initial states of the targeted agent – and see what further states the mechanism produces. For example, to predict someone else's choices, one can feed simulated desires and beliefs into a decision-making system and allow it to generate the same choice it would produce given genuine beliefs and desires. (Goldman 1995: 718)

Goldman is here offering an account of what we do when we try to ascribe mental states. But much of what he says applies to any exercise of the imagination, for whatever purpose. I am suggesting that imagining, in our favored sense, involves the generation and manipulation of what Goldman here calls "simulated desires and beliefs" – and also simulated emotions, about which more further on. Simulated beliefs are not beliefs, because they are states that do not occupy the sorts of causal roles that beliefs occupy, but they are *like* beliefs in certain respects and it is their likeness to beliefs that makes them simulations of, exactly, *belief.* In particular they are like belief in respect of inferential role and affective power. We reason from simulated beliefs in just the ways we reason from beliefs, and having the simulated belief that I am being chased by a bull can have at least some of the anxiety-making power that believing I am does. Similarly for desires and simulated desires. (Indeed, just as beliefs and desires generally operate together, as in practical reasoning and the generation of affect, so too do we generally need to consider the effects of simulated beliefs and desires together. But for the sake of simplicity I will focus mostly on simulated beliefs here; see Currie (2002) for more on desire.)

All this helps explain how putting ourselves in another's shoes can help us see how that person will respond; we can reason from the premises that person reasons from, make the decisions that person makes, and feel the emotional urgings he or she feels.

In almost all expositions of ST, its role in understanding and predicting people's decisions is emphasized, as it is in the passage from Goldman above. This is natural enough, since ST was developed as an alternative to the view that we understand others by deploying a theory about motives and behavior. But it does no violence to the view itself to distinguish two separable components within it. The first, more general (but certainly not vacuous) component asserts that human beings have the capacity to generate and manipulate simulative states such as simulated beliefs and desires. The second, more specific, claim is that this capacity is employed for understanding people's inner lives and the decisions that spring from them. But once we grant the existence of the simulative capacity itself, the question arises as to whether it plays a role in other human activities. One of these might be imaginative engagement with works of fiction. I claim that works of fiction ask us to imagine various things, and that we respond by generating appropriate simulative states which then constitute those very imaginings (Currie 1990).

Because one claim of ST is that decision-prediction is done by imaginative projection, we might think it tells us this:

1 Imaginative engagement with a fiction always involves putting ourselves in the shoes of the characters.

I agree with Matthew Kieran and Noël Carroll (Kieran 2003, Carroll 1997) that 1 is not true. They show how much of our response to fiction does not depend on any sort of imaginative identification with, or putting ourselves in the shoes of, any of the characters. So we can agree that:

2 Imaginative engagement with a fiction does not always (and may not even mostly) involve putting ourselves in the shoes of the characters.

But Kieran uses this as the basis for an argument to the conclusion that "Narrative appreciation and understanding is far more rich and complex than adversion to simulation theory seems to allow" (Kieran 2003: 87). This follows only if ST is committed to proposition 1 above (as Noël Carroll explicitly claims: Carroll 1997: 391). But 1 is not what should be claimed by someone interested in applying ST to fiction. What should be claimed is merely that engagement with the fiction involves simulation of some kind, and this need not be the simulation of characters' mental states – though I shall argue later that sometimes it is. Engagement with *Peter Pan* requires me to have various sorts of belief-like imaginings, such as that Peter is in danger, that Captain Hook is afraid of the crocodile, that the crocodile has swallowed a clock. This, according to ST, involves me in having pretend beliefs with just those contents. I use those pretend contents, and others I acquire from the work, as the basis for inferences and expectations concerning the work, as when I suppose that ticking clocks will make Hook feel nervous. The story also encourages me to have various kinds of desire-like imaginings, for example the desire-like imagining that Peter escape from Hook. These are all cases where the reader is expected to exercise simulative capacities, but they are not cases where the reader has to enter imaginatively into the mind of any character. When I imagine that Peter is in danger, I am not simulating anyone's beliefs; Peter might be unaware of the danger. I am engaged in what we might call an impersonal simulation. The idea that simulation is always simulation of someone is false. Simulations are always simulations of *something*, but there need be no interesting sense in which they are simulations of someone. When I take on the imaginative counterpart of the belief that P, I am simulating the belief that P; I need not be engaged in a project that has as its purpose that I enter imaginatively into the life of some particular person, real or imagined, who believes that P.

We might write this off as a verbal dispute: Carroll and Kieran use "simulation" in a narrow sense which covers just what I would call "character simulation" (see Carroll 1997: 388 for an explicit statement). Concerning what they call "simulation" we do not disagree. However, I suggest that it is important that we use words in ways that reflect natural distinctions. On my broad use, "simulation" refers to a psychological kind: a mental activity that manifests itself in different ways. After all, advocates of simulation theory have long argued that the mental processes we use to simulate the states of others can be put to other uses. For example, it is suggested that we assess the truth-value of at least some counterfactuals by simulating belief in the antecedent, and then seeing whether the consequent looks reasonable (Goldman 1992). On this view both mindreading tasks and the assessment of counterfactuals require simulation. We could not even say this if we insisted that simulation occurs only when the pretend belief is part of an attempt to enter imaginatively into the mind of another.

Having made this more general point, I want now to focus on the question whether, and in what ways, character-simulation is important in engagement with fiction. It is more difficult here to identify a sharp disagreement; Carroll and Kieran do not deny a role for character-simulation, though they are somewhat begrudging in their recognition of it. I wish to propose a more positive view of its significance, and to see that it can help us to understand, not only our own responses to fiction, but also structural features of works themselves, and some of the narrative strategies that authors adopt. Before I get to this, I will consider one general argument in favor of the importance of character-simulation, and indicate why it is inconclusive.

Fiction and Real Life

There is an apparently rather powerful argument for saying that character simulation plays an important role in our negotiations with a fictional work. Simulation plays an important role in our understanding real people; it would be odd if it did not play a comparably important role in our understanding of fictional people as well, at least where they occur in realistic fictions. And we do certainly need to understand fictional characters in order fully to appreciate the works in which they figure. I confess to having given some weight to this argument in the past (see for example Currie 1998); I am now less inclined to do so. I agree with its premise about our access to the minds of real people: simulation does play an important role in our understanding of the mental states of real people, though it is not the only means we have. There are different kinds of mind-reading tasks and what might loosely be called theory is appropriate to some of them, while simulation is a plausible method in other cases. I think that we can say something about which mind-reading tasks fall into which category.

However, understanding real people and understanding fictional, and especially literary, characters are very different activities, even where the characters concerned are so drawn as to embody motivational systems very like those of real people. They are different not because their results are different but because the constraints on us when we try to arrive at these results are different, and these differences may be crucial to determining the best method to use. Mind reading by simulation is a capacity that evolved in humans over a long period; it probably developed in response to the problems posed by face-to-face exchanges with conspecifics in fairly small groups, where there is much shared experience and a high probability of relatedness between the parties. In that case we would expect humans to employ simulative strategies most naturally in situations where there is little time for theorizing, where there is much in common between the parties, and where there are few other reliable sources of information. The situation in which we confront fictional characters is often not like this. While understanding real people is typically time-pressured, literary texts dictate no particular pace of engagement, and provide us with opportunities for lengthy reflection that may tip the balance in favor of theorizing. By contrast with conversation in the Pleistocene, fiction often confronts us with people historically and culturally distant from ourselves, or with whom we simply do not have much in common, calling once again for greater dependence on theory. Finally, authors of fictions (or their surrogate narrators) are often a source of reliable, and indeed authoritative, information about the characters' motives and other mental states. In conversation we do not usually have someone whispering in our ear telling us about our conversation partner's inner life – and why would we believe such an informant anyway?

The last-mentioned condition – the role of authors – introduces especially interesting and complex factors. Authors do not function merely as sources of additional evidence over and above that which might be gleaned from simulation, together with normal patterns of evidence-sifting and hypothesis formation. Their activities serve to indicate to us aspects of the narrative that can strongly affect our conclusions about characters' actions and motives. When we learn something about a fictional character because the work itself tells or suggests it, this is not at all like learning something about someone in the real world by casual observation. For what the fiction tells us comes labeled as having a special evidential relevance; we are told this *for a reason*. The reason might be that the author wants to suggest something about a character's motive, and thinks that putting this piece of evidence in our way will suggest it. But this works only because we recognize that the evidence has been put there for that very reason. Thus the world of a fiction is not one that we engage with by applying ordinary standards of evidence and probability; what is evidence is inseparable from what is a sign of authorial intention. And so we may rightly draw conclusions about motive or behavior that would be unwarranted on the same purely evidential basis in real-world situations. Elsewhere Jon Jureidini and I argue that it is characteristic of a certain kind of psychosis to see the world as if it were governed by the

Gregory Currie

sorts of forces that externally regulate the actions of fictional characters (see Currie and Jureidini 2003).

These are reasons for being hesitant about the idea that mental simulation ought to play a role in understanding fictional characters comparable with the role it plays (or is said to play) in understanding real people. They are not reasons for thinking that imaginative engagement with fictions is not mental simulation at all. All that follows is that the simulation doesn't have to be simulation of characters.

But granted the disanalogies between understanding real people and understanding fictional characters, might there still be cases where we do simulate characters? I think the answer is yes. As we shall see, this need not mean that other kinds of emotional effects are absent. Few works depend on, or could reasonably mandate, our imaginatively identifying with a character throughout, or our being so imaginatively absorbed as to have no other kind of experience. What is more common is for the work to encourage a complex mosaic of simulations which are simulations of characters, and simulations which are not.

Next I shall say something about the concept of empathy and its place in a theory of the imagination.

Empathy

A convenient way to make the distinction between impersonal simulation and simulation which constitutes imaginative projection into the situation of another is to describe the latter kind as empathy. This word may normally have some connotations that would be restrictive, given our interest. We often think of empathy primarily as a matter of shared feeling, and writers on ST have sometimes emphasized the role of such sharing in our understanding of other persons (see for example Goldman 1992, Gordon 1995). But I do not think that it can be definitive of empathy that it exclusively concerns feelings. At most we tend to assume that when I empathize with others I come to share with them mental states that have an affective component; empathizing with others' disappointment requires the mental rehearsal of their thoughts as well as of their feelings. I don't agree that the shared mental states must involve feeling, though they often do. Suppose someone is making a difficult decision, but does so coldly, without emotion. I can be said to empathize with that person's decision when I recreate his or her unemotional decision making in my own mind. The reason that empathy usually does involve feeling is that we are most conscious of using our empathic power when someone is in a disturbed or otherwise unusual state, and this usually involves some salient feeling. But where empathy does involve the recreation of another's emotion or feeling, ST can very well account for this, in terms of the common affective power of beliefs/desires and simulated beliefs/desires.

Empathy, as commonly understood, also carries with it implications of sympathy, but I shall follow more rigorous practice in thinking of empathy and sympathy as distinct (see for example Goldie 2002, Sober and Wilson 1999). I may be able to empathize with characters without sympathizing with them, though empathy may give most of us a tendency to sympathize. Perhaps the Count of Monte Cristo empathized with his enemies the better to take revenge on them.

Empathy, according to the description I have given so far, involves the sharing of another's mental state. A simulation-based account of empathy involves something less than a full sharing, because the idea is that I come to have pretend versions of your beliefs, and not those beliefs themselves; similarly for desires. This is surely reasonable: no one should claim that when I empathize with you I really come to believe and desire as you do; we cannot change our beliefs in such a way as to make that practicable. What of shared emotion? There are complex issues here to do with how we type-identify emotions. My own view is that it is possible to literally have the same emotion as others in the process of empathizing with them (Currie and Ravenscroft 2002: ch. 9). But I rest nothing on this and am content to allow that empathy provides us only with a pretend or "quasi" emotion-substitute (Walton 1990).

It is possible, within the framework of ST, to give different accounts of empathy, of different "thickness." Note that empathy does not occur simply because the reader and a character share an emotion, for two people with the same emotion do not automatically constitute a case of empathy. There must be some connection between these two emotional states stronger than coincidence. We could try an account in terms of "emotion tracking," analogous to the kind of gaze-following that we know infants and many animals are capable of. On this conception, I empathize with you only when your thoughts and feelings exercise control over mine. When you have certain thoughts (perhaps including indexical thoughts), I tend to have them also, and when you have certain feelings, I have them also. But this will not do. I might simply be subject to your influence, and generally respond to things as you do; this would not be empathy. Sober and Wilson claim that it is essential to empathy that the empathic emotion is experienced because I believe that you experience that very emotion (Sober and Wilson 1999: 234). In that case empathy could never be a source of knowledge about other people's emotions. Also, there are many cases where I empathize with you, and may end up having the same thought or feeling as you, but where my doing so is not relevantly caused by your having that thought or feeling. I wonder how you feel in a given situation; I imagine myself in that situation and come to feel a certain way; in this case I empathize with your feelings, but I do not come to empathize with you because you feel that way. The cause was, rather, my asking myself how you would feel in that situation.

One answer to these problems would be to propose a peculiar experiential aspect to empathic emotions, somewhat along the lines suggested by John Campbell in his account of joint attention, which he calls the relational experiential account (Campbell 2002, ch. 8). On Campbell's view, my jointly attending with you, to an object O, requires that your attending to O figures as a constituent in my experience of O; he argues that it is only this kind of joint attending that can make certain kinds of coordinated action rational. It is not clear how Campbell's proposal could be carried over to the case of empathizing with beliefs or desires, since his proposal concerns experiences. But it might work for emotional empathy if you think, as I do, that emotions are states much more like perceptions than they are like beliefs and desires (Currie and Ravenscroft 2002, ch. 9). However, I am inclined to think that this is not, in the end, a helpful suggestion. Certainly, we do not need to coordinate our actions with those of fictional characters. Nor, typically, do we need to imagine that we need to coordinate our actions with them. More importantly, a relational experiential account

Gregory Currie

of empathy would be self-defeating: when I set myself to get into the same mental state as a character who is thinking about a certain picture, the character's attending to the picture would appear as part of my simulative mental state, and so that simulated mental state would not have the same content as the character's. The character, after all, is not thinking about his or her own thinking.

We could try insisting that the empathizer takes a meta-propositional attitude toward the target of his or her empathy: that the empathic thought must be accompanied by the thought that, say, "I am (with this lower-level thought) trying to understand what this person thinks and how this person feels." I think we can be said to empathize even in some cases where no such meta-thoughts are present, at least at the time of the empathizing. Instead, we should see empathy in terms of the surrounding content of activity within which this feeling or thought occurs. Specifically, the feeling or thought needs to be embedded in a project with a certain kind of narrative shape. The conditions on this narrative are difficult to spell out and are certainly subject to vagueness, as I think is the question: what counts as empathy? Typical cases would be where I start by wondering how things are with the other person, and this leads to my imagining myself in the other person's position and coming to feel as that person does; this then leads me to a view about how the person feels. However, we should not insist that empathy results in an explicit belief to the effect that "That person feels this way"; it might simply be that you are justified in attributing to me a belief about the person's mental state on the basis of my going on to behave in some way that displays sensitivity to his or her feeling: helping, if I am well-motivated, or exploiting the person if I am not. In the case mentioned above, where I am much influenced by your reactions to others, this might, retrospectively come to count as a case of empathy if it resulted in my reflecting on how you feel about that person or behaving appropriately, based on an awareness (or presumption) that you and I feel the same. Empathy is a functional notion: it is the concept of a state that plays a characteristic role in a larger pattern of thought, feeling, and behavior.

Empathizing with Characters

In this final section I want to make out a case for the role of empathy in the reader's response to a literary work. As I have indicated, I will examine a specific case. While I have chosen a literary example, a cinematic or theatrical one would also have done as well (see Gaut 1999 and Smith 1997 for limited defenses of the role of empathy in film). One criticism of what follows is that it is merely an account of how the work struck me, and hence no basis for an argument. While I've tried to link claims about the work's emotional appeal to independently identifiable features of the work, we need to control our ambitions for objectivity in criticism. The failings of literary theory from structuralism onwards are partly the result of a false belief that we can replace personal sensitivity with a set of theory-driven categories; the result has been an extreme overvaluation of self-conscious artifice in narrative and an unfounded rejection of psychological realism. As Robert Alter remarked, analyzing a work's self-referential structure seems more rigorous than feeling the rightness of a character's action, but it gives a very distorted view of what's valuable in literature (Alter 1975). And to the extent that the objection about subjectivity is legitimate, it can be leveled against any account which places emphasis on emotional response; empathic responses are not more subjective than other emotions. I take myself to be arguing here with those who agree with me about the role of emotion in literature, and disagree simply about how much of that is empathic; they can't afford to throw around accusations of subjectivity.

Anne Brontë's *The Tenant of Wildfell Hall* was published in 1846, three years before her death (see Allott 1974 and Thormählen 1993 for the book's critical, intellectual, and religious context). Critical opinion at the time, including that of her sister Charlotte, was negative. A re-evaluation is underway, though one likely, I think, to generate its own misunderstandings. The book falls naturally into three sections, narrated, respectively, by Gilbert Markham, by Helen Huntingdon, and by Gilbert again. In the first Gilbert meets Helen, the mysterious new tenant of Wildfell Hall. He forms an attachment to her based on their mutual sympathy as well, no doubt, on the romantic obscurity of her situation. At the same time he is exasperated by the credence given by neighbors to rumors concerning her relations with her landlord, Frederick Lawrence. No sooner has Gilbert declared himself to Helen than he discovers apparently incontrovertible evidence of the truth of these rumors. The second part is Helen's own manuscript account of her earlier life, given to Gilbert by way of explanation. It describes her infatuation with and marriage to the worthless, tyrannical, and increasingly depraved Arthur Huntingdon, and her escape to Wildfell Hall, the owner of which is now revealed as her brother. The rumors exploded, Gilbert seeks a reconciliation. Helen sees clearly that her married state, however deplorable its circumstances, requires their separation. In the final part Helen nurses her ungrateful husband until his death, much hastened by excess, and Gilbert is prevented by reticence and misunderstanding from renewing his suit until goaded by false reports of her impending second marriage. Finally at her door and with her wealth visible around him, he reflects bitterly on the difference in their station and the unlikelihood that she will accept him. But Gilbert is wrong, though his concluding overview of their married life leaves open the question quite how satisfactory Helen herself has found it.

For all its relentlessly argumentative dialogue and clear didactic purpose, *The Tenant of Wildfell Hall* holds its reader through a variety of emotions. Not all these emotions are empathetic. Anxiety for Helen prior to what will obviously be a disastrous marriage; exasperation at her initial blindness to Arthur's wicked nature; hope that Arthur will die (apparently not shared by Helen): these are all cases of reader-emotions that are not empathetic. Conversely, some emotions experienced by characters are likely to be beyond the reach of many in a modern audience: Helen's agony of mind over the possibility of Arthur's eternal damnation, for example. And for reasons given in the earlier discussion, some cases where the reader may share an emotion with a character do not count as empathy. Along with the reader, Helen's aunt, Mrs Maxwell, feels anxiety at the prospect of her marriage to Arthur, but the reader's anxiety is probably not empathic. For this to be a case of empathy it is required (according to me) that the reader's feeling is part of some narrative of inquiry concerning Mrs Maxwell, and that does not seem to be what is going on here. Recall also that it is required for empathy that the shared emotions have the same object. I might feel relief when Helen accepts Gilbert, and partly because Gilbert is relieved, but if my relief is about Gilbert's state of mind, while his is about Helen's decision, my relief is not empathic.

Still, with all these reservations in place, I believe that empathy plays an important role in the reader's response to this novel, and that few readers would stay the course without its encouragement. The novel's three-part structure, with alternating narrators, has been variously interpreted as reflecting Gilbert's acceptance of Helen as an equal, and his attempt to control her. In my view the structure is best understood, not as suggesting relations between the characters, but as part of the work's strategy for encouraging empathy. The book's success depends on establishing, with the reader, a number of conflicting emotions concerning Helen, which Gilbert's perspective provides: we feel admiration for the spirited independence of her moral and aesthetic sensibility at the same time as we are irritated by her narrow attitudes. The second part enables us to explain all this by experiencing for ourselves something of the emotional journey that has shaped her. For this, it was essential that Helen's narrative should take the form it did: the much-criticized diary she places in Gilbert's hands. Those who would have preferred a direct telling fail to see that, being retrospective, this would have made it more difficult for us to empathize with Helen's younger self. The third part, while narrated by Gilbert, is somewhat complicated because the device of letters from Helen shifts the focus of empathy to her for some of the time. But the greater part of this, which is seen from Gilbert's perspective, sustains the narrative by reintroducing uncertainty about Helen's feelings. As I shall indicate, this is only partly successful.

Empathy serves two other functions in the book. One is to help us sympathize with attitudes and behavior that would otherwise tend to alienate us from the characters. We have seen how empathy helps us make sense of Helen's uncompromising moralism as well, incidentally, as her oddly protective attitude to her son. Just at the point where Gilbert believes the worst of Helen, Lawrence chides Gilbert for his ill-humor, saying "You have found your hopes defeated; but how am I to blame for it?" (Brontë [1846] 1976: 90). Gilbert responds by knocking Lawrence from his horse. Commentators have suggested that this suggests an affinity between Gilbert and Arthur. But while Gilbert does have significant failings, the contrast is stark: we observe Arthur's cruelty from the outside and feel only Helen's hurt, but we are encouraged to experience some of Gilbert's anger and resentment. We see how Lawrence's observation appears to Gilbert as a calculated and gratuitous addition to his humiliation. (See Neill 1996 for perceptive remarks on how empathy extends our emotional repertoire.)

The second function of empathy is to heighten and sustain certain emotions which might otherwise be compromised by our expectations about the narrative. In the first part we share Gilbert's admiration for Helen, and experience his growing attachment; we also feel something of his anguish as the result of his belief that she has formed a liaison with Lawrence – though we, as readers, may very well be convinced that this is merely a dramatic device and that Helen is innocent. In the second part we share Helen's feelings of disappointment with Arthur, and her growing recognition of his depravity, though we readers never expected anything better from this worthless character. In the final part we return to Gilbert, sharing in his uncertainty about

Helen's feelings now that she is free, though we have every reason to think, from a dramatic point of view, that all will end well for them.

I say again that empathy is just a part of our overall experience of the work. It is accompanied and modified by such other reactions as ironic distance from our own emotions, awareness of the author's manipulation of our responses, occasional doubts about plot construction, and dissatisfaction with the use of character and dialogue. It does not signal unthinking absorption or submission to authorial will. Nor does empathy with a character mean that we take that character's part in anything but the most provisional sense. Early in the novel, Gilbert and Helen debate the nature of virtue and the wisdom of sheltering children from the knowledge of vice. Here the narration encourages us to empathize with Gilbert's irritation at, as he puts it, "the continual injustice she has done me" (Brontë 1976: 22). Yet we are likely to conclude that Helen did not have the worst of the argument, and that some of her more extreme formulations are the expression of bitter experience that Gilbert has yet to comprehend. We may feel that Gilbert misjudges Helen, but we understand how easy it is for him to do so. Nor is the duration of empathy crucial in a temporal art like literature, any more than the extension of a color is crucial in a spatial art. In two paintings by Corot, *Ville-d'Avray* and *The Boatman of Montefontaine* (both in the Frick Collection), red occupies a tiny proportion of the canvas. Yet it is placed so as to profoundly affect our perception of the whole. Our experience of *The Tenant of Wildfell Hall* would be very different without those moments of empathic contact with Helen and Gilbert.

Reflection on the empathic structure of the work helps us understand, not merely our own responses, but also the author's intentions, the work's structure, and some of the factors that constrain and occasionally compromise its production. I have referred already to its three-part division, reflecting the shifts of perspective. First person narration is crucial for the empathetic effect in this novel, but the effect is heightened by the fact that both narrators are limited epistemically in ways that mirror their imperfect control over events and, occasionally, their own behavior. Fallible characters are easier to empathize with than omniscient narrators, partly because we are fallible, and we empathize better with people the more like us they seem to be (see e.g., Batson, Turk, Shaw, and Klein 1995). This creates a tension that is sometimes useful, but on at least one occasion undercuts the intended effect. The novel does not encourage empathy with Helen's early feelings of attachment to Arthur; Helen's own diary, despite its hopeful tone, makes clear his worth. This may have been intended by Anne Brontë, wishing to distance the reader from Helen's infatuation. But the device of a narrator who is, on the one hand mistaken and who, on the other, provides the reader with clear evidence of his or her mistake creates problems elsewhere. As I read it, we are intended to empathize with Gilbert's anxiety, very late in the book, about whether Helen will accept him. But the intention fails; his reporting of her demeanor indicates clearly that she will. At least, the effect is not long sustained. "There was such evidence of joyous though suppressed excitement in the utterance of those few words," notes Gilbert, on hearing Helen's reaction to his arrival (Brontë 1976: 378). The problem is not that Gilbert's perspective and ours are different; that is true, as I have emphasized, on a number of occasions in the book where we still manage to empathize with an anxious emotion even though we have good reasons to think things will turn out well. The problem is that we are expected to share his pessimism, while the grounds we have for being optimistic about the outcome are grounds we are invited to see from Gilbert's own perspective.

The Tenant of Wildfell Hall is unusual in many ways, certainly in its literary quality, and perhaps also in the extent of its dependence on empathic effects. It is, however, not alone in its use of these effects. We cannot understand or properly value it, and many other works besides, without understanding the mechanisms by which these effects are achieved. Imaginative exploration of characters is by no means all there is to literary experience, but we must be alive to its importance.

Note

I am grateful to Tamar Szabo Gendler, Paul Noordhof, and Bob Stecker for extensive commentary and discussion. This research was supported by a small grant from the British Academy.

Imagine That!

Jonathan M. Weinberg and Aaron Meskin

Introduction

Many components of our psychology may reasonably be labeled "imagination," but one such component plays an especially important role in our experience of works of fiction. We will use the term "cognitive imagination" to mark off this particular type of imagination, for it shares many of the typical properties of belief. For example, both cognitive imaginings and beliefs have propositional contents (and we thus speak both of "believing that" p and "imagining that" p). Importantly, the cognitive imagination also lacks other traits that are characteristic of belief; for example, beliefs are truth-directed and play a privileged role in causing action, and neither of those claims are true of imaginings. We will indicate here some of the cognitive imagination's explanatory value, illustrating the central role it must play in any account of a number of fundamental phenomena of our engagement in fiction. Yet we will also, at the end of the essay, suggest that an account of our interaction with fiction must look beyond the imagination as well.

So our primary aim is to present a theory of the cognitive imagination as it functions in our engagement with fiction. To do so, we first need to canvass the explananda that any such theory must accommodate. We focus in the next section on sketching two broad classes of fiction-related phenomena that any theory of the imagination must account for.

Fictional Explananda

First, the cognitive-epistemic phenomena, which have to do broadly with our ability to follow and comprehend fictional narrative:

1   *Capacity for fictional import and export.* The business of imaginatively engaging with fiction is a business of import and export. First, an important aspect of our engagement with fiction is our capacity to engage in "filling-in." Fictions do not make explicit all that is required in order to understand and appreciate them (Walton 1990: 138ff, Carroll 1998: 319–23). So we draw on background assumptions in order to flesh out the fictional scenarios that are presented to us. We do not, then, simply imagine the explicitly represented contents in fictions, but instead marshal knowledge we have both of the ordinary world and of the nature of fictions (e.g., genre conventions) to enhance the contents of our imaginings. Any plausible theory of the cognitive imagination must make sense of this general capacity for the importation into the imagination of content from our store of beliefs. We also have the capacity to export contents – in metarepresentational form – from the imagination. In fact, we are not only ordinarily capable of forming beliefs about what we do and did imagine, but this basic capacity also enables us to form beliefs about what is true in fictions. It is this latter capacity that underwrites both our memories of fictions and the pleasures we take in discussing them.

2   *Access to the inferential mechanisms.* It isn't just the heroes of detective fictions who are masters of abductive inference, so too are many of the readers of such fictions. For even as the gumshoe attempts to determine the perpetrator's identity, so too does the mystery reader curled up with the book. But this is just one example – in fact, the comprehension, appreciation, and enjoyment of much fiction requires the ability to engage in various inferences in the imagination. So the cognitive imagination must have access to whatever psychological processes underwrite our ability to perform inferences.

3   *Representational distinguishability.* While there certainly is a wide range of interaction between our store of beliefs and the cognitive imagination, it is also the case that the two capacities are functionally distinct: we do not, merely in virtue of imagining something thereby believe it; nor do we merely in virtue of believing a proposition thereby come to imagine that proposition. Also, we can deploy both capacities synchronically – imagining does not preclude belief, nor vice versa.

Next we turn to four phenomena that are related to our affective responses to fiction:

4   *Phenomenological and physiological robustness.* Most fictions elicit affective responses that feel substantive from the first-person perspective. Moreover, these fictions can be observed from the third-person perspective to have significant effects on the audience. As Colin Radford puts it: "We shed real tears for Mercutio. They are not crocodile tears, they are dragged from us and they are not the sort of tears that are produced by cigarette smoke in the theatre" (Radford 1975: 70). While a theory of the cognitive imagination need not take attributions of full-fledged emotions in response to fiction at face value, it must offer an explanation of such attributions – and, in particular, the phenomenological and physiological reactions that underlie them. We will use the term "fictive affect" to refer to these reactions, so as to remain neutral on the question of whether these responses are, in fact, full-fledged emotions.

5 *Ambiguous relationship to nonfictive affect and emotion.* Indeed philosophers have debated whether audiences of fiction typically experience such emotions as anger, sadness, or joy. For example, Kendall Walton holds that typical viewers of horror films do not literally fear the monsters that populate them, although they may feel "quasi-fear sensations," rather it is *fictional* that they feel such fear (Walton 1990). Yet Berys Gaut accuses Walton's theory of failing to respect the fact that we actually do fear fictional monsters (Gaut 1993). Given such disagreement, it would be rash to stipulate the matter in either direction. Instead, a theory here ought to treat the disagreement itself as an explanandum. There is something about fictive affect that tugs us towards ascribing the garden-variety emotions, and also something that pulls us away. This tension itself stands in need of an explanation.

6 *Fiction-directed affective intentionality.* Fictive affect does not just feel real – it is also experienced as character- (and event-) directed. While reading or watching *The Lord of the Rings*, we feel both pity *for* and disgust *with* Gollum, and fear *for* the characters fighting the Uruk-hai. Many of our affective responses to fictions are experienced and described in such intentional terms. Moreover, we take it *prima facie* to be the case that people are correct in those descriptions.

7 *Behavioral circumscription.* Audiences experiencing fictive affect will display a small but significant set of relevant behaviors, but will fail to demonstrate other behaviors that would be expected of someone experiencing its nonfictive analogue. As the Radford quote above indicates, we do exhibit some of the *behavioral* responses that typically go along with the emotions. Yet we do not (generally) find audience members behaving fully as they do when they have emotional responses in ordinary (i.e., nonfictive) life. Horror movie viewers do not typically flee the cinema screaming. Fictive affect's behavioral range is typically quite circumscribed.

There is one further major explanatory constraint on a theory of the imagination: the theory must predict not just that we have affective responses as characterized by (4)–(7), but it must furthermore correctly predict the *particular* responses we have to particular fictions. If a theory predicts that we have fictive affect, but predicts the wrong affective responses (e.g., fear of Frodo, admiration for the Uruk-hai), then such a theory must obviously be rejected.

Towards Minimal Nondoxastic Cognitivism

Once these explananda are recognized, several theories of the cognitive imagination that otherwise might have seemed attractive can be seen to be absolute nonstarters. Despite the popularity of the slogan "suspension of disbelief," any theory claiming that engaging with fiction involves our coming literally to believe the contents of a fiction runs immediately afoul of the distinguishability explanandum. Moreover, unless such an "illusion theory" supplements itself with some account of how our action-guiding system is disconnected during the course of the cognitive illusion, it would seem to entail that, for whatever time we were really believing the contents, we would act accordingly – and thus it would fail to accommodate behavioral circumscription. Such an account will have no problem explaining import, since non-

Jonathan M. Weinberg & Aaron Meskin

imaginative beliefs will be able to interact with "imagined" representations in just the same way that all our beliefs can interact with each other. But it is unclear how we could infer in-the-story-it-is-true-that-p from a mere belief that p, so our capacity to export is left unexplained. It is also not clear that the illusion theory will predict the *right* fictive affect. In some contexts (such as black comedies), our affective responses to fictional events are quite different from what they would be if we believed them to be happening (see S. Nichols forthcoming).

The failures of the illusion theory suggest a different belief-based theory: to imagine the fictional content p is simply to hold the belief about the fiction that in-the-story-it-is-true-that-p. Although the "metarepresentational" theory clearly entails behavioral circumscription (since such beliefs about a fictional story will rarely prompt us to an action), it also seems unable to explain phenomenological/physiological robustness. Fearful affective responses, for example, seem to require representations of the form *S is in danger*, where S is someone we care about. But it is not enough for the representation to be a subpart of another representation. For example, if you believe, not that *the slime is threatening*, but that *a friend think the slime is threatening*, your only fear will be for that friend's sanity; similarly for a belief that *it is metaphysically possible that a slime is threatening*. So a belief like *in the novel it is true that S is in danger* is not of the right form to generate correct affective responses.

A further problem for the metarepresentational theory is that we often have affective responses to imaginings that are not derived from any fiction. Merely imagining a close friend's being in great pain may be enough to produce a pang of pity, without there being any work of fiction at all concerning your friend and his or her suffering (cf. Gaut 2003). While it might seem tempting to suggest that in such cases a minimal story is created, such a view leaves open the question of what it is to be a story. And the metarepresentational theorist cannot explain what a story is in terms of imagining, since that would lead to vicious circularity.

The upshot of these failures is that beliefs themselves are inappropriate to be the representations of the imagination. But we know that the cognitive imagination must involve something very much like beliefs. Fiction-directed intentionality, for example, is most easily explained in terms of imaginative representations having basically the same semantic properties as beliefs. That we can import beliefs into the imagination, and export them out again, indicates a certain structural affinity between belief and imagination. Imagination should have representations that are belief-like; but such phenomena as behavioral circumscription and distinguishability indicate that they cannot be *too* belief-like. So the first substantive lesson about the imagination that we learn from considering the explananda is what we will call *minimal nondoxastic cognitivism* (MNC): (1) the mental representations of the cognitive imagination share the basic syntactic and semantic properties of beliefs, and (2) they can interact with both the inferential and affective systems in much the same way as beliefs, but (3) they lack other of the causal properties of beliefs, especially the capacity to direct our action-control systems. We claim that any successful theory of the cognitive imagination will endorse MNC.

As noted already, any MNC theory should also do fine with fiction-directed affective intentionality, because the representations in the imagination can take the fictional characters and situations as their objects. That an MNC's mental representations are both similar and dissimilar to beliefs furthermore accounts for the difficulty in deciding whether fictive affect is real emotions or not. To whatever extent the representations drive our affect systems in the same way that beliefs do, to that extent we will be inclined to call those reactions real emotions; to whatever extent the representations fail to drive our action-systems in the way that is usually associated with emotions like fear, to that extent we will be inclined to withhold the title of real emotions from them.

Moreover, MNCs seem to be halfway in the right direction towards explaining the epistemic-cognitive aspects of our engagements with fictions. By having two distinct types of representation, it clearly has the right raw materials for representational distinguishability. Moreover, recall that an MNC insists that imaginative representations can interact with our inferential mechanisms in much the same way that beliefs do. Thus inferential access will be automatically accommodated. Now, in order to explain import and export, an MNC would have to be filled out to posit some sorts of mechanisms or processes underlying those capacities, but there is no reason to expect that this could not be done successfully.

Given these moderately rich explanatory resources, is MNC sufficient as a theory of the cognitive imagination? Unfortunately, it is not enough. For example, we do not wish to explain merely that *some* sort of affective responses can happen, but moreover to explain the *particular* sorts of responses that we do in fact have. We do not wish merely to explain the raw possibility of import and export, but moreover to explain the particular ways in which those capacities are exercised. In short, endorsing MNC is enough to point us towards good candidates for explanations of the cognitive imagination, but does not of itself provide us with a sufficient account.

One way we can see that MNC is explanatorily insufficient is by noting that a variety of different and apparently opposed theories are consistent with the minimal constraints that MNC places on any acceptable account of the cognitive imagination. Various "simulation theories" (Currie 1995a, 1995b, and this volume), "thought theories" (Carroll 1990: 79–87), and the "possible-worlds box" approach we articulated in an earlier paper (Meskin and Weinberg 2003) all look to be consistent with MNC. This supports our contention that MNC is not enough to count as a full-fledged theory of the cognitive imagination. Those interested in the cognitive imagination will therefore want to explore possible ways of enriching MNC.

Imagination as Simulation?

One metaphor that has proved very fertile in providing possible enrichments of MNC is that of *simulation*: to imagine that p is, in some sense, to simulate believing that p. Left merely as a metaphor, though, the simulation idea stands as nothing more than an adherence to MNC. Though many philosophers have agreed that there is *something* to this idea of imagination as simulated belief, distinct ways of cashing out the metaphor into a theory have proliferated. We will consider three such glosses here, in terms of *cognitive architecture, character identification,* and *psychological explanation.*

Jonathan M. Weinberg & Aaron Meskin

Since the notion of mental simulation has its original home in psychology and the philosophy of mind, it is unsurprising that one popular way of fleshing out simulation has been in terms of cognitive architecture (Gordon 1986, Goldman 1989, Currie 1995a, Walton 1997, Nichols and Stich 2000). The *architectural hypothesis* claims that, when we use our imaginations, we take our belief-system "offline," disconnecting it from the systems that normally produce action and most behaviors, while leaving it connected to the inferential and affect systems. When imagining that p, we thus use our own belief system containing a representation that p to simulate being a p-believer. This hypothesis also requires some system for temporarily disabling any ordinary beliefs we might have which we are not also imagining, such that they will not interfere with the imagination but can be restored when we go back "online." Moreover, the system must mark the imagined representations as such, so that they can be expelled from the system at the simulation's end, and return the belief system to its previous, nonimagined state (with added ordinary beliefs about what happened in the story, thereby enabling exportation).

This idea of a redeployed belief system nicely fits the bill for MNC: the offline system retains just the right links to the other cognitive systems to enable the explanations that MNC wishes to make, allowing us to make inferences in the imagination and feel emotional responses. But it avoids any bizarre behavioral consequences, by having the action systems offline during the simulation, and by purging the fiction's contents at the end of the simulation.

Nonetheless, the architectural reading of simulation fails badly on other explananda. The hypothesis is badly inconsistent with representational distinguishability. We very frequently engage in both ordinary belief-involving cognition and imaginative cognition at exactly the same time. But when the belief system is being redeployed to act as our imagination, it cannot at that time also operate in ordinary cognition. That fact also indicates that the architectural hypothesis cannot explain the particulars of the importation phenomena. Our ordinary beliefs must be rendered inoperative during the simulation, or else they will automatically count as being imagined. Yet, while they are inoperative, unable to interact with their fellow beliefs and with the inferential and other cognitive mechanisms, they therefore cannot be drawn upon for the purposes of filling out the imagined situations. The view can explain the possibility of *some* importation, by allowing appropriate beliefs to be added in as simulated beliefs at the beginning of the simulation. But ongoing importation during simulation cannot be so accommodated. So, despite its popularity, we must reject the architectural hypothesis.

Another popular way of adding some substance to the simulation metaphor is suggested by the notion of character identification. Readers often speak in such terms (see below), and this construction suggests that engaging with fiction centrally involves a process of taking on a character's or characters' beliefs as if they were our own. Certainly many philosophers have been attracted to this idea (Currie 1997, Walton 1997). Although it has sometimes been packaged with the architectural hypothesis, we can consider the idea of character identification independent of any particular psychological implementation of it; we'll call this the *character identification hypothesis*. This view adds to MNC its claims about what particular belief-like representations we ought to entertain, when engaging with fictions – namely, the representations with the same contents as the beliefs of some character or characters. Since characters engage in inferences, so would we when identifying them; since characters feel emotions, so would we enjoy analogous affective responses.

However, the character identification hypothesis quickly runs into irremediable difficulties. For starters, this proposal entails that our emotions should track those of the characters; yet often we have emotions that they do not have (Carroll 1998, Meskin and Weinberg 2003). We may know the heroine is in danger, yet she is blissfully ignorant of the faceless chainsaw-wielding zombie just off screen. Moreover, there are cases where readers apparently imagine things that are not believed by any character in the fiction at all. Some fictions, such as Ray Bradbury's "There Will Come Soft Rains," do not really have any characters who are psychological entities at all.

Recognizing these difficulties, some philosophers have suggested that in addition to being able to simulate the explicit characters in the fiction, we can simulate being someone who is taking the fiction to be a veridical account of actual events. Indeed, some fictions, such as epistolary novels, seem to require not just imagining their contents but imagining that we are reading their contents. So perhaps that kind of imagining can be generalized to all fictions. Gregory Currie has argued for such a view in his earlier work: "As a reader of fiction, I simulate (put myself in the shoes of) someone who is reading a factual account" (Currie 1997: 68–9). Clearly such a "reader of fact" could have all sorts of beliefs and affective responses that no explicit character in the story has.

But other aspects of our responses to fiction cannot be explained by this version of the character identification hypothesis. In particular, some fictions seem inconsistent with the existence of such an imagined reader. Consider a science fiction story about a psychological virus that spreads uncontrollably, destroying the minds of all who contract it. Medical science is unable to contain this unprecedented affliction, and the story ends tragically after the death of the last psychological being in the universe: "The mind–body problem was solved once and for all, and there was no one left to dispute that body was now, and eternally, the victor." There is simply no way to simulate reading that story as a veridical account. Who is supposed to have written the account? Moreover, who are *we* supposed to be, to now be reading it? Simulating believing the story to be true is inconsistent with our simulating believing ourselves to be engaged in any sort of mental activity at all, either the imagining of the contents or the sadness that results from it.

In short, the character identification hypothesis fails because it requires that we have some sort of target psyche for our simulations, and many fictions simply lack appropriate targets for us to be simulating. An adherent to MNC need not insist that we never simulate particular entities – perhaps that is how they would explain instances of empathetic responses to some fictions – but it had better not require that we always do so.

Currie recognizes this problem: "Simulations are always simulations of *something*, but there need be no interesting sense in which they are simulations of someone" (Currie, this volume: 213, emphasis in original). Currie thus has come lately to prefer what he terms "impersonal simulation." But what, beyond mere adherence to MNC, could the idea of "impersonal simulation" amount to? We offer one conjecture here.

Jonathan M. Weinberg & Aaron Meskin

Currie does reject the claim that in simulating a belief that p, we are simulating being any particular p-believer. Nonetheless, he is still committed to the idea that the reader's imagination-involving psychological responses and activities with the fiction are fundamentally analogous to the activities of a parallel individual with identical but nonimaginary beliefs and desires. (See, for example, Currie's discussion of *Peter Pan* in this volume.) So let us consider Currie's idea of impersonal simulation as amounting to this hypothesis: we can explain the particular psychological transactions of a reader using imagined beliefs, desires, and so forth in the exact same way that we can explain parallel transactions by a person with the corresponding real beliefs, desires, and so forth. In essence, the folk psychological hypothesis claims that we can supplement MNC with the general principles of folk psychological explanation (excluding those that predict action), as expanded to cover imaginative states in just the way it is usually taken to cover their nonimaginative counterparts; and that, if we do so, we can generate a complete psychological explanation of our dealings with fiction. For example, we can explain our apparent sadness for Anna Karenina, by appeal to our simulated beliefs about her awful situation (and perhaps simulated desires, see below), plus some basic principles about what sorts of beliefs typically lead to feelings of sadness.

How does this view differ from the character identification hypothesis? It differs in that the *total* set of imagined beliefs need not correspond to the *total* set of any even possible person's beliefs, but the *local* activities of those imagined beliefs should be explicable in exactly the way we would explain the particular activities by someone who had those beliefs (and other mental states, of course). For example, Currie could explain our apparent sadness at the end of the earlier sci-fi short story in the following way. We have the simulated belief that the last enpsyched creature has died, and the simulated desire that the death of all thinking things not happen; fictive affect results, with at least the phenomenological and physiological correlates of sadness. So our sadness-like response can be explained in the exact same way we would explain the actual sadness of someone whose belief that p collided fatefully with his or her desire that not-p. The view does not, however, require that our simulated beliefs more generally model those of any character, and so it does not encounter the "no target" problem faced by the character identification idea of simulation.

Despite the advantages that the folk psychological hypothesis has over other glosses on the simulation idea, we contend that its resources are insufficient to account for many important aspects of our imaginative engagements with fiction. Problems for the view take the form of psychological phenomena common to such engagements that cannot be explained by appeal only to our simulated psychological states and the explanatory principles of folk psychology. In particular, there are cases in which we need to appeal to both the simulated states and our ordinary, nonsimulated states *at the same time*. There is no parallel to such psychological activities in our ordinary cognition – it would be like having two distinct, mutually inconsistent, but interacting belief systems. For any bit of our psychology requiring a psychologically mixed explanation, it will not suffice merely to expand the principles of folk psychology concerning beliefs, desires, and the like to cover "belief-like" imaginings and "desire-like" imaginings. For there is nothing in those principles to cover transactions between imaginings and beliefs, yet such transactions are exactly what we need to have explained. While these sorts of phenomena are quite common, we will document here only two kinds requiring such mixed explanations: genre knowledge and star power.

First, our imaginings, and our expectations about those imaginings, presuppose knowledge of how various sorts of fictions work. We expect that the hero can hold off the vampire with a cross, not because we have an importable belief that real vampires can be so thwarted, but because we know that this is a standard convention of certain horror stories. But how do we know to bring in that kind of information? Presumably we recognize various cues – moody lighting, creaky floorboards, spooky music – and infer from them that the story is probably a horror story. And extrafictional factors may be relevant, like an author's reputation, the shelf category head in the bookstore, or even the font of the book's title. Suppose we imagine that a cross is placed prominently in the protagonist's bedroom, and come as a result to expect that that cross will play a role in some future supernatural struggle. Can the formation of that expectation be explained with the resources of the folk psychological simulation hypothesis? It would seem not. These recognitions are clearly not happening inside the imagination – we don't typically imagine anything *about* horror stories, but rather imagine the contents *of* a horror story. So the explanation of that expectation would require the following extraimaginative steps: an inference from the genre cues to a belief about the fiction's genre; an inference from the genre to the presence of its conventions; and, finally, the formation of the expectation based on the genre conventions and the imagined content of the cross.

"Star power" is another factor that influences our experience of fiction, but which falls outside of the purview of Currie's current theory. In *The World Viewed*, Stanley Cavell has suggested that the film star's identity as star carries significant weight, perhaps even more than the weight of the character he or she is portraying in any given film (Cavell 1971). Cavell interprets the weight of stardom ontologically, but a less contentious psychological reading will suffice for our purposes. When a film star is in a movie, both the character's identity and the identity of the star are psychologically salient. For example, Bogart plays Bogart as much as he plays any particular private eye or proprietor of a North African café, and his Bogeyness informs our experience of his films. And this psychological doubleness is no mere side-effect or cognitive quirk. Rather, filmmakers count on it and exploit it.

V. F. Perkins describes an excellent example of this in his discussion of how Hitchcock pulls off a brilliant transfer of our sympathies and expectations approximately one-third of the way into his film *Rope* (Perkins 1972). For the first half-hour, we find ourselves sympathizing with the young perpetrators of the heartless murder that launches the film. For example, as their housekeeper draws ever closer to almost discovering the corpse, we feel a gnawing fear on their behalf. But once the character Rupert enters, played by James Stewart, our sympathies begin immediately to switch over to him, and as his idle curiosity is further roused, even though "we originally wanted nothing to interfere with the success of the criminals' enterprise, we spend the final half-hour of the film longing for our new hero to expose the murder" (Perkins 1972: 143). Perkins observes that this reversal is facilitated by not just the movie convention that crime must not pay, but also the convention of "greater star-power (James Stewart as the detective versus Farley Granger and John Dall as the murderers)" (p. 143). Perkins's observation corresponds quite closely with our own phenomenology

Jonathan M. Weinberg & Aaron Meskin

of that movie. When the character of Rupert comes onscreen, we cannot but see him as *James Stewart*, and our affective proclivities begin to reconfigure accordingly.

So our recognition of who plays what role can deeply inform both our expectations as well as our affective responses to the fiction. Yet we do not in any sense imagine that a character is being played by any actor. Indeed, we almost never imagine any contents about characters *qua* fictional entities. To explain our sympathy for Rupert we must look beyond the imagination, and include our nonimaginative recognition of Stewart, and our beliefs about his typical roles. This transfer of sympathies thus falls outside of the explanatory ambit of the folk psychological hypothesis.

An Alternative Account of the Cognitive Imagination

Let us suggest another way of supplementing MNC, without relying on the simulation metaphor. We start with an explicit rejection of the architectural simulation hypothesis, by postulating a *distinct* representational system in which the imagined contents are entertained (Nichols and Stich 2000, Meskin and Weinberg 2003). This "imagination system" is very similar to the belief system, but with key differences rendering it appropriate for MNC. The representations in the imagination system are of just the same form as beliefs; for example, they are propositional. Furthermore (and in virtue of this), imagined contents interact causally with many of the same systems, and in much the same way, that beliefs do. For example, both systems can take input from the perceptual systems, and both systems can input to and receive output from our inferential mechanisms. Moreover, both systems can drive our affect systems. But the two systems are not functionally identical. Importantly, the imagination system is not connected to the action guidance system in the way that the belief system is. And, of course, the general function of the imagination is not to represent the world as it is (as is the function of belief).

This "double representational system" architecture suggests some very easy explanations of some of the MNC phenomena. The imagination system's representations have just the right connections to account for phenomenological/physiological robustness and access to the inferential systems, as well as the sense that our affective responses to fiction have something deeply akin to regular emotions. And they lack just the right connections to respect behavioral circumscription and our sense that our affective responses to the imagination are not full-fledged emotions. Representational distinguishability and the possibility of simultaneous belief and imagination fall right out of there being two separate systems, whereas we get fiction-directed intentionality from imaginative representations' having the same format as regular beliefs. The import/export phenomena can be explained by positing mechanisms that bridge the two systems; such mechanisms are unproblematic precisely because the two systems use the same format for their representations. Basic export just requires some sort of monitoring system that can track what contents are in the imagination, a very simple mechanism that tacks "What I am imagining is that . . ." onto the front of any content in the imagination system, and the capacity to post the result to the belief system (cf. Nichols and Stich 2002 on self-knowledge). In order to form beliefs about what is fictionally the case, there must also be a way of keeping track of the source of the imaginative contents. Import is only somewhat more complicated, but more on that in a moment.

We need to show that the double-system theory avoids the problems that the other theories we have seen so far have encountered. It obviously succeeds better than the illusion and metarepresentational theories, since it is an MNC theory. But what about the different simulation hypotheses? It is superior to the architectural hypothesis, because it has no trouble with the simultaneous use of belief and imagination. And it is superior to the character identification approach, because there is no requirement that the body of representations in the imagination system correspond to the beliefs of any being at all, real or fictional.

Moreover, the double-system theory is superior to the folk psychological hypothesis precisely because we can offer explanations about how the two systems interact and influence each other – a kind of explanation not available to the latter account. We first need to add an element to our theory: imaginative voluntarism. That is, we can often simply decide to imagine anything that we have the conceptual resources to represent in the first place. We need not be committed to the claim that we can always do this, and certainly not to any claim that we don't often find ourselves imagining things totally outside of any deliberative control. All we need is that we have some appropriate mechanism connecting our decision systems and the imagination system, which can take a decision to imagine that p as input, and thereupon output a p-representation into the imagination system. There should be no difficulty in appealing to such a mechanism since it is already required to explain other imaginative capacities such as hypothetical reasoning and pretend play.

With this mechanism in place, it is easy to explain the complicated import-involving phenomena underlying our use of genre knowledge and star powers. We can believe (via export) that various genre-appropriate characteristics have been manifested in the fiction, and infer from those beliefs that the work is in that genre, and from there form appropriate expectations as well as appropriate filling in of the fictional world. And star power arises from our simultaneously believing that, for example, Rupert is being played by James Stewart, and that James Stewart characters tend to be trustworthy protagonists, and our imagining that Rupert is suspicious of the boys' behavior. These sorts of explanations centrally involve the coordination of the two distinct representational systems, and thus they are unavailable to any of the simulation hypotheses we have considered here.

The resulting picture is one in which imagination plays *a* central, but not *the* central, role in the psychology of fiction. The imagination is actively managed by the rest of our cognition, which in turn is influenced by the imagination (primarily by the latter's driving our affect systems and the monitoring systems underlying export). Hence our fundamental claim here is that fiction may all be in our heads, but it's not all in our imaginations. We will conclude our argument by clarifying our view with respect to two possible worries: whether we need to posit yet another system to account for pretend desires; and whether we can, having abandoned simulation, make sense of the very idea of character identification.

Jonathan M. Weinberg & Aaron Meskin

Desire and Imagination

In recent writings (Currie 1999, 2002, Currie and Ravenscroft 2002), Currie has empha-sized the role that desire-like imaginative states play in our engagement with fiction. Such states – if they existed – would be functionally akin to, but not identical with, ordinary desires. In particular, they would interact with belief-like imaginings in much the same way that desires interact with beliefs, albeit in a manner consistent with behavioral circumscription. Moreover, rather than representing the world as we would like it to be (as desires do), desire-like imaginings presumably represent things as we would hypothetically like them to be.

While there is nothing in our theory as sketched so far that precludes the existence of imaginative states that are functionally akin to desires, we are skeptical of the arguments for their existence that Currie presents. In fact, we are skeptical of the need to posit anything at all like desire-like imaginings in order to explain any imagina-tion-related phenomena. Full-fledged desires, as well as belief-like imaginings that one desires, appear to be enough to explain the features of our imaginative experi-ence to which Currie points.

Currie argues that any theory of the imagination will have to posit the existence of desire-like imaginings to explain our ability to engage in practical reasoning in the context of imagining (Currie 2002: 210–11). While we agree with Currie that some-thing other than ordinary desires must be posited in order to explain imaginative practical reasoning, we see no reason why we need posit anything other than belief-like imaginings. In such cases, we simply need to *imagine that we desire something*. But such states are not desire-like, they are belief-like imaginings about desires.

Currie argues that we must posit the existence of desire-like imaginings to explain why we have the particular affective responses to fictional characters that we do (Currie 2002: 211–13). For example, the death of a fictional hero typically affects us very differently than the death of a villain. And the difference in our responses does not seem as if it can be explained merely in terms of differences in beliefs or belief-like imaginings about those characters. The best explanation for the difference looks to be that some desires or desire-like states are involved in the generation of our emo-tional responses. Furthermore, we do talk of what we want for certain fictional char-acters (see the Perkins quote above). But Currie argues that we cannot be referring to real desires. And belief-like imaginings about desires won't do the trick here – having a desire within the scope of belief-like imagining does not look as if it could inter-act with belief in order to produce affect. So Currie reasons that it must be desire-like imaginings that play a role in generating fictive affect.

But why couldn't ordinary character-directed desires work to explain our differ-ential responses to heroes and villains? Currie suggests that the only way we can make sense of nonimaginative desires directed towards fictional characters is by understanding them as desires that *in the fiction* certain things about those charac-ters be the case. But this, he argues, fails to make sense of our attitudes and responses towards fiction. First, when we are sad about the fate of a character we are not, thereby, sad that the fiction is such that the character suffers that fate. Second, the (often pleasurable) tension that we frequently feel when appreciating a tragedy seems to involve conflict between desire-like character-directed imaginings (e.g., that the character fare well) and genuine desires that the tragedy be such that those character-directed desires are unsatisfied (Currie 2002: 212).

We find Currie's reasoning here quite odd. While there does seem to be an inner tension between our desires for Desdemona and our desires about how *Othello* will turn out, the natural explanation of such a tension would be in terms of conflicting full-fledged desires. In fact, conflict between ordinary desires strikes us as a much more plausible story of the psychological tensions that tragedies tend to produce than the account that Currie offers. After all, one does not feel tension when one believes and imagines propositions that are inconsistent; why would one feel tension when one's desires and desire-like imaginings were in conflict? Moreover, it does not seem at all implausible that we both desire that it is true that in the fiction Desdemona does well while also desiring that the fiction that we are reading or watching is of a tragic sort. For even if Desdemona's doing well would entail that *Othello* was radically different than it is, our desiring the former does not entail our desiring the latter (Neill 1993, Gaut 2003). (Compare: both authors desire to be professional philosophers, but neither desires to be penurious, even though they know that pursuing the former may well lead to becoming the latter.)

We believe, then, that we need not add anything to our theory in order to explain the phenomena to which Currie points. In fact, there is a perfectly good explanation for the fact that "desire-like imaginings don't seem to figure much in folk-psychological thought and talk about the imagination" (Currie 2002: 213): there simply are no desire-like imaginings. There are real desires and there are belief-like imaginings about desires. The former play a significant role in our engagement with fiction. The latter are crucial to imaginative practical reasoning. But we need not posit the existence of any desire-like states over and above these. (See Nichols 2004 for related criticisms of the desire-like imagining proposal.)

Identification and the Imagination

We have, to this point, said little about imaginative identification other than to dispute the view that our engagement with fiction is essentially a matter of identifying with characters. This may seem to be a lacuna, since it is a commonplace that our engagement with fiction centrally involves a process of identification with characters, and it is natural to assume that this process takes place in the imagination. Moreover, folk wisdom seems to hold that the quality of some fictional works is, at least in part, dependent on the extent to which they elicit character identification. Hence, the frequent complaint that "I didn't like the movie, because I couldn't identify with any of the characters." Many authors take these bits of folk wisdom quite seriously (Gaut 1999: 200).

We agree that consumers of fiction appear to be referring to *some* phenomenon (or phenomena), related largely to care and concern for characters, when they talk of identification. But neither the term nor its ordinary usage license any assumptions about the psychological processes and mechanisms underlying the phenomena it picks out – for example, whether it essentially involves imagining about the self or even whether it is an imaginative activity at all.

Jonathan M. Weinberg & Aaron Meskin

Our theory of the cognitive imagination has the resources to make sense of at least two very distinct activities, both of which might plausibly be thought of as species of identification (although only the first one could be reasonably thought of as species of *imaginative* identification). In particular, we distinguish *imaginative character identification* from *doxastic character identification*. Both can be easily explained on our account of the imagination.

Let us first consider imaginative character identification. What does this consist in? The etymology of the term "identification" has suggested to many that it must indicate an imagined numerical identity between the self and a fictional character. But we are sympathetic to the view that full-fledged identity (even in the imagination) is not required for identification. Instead, we follow Gaut in thinking that identification is (at least typically) aspectual (Gaut 1999). Exercise of the imaginative identification merely requires that one imagine that one is similar-in-certain-respects to a fictional character (i.e., that one shares properties with the character). For example, while reading a comic book one might imagine that one is similar to Superman with respect to his moral fiber while not imagining that one is similar to him with respect to strength. Our account of the imagination – in fact any account that is committed to MNC – has no problem accommodating such belief-like states. And such states might well play a role in our engagement with fiction, particularly in generating empathetic responses to fictional characters.

But just as we might imagine that we share various properties with a fictional character, we might also come to believe that we are similar in certain respects to a fictional character. For example, when one imagines that Frodo is brave, one will (via export) typically come to believe that it is true in the fiction that Frodo is brave. And if one happens also to believe that one is brave, then one can easily infer that one is similar to Frodo with respect to bravery.

We suggest that one thing that much of the talk about identifying (or failing to identify) with fictional characters has to do with is the presence or absence of such *beliefs* about similarities between the self and fictional characters – that is, doxastic identification. Again, this identification is most plausibly understood to be aspectual. It is not plausible that normal consumers of fiction ever come to literally believe they are the fictional characters they read about. But we believe that consumers of fiction frequently come to believe that they are like (or unlike) those fictional characters in salient ways. If reference to identification is required to explain certain fiction-related phenomena, then we suggest that doxastic identification may often do the trick.

References for Chapters 13 and 14

Allott, M. (ed.) (1974). *The Brontës: The Critical Heritage*. London: Routledge and Kegan Paul.

Alter, R. (1975). *Partial Magic*. Berkeley: University of California Press.

Batson, C., Turk, C., Shaw, L., and Klein, T. (1995). "Information Function of Empathic Emotion." *Journal of Personality and Social Psychology*, 68: 300–13.

Brontë, A. ([1848] 1976). *The Tenant of Wildfell Hall*. London and New York: Dent/Dutton Everyman Library.

Campbell, J. (2002). *Reference and Consciousness*. Oxford: Clarendon Press.

Carroll, N. (1990). *The Philosophy of Horror, or, Paradoxes of the Heart*. New York: Routledge.

Carroll, N. (1997). "Simulation, Emotions and Morality." In G. Hoffmann and A. Hornung (eds.), *Emotions in Postmodernism*. Heidelberg: Universitätsverlag C. Winter.

Carroll, N. (1998). *A Philosophy of Mass Art*. Oxford: Oxford University Press.

Cavell, S. (1971). *The World Viewed: Reflections on the Ontology of Film*. New York: The Viking Press.

Collingwood, R. (1938). *The Principles of Art*. Oxford: Clarendon Press.

Currie, G. (1990). *The Nature of Fiction*. New York: Cambridge University Press.

Currie, G. (1995a). "Imagination and Simulation: Aesthetics Meets Cognitive Science." In M. Davies and T. Stone (eds.), *Mental Simulation* (pp. 151–69). Oxford: Blackwell.

Currie, G. (1995b). *Image and Mind: Film, Philosophy, and Cognitive Science*. New York: Cambridge University Press.

Currie, G. (1997). "The Paradox of Caring: Fiction and Philosophy of Mind." In M. Hjort and S. Laver (eds.), *Emotion and the Arts* (pp. 63–77). New York: Oxford University Press.

Currie, G. (1998). "Realism of Character and the Value of Fiction." In J. Levinson (ed.), *Aesthetics and Ethics* (pp. 161–81). New York: Cambridge University Press.

Currie, G. (1999). "Narrative Desire." In C. Plantinga and G. Smith (eds.), *Passionate Views: Film, Cognition, and Emotion* (pp. 183–99). Baltimore, MD: The Johns Hopkins University Press.

Currie, G. (2002). "Desire in Imagination." In T. Gendler and J. Hawthorne (eds.), *Conceivability and Possibility* (pp. 201–21). Oxford: Oxford University Press.

Currie, G. and Jureidini, J. (2003). "Art and Delusion." *Monist*, 86: 556–78.

Currie, G. and Ravenscroft, I. (2002). *Recreative Minds: Imagination in Philosophy and Psychology*. Oxford: Oxford University Press.

Gaut, B. (1993). "The Paradox of Horror." *British Journal of Aesthetics*, 33: 333–45.

Gaut, B. (1999). "Identification and Emotion in Narrative Film." In C. Plantinga and G. Smith (eds.), *Passionate Views: Film, Cognition, and Emotion* (pp. 183–99). Baltimore, MD: The Johns Hopkins University Press.

Gaut, B. (2003). "Reasons, Emotions, and Fiction." In M. Kieran and D. Lopes (eds.), *Imagination, Philosophy, and the Arts* (pp. 15–34). New York: Routledge.

Goldie, P. (2002). *The Emotions*. Oxford: Clarendon Press.

Goldman, A. (1989). "Interpretation Psychologized." *Mind and Language*, 4: 161–85.

Goldman, A. (1992). "Empathy, Mind, and Morals." *Proceedings and Addresses of the American Philosophical Association* 66: 17–41.

Goldman, A. (1995). "Simulation and Interpersonal Utility." *Ethics*, 105: 709–26.

Gordon, R. (1986). "Folk Psychology as Simulation." *Mind and Language*, 1: 158–71.

Gordon, R. (1995). "Sympathy, Simulation, and the Impartial Spectator." *Ethics*, 106: 727–42.

Heal, J. (1986). "Replication and Functionalism." In J. Butterfield (ed.), *Language, Mind and Logic* (pp. 135–50). Cambridge, UK: Cambridge University Press.

Kieran, M. (2003). "In Search of a Narrative." In M. Kieran and D. Lopes (eds.), *Imagination, Philosophy, and the Arts* (pp. 69–87). London, Routledge.

Meskin, A. and Weinberg, J. (2003). "Emotions, Fiction, and Cognitive Architecture." *British Journal of Aesthetics*, 43: 18–34.

Neill, A. (1993). "Fiction and the Emotions." *American Philosophical Quarterly*, 30: 1–13.

Neill, A. (1996). "Empathy and (Film) Fiction." In D. Bordwell and N. Carroll (eds.), *Post-Theory: Reconstructing Film Studies* (pp. 175–94). Madison: Wisconsin University Press.

Nichols, S. (2004). "Review of G. Currie and I. Ravenscroft's *Recreative Minds: Imagination in Philosophy and Psychology*." *Mind*, 113: 329–34.

Nichols, S. (forthcoming). "Just the Imagination: Why the Imagination Doesn't Behave Like Believing." *Mind and Language*.

Nichols, S. and Stich, S. (2000). "A Cognitive Theory of Pretense." *Cognition*, 74: 115–47.

Nichols, S. and Stich, S. (2002). "How to Read Your Own Mind: A Cognitive Theory of Self-Consciousness." In Q. Smith and A. Jokic (eds.), *Consciousness: New Philosophical Essays* (pp. 157–200). Oxford University Press.

Perkins, V. F. (1972). *Film as Film: Understanding and Judging Movies*. New York: Penguin.

Radford, C. (1975). "How Can We Be Moved By the Fate of Anna Karenina?" *Proceedings of the Aristotelian Society*, Supp. vol. 49: 67–80.

Scruton, R. (1974). *Art and Imagination*. London: Routledge & Kegan Paul.

Smith, M. (1997). "Imagining from the Inside." In R. Allen and M. Smith (eds.), *Film Theory and Philosophy* (pp. 412–30). Oxford: Clarendon Press.

Sober, E. and Wilson, J. (1999). *Unto Others*. Chicago: University of Chicago Press.

Thormählen, M. (1993). "The Villain of Wildfell Hall: Aspects and Prospects of Arthur Huntingdon." *Modern Language Review*, 88: 831–841.

Walton, K. (1990). *Mimesis as Make-Believe: On the Foundations of the Representational Arts*. Cambridge, MA: Harvard University Press.

Walton, K. (1997). "Spelunking, Simulation, and Slime: On Being Moved by Fiction." In M. Hjort and S. Laver (eds.), *Emotion and the Arts* (pp. 37–49). New York: Oxford University Press.

Further Reading for Chapters 13 and 14

Davies, M. and Stone, T. (eds.) (1995). *Folk Psychology: The Theory of Mind Debate*. Oxford: Blackwell.

Davies, M. and Stone, T. (eds.) (1995). *Mental Simulation: Evaluations and Applications*. Oxford: Blackwell.

Gallese, V. and Goldman, A. (1998). "Mirror neurons and the simulation theory of mind-reading." *Trends in Cognitive Sciences*, 2: 493–501.

Gopnik, A. and Wellman, H. M. (1992). "Why the Child's Theory of Mind Really Is a Theory." *Mind and Language*, 7: 145–71.

Kieran, M. and Lopes, D. (eds.) (2003.) *Imagination, Philosophy and the Arts*, London: Routledge.

Prinz, J. (2004). *Gut Reactions: A Perceptual Theory of Emotion*. New York: Oxford University Press.

Rall, J. and Harris P. L. (2000). "In Cinderella's Shoes? Story Comprehension from the Protagonist's Point of View." *Developmental Psychology*, 36: 202–8.

CAN EMOTIONAL RESPONSES TO FICTION BE GENUINE AND RATIONAL?

CHAPTER FIFTEEN

Genuine Rational Fictional Emotions

Tamar Szabó Gendler and Karson Kovakovich

The Paradox

The "paradox of fictional emotions" involves a trio of claims that are jointly inconsistent but individually plausible. Resolution of the paradox thus requires that we deny at least one of these plausible claims.

The paradox has been formulated in various ways (some of which we discuss below), but for the purposes of this chapter, we will focus on the following three claims, which we will refer to respectively as (1) the response condition, (2) the belief condition, and (3) the coordination condition.

Regarding certain fictional characters (and situations) F, it is simultaneously true that:

1   We have genuine and rational emotional responses towards F;
2   We believe that F is purely fictional;

At the same time, it is also true that:

3   In order for us to have genuine and rational emotional responses towards a character (or situation), we must not believe that the character (or situation) is purely fictional.

The inconsistency among the three claims is clear: the response and belief conditions together tell us that we can have genuine rational emotions towards F while believing F to be purely fictional; the coordination condition denies that this conjunction is possible. So while any pair of the trio can be consistently maintained, endorsing all three at the same time results in a contradiction. But each of the three claims is also *prima facie* plausible. We do seem to have genuine and rational emotional responses towards purely fictional characters and situations (as when we shed authentic, appropriate tears at the report of Anna Karenina's demise); at the same time, we seem to believe that those characters and situations are purely fictional (we do not expect to read a report of Anna's suicide in the annals of the Leningrad Railroad Authority, nor do we expect to be able to intervene in any way regarding the events described in the novel). Still, there seems to be something irrational, inauthentic, or even impossible about responding emotionally to things we believe to be purely fictional. (How can we rationally feel genuine fear for something we know to be merely imaginary, or authentically respond with anger to something we know could never have happened?)

Since they cannot be true simultaneously, it must be that one of the *prima facie* plausible claims is, in fact, false: but which one? Each has been forcefully denied by well-respected figures in the literature – and important insights about the nature of our emotional responses underlie each of these denials. At the same time, we will argue, those who attempt to resolve the paradox by denying either the response or belief condition tend to rest their attempts on a distorted conception of the relations between emotions, beliefs, and actions. Careful examination of these connections in light of recent empirical research on the nature of emotions offer grounds for thinking that it is the coordination condition that should be denied. Drawing on research by Antonio Damasio and insights of Paul Harris, we will suggest that it is *not* a condition of our having genuine and rational emotional responses towards a character (or situation) that we believe the character (or situation) to be nonfictional. Rather, we will suggest, our cognitive architecture is such that without the tendency to feel something relevantly akin to real emotions in the case of merely imagined situations, we would be unable to engage in practical reasoning (Damasio 1997, 1999, Harris 2000).

Before continuing, four caveats about what we will and won't be doing in this chapter. First, given limits of space, we will have little to say about the nature of emotion. In particular, we will set aside important questions about whether the collection of attitudes and feelings generally referred to as "emotions" forms a natural class, whether there are correctness-conditions for feeling emotions, and whether emotions are – strictly speaking – attitudes directed at particular entities. Instead, we will focus on two classic examples from the literature – pity and fear – each of which is at least a plausible example of an emotional response that, at least in certain cases, seems to be object-directed and correctness-evaluable. Second, the notion of rationality at play in our discussion will be an extremely thin one: in calling an emotion "rational" we are claiming only that it is *not irrational* – that it does not interfere with our capacity to function as agents who make effective use of means–ends reasoning, and that it does not directly involve us in inconsistent belief. In so doing, we neglect a number of important distinctions – between instrumental and intrinsic rationality, between theoretical and practical rationality, and between "act-rationality" and "rule-rationality." (The issue of rationality of emotions is discussed in more detail in Derek Matravers's chapter.) Third, we will help ourselves to a loose notion of "fictional" – contrasting here with "nonfictional" – where characters such as Anna Karenina and places such as Oz are fictional in the sense that we do not consider them to be concrete denizens of the actual world, or plausible continuations of the

Tamar Szabó Gendler & Karson Kovakovich

actual world. (We here ignore a number of important issues relating to authorial intent, truth in fiction, and – except for a brief discussion below – the ontology of fictional characters.) Finally, we will assume it to be common ground among all parties that each of the three conditions in the paradox has at least *prima facie* plausibility, but is in principle deniable. So we will have little to say about views that stipulate at the outset that we can feel genuine or rational emotions only towards entities that are actual, making the truth of the coordination condition a definitional matter, or views according to which we do not even *seem* to have emotional responses to fictional characters, rendering the response condition trivially false. Of course, it is not always an easy matter to separate terminological from substantive disputes, particularly when one is engaged in conceptual analysis – but we will do our best.

In order to remain focused on substantive issues, we will devote most of our discussion to characterizing the descriptive and normative conditions governing our emotional responses to various sorts of real and imaginary situations, devoting the final sections to applying this characterization to a number of proposed resolutions to the paradox. For ease of presentation, we will use the term "fictional emotion" to refer to emotional responses that we apparently have towards characters and events that we believe to be fictional, and "actual emotion" to refer to emotional responses that we apparently have towards characters and events that we believe to be actual. So, "fictional emotion" as we use the expression does not refer to an emotional state of a fictional character (Anna's anguish), but to an actual person's apparent emotional response to such a character (your pity). We can then state our fundamental questions as follows: what is the significance of the manifest similarities between our fictional and actual emotional reactions, and what is the significance of their manifest differences? Is this configuration of similarity and difference indicative of something problematic in our emotional responses to fiction? And does this pattern of similarity and difference suggest that fictional and actual emotions are two species of the same genus?

In our discussion below, we will argue that the manifest similarities between fictional and actual emotions *are* significant, even in light of their differences, that this configuration of responses *is not* a pathological one, given facts about our cognitive architecture, and that it *is* reasonable to employ the expression "genuine, rational emotion" in describing both actual and fictional emotions. While those who deny the response condition are correct to note that our fictional and actual emotions differ in their subject-matter and motivational force, this difference is not sufficient to render fictional emotions either inauthentic or irrational. And while those who deny the belief condition are correct to note that the similarities between actual and fictional emotions indicate that we treat their apparent objects in comparable ways, this comparable treatment need not be a reflection of a belief in the actuality of fictional entities. Rather, we will contend, it is the coordination condition that articulates a false constraint on our emotional reactions: it is crucial to our ability to make rational decisions about various courses of action that we respond with genuine emotions to situations that we know to be nonactual.

The bulk of this chapter will be devoted to articulating and defending this claim. But before turning to this, we need to undertake two matters of housekeeping. In stating the paradox, we spoke of having genuine and rational emotional responses towards fictional characters. But there are important philosophical questions about what it even means to say that we feel fear or pity for something that does not exist; we discuss these issues briefly and inconclusively in the next section. Second, it is important to realize that there has been an extensive literature on the topic of fictional emotions (including several book-length treatments of it), and while this is not the place for a full literature review, we devote the subsequent section to showing how our own presentation of the puzzle accords with some of the most influential of these discussions. With this groundwork in place, we then turn to a presentation of our own view, followed by a closing section where we contrast our approach with a number of other extant approaches.

Fictional Characters

In our statement of the paradox, we spoke of "having genuine and rational emotional responses towards F" where F is a fictional character or event. But this raises certain puzzles. On most standard semantics, when a name occurs as the direct object of a verb or in a that-clause of an emotional attitude verb ("I pity Anna Karenina" "I fear that Anna is going to kill herself"), we can quantify into the name position, and conclude that something exists that is referred to by the name ($\exists x \ (x = \text{Anna Karenina})$). (A similar puzzle arises with the prefix "It is true in the story that . . ." – from "It is true in the story that Anna Karenina killed herself" we can, it seems, conclude that Anna Karenina exists.) *Prima facie*, however, we seem committed to saying both that we pity Anna Karenina and that she does not exist. How is this puzzle to be resolved?

Four strategies suggest themselves, each with costs and benefits. The first is to reject the standard semantic picture that gives rise to the puzzle in the first place. Contrary to common assumption, we cannot, in general, quantify into name slots. So in saying that we pity Anna, we are not committed to her existence. Many find such revisionary semantics unpalatable. The second is to claim, following Meinong, that there *are* things, such as fictional characters, that do not *exist*. We might then distinguish a broad quantifier that can range over both existent and nonexistent entities from a narrow quantifier that can range only over things that exist. While quantifying in with the broad quantifier is legitimate, quantifying in with the narrow quantifier is not. So in saying that we pity Anna, we are committed to *there being* Anna, but not to her existence (Parsons 1980, Crittendon 1991). Many find such a view ontologically suspect.

The third strategy accepts both the standard semantic picture and a non-Meinongian ontology, and thus accepts that in saying that we pity Anna, we are indeed committed to Anna's existence. On one substrategy of this view, fictional characters exist but they do not inhabit our actual world; rather, they exist as flesh-and-blood entities in some other world spatiotemporally and causally isolated from our own. On another substrategy, fictional characters are abstract entities, such as abstract individuals (see van Inwagen 1977, Salmon 1998 among others), or abstract roles, kinds, or sets of properties (Wolterstorff 1980, Lamarque 1981). Each bears costs. The first substrategy requires acceptance of something akin to Lewis's unpopular ontol-

Tamar Szabó Gendler & Karson Kovakovich

ogy (cf. Lewis 1978); moreover, it violates our sense that fictional objects are not the sorts of things that exist concretely in any world whatsoever. The second has the unpleasant result that we bear attitudes towards *abstracta* (such as pity) that seem appropriately borne only towards *concreta*.

A final strategy holds that when we use fictional names, directly or in the context of attitude-ascriptions, we engage in make-believe, pretending that the names refer when they do not. On such a view, sentences such as "Anna is sad" do not really express propositions, and sentences such as "I pity Anna" do not really express propositional attitudes, though we pretend that they do. While it is not literally true that Anna Karenina exists, it is true in the fiction that she does, and we can fruitfully speak (in certain contexts) as if that fiction were true (cf. Evans 1982, Walton 1990, Brock 2002). This has the result that we do not have genuine emotional attitudes towards fictional characters. We discuss this issue in more detail below.

It is beyond the scope of this chapter to evaluate which of these strategies is ultimately most successful. We thus put the special semantic puzzles raised by names of fictional characters to one side.

Traditional Formulations of the Paradox

As we have noted, the problem that gives rise to the paradox is that we seem to respond to fictional scenarios in two different ways: emotionally, we respond to them as if they might be actual; cognitively, we respond to them as if they could not be actual. And, in general, we expect our cognitive and emotional responses to run in synchrony. So there is a mismatch between two of our responses in a circumstance where we expect no such mismatch.

While a number of related issues concerning our emotional responses to fiction are addressed in the writings of Plato and Aristotle some 2,500 years ago, specific attention to this particular puzzle finds its first hints in the work of Samuel Johnson in the mid-eighteenth century and Samuel Taylor Coleridge some 50 years later (Plato 1992, Aristotle 1984, Johnson [1765] 2004, Coleridge [1817] 1985). But it was only in the late twentieth century – with the publication of Colin Radford's "How Can We Be Moved by the Fate of Anna Karenina?" and Kendall Walton's "Fearing Fictions" – that the paradox was explicitly formulated in a way that captured widespread professional attention (Radford 1975, Weston 1975, Walton 1978); the result has been something of a cottage industry in (analytic) aesthetics. (For a comprehensive bibliography, see Hjort and Laver 1997.)

Although they do not state the paradox in these stark terms, with a bit of excavation and reconstruction, we can see that both Radford and Walton are concerned with some variant of the issue we have identified. So, for example, in his seminal essay "How Can We Be Moved by the Fate of Anna Karenina?" Colin Radford makes the following observation: "It would seem then that I can only be moved by someone's plight if I believe that something terrible has happened to him. If I do not believe that he has not and is not suffering or whatever, I cannot grieve or be moved to tears" (Radford 1975: 68). At the same time, he notes: "we are moved by the death of Mercutio and we weep while knowing that no one has really died" (Radford 1975: 71). It is reasonable to think that the first of these quotes essentially articulates the coordination condition, while the second points out a case where we simultaneously satisfy the response and belief conditions.

In the same way, one can map Kendall Walton's early discussion of the puzzle onto our formulation. In "Fearing Fictions" Walton notes that: "It would seem that real people can, and frequently do, have psychological attitudes toward merely fictional entities, despite the impossibility of physical intervention" (Walton 1978: 5–6; response condition). At the same time, he notes, when confronted by a cinematic representation of approaching green slime, the filmgoer "knows perfectly well that the slime is not real and that he is in no danger" (Walton 1978: 6; belief condition). But, Walton suggests, "it is plausible that" psychological attitudes such as "pity, worry about, hate, and envy are such that one cannot have them without believing that their objects exist, just as one cannot fear something without believing that it threatens them" (Walton 1978: 21, n. 15; coordination condition). (Comparable mappings can be offered for the other highly influential formulations: see, for example, Lamarque 1981: 291, Carroll 1990: 62, Currie 1990: 187.)

Our Resolution: Overview

Walton and Radford propose solutions to the paradox that involve the denial of the response condition: Walton contends that fictional emotions are not genuine; Radford holds that they are not rational. Others have suggested that it is the belief condition that is false: when we respond emotionally to fictional characters, we lose track of our belief that they are fictional. (We discuss these views in more detail below.) Our own resolution to the paradox involves endorsing the response and belief conditions while denying the coordination condition. In so doing, it will be helpful to have a particular case in mind. So consider the classic example of feeling pity for Anna Karenina (Radford 1975). What we contend is that, in keeping with the response condition, the pity that we feel for Anna is both genuine and rational, even though, in keeping with the belief condition, we believe Anna to be a purely fictional character. (We are, recall, bracketing ontological issues concerning the precise content of this apparent attitude.)

There are reasons to find each of these claims suspect. After all, in ordinary cases when we feel pity for a (living) person, we are at least in principle motivated to take some sort of action regarding that person – but to the extent that we realize that Anna is purely fictional, we seem to feel no such motivation. This suggests that our actual emotions are sufficiently different from our fictional emotions to render them different in kind: the former are genuine; the latter are not. If, instead, we hold that both actual and fictional emotions are instances of genuine emotion, then the latter seem somehow defective: if emotional responses are intimately tied to motivation, then an emotional response whose object is rightly believed to be fictional is surely irrational. The only apparent way to avoid this conclusion is to hold that when we experience fictional emotions, we temporarily fail to believe their objects are purely fictional (contra the belief condition). If this line of reasoning is correct, then the coordination condition expresses a genuine constraint on our emotional responses.

Tamar Szabó Gendler & Karson Kovakovich

Below, we discuss each of these objections in some detail. Our goal in this portion of the chapter is to make a positive case for our own position. Our view finds its source in recent empirical research (by Antonio Damasio and others) showing that when we make practical decisions about our own futures, our reasoning is action-guiding only in cases where we imaginatively engage with potential consequences to produce emotional responses that are then somatically encoded – that is, that result in particular sorts of bodily changes. (We describe this research in the next section.) This suggests that, far from being exceptional, emotional responses to nonactual situations are a fundamental feature of our cognitive repertoire. Moreover, because of the role they play in underpinning practical reasoning (allowing us to act on our preferences by somatically encoding our evaluations of potential outcomes), it is crucial that they resemble actual emotions as precisely as possible. Together, these features suggest that it is legitimate to consider such emotional responses to be both genuine and rational. (We defend this claim in more detail below.) Moreover, we will contend, despite their resemblance to actual emotions, fictional emotions do not rest on a confusion in belief about what is merely fictional. As we will argue below, we tend to initially interpret all cognitive and sensory input as indicative of the presence of the ordinary source of phenomena of its type. Such instantaneous interpretations are not sufficiently robust to be properly considered beliefs. Together, these considerations suggest both that we should embrace the response and belief conditions, and that we should reject the coordination condition.

The Damasio results

Individuals with damage to their ventromedial prefrontal cortex display a typical set of behaviors. Most strikingly, they manifest extraordinary difficulties in day-to-day activities: though they are able to articulate reasons for pursuing various courses of action, they are unable to use those reasons as bases for behavior, acting instead in ways that seem erratic and unplanned, and that are often counterproductive and anti-social. In addition, they exhibit a number of patterns that are detectable in laboratory settings. So, for example, while they are easily able to identify whether a photograph is "disturbing," and even to articulate why ("its front paw is caught in a trap" "the bodies are piled atop one another"), they typically lack autonomic reactions to such emotionally distressing images. This contrasts strikingly with normal patients, who consistently display such responses (Harris 2000: 85, describing Damasio, Tranel, and Damasio 1991).

A similar pattern of deficits reveals itself in a testing paradigm developed by Damasio's team. Experimental subjects are given four decks of cards and a pile of play money, with the goal of maximizing their profit by turning over cards one at a time from any one of the four decks. Cards from the four decks are preassigned values so that for each card from deck A or B that the subjects turn over, they earn a sizable reward, while for each card from deck C or D, they earn a significantly smaller reward. But decks A and B are also associated with high penalties, whereas decks C and D are not, so that playing with decks A and B results in a net loss, whereas playing with decks C and D results in a net gain (Bechara, Damasio, Damasio, and Anderson 1994).

When normal subjects are presented with this task, they initially sample from all decks, but eventually settle on decks C and D (the overall advantageous decks with lower immediate rewards), and their performance continues to improve over time. By contrast, when the task is presented to subjects with damage to the prefrontal cortex, results are strikingly different: they soon settle on decks A and B (the overall disadvantageous decks with higher immediate rewards); moreover, they show no improvement in performance over time.

As normal subjects successively experience the consequences of choosing from the high-risk decks, they begin to exhibit skin conductance responses in anticipation of such selections. Soon afterwards, they begin expressing a "hunch" that these decks are more risky, and begin avoiding them in favor of the lower-risk decks; ultimately, many of them are able to articulate the basis for this avoidance. By contrast, subjects with damage to the prefrontal cortex exhibit no such skin conductance responses in anticipation of their high-risk deck selections, and no tendency to avoid such decks in their own selection process. This is so even when they are able to articulate conceptually the relative risks involved. (Summary based on Harris 2000: 86–7.)

What Damasio, Bechara, and others have concluded on the basis of this research is that autonomic responses play a central role in practical reasoning. Some sort of somatic realization of the potential consequences of a risky action seems crucial to prudent decision making. Without it, the theoretical advantages of one or another course of action may be apparent, but these will not translate properly into action-guiding behavior.

This research seems to show that our ability to engage in practical reasoning rests on the following sort of process: we imaginatively engage with the potential consequences of various courses of action, thereby activating our emotional response mechanisms, and we encode the results of these simulations somatically; the presence of these "somatic markers" then helps to guide our future behavior. Call these emotions "simulated emotions." It is clear that simulated emotions are a fundamental feature of our cognitive repertoire. It is also clear that there are striking resemblances between *simulated* emotions and *fictional* emotions, so much so that if we can establish that simulated emotions are both genuine and rational, then we will have done most of the work required for establishing the faultiness of the coordination condition.

Genuineness

There are at least two dimensions along which fictional and simulated emotions differ from actual emotions that seem relevant to whether the former are rightly considered genuine. Whereas the apparent objects of actual emotions are actual individuals and events, the apparent objects of simulated and fictional emotions are ostensibly non-actual. And whereas actual emotions feed directly into behavior in certain predictable ways (we move away from objects that we fear, and intervene on behalf of individuals that we pity), fictional and simulated emotions are not directly tied to action in this fashion.

Famously, Kendall Walton has contended that these differences mean that we do not feel genuine emotional responses to fictional scenarios. Instead, he contends, we experience phenomenally indistinguishable *quasi-emotions* that differ from genuine

Tamar Szabó Gendler & Karson Kovakovich

emotions along two dimensions: in contrast to genuine emotions, they do not require that we be existentially committed to their apparent objects; and they are not intimately connected to motivation and action (Walton 1990; an alternative view is presented in Walton 1997). So, for example, he writes concerning the first requirement: "Grief, as well as pity and admiration, would seem to require at the very least awareness of the existence of their objects. It is arguable that for this reason alone appreciators cannot be said actually to pity Willy [Loman] or grieve for Anna [Karenina] or admire Superman" (1990: 204). And, concerning the second:

> Fear is *motivating* in distinctive ways, whether or not its motivational force is attributed to cognitive elements in it. . . . To deny this, to insist on considering . . . [a] nonmotivating state to be one of fear of [its purported object] would be to reconceive the notion of fear. Fear emasculated by subtracting its distinctive motivational force is not fear at all. (Walton 1990: 201–2)

Regarding the first quotation, there is the risk of degenerating into terminological debate. If one defines "genuine" (or "actual") emotion so that such emotions "require . . . awareness of the existence of their objects," then Walton is surely correct; the substantive question is whether such a restriction effects a natural cut in conceptual space. (We here ignore the difference between nonexistence and nonbeing; see the section "Fictional Characters" above.) An argument can be made that there is a continuum of cases – from cases where the object of the emotion is an entity that exists only in the past (where I pity someone who has died), to cases where the object of the emotion is a situation that may or may not occur in the future (where I fear a stock market crash), to cases where the object of the emotion is an entity that may or may not exist in the future (where I pity the oldest daughter of my great-grandson), to cases where the object of the emotion is a situation that is explicitly fictional (where I fear the flood that may drown the inhabitants of Alpha Centauri), to cases where the object of the emotion is an entity that is explicitly fictional (where I pity Anna Karenina). We have no inclination to withhold attributions of genuineness from cases involving past or future or merely possible persons or events ("She doesn't *fear* a stock-market crash, she just *quasi-fears* it"). It thus seems that we do not require that the target of a genuine emotion exist in the here and now. What, then, would incline us to withhold such attributions in the case of explicitly fictional persons and events? The source seems to be either worries about empty names ("She doesn't pity Anna Karenina – there is no Anna Karenina") or related worries about misattribution ("What he fears isn't the bear in the closet – there is no bear there – what he fears is the sound of the wind"). We are setting aside worries of the first sort. And it is interesting to note that worries of the second sort dissipate somewhat when we are explicitly aware of the fictionality of our character. When someone (apparently) feels pity for Anna Karenina, knowing full well that Anna is a fictional character, we are not inclined to think that this person has misidentified the target of his or her emotion. In short, unless we stipulate at the outset that attitudes such as fear and pity can take as their targets only certain sorts of entities, then, assuming a standard picture of what exists and what does not, and setting aside legitimate worries about empty names, it seems arbitrary to insist that they are genuine only when their objects exist.

Regarding the second quotation from Walton, it is far from clear that fictional and simulated emotions differ from actual emotions to the degree that Walton seems to be suggesting. Note first that in order for the reasoning process described above to operate effectively, our simulated emotions and our actual emotions must line up as closely as possible: otherwise, the process of considering alternative outcomes would not give us proper information about how we would respond once one of those outcomes became actualized. So simulated emotions and actual emotions should be, in a well-functioning person, as similar as possible. This nonaccidental similarity provides grounds for considering simulated emotions to be genuine, and insofar as fictional emotions exploit similar mechanisms, it provides parallel grounds in that case. (It is in this regard that part of the truth about fictional emotions is captured by the position known as "factualism," according to which the objects of our emotional responses to fiction are actual people in situations literally or metaphorically akin to those described in the fiction. For various versions of this position, see Paskins 1977, Johnson [1765] 2004, Weston 1975, McCormick 1988.)

Moreover, if Damasio is right, both simulated and fictional emotions produce bodily changes akin to those produced by actual emotions. That the latter feed directly into action whereas the former feed only indirectly into action can be traced, we propose, to a difference in processing, not in motivation (modulo differences in vivacity of stimulus). An alarm clock set five minutes fast can motivate us to rise, even if we are fully cognizant of the misinformation it gives; we are reluctant to pull the trigger in a bulletless version of Russian roulette, even when we are certain that the gun is completely empty. (See also our discussion of optical illusions below.) So while Walton is surely correct to note that fictional emotions do not feed into behavior in the ways that actual emotions do, it does not follow that they do not have similar motivational structure.

But this line of thought brings out a certain tension in our view. We have been emphasizing the similarities among fictional, simulated, and actual emotions. One elegant explanation of these similarities would be that we momentarily lose track of the nonactuality of the simulated and fictional stimuli when we respond emotionally to them. If so, then perhaps it is the belief condition that is at fault (insofar as the response condition holds. (This is the explanation given by advocates of the position known as the "momentary confusion" or "suspension-of-disbelief" view.)

As before, there is a risk of turning a substantive dispute into a terminological one: if "belief" is used thinly enough, then the belief condition may indeed be inapplicable as stated. The substantive question is whether there are other reactions to non-standard stimuli where we are not inclined to say that the similarity between ordinary and divergent cases rests on a false belief. We think there are many. In cases of optical illusions, for example, we may perceive a bent stick as being straight – or perceive the two lines in the Muller–Lyer illusion as being of different lengths – without *believing* that things are as they seem. If we stand near the edge of a high glassed-in platform, we may recoil slightly, without *believing* that we are at risk of falling. One explanation for this and other such cases is that we respond to nearly all cognitive and sensory input as being indicative of the presence of its ordinary stimulus-source. (So, for example, objects exhibiting the retinal-stimulation pattern of the water-embedded stick are, in ordinary cases, objects that are bent; situations exhibiting the

Tamar Szabó Gendler & Karson Kovakovich

retinal-stimulation pattern of the glassed-in high platform are, in ordinary cases, dangerous.) But precisely because these initial response patterns are so evidence-resistant, there is good reason to think that they are subdoxastic. If a response-pattern cannot be changed in reaction to the presentation of reasoned evidence (we cannot "talk ourselves out of" optical illusions), it seems misleading to categorize it as belief-involving. So the similarities between simulated and actual responses need not be seen as impugning the belief condition.

In sum, there are similarities and dissimilarities between fictional and actual emotions. Whether the differences are sufficient to warrant referring to them with distinct expressions is to some extent a terminological dispute. The substantive issue concerns what forms these similarities and dissimilarities actually take. It is our contention that the similarities are more striking than the differences.

Rationality

In a series of some dozen articles over nearly a quarter of a century, Colin Radford has contended that fictional emotions are irrational. As with Walton, part of our dispute with Radford may be terminological. Radford writes:

> What is necessary for the occurrence of these [emotional] responses is missing when the objects which elicit them are (believed to be) fictional. There is then literally, nothing to be concerned about, no one – indeed nothing – to pity. . . . However natural, almost universal, such responses are, we can and do come to see that they are irrational, do we not? (Radford 1989: 96)

These remarks are somewhat perplexing: if "what is necessary for the occurrence of these [emotional] responses is missing" then it is hard to see how such responses could be "almost universal." If, with Walton, Radford is suggesting that the very concept of emotional response precludes our responding emotionally to the nonactual, then our reply is as above. But this does not seem to be his primary worry. Rather, the source of discomfort for Radford seems to be the thought that fictional emotions somehow involve us in competing, even contradictory, commitments. He writes: "we are frightened for ourselves of characters we know to be fictional and are irrational, incoherent, and inconsistent in being thus frightened" (Radford 1995: 75).

By employing the terms "incoherent" and "inconsistent," Radford seems to be suggesting that in feeling fictional emotions, we reveal ourselves to be holding contradictory beliefs. The thought behind such an analysis might be the following: when we respond with genuine emotion to a character, or describe someone as responding with genuine emotion to a character, we reveal that we believe that character to be actual; but when we believe a character to be fictional, we believe that character not to be actual; so when we respond with genuine emotion to a character that we believe to be fictional, we believe that character to be actual and not to be actual. But this reasoning, as we have argued at the end of the last subsection, is flawed: it is a mistake to think that feeling genuine emotions requires a belief, temporary or otherwise, in the actuality of its purported target.

Alternatively, perhaps Radford's worry is that in responding to fictional characters with genuine emotion, we violate a norm that we tacitly hold: that we should respond emotionally only to things that we believe to be actual. The irrationality of our behavior would thus consist in repeatedly violating a principle that we reflectively endorse (in the same way that it would be irrational for someone who had a principled commitment to vegetarianism regularly to eat meat). But it is far from clear that we *do* (or *should*), on reflection, subscribe to such a principle. If, as we have suggested above, simulated emotions play a central role in allowing us to make and act on decisions about our future well-being, then far from impeding our capacity to act as agents who make effective use of means–ends reasoning, they contribute directly to it. If so, it is hard to see why we would want to endorse a principle telling us that we should respond emotionally only to things that we believe to be actual (even if, as a practical matter, this ideal proves unattainable).

But a residual issue remains about whether we would want to endorse a weaker principle according to which we should not respond emotionally to things we explicitly believe to be fictional. After all, one might contend, fictional emotions do not seem to play the same direct role in our capacity for practical reasoning that simulated emotions do, so we should aim not to feel them. But it is not clear that even this weaker line of argument can be successfully maintained. One line of thought, stemming from Aristotle and emphasized more recently by thinkers such as Susan Feagin and Martha Nussbaum, stresses the instrumental role of fictional emotions in the cultivation of moral and intellectual character (Aristotle 1984, Feagin 1983, Nussbaum 1986, 1990). By engaging emotionally with fictional characters and situations, we broaden our range of simulated encounters, gaining insights about others' experiences that are processed much as if they had been our own. Without such a capacity, actual experience would be our only source of such emotional encounters, severely limiting the range of our reactive possibilities. So fictional emotions may contribute to our capacity for rational action through the role they play in educating our sensibilities. If so, then there is little reason to think that we should endorse a categorical principle according to which we would, ideally, fail to feel such emotions.

In saying this, we are not denying that there are plenty of circumstances where such emotional responses are very much out of place. Cases where emotional investments in the fictional exceed corresponding investments in the actual are exemplary instances of irrationality (as both psychoanalytic theory and common sense remind us). And cases where prop-based pretense produces responses that, given ordinary practice in such games of make-believe, are unprompted are likewise paradigmatically irrational (as, for example, when a child feels genuine fear that its stuffed animal will catch a cold). But the existence of such cases does not impugn the possibility of rational genuine emotional responses to certain sorts of fictional scenarios. (Though they do reveal that our assessments of rationality and irrationality are, here as elsewhere, governed by conventional norms of appropriateness.)

Tamar Szabó Gendler & Karson Kovakovich

Conclusion

As we have formulated it, there are three basic ways to resolve the paradox of fictional emotions, by rejecting the response condition, the belief condition, or the coordination condition.

Those who reject the response condition deny that we have genuine and rational emotional responses to fictional characters or situations. But grounds for rejecting the position vary widely. Those who endorse *the quasi-emotion theory* and *irrationalism* hold that we do have emotional responses to fictional characters and situations, but that these responses are either *nongenuine* (quasi-emotion theory) or *irrational* (irrationalism). Those who endorse *factualism or nonintentionalism* hold that, contrary to appearances, we do *not* have emotional responses to fictional characters and situations; rather, our fictional emotions are actually directed at real-world analogues of their apparent targets (factualism), or are not directed at anything, instead being diffuse, objectless moods (nonintentionalism). We have discussed the first and second of these (*quasi-emotion theory and irrationalism*) in some detail above. Regarding both the third (*factualism)* and the fourth (*nonintentionalism*), we note that while they provide plausible explanations for certain cases, they do not seem to have the generality required for a full solution. In too many cases, there is no plausible real-world analogue to serve as the requisite surrogate. And in too many cases, the emotional response is far too focused to be classified as merely a mood.

Those who reject the belief condition hold that when we respond emotionally to fictional scenarios, we do not believe them to *be* fictional. So the similarity between our emotional responses to actual and nonactual scenarios can be traced to a certain sort of (albeit temporary) confusion. Although this view brings out the importance of recognizing similarities among actual, simulated, and fictional emotions, as we noted above, it overstates its case in claiming that these similarities arise from a false belief about the fictionality of the scenarios in question.

Those who reject the coordination condition allow that we can respond with genuine, rational emotions to targets that we believe to be fictional. Above, we have offered reasons for holding such a position.

Note

For comments on an earlier draft, we are grateful to Gregory Currie, John Hawthorne, and Zoltán Gendler Szabó.

The Challenge of Irrationalism, and How Not To Meet It

Derek Matravers

The apparent phenomenon of our feeling emotions towards fictional characters generates at least four different problems. These need to be considered separately, although the solution to any one of them may influence the solution to one or more of the others. The first is a matter of causation: how can a situation we believe not to exist cause us to feel an emotion (or emotion-like state)? The second concerns the correct way to describe the mental state that is caused: can such a state be an emotion, in the absence of the relevant belief (or connection with motivation)? The third concerns the ontology of the object of the emotion (or emotion-like state): on what is the object directed, given that we know fictional characters do not exist? Finally, there is a question of whether we are rational to feel an emotion in circumstances in which we do not have the relevant belief.

What is the Nature of the Mental State?

The second of these is the problem that has received most attention. I shall briefly review this and my favored solution, before going on, in the body of this paper, to discuss whether this solution might prove too much. In more detail, the second problem is this. We are reading a text, which we believe to be a novel (*The Return of the Native*), and find in it some situation in which a character (Mrs Yeobright) is in a perilous state (having been bitten by a snake). This causes in us a mental state that feels very much like, and we are inclined to describe as, pity. One account of the emotions, however, is that they necessarily involve a relevant belief. I shall refer to this as the "narrow cognitive theory," as opposed to "the broad cognitive theory" which agrees that emotions involve some cognitive component, but allows such a component to be a state other than a belief. Given the narrow cognitive theory, pity involves the belief that the object of the emotion is suffering. As we know Mrs Yeobright never existed, hence was never bitten by a snake, we lack the belief that the object of our emotion (given we can make sense of that) is suffering. Lacking this belief, what we feel cannot be pity. Hence the problem: our apparent emotion of pity cannot really be pity, as we lack the relevant belief.

One way to resolve the problem is by rejecting the narrow cognitive theory. Indeed, one could go further and argue that feeling an emotion such as pity for a fictional character is a clear counterexample to this theory. Narrow cognitivists standardly appeal to the link with motivation to support their case. In the real world, pity includes a disposition to action so as to prevent or alleviate the object's suffering. We have no such disposition in the case of fictions. It is logically impossible for us to help Mrs Yeobright, and, perhaps because of this, we feel no disposition to help. Hence, we get a neat divide. On the one side we have the real world, beliefs, and a possibility of action. On the other side we get fictions, absence of beliefs, and no possibility of action. This seems sufficient for us to reserve the term "pity" for the real world cases. Kendall Walton, who has done more than anyone else to sort these problems out, puts the matter thus:

> To allow that mere fictions are objects of our psychological attitudes while disallowing the possibility of physical interactions severs the normal links between the physical and the psychological. What is pity or anger which is never to be acted on? What is love that cannot be expressed to its object and is logically or metaphysically incapable of consummation? We cannot even try to rescue Robinson Crusoe from his island, no matter how deep our concern for him. (Walton 1990: 201–2)

The problem with this reply is that the divide is not so neat. The possibility of acting on our motivations does not divide the real world from the fictional world. There is a division between situations with which we are confronted, and situations that are represented to us. It is characteristic of the former case that our emotions can cause us to act on the object of the emotion. It is characteristic of the latter case that they cannot. Examples of the former will be acting on my fear of the charging bull, and acting on my pity for the injured pedestrian. Examples of the latter are fear for my daughter (who is traveling abroad), and pity for the wounded at Waterloo – neither of which cause action towards their objects. What characterizes the latter case is the absence of beliefs that would enable us to act towards the object of our emotion (what I have called "instrumental beliefs") (Matravers 1998: 22). In some cases (such as fear for my daughter traveling abroad) this is a contingent matter. I could have had the relevant instrumental beliefs (if I knew where she was and knew how to wire her money). In such cases, I could turn a situation that is represented to me into a confrontation by acquiring the relevant instrumental beliefs. In other cases (such as emotions felt towards those in the past) there are no instrumental beliefs that I could have. In all such cases, we have the real world, beliefs, and no possibility of action. With respect to the absence of motivation (or the possibility of motivation) fiction is on a par with emotions felt towards actual objects for which we lack the relevant instrumental beliefs.

Hence, we are faced with a choice. We could accept that the link between feeling emotions and motivation must be preserved, and accept the conclusion that there is something wrong with our feeling emotions towards situations with which we are not confronted. Alternatively, we could allow emotions in the absence of motivation, in which case this argument (at least) for there being something problematic about feeling pity for Mrs Yeobright disappears. In my book I favored the latter option (Matravers, 1998: 68–70), arguing, as I have done here, that the detour via motivations does nothing to show there is anything particularly problematic about feeling emotions for fictional characters (given solutions to the other problems I mentioned at the start).

The Rationality of Feeling Emotions Towards Fictions

I shall call the view that the emotions we feel towards fictions are (1) genuine and (2) rational, "emotionalism." In this essay, I am going to assume (1) and consider (2). That is, assuming that what we feel towards Mrs Yeobright is genuine pity, is this state rational? Someone who thinks it is not is Mr Keith, a character in Norman Douglas's novel, *South Wind*:

> It saddens me to see grown-up men and women stalking about in funny dressing gowns and pretending to be Kings and Queens. When I watch *Hamlet* or *Othello*, I say to myself: "This stuff is nicely riveted together. But, in the first place, the story is not true. And secondly, it is no affair of mine. Why cry about it?" (quoted in Matravers 1998: 2)

Mr Keith is not bothered about whether the mental state provoked by fictions is or is not an emotion. (As an aside, Hamlet is not bothered by this either; when he asks "What's Hecuba to him or he to Hecuba?" (II ii 543) he is more worried by the same kinds of thing as is Mr Keith). His principal claim is that it is not reasonable to cry over something that is not true. I shall call this position "irrationalism." He has a second (and I think quite interesting) claim that it is not reasonable to involve oneself emotionally in matters that are not one's proper concern. I shall not focus on this second claim, although it will resurface later when I discuss the motivation we have for engaging with fictions.

One notable irrationalist is Colin Radford. In the conclusion of a paper that did much to reintroduce the debate about feeling emotions towards fictions to contemporary philosophy, he says: "I am left with the conclusion that our being moved in certain ways by works of art, though very 'natural' to us and in that way only too intelligible, involves us in inconsistency and so incoherence" (Radford [1975] 2002: 248). Radford supports his conclusion with the following consideration. Imagine someone telling you a story about his sister that brings it about that you feel great pity for her. He then says that he does not have a sister (Radford [1975] 2002: 239–40). One can put aside the question of whether or not your pity will vanish as being a matter for psychology. The question is whether it not vanishing would be a case of irrationality. The irrationalist's claim – which has some intuitive force – is that it would.

One further strength of the irrationalist position is that it avoids a perennial danger for emotionalism. There are several grounds on which one could argue that emotions felt towards fictions are genuine and rational. In this volume, Gendler and Kovakovich argue against "the coordination condition": namely, they deny that "in order for us to have genuine and rational emotional responses to a character (or situation), we must not believe that the character (or situation) is purely fictional" (p. 241). Clearly, there are many and varied genuine emotional responses to a character or situation that we do not believe to be actual that are irrational – a claim with which I am sure Gendler and Kovakovich would agree. As an example of such an irrational emotion, consider that which many have towards flying. This is a genuine fear towards a situation they do not believe to be actual (it is not that people who fear flying do not believe the statistics). It is always a good question for the emotionalist as to whether they are able to make this distinction. It is unclear to me whether Gendler and Kovakovich (in their chapter in this volume) are able to or not. They seem to argue that *any* emotion that can perform the role in decision making they specify will thereby be rational. The principle would seem to be that any means that serves a rationally defensible end is itself rational. I discuss (and reject) this below.

What is it that justifies a particular instance of an emotion? A simple cognitive account would be as follows. An instance of an emotion (E) is justified if and only if

1   We are justified in holding the cognitive aspect of E
2   E is a reasonable response given that cognitive aspect
3   E is of an appropriate intensity.

For example, if I see a shadowy figure in my kitchen putting my expensive espresso-maker into a bag, I am justified in forming the belief that there is a burglar in the kitchen. Fear is a reasonable reaction to this, and even quite intense fear. Hence, this situation is one in which intense fear would be justified. In the normal run of things, if I am told a colleague has taken my pencil, I am justified in forming that belief. Irritation is one reasonable response, but perhaps only a fairly mild irritation. Jumping up and down and demanding they be removed from their post would violate (3).

If we apply this account to our pity for Mrs Yeobright, the results are inconclusive. The reader is justified in being in the cognitive state of imagining that Mrs Yeobright is in a perilous state. The irrationalist's first option would be to assert narrow cognitivism: that is, assert the claim that to count as feeling pity, it is necessary to *believe* that Mrs Yeobright suffered. Of course, we have no such belief. The independent arguments for narrow cognitivism are, however, weak so that reply seems simply to make the irrationalist's opponents' position false by a contested definition. A stronger response would be to ground the claim of irrationality on the denial that actual pity is a reasonable response given a proposition imagined rather than a proposition believed. It is not reasonable to feel actual pity towards someone who has not actually suffered.

Although I think irrationalism has some prima facie plausibility, the costs of holding it are high. In a recent paper, Berys Gaut (2003) presents two such costs as arguments against irrationalism (in fact, he gives three, but the third is in support of a Waltonian nonrealist position that I am not considering here). First, the irrationalist is committed to the claim that all emotions held towards fictions are unjustified.

As Gaut says, it is hard to accept the consequence of this, namely that "almost every response to fiction would be tainted by irrationality" (Gaut 2003: 25). Second, the irrationalist cannot make discriminations that critics need to make. The reader who feels some degree of sympathy for George Eliot's Mr Causabon is responding more reasonably than the reader who feels nothing but impatience and contempt. The irrationalist has to, in this case, bite the bullet. Almost every response to fiction is tainted with irrationality and we simply have to accept that we cannot make the discriminations like those mentioned: they are all equally unjustified. Gaut's arguments have the structure that, if irrationalists are not going to count our pity for Mrs Yeobright as justified, then there are a lot of other things that they will not be able to count as justified. The best response is to agree: they are all unjustified. This does not imply that we ought not to feel emotions towards fictions. That is, there might be reasons why we should be irrational.

A positive argument the emotionalist could deploy would be to reject the parallel drawn between feeling pity for a fictional character and feeling pity (in real-life cases) for someone after learning they do not exist. The case of Mrs Yeobright and the case of the nonexistent sister are not analogous. According to the assumptions laid out at the beginning of this essay, *The Return of the Native* supports an imaginative construction that makes "Mrs Yeobright is in a perilous state" an appropriate cognitive content for a mental state that it is correctly described as pity. There is no such imaginative construction in one-off thoughts about a nonexistent sister, hence no appropriate cognitive content. This should not, however, impress the irrationalist. Why should having a place within an imaginative construction render an emotion felt towards a nonexistent person rational? If paying real money for tiny plastic houses is irrational, then it is not made more rational by the transaction taking place within a game of *Monopoly*.

Richard Joyce has produced a more sophisticated version of this argument. He distinguishes two frameworks for rational assessment: "doxastic rationality" and "practical rationality." Doxastic rationality (as its name suggests) relates primarily to the assessment of beliefs:

> We have an established theory of doxastic rationality, distinct from our way of rationally appraising action, and it is clear why: having a belief system fulfils a purpose that acting does not. We form beliefs in order to have an accurate representation of the world, and to do so successfully requires sensitivity to available evidence. (Joyce 2000: 220)

Practical rationality relates to the assessment of actions:

> A person has interests, and if there is something she can do to satisfy those interests, we may say that she has an "objective reason" to do that thing. When she is justified in believing herself to have an objective reason, then she has a subjective reason. She is rational insofar as her actions are guided by her subjective reasons. (Joyce 2000: 215; Joyce cites Cullity and Gaut 1997: 2 as the source for this account)

Joyce believes that having emotions towards fictional characters is in an agent's interest. There is much in the literature to support this (de Sousa 1987: 182, Greenspan

Derek Matravers

1988: 144). Hence, according to Joyce, the agent has a subjective reason to have an emotion towards a fictional character, and would be rational in acting so as to bring that about. We can act so as to bring it about that we feel pity for Mrs Yeobright; that is, we simply pick up *The Return of the Native* and start reading. Hence, feeling pity for Mrs Yeobright is rational.

There is a missing step in the argument as I have laid it out above, which is the step that causes Joyce most trouble. Clearly reading *The Return of the Native* is an action, and so subject to assessment by practical rationality. Reading the book causes the pity we feel for Mrs Yeobright. However, does it follow that the pity we feel for Mrs Yeobright is an action and so is subject to assessment by practical rationality? Joyce commits himself to the following claim (which he numbers (7)): "If a person performs action Φ, believing that ψ will likely result – and no other agency is involved – then, if ψ does result, that person is deemed not merely responsible for ψ, but to have performed action ψ" (Joyce 2000: 218). He gives an example to back this up: "If I cut down a tree, knowing that the birdhouse in its branches will likely be damaged – and it is – then I have performed the action of damaging the birdhouse" (Joyce 2000: 218). Despite the support of this example, Joyce concedes (7) does not seem in general correct, as he shows by the following:

> Suppose there were a pill I could take which would cause me to form the belief that Napoleon won Waterloo (Φ is taking the pill). The conclusion – that believing that Napoleon won Waterloo is an *action* that I perform – is unpalatable. More importantly, even if (7) were true – even if I did take the pill, thus performing the action of forming that belief – and even if I did so because I could see that believing that Napoleon won Waterloo was going to be, in some fashion, of immense instrumental value – none of this would suffice to make that belief rational. (Joyce 2000: 219)

Joyce's final pump of our intuitions on this question asks whether, in such circumstances, the *person* is or is not rational: "If a person, P, performs action α, justifiably believing that β will likely result, and justifiably believing that β will serve his ends, then (i) α is a rational action, and therefore (ii) P is (*ceteris paribus*) rational" (Joyce 2000: 219). This holds, Joyce thinks, even if α is "taking a belief pill" and β denotes the formation of a belief. In the circumstances relevant to this paper, P believes that thinking about Mrs Yeobright will cause the other elements of the emotion which, together with the thoughts about Mrs Yeobright, constitute pity. P also believes that such a feeling of pity is instrumentally valuable. Hence P is (ceteris paribus) rational.

Even if Joyce is right that P has a subjective reason to bring about his pity for Mrs Yeobright, and is to that extent rational, this does not undermine the claim that the resulting emotion is irrational according to doxastic norms. However, given that P is rational and the action is practically rational, the irrationalist's position looks a little thin. What are the grounds for insisting that the pity is irrational according to doxastic norms? Joyce focuses his attention on the analogies Radford draws between feeling emotions for fictions and cases of prima facie irrationality such as phobias. I am not going to explore that debate, if only because the best way to describe phobias in terms of belief-desire psychology seems no more clear than the best way to describe our attitudes to fictions. If we put that to one side, along with the assertion of narrow

The Challenge of Irrationalism

cognitivism, what is left is the mere insistence, by the irrationalist, that an emotion felt towards a nonexistent person is not reasonable.

There is, however, a problem in Joyce's argument, which lies in his characterization of practical rationality:

> A person has interests, and if there is something she can do to satisfy those interests, we may say that she has an "objective reason" to do that thing. When she is justified in believing herself to have an objective reason, then she has a subjective reason. She is rational insofar as her actions are guided by her subjective reasons. (Joyce 2000: 215)

This works for Joyce's example of having reason to acquire a false belief. If I am promised a sum of money for believing Napoleon won Waterloo, my actions in taking the pill are guided by my desire for that false belief. However, it is not clear it works for the other cases. There are (possibly) two different interests we have for going on a fairground ride. First, there is the thrill it will generate. Second, there might be some further instrumental good to do with hardening us against danger or exploring the far reaches of our emotions. The first plainly guides our actions in going on the ride, the second (putting aside some exceptional cases) does not.

Joyce argues that the benefit of feeling emotions for fictional characters is (roughly) learning about our capacity to feel such emotions. The irrationalist can grant that people have this objective reason. If these people are reflective, and believe themselves to have this objective reason, they also have a subjective reason to feel the emotions. However, it is plain that our actions in reading a novel (and thus generating these emotions) are not guided by our subjective reasons. That is, although our reading of novels could be guided by some desire for self-improvement with respect to our knowledge of our emotional selves, that would be quite exceptional (and rather sad). Our motive for engaging with fictions, as with engaging with any of the arts, is the intrinsic rather than the instrumental value it brings.

Situations in which a person has an objective reason for doing something, yet not one that provides a motive for doing it, have been much explored in ethics (Williams 1981). We do not need to decide on that issue, however, for, by Joyce's definition, a person is rational "insofar as her actions are guided by her subjective reasons," and, in the case of fictions, they are not. Joyce's argument provides no independent reason for the irrationalist to concede that a person is being rational. We have the same stand-off between those who think the rationality of emotions is "reality-indifferent" and those that do not.

The same consideration applies to the contribution of Gendler and Kovakovich in this volume. Drawing on empirical considerations, they show that people need to engage with simulated emotions in order for our decision making to function effectively. In this case, it is plausible that the motivation we have for simulating emotions is to help in a situation in which we are called upon to decide something. In as much as our actions are guided by our subjective reasons, these emotions are (by Joyce's definition) rational. However, it would be exceptional – even bizarre – for our actions in picking up and reading a novel to be guided by such reasons. Once again, such considerations do nothing to show that in reacting with emotion to a fiction a reader is being rational.

A different line the emotionalist could take against the irrationalist would be to insist upon irrationalists paying the price for their position. One should not simply be happy with irrationality; something should be done to avoid it. More precisely, irrationalists are committed to three uncontroversial claims which together militate against their position. First, fictions do cause emotions in the absence of the belief that the object of the emotion actually existed. Second, people ought to be sensitive to reasons. That is, if we believe we have a mental state that is irrational or unreasonable, we ought to feel a pressure to change or rid ourselves of that state. Finally, readers feel no pressure to change or get rid of that emotion.

Irrationalists can reply to this in at least the following two ways. First, they could argue that, in deciding whether or not to get rid of these emotions, we are reflecting on the good (or not) this will do us. From this position, we could reflect on the objective reasons we have for engaging with fiction and take the view that the instrumental value of emotions gives us reason to keep them, which overrides whatever reason we have to change or get rid of them because of their doxastic irrationality. To support this, the irrationalist might contrast mechanisms by which people can induce fear for themselves (such as fairground rides, flight simulators, and transparent floors) with circumstances in which people were in real danger. There is surely a difference in reasonableness between fear felt for oneself in these two sets of circumstances, even though people are motivated to feel the emotions (and to continue to feel the emotions) in the former set. To this the emotionalist would give the now familiar reply that, although there is a difference to be marked, it is misleading to do so by appeal to rationality. In other words, appeal to further cases does not sort the problem out as the disagreements the two sides have over fiction will simply reappear for those cases. This is where the disagreement between the emotionalist and irrationalist such as Radford appears to rest.

Fiction and Sentimentality

If we return to the criticism I made of Joyce's argument and explore what does guide a person's actions in bringing about emotions felt for fictional characters, there is room for a perhaps more idiosyncratic irrationalist to continue the argument. The reply the idiosyncratic irrationalist should give is that, although people do not generally feel a pressure to change or rid themselves of an emotion held towards a fiction, they ought to. The three claims which – according to the emotionalist – the irrationalist should accept are not formally inconsistent. The first is that people ought to be sensitive to reasons and the third is that, in fact, they are not. However, it might be that people are not doing what they ought to do. To pursue their case the idiosyncratic irrationalist should, I think, abandon the claim that emotions felt towards fictions are irrational and instead argue that there is something wrong with them on other grounds (although I shall continue to use the term "idiosyncratic irrationalist"). After all, Mr Keith is "saddened" by emotions felt for fictions, not puzzled by them.

Let us put fictions to one side for the moment and explore, briefly, emotions felt in central cases. The problem with Joyce's (7) is that one is deliberately bringing about the emotion. There are certain mental states – pleasure being the obvious example – for which our bringing them about raises no problems. Emotions such as sympathy, pity, sadness, joy, and so on (the emotions characteristically felt for fictional characters) are not like that, however. Consider the following paradigm case. I open a letter and come to believe that a loved one has died. This belief causes various other phenomenological and physiological changes, which, all together, constitute my sadness at the death of a loved one. It is important that the sadness follows involuntarily from the belief. Indeed, it is difficult to make sense of voluntariness entering at this stage: that is, difficult to make sense of acquiring the belief and deciding to feel sad. A consequence of this is that it would not really make sense to ask the person involved why, in addition to having the belief, they felt sad. It would not make sense because the belief *causes* the sadness: it is not under the person's control. Although there may be many instrumental benefits to feeling sad, those are not the motives the person has for feeling sad. Given that the person has the relevant belief, the question of a motive for feeling sad (or not feeling sad) does not arise.

The question the idiosyncratic irrationalist poses concerns the *motives* we could have for the voluntary generation of emotions such as those we are considering. Clearly, there are some motives that are appropriate. For example, we might have a moral duty to acquire beliefs about the suffering of those less fortunate than ourselves. This awareness, let us say, causes us to feel pity. The motive is healthy (benevolence) and the induced emotion is part of a package that includes links to motivation. Given this, it is appropriate for us to generate emotions through reading documentaries about morally troubling events. However, there are also clear cases of motives for generating emotions that are inappropriate. Consider the following discussion of sentimentality by Michael Tanner:

> ... feelings tend, after a certain point, to dislocate themselves from their objects, if they have them ... once the dislocation has taken place, there is a tendency to auto-generation, so that it isn't so much inappropriate strength or object that is in question, but a disturbing autonomy which retains the *cachet*, if any, of the emotion when it was in more or less proper relationship to its object, which may have been a perfectly worthy one. The element of dishonesty, probably of self-deceit, that is agreed to be characteristic of attitudes, people or whatever when they are sentimental is connected with the sense of the developed feeling having lost touch with their origins, in insidious and dangerous ways. And there is a general implication, though not a universal one, that the self-development is illicitly pleasurable. (Tanner 1976–7: 132–3)

What can we say about the motive for the voluntary generation of emotion through fiction? As we have seen, this question is avoided in the argument of Joyce (and Gendler and Kovakovich), as that focuses on the instrumental benefits of the emotion. The motive for engaging with fictions, as with engaging with any of the arts, is the intrinsic rather than the instrumental value it brings. The emotionalist would argue that there is no single motive for involving ourselves with fiction. There are some fictions (trashy romantic novels, for example) where the motive might be to generate an emotion in which one can then wallow. This seems tied to the characterization of sentimentality that Tanner gives above. However, other fictions (those of a

Derek Matravers

character likely to appeal to F. R. Leavis) raise appropriate emotions of appropriate intensity. In such cases, the accusation of sentimentality does not carry conviction.

The idiosyncratic irrationalist would argue that there are features of our generating emotions through fictions that cast doubt on the appropriateness of *any* motive we have for such engagement. The motive in the moral case was appropriate because the emotions were not being generated for their own sake. Rather, bringing them about forms part of what it is to be properly morally motivated. Indeed, as Tanner brings out in the following remark about righteous indignation, there is something suspect about the generation of emotion without any link to action: "The kind of feelings I am thinking of are righteous indignation on the basis of which no action can be taken, and in general that range of feelings which help to increase one's sense of one's own superiority so long as no activity is required" (Tanner 1976-7: 139-40).

The emotions we feel towards fictions cannot link to action. In reading fictions we are generating emotions for no further end. Of course, doing so might have some instrumental value in the long term, but, as stated above, this cannot be our motive for picking up a book and reading it. The idiosyncratic irrationalist's worry is that, in a world in which there are so many situations deserving of our emotional attention (and consequent action) having a motive for the generation of emotions for no further end looks to be self-indulgence. I think this is, fundamentally, what drives the irrationalist's case. If so, then they are not so idiosyncratic after all. The charge that putting an interest in the arts above pressing moral concerns is self-indulgent has a distinguished philosophical pedigree, including – of course – Plato and Rousseau (Rousseau [1750] 1987, Plato 1992). What the emotionalist has to do in reply is to defend taking an interest in the arts against this moralistic charge. There are such defenses (and replies to such defenses), but I am not going to be able to sort out this "ancient quarrel" here. The point, however, is that it is *this* charge that needs to be answered, hence the appeal to the instrumental value of fiction is irrelevant.

We have to enter a caveat here to the idiosyncratic irrationalist's case. By claiming that emotions felt for fictions are inappropriate, the idiosyncratic irrationalist might have proved too much. Initially, the charge of irrationality involved the following divide. To be rational, it is necessary that an emotion be directed to an actual object. These include emotions felt towards objects in both confrontations and documentaries – that is, representations of actual events distant in time or place (or time and place). Emotions felt towards objects in fictions were, by contrast, irrational. The charge of inappropriateness threatens to divide matters up differently. I suggested that it is appropriate for us to generate emotions through reading documentaries about morally troubling events, provided the emotions were connected with motivation. However, there are many such documentaries where there could not be a connection to action: reports of events for which we lack the instrumental beliefs to bring about action.

There are two ways in which idiosyncratic irrationalists might answer this question. First, they might maintain that emotions felt towards objects in documentaries are not subject to the same criticism as emotions felt towards objects in fictions. Given their general view, it is likely that they would not regard an interest in documentaries as being on a par with an interest in fictions. Actual people in actual situations share a moral community with us in a way that fictions do not. Part of Mr Keith's original complaint was that fictional events are "no affair of mine." Actual events, however, are an affair of ours. It is part of our general moral obligations to acquaint ourselves with them. Thus, using documentaries to generate emotions is not voluntary in the way that using fictions to generate emotions is. As such a reply is vulnerable to the comments Tanner makes on righteous indignation, the irrationalist might be wise to try a different – more conciliatory – approach. While we do have some moral obligation to explore the actual world beyond our immediate acquaintance, this will not excuse interaction with all documentaries. The argument is that emotions felt towards fictions have none of the standard package of beliefs, desires, and motivations. Reports of actual situations have at least beliefs, but the rest of the package will vary according to cases. Emotional reactions to objects in some documentaries will be subject to the same accusation of inappropriateness as emotional reactions to fictions.

This chapter is an attempt to evaluate the claim that feeling emotions for non-existent people is irrational. There have been two conclusions. First, I have not been able to find a decisive refutation of irrationalism. We arrive at a stand-off in which the irrationalist asserts that the absence of the relevant belief rendered the emotion irrational, a claim the emotionalist denies. Although defensible, the irrationalist's position does not seem to me a happy one on the simple grounds that we should be uncomfortable in attributing irrationality to the mental states of all consumers of fiction. If we think there is some plausibility in the irrationalist case, this provides support for a different approach altogether: one in which the emotions felt towards fictions are not actual emotions, but make-believe emotions. The irrationalist need not be worried because there is no reason to think make-believe emotions should have actual objects, and the emotionalist can be satisfied in that make-believe emotions have all the instrumentally valuable properties of actual emotions. We can learn about finance playing *Monopoly* with *Monopoly* money, just as well as we would learn playing with real money. My second conclusion would tell against a Waltonian approach as much as against an approach that claimed that the emotions we feel are real. This grounds the motivation for irrationalism in the perennial thought that art is a distraction from the proper concerns of morality. Ironically, the puritanical flavor of this would horrify nobody more than it would the fictional Mr Keith.

Note

I am grateful to Berys Gaut for useful comments on an earlier draft of this paper, and to the editor for his suggestions for improvement.

References for Chapters 15 and 16

Aristotle (1984). *The Rhetoric and the Poetics of Aristotle*, trans. R. Roberts, introduction I. Bywater. New York: McGraw Hill.

Bechara, A., Damasio, A. R., Damasio, H., and Anderson, S. W. (1994). "Insensitivity to Future Consequences Following Damage to Human Prefrontal Cortex." *Cognition*, 50: 7–15.

Brock, S. (2002). "Fictionalism about Fictional Characters." *Noûs*, 36: 1–21.

Carroll, N. (1990). *Philosophy of Horror*. New York: Routledge.

Coleridge, S. T. ([1817] 1985). *Biographia Literaria*, ed. James Engell and W Jackson Bate. Princeton, NJ: Princeton University Press.

Crittendon, C. (1991). *Unreality*. Ithaca, NY: Cornell University Press.

Cullity, G. and Gaut, B. (eds.) (1997). *Ethics and Practical Reason*. Oxford, Clarendon Press.

Currie, G. (1990). *The Nature of Fiction*. Cambridge, UK: Cambridge University Press.

Damasio, A. R. (1997). *Descartes' Error*. New York: Grosset/Putnam.

Damasio, A. R. (1999). *The Feeling of What Happens*. New York: Harcourt.

Damasio, A. R., Tranel, D., and Damasio, H. (1991). "Somatic Markers and the Guidance of Behavior: Theory and Preliminary Testing." In H. S. Levin, H. M. Eisenberg, and A. L. Benton (eds.), *Frontal Lobe Function and Dysfunction* (pp. 217–29). New York: Oxford University Press.

de Sousa, R. (1987). *The Rationality of Emotion*. Cambridge, MA and London: MIT Press.

Evans, G. (1982). *The Varieties of Reference*. Oxford: Oxford University Press.

Feagin, S. (1983). "The Pleasures of Tragedy." *American Philosophical Quarterly*, 20: 95–104.

Gaut, B. (2003). "Reasons, Emotions and Fictions." In M. Kieran and D. M. Lopes (eds.), *Imagination, Philosophy and the Arts* (pp. 15–34). London: Routledge.

Greenspan, P. (1988). *Emotions and Reasons*. New York and London: Routledge.

Harris, P. L. (2000). *The Work of the Imagination*. Oxford: Blackwell.

Hjort, M. and Laver, S. (ed.) (1997). *Emotion and the Arts*. New York: Oxford University Press.

Johnson, S. ([1765] 2004). *Preface to Shakespeare's Plays*. Whitefish, MT: Kessinger.

Joyce, R. (2000). "Rational Fear of Monsters." *The British Journal of Aesthetics*, 40(2): 209–24.

Lamarque, P. (1981). "How Can We Fear and Pity Fictions?" *British Journal of Aesthetics*, 21: 291–304.

Lewis, D. (1978). "Truth in Fiction." *American Philosophical Quarterly*, 15: 37–46.

Matravers, D. (1998). *Art and Emotion*. Oxford, Oxford University Press.

McCormick, P. J. (1988). *Fictions, Philosophies, and the Problems of Poetics*. Ithaca, NY: Cornell University Press.

Nussbaum, M. (1986). *The Fragility of Goodness*. New York: Cambridge University Press.

Nussbaum, M. (1990). *Love's Knowledge*. New York: Oxford University Press.

Parsons, T. (1980). *Nonexistent Objects*. New Haven, CT: Yale University Press.

Paskins, B. (1977). "On Being Moved by Anna Karenina and *Anna Karenina*." *Philosophy*, 52: 344–7.

Plato. (1992). *Republic*, trans. G. M. A. Grube, rev. C. D. C. Reeve. Indianapolis, IN: Hackett.

Radford, C. (1975). "How Can We Be Moved by the Fate of Anna Karenina?" *Proceedings of the Aristotelian Society*, supplementary vol. 49: 67–80.

Radford, C. (1989). "Replies to Three Critics." *Philosophy*, 64: 93–7.

Radford, C. (1995). "Fiction, Pity, Fear, and Jealousy." *Journal of Aesthetics and Art Criticism*, 53: 71–5.

Radford, C. ([1975] 2002). "How Can We Be Moved by the Fate of Anna Karenina?" In A. Neill and A. Ridley (eds.), *Arguing About Art* (pp. 239–49). London: Routledge.

Rousseau, J.-J. ([1750] 1987). "Discourse on the Sciences and the Arts." In *Jean-Jacques Rousseau: The Basic Political Writings*, ed. and trans. D. E. Cress (pp. 1–21). Indianapolis, IN: Hackett.

Salmon, N. (1998). "Nonexistence." *Noûs*, 32: 277–319.

Tanner, M. (1976-7). "Sentimentality." *Proceedings of the Aristotelian Society*, 77: 127–47.

van Inwagen, P. (1977). "Creatures of Fiction." *American Philosophical Quarterly*, 14: 299–308.

Walton, K. L. (1978). "Fearing Fictions." *Journal of Philosophy*, 75: 5–27.

Walton, K. L. (1990). *Mimesis as Make-believe*. Cambridge, MA: Harvard University Press.

Walton, K. L. (1997). "Spelunking, Simulation, and Slime: On Being Moved by Fiction." In M. Hjort and S. Laver (eds.), *Emotion and the Arts* (pp. 37–49). New York: Oxford University Press.

Weston, P. (1975). "How Can We Be Moved by the Fate of Anna Karenina?, II." *Proceedings of the Aristotelian Society*, supplementary vol. 49: 81–93.

Williams, B. (1981). "Internal and External Reasons." In *Moral Luck* (pp. 101–13). Cambridge, UK: Cambridge University Press.

Wolterstorff, N. (1980). *Works and Worlds of Art*. Oxford: Clarendon Press.

Further Reading for Chapters 15 and 16

Dadlez, E. (1997). *What's Hecuba to Him?: Fictional Events and Actual Emotions*. Pennsylvania, PA: Pennsylvania University Press.

Feagin, S. L. (1996). *Reading With Feeling: The Aesthetics of Appreciation*. Ithaca, NY and London: Cornell University Press.

Thomasson, A. L. (1999). *Fiction and Metaphysics*. Cambridge, UK: Cambridge University Press.

Yanal, R. J. (1999). *Paradoxes of Emotion and Fiction*. University Park: Pennsylvania State University Press.

IS ARTISTIC INTENTION RELEVANT TO THE INTERPRETATION OF ARTWORKS?

Interpretation and the Problem of the Relevant Intention

Robert Stecker

A Brief Introduction to the Philosophy of Art Interpretation

This chapter focuses on one among the nest of problems that crisscross in debates about the interpretation of works of art, namely the relevance of the intentions of artists to the interpretation of their works. This topic is plausibly the one that was at the center of attention when interpretation first became an important issue in the philosophy of art and in literary and art theory. The early debate often had an all or nothing character with anti-intentionalists arguing that reference to artists' intentions are simply irrelevant to the interpretation of their works and intentionalists arguing that the meaning of works are to be identified with such intentions. Sixty years later, this issue is still with us, but it is now intertwined with a number of others, and the positions about the relevance of intention are both more subtle and more moderate.

Several distinct issues have emerged in the debate about the nature of art interpretation. Most relevant to the intention debate are the following three. One is *the proper aim issue*. This concerns what interpretations of artworks are trying to accomplish, and whether this can be expressed in terms of one central proper aim or whether there are multiple central proper aims. Another is *the critical monism/critical pluralism issue*. This concerns whether there is a single correct interpretation of an artwork or whether there can be multiple, noncombinable acceptable interpretations. Notice that both of these first two issues have to do with multiplicity and plurality, of aims in the first instance and of interpretations of individual works in the second. Finally there is *the work meaning issue*. Is there something that we can identify as the meaning of the work, and is identifying this at least one, if not the only, aim of art interpretation?

Of equal importance is another trio of issues, though ones that operate at a different level than those just mentioned – a level that is beyond the concern of this chapter. First, do our attempts to understand art always involve interpretation or can we sometimes understand without interpreting? Answering this question requires distinguishing interpretation from other forms of understanding. Secondly, what exactly are the objects we interpret? They are artworks, of course, in the cases that concern us, but there is much debate about what sort of objects these are and the answer we give to this question can have a bearing on what is going on when we interpret these objects. Finally, a very large and important issue is about the extent that interpretations change or even create their objects. The most conservative view on this issue is that they don't change them at all, but simply, when successful, discover what is already there. The alternative view is that interpretations participate to a greater or lesser extent in creating the object being interpreted. (A detailed discussion of these issues is found in Stecker 2003.)

The Place of Intention in the Interpretation Debate: Interpretive Aims

Questions about intention enter the interpretation debate at two chief locations: with regard to the proper aim issue and with regard to the work meaning issue. (For their bearing on the critical monism/critical pluralism issue, see "Conclusion" below.) This section concerns the question whether it is a proper and central aim of art interpretation to identify the intentions of actual artists.

On the face of it, it seems obvious that interpreters of artworks do have available to them the aim of figuring out the intentions of artists in making their works. After all, critics and ordinary art lovers still make such inquiries, and their doing so seems to be in keeping with other interpretive practices. To stick to matters that are completely nontendentious, when we need to interpret conversational utterances, instructions, official statements, policies, expressions of thought such as philosophical works, we routinely and uncontroversially inquire into the intended meaning of these items.

One thing that adverting to these other practices shows is that one of the most common worries about this interpretive aim – whether we can ever know about the intentions of others – is overblown. In conversation, we believe that we can grasp the intentions of our interlocutors normally without asking for clarification (or else asking for clarification would be pointless). It might be replied that this is because we share a rich context of utterance when involved in conversation, but that this is the main reason we can often infer intention is belied by the fact that we bring the same belief to the interpretation of philosophical works from the past. We may have to know about the context of utterance to have a good basis for inferring intentions, but that doesn't mean we have to operate from within the same context.

Reference to other interpretive contexts does not ward off a different kind of objection. This is the claim that art interpretation has a special dominant aim not found in these other practices that precludes the aim of identifying an artist's actual intention. The claim here is that *the* aim of art interpretation is to achieve a certain sort of payoff: an appreciative experience, enhanced aesthetic appreciation, making the work the best (object of appreciation) it can be (see Davies 1991: 181-206, Dworkin 1986: 45-86, Lamarque 2002). The basic proposal is that interpretations of artworks are for the purpose of better appreciating them. The subsidiary claim is that focus on

Robert Stecker

the intention of the artist is not the best route to achieving this, or alternatively, it is to shift our attention from *the* proper aim of interpretation to a different improper aim.

There is undoubtedly at least one valuable point to be derived from this objection. It is that identifying the actual intention of the creator of an artwork is not the only aim we have when interpreting a work. We do sometimes aim at the sort of enhanced appreciation the objection trumpets. However, beyond this important point, there is little to be said for the objection, and to the extent that its point is to rule out the identification of intention as *a* proper aim of art interpretation, it is ineffective. This is so for at least three different reasons.

The first reason is that intention-oriented criticism can be just as appreciation-enhancing as any other. While it is not necessary that the interpretation that captures the artist's intention gives us the "aesthetically best" interpretation, it is as likely to do so as any other. At the very least, it will add to the variety of reasonable interpretations of the work, which itself can add to the work's appreciation as is recognized even by some who take the view that the purpose of interpretation is appreciative experience (Goldman 1990).

Second, it's not clear that the primary or initial aim of *any* interpretation is to enhance appreciation. Rather, it is to do this by pointing to something in the work that is not obvious, or at least by pointing to a nonobvious way the work could be taken. That is, we seek to appreciate a work by forming a deeper understanding of it or by arriving at *an* understanding which delivers a richer appreciative experience. So the aim that the proponents of the objection under consideration should be pushing is better described as appreciative understanding, and one route to this is via the actual intentions of artists.

Finally, it is simply dogmatic to maintain that enhanced appreciation is *the* goal of art interpretation. Someone may simply want a better understanding of a work, or, more narrowly still, be curious about what an artist intended to do in it. It's plausible that we interpret with a number of different aims, no one of which is the supreme one. (See Stecker 2003 for a defense of this thesis.)

There is one other objection to taking the identification of actual intentions as an aim of art interpretation. This objection does not deny that we try to figure out this sort of thing but denies that it has anything to do with the interpretation of artworks. Rather, it is claimed, it is concerned with the biography of the artist. The argument behind this objection is simple. Intentions belong to people, not things. Artists are people; works are things. Therefore, discovering intentions is finding something out about artists, not artworks.

This is an admirably straightforward argument. Its premises are straightforwardly true. Unfortunately, it is just as plain that the conclusion does not follow. This is because, although people have intentions, and things don't, people's intentions transmit properties to the things those people do and make that are ontologically dependent on those intentions. So one can't understand those properties of things without understanding the intentions constitutive of them. Hence, when we discover art intentions, though we do find something out about the artist, we also find something out about the work. To see this, consider first an example outside the arts. Suppose you visit my house and you see, near the fireplace, a large tree stump. You wonder if it serves as a seat, but I wave you off. It is a wood-splitting platform by virtue of my intention to use it for that purpose. On the table near the fireplace is a manuscript entitled "A Chronicle." You say that you did not know I engaged in historical research. I inform you that it is a work of fiction. What makes it fiction rather than a real chronicle, in part, is my intention to produce a certain type of work.

The examples given so far are untendentious illustrations that intentions bear on the nature of things though they belong to people, and so an investigation into the identity of certain intentions is not merely biographical. That is, it is widely accepted that we have to appeal to certain "constitutive" intentions to understand or correctly identify certain items (see Levinson 1996: 188-9). What is the subject of greater controversy is whether actual intentions bear not just on the type of thing done or produced, but on what such a thing means or communicates (when it is the sort of thing that means or communicates at all). Settling this controversy brings us to the second way that intention enter the interpretation debate: with regard to the meaning of artworks. To understand artwork meaning, do we need to understand the artist's intentions?

Actual Intentionalism as a Theory of Meaning

The most extreme intentionalist view, which was the object of those early attacks on intentionalist accounts of meaning mentioned at the beginning of the chapter, is the identity thesis: that the meaning of a work is identical to what the artist intends to convey or express in the work. There are decisive objections to this sort of intentionalism. One such objection will suffice here. People, including artists, do not infallibly succeed in realizing everything they intend to do. The meaning of a work could hardly be identical to an *unrealized* intention. Yet this is among the implications of the identity thesis. Hence the thesis must be false, since it has a false implication.

As it turns out, the identity thesis never has had many defenders. (Perhaps the only unequivocal proponents of it are Knapp and Michaels 1985). However, targeting this thesis does help to isolate a necessary condition for an intentionalist theory of meaning that has a chance of success. Unrealized intentions must be excluded from the meaning-determining intentions. But there is disagreement over when an intention is unrealized, which leads to different intentionalist theories. In setting these theories out, it is easiest to begin with cases of linguistic meaning. We can ask later how the most viable theories can be extended across the arts.

One popular view is that intentions select a meaning when linguistic conventions leave an utterance ambiguous or indeterminate. Analogously, the intention of the author is what disambiguates literary works that would otherwise have two or more viable readings (Carroll 2001: 198, Iseminger 1992). The conception of a realized intention, on this view, is an intention consistent with the framework provided by the operative conventions. An intention would fail to be operative that violates such a convention. Thus Mrs Malaprop frequently fails to say what she intends because she constantly violates the conventions of English. When she says, "there's a nice derangement of epitaphs," her utterance just can't mean that there is a nice arrangement of epithets, because arrangement is not one of the conventional meanings of "derangement" and similarly for "epitaph" and epithet. On the other hand, it is open to me to make my words refer to a riverside appointment, when I say I will meet you at the bank, because a riverside is one of the conventional meanings of "bank." Call this *convention-constrained intentionalism*.

There are two main problems with this suggestion. One is that its account of a realized intention is too narrow or restrictive. There are many uses of language, both in conversational and literary contexts, where we use words in a way that extends or departs from conventional literal meaning, without failing to realize our intentions. One example of such a case is irony. If you say to an acquaintance particularly prone to callous behavior that you have always been impressed with his sensitivity and compassion, the meaning of your words will be clear to most of your audience with the possible exception of the individual being addressed, who may be too conceited to take in the irony. Yet convention-constrained intentionalism implies that you necessarily failed to say what you meant since callousness is not one of the conventional meanings of "compassion" any more than arrangement is one of the conventional meanings of "derangement." Irony is usually regarded as a use of language that provides one of the best cases for actual intentionalism about meaning, and an intentionalist view that cannot accommodate it is clearly inadequate. However, there are many cases where we intend to convey something that goes beyond the conventional meaning of our words. For example, I might say, "the bus is coming," in order to tell the children to go to the bus stop. In the context of a game of bridge, you might point out that Mary doesn't have a heart to convey that she can't trump her opponent's ace. The conventions of language permit us to convey all of these things, but what we convey are not conventional meanings.

While convention-constrained intentionalism is too restrictive in some cases in its account of realized intentions, in other cases, it is too broad or permissive. This is the second problem with the account. The reason for this is that it ignores context, which is just as important as convention in fixing meaning. For example, suppose I am your real estate agent, and I say, "We will close on the house [you have bought] at the bank," meaning the river bank (because I think it would be just lovely to perform the official transfer of ownership at such a pretty spot). I probably have not done enough to convey my intention and override the contextually supported assumption that I am referring to the offices of the institution financing the purchase. Here context supplies a referent to "bank" *independently of* my intention, and in order to realize my intention that my words refer to a riverbank, I need to draw your attention to this fact and away from the contextually supplied referent.

Given the problems with convention-constrained intentionalism, one might be attracted to its polar opposite: *whatever-works intentionalism*. (This view is inspired by, but should not be attributed to, Davidson 1986.) According to this view, intentions are realized if one manages to communicate them. Otherwise, they are unrealized. This view has no problem explaining the successful use of irony, figures of speech, or contextually based extensions of meaning such as the use of "the bus is coming" to tell children to go to the bus stop. More dubiously, according to this view, if Mrs Malaprop can convey to us (with an assist from context) that she means a nice arrangement of epithets by "a nice derangement of epitaphs," then her intention is successfully realized and her utterance has that meaning. It is simply of no consequence that her success has no basis in the conventionally fixed referents of the words she happens to use.

One problem with whatever-works intentionalism is that it is unable to make the important distinction between what someone says on the occasion of utterance and what is conveyed by the utterance on that occasion. This is because its whole focus is on what is conveyed. But, even in conversational contexts, we are often interested in distinguishing between what a speaker intends (which if grasped is obviously conveyed) with what is actually said. This is almost always true in official conversation: for example, one's boss explaining the conditions for promotion, but it is true on many other occasions as well. In making this point, I am not claiming that the meaning of an utterance should simply be identified with what is said rather than conveyed, but I would suggest that not everything conveyed is part of utterance meaning. For example, if one manages to convey something despite, rather than because of, the conventional meaning of one's words (as is the case with Mrs Malaprop) then that is not part of utterance meaning.

What we need is a conception of a realized intention and a related conception of utterance or work meaning, that is intermediate between the two views we have discussed so far. Such a view might go as follows: an utterance means X if the utterer intends X, the utterer intends that his or her audience will grasp this in virtue of the conventional meaning of the words or a contextually supported extension of this meaning permitted by conventions, and the first intention is graspable in virtue of those conventions or permissible extensions of them. If the conditions are met, the intention to convey something with an utterance has been realized. This intention can be realized in other ways (as whatever-works intentionalists understand) but not ways that guarantee the utterance will mean what it manages to convey.

This view – call it *the intermediate view* – has the advantage of coopting the plausible intuitions behind convention-constrained and whatever-works intentionalism, while avoiding their unattractive consequences. Intentions that determine utterance (work) meaning are tied to operative conventions, but not restricted to the literal, conventional meaning of words. The role of context is also recognized. However, certain intentions conveyed (realized) via contextual pointers are ruled out as meaning-determiners, because they are not permitted extensions of operative conventions.

The intermediate view can be extended to all sorts of art forms beyond literature. To do this, one has to hook intentions up to the routes through which meaning is conveyed in a given art form, which may not always be convention. For example, pictorial representation may operate via natural, innate, species-wide, recognitional abilities alongside the conventions associated with a style, genre, or period. A painting will represent X if the painter intends to represent X, intends to do this via the audiences' recognitional abilities, relevant conventions, or permissible contextually supported extensions of the conventions, and the audience can recognize X through these factors.

Finally, the intermediate view needs to be regarded, not as a freestanding account of utterance (work) meaning, but as part of a larger account which can also include some nonintentional determinates as well. The real estate agent's proposal to meet at the bank might be an example where the intended referent of "bank" (riverbank) is less salient than, and for that reason overridden by, the contextually supplied refer-

Robert Stecker

ent (financial institution). In a somewhat different vein, a literary work, *in addition to* what it intentionally does, may inadvertently express attitudes toward a race or a gender, for example, which may also be part of the meaning of the work. For example, as Noël Carroll has noted (2001: 186), although Jules Verne's novel, *Mysterious Island*, intentionally and explicitly opposes the institution of slavery, it also, no doubt unintentionally but no less actually, expresses a residual racism in representing the former slave Neb as a superstitious, docile, naive, childlike individual with a curious affinity with a domesticated monkey.

Criticisms of Actual Intentionalism

We have now given a role to the actual intentions of utterers and artists in fixing the meaning of utterances and artworks. It is a modest role because it is nothing like the claim of the identity theorist, that the meaning of these items just are the intentions of their makers. The intermediate view recognizes that actual intentions are one factor among several that fix meaning and that meanings can sometimes be unintended in virtue of the operation of these other factors.

Even the most moderate intentionalism has its critics who fail to be convinced that intentions have any role in fixing meaning. In this section, we will look at some of the most serious criticisms of actual intentionalism per se.

The *first objection* is the *publicity paradox*. It argues that once we take seriously a certain intention shared by all artists, this rules out the consideration of other intentions as determinative of artwork content. The widely shared intention is to create an object for public consumption, an object available to a public absent the artist. Such an object must, as it were, stand on its own. So one might conclude that the initial intention with which works are made is the intention that one's intentions not be consulted. So intentions are not relevant to work meaning (content).

Unfortunately, the reasoning behind the publicity paradox is fallacious. First, there is no paradox, and so there is no reason to reject intentionalism because it leads to contradictory conclusions (i.e., to the paradox that we should both consult and not consult the artist's intentions). Rather the point that the publicity "paradox" is making is that if we consult one intention that all artists have (to produce an object for a public), that precludes the consultation of other intentions. The first intention is constitutive: it determines the type of object we are dealing with. The intentions that we purportedly should not consider are meaning-determining. The claim that the above mentioned constitutive intention with which artworks are made rules out consulting the meaning-determining intentions of artists is either true or false, but not both true and false. Of course, if it is true, that is still devastating for even moderate intentionalism.

The second point, though, is that the claim is not true. A minor problem with the claim is that it falsely assumes that all artists make their works with the "publicity intention." Some artists seem to work primarily for themselves rather than for an autonomous public, while others, especially in recent art history, attach all sorts of explanatory appendages to reveal their intentions in the absence of their person. The main reason, however, that the claim is false is that the fact that works are intended for public consumption in no way implies that the artists intend that their meaning-determining intentions not be consulted. Just as compatible with the public nature of works is the idea that they reveal the artist's intention without further consultation. This latter idea captures the way many other forms of public communication work. If I post a set of rules for behavior in a given environment (e.g., a classroom), I assume that people will understand what behavior they are intended to elicit or prohibit, and that they will act accordingly without further consultation. If I write a philosophy paper, once again the aim is not that readers won't consult (attempt to identify) my intentions, but rather that they won't need to consult me to identify those intentions, but only my paper. In short, publicity is perfectly consistent with an interest in intentions. It at most implies that interest is primarily satisfied by means of work itself.

It might be thought that publicity has one further implication that is still damaging to actual intentionalism. This implication is that the range of evidence of intention compatible with publicity is *limited to* consulting the work. While intentionalism can recognize the work as the primary source of information about intention, it cannot confine admissible evidence to it. After all, there are often disputes about the intention of a work, and if we really want to settle these, any available evidence ought to be relevant. However, once again the claim about what publicity requires is inaccurate. This is clearest after we acquire a historical distance from a work. Then, more collateral information may be needed to access its meaning, even if its meaning-determining intentions were initially transparent. However, it is reasonable to assume that some such information is always needed as works are not only public objects but contextualized ones connected to a culture, to traditions, as well as to an individual (or group) creator. To think of a work as a public object is at best to have a partial understanding of its nature. Publicity couldn't imply that works are self-contained modules accessible without any collateral information, because such a claim is just not true.

A *second objection* to moderate actual intentionalism based on the intermediate view is *the knowledge of intention dilemma* (Trivedi 2001). To understand the objection, recall first that unrealized intentions (indeed, even some realized intentions) do not determine work meaning. The intermediate view selected a class of realized intentions and claimed that they are meaning-determining. The current objection falls into place once we ask: how do we know when we have such an intention? The objection claims that there are two possible answers to this question, and neither is palatable to the intentionalist. The first answer is that we have to figure out the intention, figure out the work meaning, and then see if they match. The problem here is that if we can figure out the work meaning independently of figuring out the intention, then intentions are not needed to identify work meaning, and work meaning can be defined without mentioning intentions. On the other hand, suppose work meaning cannot be identified independently of identifying the properly realized intentions. Then we could never find out whether intentions are properly realized, and work meaning would forever be unavailable.

If the identity thesis were true, this dilemma would clearly be fallacious. For then, where we determine meaning, we would also determine properly realized intention and visa versa. To see this, consider an entirely different sort of identity: that of water and H_2O. Notice that we have developed two distinct sets of tests, water tests and H_2O

tests. Water tests are based on appearances – looks, tastes, feels – and on functions: what we can do with the stuff. H_2O tests involve chemical analysis. One might say that, since we can figure out what water is independently of H_2O tests, water and H_2O are logically distinct. But this is not so. In reality, water tests are H_2O tests and visa versa. However, since moderate actual intentionalists recognize that there are nonintentional sources of meaning, there is not a mapping from one concept to the other as there is with water and H_2O.

The complexity of work meaning makes it harder to see that the dilemma is fallacious, but fallacious it is, and the chief problem is the second horn, the claim that if work meaning cannot be identified independently of properly realized intentions, we will never be able to determine either. We can determine both, under the given assumption, through a process of mutual adjustment of hypotheses. To see how this works, first consider a conversational case. We are at the airport check-in, and I say, "This bag is heavy." You can identify a literal meaning of my words without regard to intention: that this suitcase weighs more than the average in the appropriate comparison class. However, you also know that I am not uttering those words simply to make a factual observation regarding the weight of my bag, so your next step is to form a hypotheses about my intention in making the utterance, which may be to request help in moving the bag or to express the fear that I will have to pay an overweight charge. Context (e.g., some bag struggling) will help to choose among these hypotheses. All this will result in reading my remark as a request for help, which identifies its utterance meaning as well as successfully realizing my intention.

The process is not very different when we are interpreting artworks. We constantly are forming hypotheses about the point or function of this or that bit in the overall economy of the work. For example, we read in James Joyce's story, "The Dead": "He asked himself what is a woman standing on the stairs in the shadow, listening to distant music, a symbol of" (Schwarz 1994: 48). "He" is the protagonist, Gabriel, and the woman is his wife, Gretta. There is no problem knowing the literal meaning of the sentence. We want to know its *point*: why it is put there. Are we to ask the same question as Gabriel, and is the answer more accessible to us than to him? Or are we to realize he is asking the wrong question at this moment, a fact that reveals an alienation on his part from the flesh and blood Gretta? The default assumption is that this is a hypothesis about Joyce's point (intention), and only if we can't make that assumption work do we look for alternative determinants of meaning. In the case of other questions about work meaning, the default assumption may not be that we are identifying an intention. For example, if our question is: what attitude does *Joyce* express toward women in "The Dead," we may not start out with the assumption that the predominant attitude is one that Joyce intended, but we may nevertheless end up with the view that indeed it is (Norris 1994). Notice that we don't reach these conclusions by matching two independent statements: one about Joyce's intention, a second about work meaning. Rather we form hypotheses, and attempt to figure out if they are true and how they should be characterized (as pertaining to intentions or not.) Hence we can reject the second horn of the dilemma.

A *third objection* to actual intentionalism claims that *reference to intentions is eliminable*, and hence inessential to an account of work meaning. To flesh out this objection, recall that on several occasions above, I have appealed to convention and context to help fix properly realized intended meaning. It is also true, though this was not made explicit above, that when there is no properly realized intention to fix meaning, it is plausible that this is accomplished by convention and context directly. Consider a case where I misspeak: I say, "There is a fly in your suit," whereas I intended to say that there is a fly in your soup. Assuming that context provides the appropriate articles of clothing (in virtue of your wearing a suit), I say, on this occasion, that there is a fly in your suit, and this is fixed by the conventional meaning of my words, and the immediate context in which they are uttered but not by my unrealized (or improperly realized) intention. So in a case where I mean to say that there is a fly in your suit, why shouldn't we say that here too, convention and context do all the work in fixing utterance meaning? What contribution is left to be made by my intention to say this? On this occasion, at least, the answer appears to be none.

I believe that this example may appear persuasive because in many cases intentions that are properly realized are straightforwardly conveyed by convention and context so that we don't have to *figure out*, at every turn, what is being communicated. Even in these very straightforward cases, there may often be an assumed (as well as actual) communicative intention that an audience appeals to in, for example, disambiguating words before context and convention can do their job. (For example, in the case where I say, "Mary doesn't have a heart," while watching her play bridge, my audience has to decide whether I mean to refer to the card suits in her bridge hand, her style of playing, her general attitude toward other people, among other possibilities.) However, once we leave these most straightforward or literal cases, we generally won't be able to fix what is being said without thinking about the intention or point of saying it. If this is sometimes true in conversational contexts, it will be even more common in artistic ones. We won't be able to recognize irony, allusion, parallelism, imagery, or symbolism without being directly involved in figuring out communicative intention. Recall the sentence quoted above from "The Dead." The operative question about it is: what is its point? It is always possible that the answer we are forced to is that these words could not convey any plausible intention of the author, and so must be understood in other terms. However, when the interpretive question is what is the point, such an answer will be atypical. Hence we can set aside this last objection.

Hypothetical Intentionalism

Although I have not set out every serious objection to moderate actual intentionalism (others are set out and countered in Stecker 2003), it is more crucial to devote the remaining allotted space to an assessment of a plausible and popular alternative to the view we have been defending. This alternative is hypothetical intentionalism (HI). It is important to consider because it accepts a central intuition employed in replying to the above objections but claims there is a better way of deploying it. Hypothetical intentionalism accepts that when we interpret in order to identify utterance or work meaning, we inevitably look for an intention or a point with which something is said or presented. That is the common intuition it shares with actual intentionalism. Hypothetical intentionalism denies, though, that the intention we are looking for is the actual intention of the utterer or artist. It is rather a virtual intention suggested by the utterance or work. Different proponents of HI define this intention differently, but what I will consider here are two importantly distinct alternatives. According to the first, a hypothetical intention is an ideal audience's best hypothesis regarding the actual artist's (utterer's) intention, given a certain restriction on available evidence. An ideal audience is one that is historically situated so that it knows the corpus of the artist's work as well as other publicly available features of the context of creation. A best hypothesis is one that is most justified by the evidence, and where there is a tie among such hypotheses, one that makes the work aesthetically better. The restriction on evidence is that direct pronouncements of intention by the artist are off limits (Levinson 1996: 175–213). When all these conditions are met, the hypothetical intention identified is the meaning of the work. It way well coincide with the artist's actual intention, but it needn't.

A second version of HI abstracts still further from actual intentions. It claims that the meaning of an utterance or work is fixed by the intention of a hypothetical utterer or artist who is fully aware of context and conventions and uses them flawlessly to say or do what he or she intends (Nathan 1992).

What is attractive about HI, and why would anyone suppose that utterance or work meaning is identified by a hypothetical intention? There are three reasons. First, it is a plausible solution to a semantic problem regarding utterance meaning (and work meaning if it is to be understood on the model of utterance meaning). We have already seen that neither the meaning of utterances nor works should be *identified with* intended meaning. But we have also seen that they are not to be identified with the conventional or literal meaning of the words or sentences that constitute linguistic utterances and literary works. (The meaning of other artworks couldn't possibly be so identified.) Hypothetical intentionalism offers an alternative to these unacceptable options. Of course, the version of moderate actual intentionalism defended above is another such alternative. However, when we compare these two views, hypothetical intentionalism is the more elegant proposal. Moderate actual intentionalism says that sometimes a properly realized actual intention determines meaning. Sometimes nonintentional considerations do so. These nonintentional factors include a variety of conventional and contextual considerations, which are also in play in conveying properly realized intention. In contrast to the nest of considerations that moderate actual intentionalism appeals to, hypothetical intentionalism offers a single explanation of utterance/work meaning. This superior elegance is the second reason for adopting it. The third reason is that it gives works of art a greater autonomy from the creative artist since, according to HI, the actual intentions of artists play no direct role in fixing their meaning. Of these reasons, the last is the most controversial, since not everyone agrees that artworks have the degree of autonomy hypothetical intentionalism attributes to them. In fact, since the second version of this view gives works a greater degree of autonomy than the first, even hypothetical intentionalists do not agree among themselves about what degree of autonomy is the right one.

Whatever precisely has motivated its acceptance by some, and despite its superior elegance, hypothetical intentionalism faces some counterexamples that disqualify it from being a viable alternative to moderate actual intentionalism. I conclude by briefly setting these out.

Let us begin with the first version, which says that the meaning of a work is the intention an ideal audience would attribute to the actual artist based on the total admissible evidence and, where needed, considerations of aesthetic merit. There are two counterexamples to this. The first counterexample consists in cases where a work W means p, but p is not intended and the audience of W is justified in believing that p is not intended. In such a case, the present version of hypothetical intentionalism implies, ex hypothesis wrongly, that W does not mean p. Here is an example. According to the Sherlock Holmes stories, Dr Watson received a wound during his service in the British Army. Unfortunately the stories give the wound two different, incompatible locations – his leg in one story and his shoulder in another. We know that Conan Doyle did this unintentionally because it is impossible for one wound to be in two such different locations, and the realistic style of the stories precludes the fictional assertion of impossibilities. Nevertheless, such an impossibility is fictionally asserted and is part of the meaning of the story. However, an ideal audience would not attribute to Conan Doyle the intention to fictionally assert an impossibility, so it would falsely deny that it is part of the meaning of the story.

The second counterexample is the case where the artist intends W to mean p, it is known that the artist has this intention, but W does not mean p but q. In this case, hypothetical intentionalism implies, falsely, that W means p since an ideal audience would attribute to the artist the intention to mean p. That the two objections are closely related can be seen from the fact that an ideal audience would attribute to Conan Doyle the intention to give Watson's wound a single location, which falsely implies, on the present version of HI, that the story does this. Here is another, non-literary example. Suppose someone says, "You are a very perspicuous fellow." The best hypothesis is that the speaker intends to say that the person addressed is perspicacious (i.e., someone with acute judgment), but it doesn't follow that the speaker did say this. In fact, it seems quite certain that the speaker didn't but rather uttered the nonsense that the person in question is expressed very clearly.

Turning to the second version of HI, it fares no better with the second example. How can it explain how a hypothetical flawless user of the language can utter nonsense? At least, it appears to escape the first counterexample. The hypothetical artist, being a flawless user of the language, must have meant to give Watson's wound two locations if his words imply as much. The trouble is that this hypothetical author can't be both a flawless user of the language and, at the same time, a flawless purveyor of the realistic style. Hence, it is not so clear that the second version of HI can handle this example any better than did the first version. Furthermore, this version of HI attributes the right meaning to this bit of the Sherlock Holmes Stories for a very odd reason: a cooked-up hypothetical author intended it. Whereas moderate actual intentionalism seems to find the right explanation: in this instance, Conan Doyle failed to properly realize his intention and as a result, says something other than he intended in virtue of the conventional meaning of his words, and the fictional context.

Conclusion

The question whether artists' actual intention is relevant to the interpretation of their artworks turns out to splinter into a number of subquestions. I have attempted to answer two such subquestions here: (1) "Is identifying the artist's actual intention a proper and central aim of art interpretation?" and (2) "Is artwork meaning defined, in part, in terms of artist's actual intentions?" This chapter has defended affirmative answers to both questions, although we have also seen that great care is needed to define the role of intentions in fixing work meaning, and in not overstating the importance of this role. Finally we have seen that, while hypothetical intentionalism provides a more elegant account of work meaning, it is vulnerable to serious counterexamples.

Let me conclude by pointing out that we are now in a position to comment on a third central issue in the philosophy of interpretation: the critical monism/critical pluralism issue. That there can be a plurality of acceptable interpretations of the same work is supported by the fact that there are several proper and central aims of interpretation. However, with regard to the aim that we have focused on for much of this chapter – identifying the meaning of a work – it looks like this would ideally be captured by a single best interpretation that identifies what the artist does in a work in virtue of his or her properly realized intentions, relevant conventions, and the historical context in which the work is created.

CHAPTER EIGHTEEN

Art, Meaning, and Artist's Meaning

Daniel O. Nathan

Introduction

Interpretation of works of art is to be the general topic of this chapter, so a few words must be said about what I will take to fall under that heading. The scope of this project will be limited to what ought to be called "critical interpretation." I so label it, not by way of pointing strictly toward the activities of professional critics as much as to distinguish it from the sort of interpretation that performers might be said to do in carrying out scripts or scores. No doubt the interpretations made in performance will often (perhaps always) involve some sort of critical interpretation as well, and it is unlikely that there is a terribly bright line separating the two. But the former raise additional issues that I must leave outside the scope of the present chapter. The type of critical interpretation to be focused upon here might informally be described as the discovery or disclosure of the meaning of a work of art – an activity that is as often the domain of the average audience member or museumgoer as of the professional critic. Interpretation then is an ordinary activity, and one within which each of us participates and with which each of us is familiar. The very fact of its ordinariness may be falsely taken to imply that it does not admit of standards. But I hope to show that appearance to be misleading.

In describing interpretation as disclosure of meaning, "meaning" is to be understood broadly, that is, as not limited to the sort of semantic interpretation associated with interpreting a linguistic text, but to include grasping representational and expressive properties of works of visual art or music. Meaning, then, is the product of coming to understand a work, where understanding encompasses a full range of kinds of awareness of the artistically pertinent properties of the work in question. Some theorists have it that critical interpretation amounts to "explaining why artworks have the features, including meanings, that they possess" (Carroll 2000: 75), but I will suggest that phrases like "explaining why" invite a sort of confusion between causal explanation and interpretive justification that ought to be avoided. It is the latter that is called for in interpretation.

The focus on interpretation in this chapter needs to be sharpened further to consideration of the place intention holds in interpretation. The issue taken up here is that of the relevance of artist's intention to the interpretation of their work; specifically, whether the artist's intention can determine the correct interpretation, or even limit the range of possible interpretations of the work of art. The debate over this question is not new, and some of the tracks of the arguments are very well trodden. Still, there are some new directions that have lately been taken, or could profitably be taken, and in order to grasp their significance we must first attend to some of the seminal points of departure in the debate.

There can be little question that the modern discussion of interpretation and intention began with William Wimsatt and Monroe Beardsley in their 1946 essay, "The Intentional Fallacy." In their well-known discussion, the two argue against intentionalistic description, interpretation, and evaluation of works of literature. In succeeding works, Beardsley (1958, 1970) further develops the position and extends it to all of the arts. The essential argument throughout is simple, powerful, and seemingly decisive: either the artist's intentions are successfully embodied in the work or they are not. If they are, then any external reference to the artist's life will add nothing. If they are not, then the artist has failed and such external information can only succeed in taking us away from the work itself into irrelevancies. To advert to such additional information will result in reading a meaning *into* the work, not reading the work itself.

It is essentially that anti-intentionalist position I wish to defend in the present essay. The view is in need of defense because of a number of recent arguments and alternative positions that have made it seem increasingly suspect as an intellectual stance. Explaining what vulnerabilities have been seen in the anti-intentionalist view will be the first task of the present essay. Once that is done, a more complete development of the anti-intentionalist position will be mounted, and several new arguments will be offered in its defense.

Criticism of Classic Anti-intentionalism

As intuitively appealing as the basic anti-intentionalist position is, even its best classic statements were prone to some problems. Thus, when Beardsley (1958) developed his position, he grounded his criteria of critical relevance in terms of perceptual/phenomenological properties alone. The aesthetically relevant properties were identified as the ones internal to the work itself, where "internal" evidence was defined as "evidence from direct inspection of the object" (1958: 20). The truth of critical descriptive and interpretive statements about a painting, for example, are confirmable "by direct perception of the painting itself" (1958: 30).

Beardsley's examples actually suggest a far richer understanding of what constitutes the internal aspect of works of art, and he explicitly allows that the ability to fully appreciate aesthetic objects depends upon what he calls "a large apperceptive mass" (1958: 53). Still, the view was left open to the objection that as stated it was far too limiting to make adequate sense of critical description and interpretation. "Mere scrutiny," as Richard Wollheim (1980) labels it, is too thin a ground for critical analysis. Seeing a patch of paint as representing a house, a set of marks as part of a language, flickering images on a screen as persons moving through space, or hearing sounds as music, or movements as belonging to a single musical work, each in its own (very) different fashion requires access to external facts, facts not simply perceivable in the immediate encounter with the art object itself. Beardsley did acknowledge that recognition of representational, expressive, and semantic properties presuppose stepping outside the immediate experience. "Scores and scripts" he wrote, "are written in a language that has to be learned" (1958:24), and proper response to aesthetic objects may require "some previous acquaintance with the general style of the work, or of other works to which it alludes, or of works with which it sharply contrasts" (1958: 53). Once that is allowed, however, the clarity of the internal/external distinction begins to seem like a mirage. And with it part of the structure of the core argument is weakened. What, one must ask, now counts as "embodied in the work" if some external facts are called for in proper understanding. Further arguments, like those of Kendall Walton (1970), asserting the dependency of expressive properties on proper categorization of works of art and the dependency of categorization on an array of factors external to the work, show that perceptual qualities themselves cannot be isolated from historical and other facts. The inevitable conclusion Walton leads us to is that most, if not all, interesting aesthetic and artistic properties turn out to be relational in some way.

The new question becomes "relational to *what?*" Beardsley allowed that apperceptual information was relevant, but drew the line at information concerning the biography (especially, the aims and intentions) of the artist. But if, as Walton (among many others) successfully argued, the historical context of production is clearly relevant to interpretation (linguistic context being the clearest example), then it might appear that Beardsley's way of drawing the line is ad hoc. Beardsley's argument largely relied on the intuitive appeal of his basic position, specifically when considering cases of conflict which seem to resolve away from artist's intentions – thus, in his example, one would hardly conclude that a statue that we perceive as rough and pink is really smooth and blue just because the sculptor insists the latter was his intention. But, given the complexity of interpretation, the range of more controversial cases, and the development of less naive versions of intentionalism, such a defense quickly appears too simplistic.

There are other problems, addressed not so much at Beardsley's characterization of the position as at anti-intentionalism in general. Some authors argue, for example, that no such view can account for specifically literary uses of language like irony and metaphor. The meaning of a literary text, on a standard anti-intentionalist analysis, depends on its internal properties, its words and literary structure understood under the public conventions of linguistic usage that applied at the time. But it has been suggested that even such an elaborated approach would yield only literal meanings to texts, and that the interpretive turn called for by ironic or metaphoric expressions requires reference to the author's intention after all. The idea is that a metaphor means, in effect, something different from what is said; that the meaning of one's ironic utterance is in fact quite the opposite of what one says.

Daniel O. Nathan

It is indeed clear that the meaning of a metaphor is not to be found directly in the standard literal meanings of its components alone. One cannot properly analyze the meaning of an ironic statement by focusing on the word sequence present in the statement alone. However, these facts are not unique to irony and metaphor. Shorn of a larger context, most linguistic expressions (literal or otherwise) cannot be properly understood. The anti-intentionalist response then is to point to this larger context to identify the meaning of a metaphor or the ironic sense of some expression. In all cases, the context must be understood broadly enough to include linguistic clues running the gamut from the complete text in which the expression appears, to the full connotative richness of the words in their historical context, and even the gestures and vocal intonations that accompany the utterance of the expression. Thus, the anti-intentionalist insists that it is not Swift's intention that makes his suggestion in "A Modest Proposal" that we fricassee children ironic; it is a confluence of the linguistic clues found in the text of the essay as a whole and the connotations words like "fricassee" hold in the linguistic community at the time of expression that entail the suggestion ought to be read as ironic. Lacking such indicators, no amount of authorial intention could make a text ironic. Possessing such indicators, no effort on the author's part could prevent "A Modest Proposal" from being ironic (Nathan 1982). Similarly, an author cannot constitute a literal expression (whether it be true or false) as metaphorical just by willing it to be so.

It is essential for the anti-intentionalist that these clues all be publicly accessible, and that the relevant context be understood as logically (though, of course, not causally) distinct from what the author may have intended and from the attitude the author may have taken. But there is, by necessity, yet more that needs to be said about this broad public context. In all linguistic interpretation there are nonlinguistic background assumptions, among them factual assumptions about the nature of the world, upon which any interpretation must proceed. There are also metalinguistic assumptions, like the assumption that for something to be taken as an utterance there must be an utterer. And there are assumptions that normal speakers and hearers make about the world in which they live. Thus, for example, it is a matter of standard background assumptions that rule out several possible meaning of "bank" in "With the stock market as it is, I plan to leave my money in the bank." "Bank" here is properly understood as a financial institution, not as a seashore or a billiards shot. This comes not as a consequence of any particular speaker's intention, but because of such default background assumptions as that money is more typically kept in a financial institution than at the edge of a body of water. What these default background assumptions are is a matter of independent objective fact, not, it must again be noted, a matter of what the actual author takes the context to be. One would have to *do* something explicit (through, for example, building in a different linguistic context, "even though it is bound to get sandy") in order to defeat the background assumptions at work here. To fail to do so leaves the default meaning in place. Were such an explicit act of defeating the assumptions not necessary, a speaker could change unambiguous utterances into ambiguous ones, or alter the overt meaning of an utterance through a merely private mental act of assuming an alternative set of background assumptions. This would have the consequence of making all ordinary discourse impossible, or at best accidental. It goes to the heart of the conventions of a public discourse, to the possibility of language itself.

The anti-intentionalist must and does insist on the relevance of these default background assumptions to make sense of public meaning (Nathan 1992: 192-6). Acknowledgement of the relevance of background assumptions such as these makes the relational complexity of the enriched anti-intentionalist position more apparent. But it should be clear that this complexity need not, thus far, undercut the fundamental anti-intentionalist stance that the relevant context is not dependent upon the actual author's mental state or intention or understanding of that context. Still, there remains a further elaboration of the anti-intentionalist view that is required. Its source, once again, is by way of response to a certain type of criticism, a criticism made first and most clearly by Guy Sircello in *Mind and Art*. There Sircello argued through a series of examples across the arts, that the attribution of expressive properties to works of art sometimes requires knowledge of certain facts about the specific artist. Among the most successful and provocative of these illustrations is an interpretation of Breughel's *Wedding Dance in the Open Air* (Sircello 1972: 43). Sircello's claim is that the ironic quality of that painting, which depends on the particular juxtaposition of the dull-looking peasant faces against celebratory surroundings, presupposes that Breughel could have painted the peasant faces differently. That is, Sircello claims that if the character of the faces were strictly a function of Breughel's lack of skill, then the attribution of irony to the work would be misplaced.

It does seem that there is a sense in which the competency of the artist is implicated in the attribution of certain artistic qualities. But as the anti-intentionalist should be quick to point out, in quite ordinary cases such judgments do not necessarily presuppose that the actual author or speaker have competency or, for that matter, even exist outside of a fictional world. Thus, in the most obvious sort of example, when we attribute meaning to the utterances of Oedipus in Sophocles's *Oedipus Rex*, we do not assume that the utterer is an actual person. Nor, in performance of that play, does one really attribute any particular mental state to the actor portraying Oedipus in our grasp of the meaning of Oedipus's utterances. And assumptions about Sophocles's mental state have no direct connection to the expressive quality of Oedipus's utterances. Sophocles need not feel despair, or intend despair be expressed, or even have actually had the capacity to have used other words, for Oedipus's utterance of "What shall I do with eyes where all is ugliness?" to be one of utter hopelessness and remorse.

No investigation of the mental dexterity of the actual author is ever undertaken or even considered in rendering an interpretation. The reason for this is that the "competency" that is assumed is strictly hypothetical. As such it is embedded in the conventions of interpretation itself. Naturally, the conventions themselves rest on a history of successful acts of expression that have reflected the actual competency of speakers, that is, the actual choices by flesh and blood speakers. But, once the conventions of meaning have been established, they apply without the requirement of any particular mental state of any particular person. It is precisely on this basis that one can speak of the meaning of the expressions of fictional characters or implied authors and, in turn, of works of art themselves.

What we do presuppose, it would seem, is that *imaginarily* Oedipus could have felt and acted differently; that he, fictionally, is a flesh and blood, feeling and thinking

Daniel O. Nathan

person. An anti-intentionalist (of this author's ilk) would insist that it is only and precisely this sort of fictionalized attribution that is required to make sense of the attribution of expressive qualities of works like those in Sircello's examples, that the artistic acts that he speaks of are hypothetical, not necessarily real. Thus, when we identify the ironic quality in Breughel's *Wedding Dance*, what we are doing is a reflection of a certain conventionalized approach to artistic interpretation generally. Specifically, essential to interpretation of art is the assumption that all features of a painting are there *on purpose*. That is, we *assume* that the object could have been otherwise. That sounds as though the actual artist might have chosen to have done something other than what he or she did. But, in fact, no actual fact about the artist should prevent us from taking *any* feature seriously, so long as it bears any potential of producing an interesting interpretation. Were there actual evidence that the artist had not noticed or intended the feature deemed significant, interpreters tend to dismiss the evidence. The presence of the feature and how it fits into a reading suffices. On the present view, then, the artistic "competency" at work now begins to appear to be the competency of some fictional ideal artist, not at all necessarily that of the actual historical one.

At least one contemporary intentionalist has responded to a related line of argument by insisting that sometimes the author of a work of fiction may not just be *representing* the occurrence of an illocutionary act (like Oedipus's), but is actually performing an illocutionary act. Noel Carroll (2000) claims that Hugo is actually asserting a history of symbols in parts of *The Hunchback of Notre Dame*, Melville a discourse on whales in *Moby Dick*, and Tolstoy a philosophy of history in *War and Peace*. Perhaps some works of art do reflect the actual views of the artist such that they *could* be understood as illocutionary acts of assertion. But why should we understand that as more than an accident of what just happens to be the actual mental state of the artist? In fact, it seems quite plausible to say that whether the theory to be found in the novel reflects the actual view of the author or just the "view" of some dramatis personae is not relevant to interpreting the theory. It is similarly hard to see how the meaning of the entire text is affected by being asserted by its actual author or merely by its implied author. Were we to discover that Tolstoy did not believe in the philosophy of history reflected in *War and Peace*, it would not affect what was fictionally asserted in the book. Nor, of course, would that discovery alone make the representation of the view as ironic within the novel. Of course, nothing here aims to deny that the texts produced by an author, like any other behavioral manifestation, can be taken to be evidence of authorial intentions, beliefs, politics, and so forth. It is only the strength and relevance of the evidential connection in the opposite direction that is being questioned.

Moderate Intentionalism and the Conversational Model

Recent moderate formulations of actual intentionalism, like those of Carroll, Savile (1996), and Stecker (1997), are more subtle than the sort of intentionalism that Beardsley first reacted against, and avoid many of the pitfalls of previous versions. Most significantly, they purport to take seriously the centrality of the text in interpretation.

In so doing, they move to steal one of the central appeals of anti-intentionalism. How does this go?

First off, the moderate view accepts that one cannot mean just anything by one's utterance. One can only be understood to relevantly intend what the text or work *can* mean. And the range of possible meanings the text can have is determined by those public (and background) facts that the anti-intentionalist is content to leave as the final determinant of meaning. Thus, the moderate intentionalist asserts that one ought to discount a pronouncement of authorial intent when it departs radically from what can be observed in the work (Carroll 1992: 98-102, 2000: 76-7). According to some intentionalists, such pronouncements of intent can be taken to be insincere or possibly ironic, though I think it is hard to see why and in which cases we ought to draw such an inference. Surely not all artists can be assumed to have an objective grasp of their work or its properties.

How then does intention become relevant to meaning on the moderate view? It is relevant in cases where the intention can tell us which, among various *possible* meanings the text has, is the *actual* meaning. I take this to mean that it is only when a work appears to ground more than one interpretation that the artist's intention becomes a determining factor. That the actual artist's intention is the final determining factor in interpretation makes this view fundamentally intentionalist, but one must consider what it is that justifies this residual, but crucial, intentionalist approach.

One important justification of intentionalism can be found in a renaissance of and emphasis upon understanding art and art criticism as a communicational process. The source for this is Noel Carroll's argument that we have what he calls "conversational" interests when we approach works of art. He begins from the commonsense suggestion that artworks ought to be interpreted as "we customarily interpret other conduct and action" (1992: 102). He develops the point by saying that:

> aesthetic satisfaction is not the only major source of value that we have in interacting with artworks; the interaction is also a matter of a conversation between the artist and us – a human encounter – in which we have a desire to know what the artist intends, not only out of respect for the artist, but also because we have a personal interest in being a capable respondent. (Carroll 1992: 122)

Carroll contends we ought not here to ignore the "value we might place on having a genuine conversational exchange with another human being" (1992: 122). If one can profitably think of oneself as in a genuine conversation with the artist, then the significance of the mental state of the actual artist seems to rise to the fore. This also implies a responsibility to understand what the actual artist has in mind in his or her act of expression. One does not have conversations with hypothetical artists or implied authors. And, in real conversations, one is not simply interested in taking aesthetic pleasure in the words spoken. The goal in conversation is to acquire an understanding of what the real person meant to say, specifically to grasp the person's intentions.

This model of interpretation spins the process toward intentionalism in a provocative and interesting way. One of the best examples of its use, and one representative of a general and genuine concern raised by many moderate intentionalists, is Carroll's own richly developed example of the films of Ed Wood. Here is the thrust of the case.

Daniel O. Nathan

Ed Wood, a famously mediocre director of low budget, second-rate films, produced an equally famous bad film, *Plan 9 from Outer Space*, a movie that tops a number of lists of the worst commercial films ever made. That film was

> a cheap, slapdash attempt to make a feature film for very little, and in cutting corners to save money it violates – in outlandish ways – many of the decorums of Hollywood filmmaking that later avant-gardists also seek to affront. So insofar as the work of contemporary avant-gardists is aesthetically valued for its transgressiveness, why not appreciate *Plan 9* . . . under an analogous interpretation? (Carroll 1992: 119)

Intentionalists argue that it is only the evidence that Wood had no such subversive *intentions* that keeps us from the absurd conclusion that he should be seen as an especially insightful anticipator of the postmodern movement in film.

I will set aside several questions I have about the particulars of this case, for example, about whether the transgressive reading of Wood would be ruled out anyway as being anachronistic (would violate, that is, the impersonal historical considerations that an anti-intentionalist would take to be relevant), or whether there fail to be sufficient indications in the film itself to seriously assert that an overall subversive message was being conveyed by the film (just as in the case of irony, it is not sufficient to say surprising – or transgressive – things, one must also signal to the reader that what is being said is *other* than it first appears). If an affirmative answer to either of these two questions is forthcoming, then there would simply be no obvious reason to appeal to the real intentions or capabilities of Mr Wood in order to rule out deeming *Plan 9* a thoughtful example of avant-garde film-making. But suppose it is possible to meet these challenges. On that assumption, the anti-intentionalist must face whether appeal to particulars about the artist is proper in such a case. I take the fundamental question to be what to do when two possible readings of a work are equally well grounded in the observable properties of the work, against its relevant background conditions. That is, what does the anti-intentionalist do in cases of real ambiguity? Does the conversational model, with its appeal to artist's intentions, provide an appropriate resolution to real ambiguities?

The case of Ed Wood echoes a point made by other moderate intentionalists. In an early example, Kendall Walton (1970, 1974) argued that, absent knowledge of particulars about the mental state of the artist, one could mistake a mediocre work for one of real merit. But it is not clear to me why one ought to be bothered by the threat of seeing as meritorious what may be, on author-particular grounds, understood as a mediocre work. Perhaps this is due to the absence of a fully convincing example of being so mistaken, but it also reflects a principle of charity in judging works. If the judgment that the work (even *Plan 9*) had merit was really defensible, absent consideration of idiosyncratic facts about the artist, then it is not at all clear why one should not just let that judgment stand.

However that may be, the conversational model itself turns out to be too problematic to be applicable. There are, in my view, overwhelming reasons for rejecting it. To begin, in attending critically to his work, we are of course not in a genuine conversation with Ed Wood. We cannot be. Not only is the interaction characteristic of conversation missing, as Carroll acknowledges, but our status is inherently that of observers, not participants in a conversation. This is reflected in a number of ways. For one, our reactions/explanations/analyses are not addressed *to* the author or artist. They may on the one hand just be addressed to ourselves; more saliently they are addressed to a community of interest, and against a certain institutional background and history. This observer status (within a community of observers) casts a different light on the sense of any communicative nature to art, as well as on the issue of the publicity versus privacy of relevant background information. Moreover, as part of this observer status, the characteristic attention paid is not what one finds typically within conversation (or even communication). Wollheim (1980) has it that our response to art lies in an attitude of enjoyment or appreciation, a kind of "deep scrutiny," as he labels it. Even if deep scrutiny is not the sole or defining characteristic of critical attention to art, it suggests a fundamental distinction between interpretation and conversation. Connected to this, there is an expectation of aesthetic excellence in our typical approach to works of art. In the process, there is a deep search for aesthetic qualities, good or bad, and typically an interest in seeking references to and comparison with other works. Nothing parallel is characteristic of (or seriously imaginable among) participants in conversations. In fact, such reactions would likely put an end to our conversations, per se. (Try it with your friends.)

One needs to understand the notion of deep scrutiny of artworks as extending beyond merely the aim of aesthetic appreciation or satisfaction, to artistic interest more broadly construed. A case can be made (though it has not been yet) that this interest in scrutiny should consistently override any conversational interests we might wish to satisfy in encounters with works of art.

However, even if we were to model our response to art on conversation, it is unclear that conversational interests really dictate that we resolve ambiguities in favor of the message merely intended by our conversant. We do not hesitate to point out that our conversational partners fail to say what they meant (even, perhaps even especially, when we can guess what they meant), or that they said something ambiguous when they may have intended to limit their meaning. What, after all, is more commonplace than people mentally filling in gaps in what they have said, internally disambiguating their ambiguous utterance, so that it makes the sense that they wished it to make? That makes sense only if the original expression was itself really ambiguous. When disambiguating material is left out, the possibility that the statement was intentionally ambiguous must remain an option. But that leaves the moderate intentionalist with something logically indistinguishable from the Humpty Dumpty problem. If we will not allow speakers to make their utterances mean what they wish just by willing it to be so in the latter case, then on what grounds are we permitted to let speakers control the meaning of their utterances in the former?

If one takes seriously, as moderate intentionalists purport to do, the idea that the relevance of the author's intent is constrained by what the text *could* mean then, in the case where the text is indeed itself ambiguous (given all available nonintentionalistic evidence, default background assumptions, etc.), it does not just *become* unambiguous by virtue of the author intending it to be so. Speakers and authors can, of course, intend their expressions to be ambiguous. The very fact that the expression reads (not just superficially, but deeply) as being ambiguous turns out to be evidence (on the neo-Wittgensteinian, moderate intentionalist view) that it *was* so intended.

Thus, though the speaker may have intended an unequivocal meaning by that ambiguous expression, it is precisely the unequivocal meaning that fails to be supported by the text. To nonetheless construe it as unequivocal has intention (unsupported by the text) trumping the public text once again. One must wonder why, if that is to be permitted in the case of ambiguous expressions, the same should not also hold for evidently literal nonironic expressions. But, as I have argued elsewhere (Nathan 1982, 1992), surely it is clear that one cannot constitute something ironic just by willing it be so. Just as we require some sort of "irony marker" to ground interpreting a work as ironic, so we would require some marker in the text to indicate that the superficially ambiguous expression really is not ambiguous after all, some way of overriding the default reading that must otherwise hold sway. Hence, in the absence of the intended unequivocal meaning being supported by the text, a disambiguating intention cannot be relevant to interpretation. It is not clear where that leaves the moderate intentionalist.

"Proving" Anti-intentionalism

It will no longer do to support anti-intentionalism with the assertion of such bromides as "one ought to see the work as it is," or "critical interest ought to aim at consideration of *the work for its own sake.*" Those can only be seen as begging several questions, among them the question of what, for these purposes, the work is. Further, the anti-intentionalist advantage that was based on its focus on the centrality of the text may have been diluted by at least the lip service that moderate intentionalists give to the primacy of text itself. It does certainly remain unproven that we have an overriding interest in maximizing the sort of aesthetic and cognitive pleasure that we seem to seek in the circumscribed but deep scrutiny of works recommended by anti-intentionalists. What is indeed lacking, and what I seek to suggest albeit in a somewhat cursory and certainly brief fashion here, is a grounding conception of why anti-intentionalism makes sense with respect to the arts. Some of this grounding has been implicit in the previous discussion of the distinctions between the interpretation of art and of conversation, but I wish to suggest a more positive side to the argument.

Unquestionably, works of art call for different types of interpretation than do conversations. At least, our objectives and interests in understanding conversations seem quite distinct from our goals confronting works of art. Even advocates of the view that we have conversational interests in our response to art do not deny such differences. And it is in that distinctive quality of art interpretation that one can find justification for a fundamentally anti-intentionalist stance regarding art. The distinctiveness itself can only be understood by looking at the ongoing institutional and historical structure of the enterprise. Indeed, just as the conversational model draws some of its appeal from a certain conception of the nature of art, namely that of communication, so too does the anti-intentionalist stance find support in the properties of art as a historically embedded practice, a practice that includes conventions that in some way set normative parameters for both artists and interpreters of art.

There are a number of features that distinguish our analysis and response to works of art and their properties from real life. This separateness is revealed in several ways.

(1) Art, insofar as it is seen as representational, is removed from the causal sphere of ordinary experience. For example, Hamlet's soliloquy is not caused by the actual mental state of any person named Hamlet; it is not a function of Hamlet's intention. And what explains the emotional quality in a visual depiction is not a function of the antecedent circumstances and beliefs of anything or anyone present in the work. The sort of interpretive explanation sought is not a causal one, but something else. One seeks reasons for attributing the qualities to the work, not explanations of their efficient causes. (2) Our response to fictional events is markedly different from the response we would have to the same events in real life. It is a commonplace that our belief that what we are seeing is fictional influences our reaction to it – we do not run away from the threatening villain on the movie screen. (3) A work of art, to borrow a phrase from Beardsley, "directs attention to itself as an object rewarding scrutiny" (Beardsley 1970: 60). At least, we take there to be special properties worth searching for in encounters with artworks, uniquely artistic ones which we would never find elsewhere, others we are less likely to find or, perhaps more accurately, do not expect to find in ordinary experience. Most obviously, we seek properties indicative of aesthetic and/or artistic excellence. (4) The relevant relational contexts within which artistic properties are taken to stand are quite distinct from the connections expected in everyday life. There are, that is, both internal connections – a unique set of internal contextual cues and relationships to other properties of the work itself (the presence of unity or foreshadowing in a novel, for example, or the balance or visual tension in a painting) – as well as external connections – links to a history of objects and events that constitute themselves as a separate class (references or allusions to previous works in the genre, for example) – that mark out an art-interpretive response. (5) Conventional practice entails that we take all that we can find in the work *as if* it were there on purpose. We try to make sense of everything that is there. Not, despite common but careless belief to the contrary, by way of discovering what design or purpose was at work in the actual creation of the object (though there might be independent interest in understanding any creative act), but rather to explain what *seems* purposeful about the object. In seeking an explanation of all features that are part of the work before us, we look toward what can be explained *as though* it had been done on purpose, whether it actually was so or not. It is only this way that we can be open to the possibility of a work that could transcend the particular intellect that produced it, a possibility that the practice does not seem at all inclined to preclude.

To be found within the distinctive features just mentioned are indices of art as it shaped itself as an ongoing social practice, ones that have potentially profound implications for the intentionalist debate. The features above make a strong case for separating consideration of the life and intentions of the artist from the interpretation of the work. Only the intention revealed in the work itself – the embodied intentions, so to speak – will matter. I will conclude with the mention of a more general way in which the distinctiveness of art implies the correctness of anti-intentionalism. Whether this might constitute a sort of proof of anti-intentionalism is of course another matter.

The proposal involves something I have labeled elsewhere (Nathan 2005) the "paradox of intention," and it involves the existence of a second-order intention with regard to art production. The broad outline of the idea is this: in producing an object

Daniel O. Nathan

for public consumption (when I create, for example, a literary text that I expect and put forth to be read by a public audience), I necessarily intend to create something that will stand otherwise independent of my intentions. Specifically, I intend the object to convey all that is needed, so that access to any intentions not already expressed in the object will not be necessary. There, then, is an element of paradox: if my assumption about the production of a public object is true, it would appear that there is presumed to be an underlying authorial *intention that one's intentions need not be consulted*. That is it in its most paradoxical statement; but the idea is that in taking part in artistic activity one intends that *extratextual* access to what might be called one's first-order intentions will not be sought or needed. For such access to be needed is an indication of my failure as an artist, for it to be sought is an indication that my work is being slighted. Respect for this overarching second-order intention is then inconsistent with investigation of the other intentions an author may have had in producing the public object in question.

There is thus an implicit hierarchy of intentions that one can find in the practice of art. Engagement in art brings with it in this manner a set of necessary commitments, commitments that the artist might not in all cases actively grasp, but ones that constrain nonetheless.

A potential of artistic detachment and its obvious importance within the creative process, suggest a need to think of the work as so detached. There is a flavor of this in John Cheever's claim that fiction "completely transcends autobiography and current history"(Donaldson 1987: 163). One might see the second-order intention implicit in Cheever's remark, as well as in a broader intention to create a work capable of out-stripping one's immediate intentions, a work that could be different in various respects from the way it was conceived in the act of writing. The second-order intention is surely implied by the expectation that unanticipated outcomes are possible, and more particularly that an outcome which is artistically better is to be preferred over one that is inferior. It is undeniably an expectation that is to be found in the institution and its participants historically. And, of course, it has obvious independent value. What this represents is more than just a contingent claim about the mental states of some imaginary and actual authors. Indeed, the claim here is that the second-order intention is a *necessary presupposition* of the artistic endeavor per se, a precondition to a work being understood as a work of literature or visual art or music. It is a matter of the conventions surrounding what is taken to be of concern within the social practice. The created world, literary or otherwise, will necessarily have features that its author may not have foreseen or intended. As mentioned above, all these unintended features no less than the intended ones become fair game for interpretation and criticism. The best interpretation then turns out to be the one that can make the best sense of the greatest number of features available in the work. The art-interpretive process appears to require no less than that.

References for Chapters 17 and 18

Beardsley, M. (1958). *Aesthetics: Problems in the Philosophy of Criticism*. New York: Harcourt, Brace and World.

Beardsley, M. (1970). *The Possibility of Criticism*. Detroit: Wayne State University Press.

Carroll, N. (1992). "Art, Intention, and Conversation." In G. Iseminger (ed.), *Intention and Interpretation* (pp. 97–131). Philadelphia: Temple University Press.

Carroll, N. (2000). "Interpretation and Intention: the Debate between Hypothetical and Actual Intention." *Metaphilosophy*, 31: 75–95.

Carroll, N. (2001). *Beyond Aesthetics: Philosophical Essays*. Cambridge, UK: Cambridge University Press.

Davidson, D. (1986). "A Nice Derangement of Epitaphs." In E. Lepore and B. McLaughlin (eds.), *Actions and Events: Essays on the Philosophy of Donald Davidson* (pp. 433–46). Oxford: Basil Blackwell.

Davies, S. (1991). *Definitions of Art*. Ithaca, NY: Cornell University Press.

Donaldson, S. (ed.) (1987). *Conversations With John Cheever*. Jackson and London: University Press of Mississippi.

Dworkin, R. (1986). *Law's Empire*. Cambridge, MA: Harvard University Press.

Goldman, A. (1990). "Interpreting Art and Literature." *Journal of Aesthetics and Art Criticism*, 48: 205–14.

Iseminger. G. (1992). "An Intentional Demonstration?" In G. Iseminger (ed.), *Intention and Interpretation* (pp. 76–96). Philadelphia: Temple University Press.

Knapp, S. and Michaels, W. B. (1985). "Against Theory." In W. J. T. Mitchell (ed.), *Against Theory* (pp. 11–30). Chicago: University of Chicago Press.

Lamarque, P. (2002). "Appreciation and Literary Interpretation." In M. Krausz (ed.), *Is There a Single Right Interpretation?* (pp. 285–306). University Park: Pennsylvania State University Press.

Levinson, J. (1996). *The Pleasures of Aesthetics*. Ithaca, NY: Cornell University Press.

Nathan, D. O. (1982). "Irony and the Artist's Intention." *British Journal of Aesthetics*, 22: 245–57.

Nathan, D. O. (1992). "Irony, Metaphor, and the Problem of Intention." In Gary Iseminger (ed.), *Intention and Interpretation* (pp. 183–202). Philadelphia: Temple University Press.

Nathan, D. O. (2005). "A Paradox in Intentionalism." *British Journal of Aesthetics*, 45: 32–48.

Norris, M. (1994). "Not the Girl She Was at All: Women in 'The Dead.'" In D. R. Schwarz (ed.), *The Dead* (pp. 190–205). New York: St. Martin's Press.

Savile, A. (1996). "Instrumentalism and the Interpretation of Narrative." *Mind*, 105: 553–76.

Sircello, G. (1972). *Mind and Art*. Princeton, NJ: Princeton University Press.

Stecker, R. (1997). *Artworks: Definition, Meaning, Value*. University Park: Pennsylvania State University Press.

Stecker, R. (2003). *Interpretation and Construction: Art, Speech, and the Law*. Oxford: Blackwell.

Schwarz, D. R. (ed.) (1994). *The Dead*. New York: St. Martin's Press.

Trivedi, S. (2001). "An Epistemic Dilemma for Actual Intentionalism." *British Journal of Aesthetics*, 41: 192–206.

Walton, K. (1970). "Categories of Art." *Philosophical Review*, 79: 334–67.

Walton, K. (1974). "Categories and Intentions: a Reply." *Journal of Aesthetics and Art Criticism*, 32: 287.

Wimsatt, W. K., Jr., and Beardsley, M. C. (1946). "The Intentional Fallacy." *Sewanee Review.* 54: 3–23.

Wollheim, R. (1980). *Art and its Objects.* New York: Cambridge University Press.

Further Reading for Chapters 17 and 18

Barnes, A. (1988). *On Interpretation.* Oxford: Blackwell.

Beardsley, M. (1982). "Intentions and Interpretations: a Fallacy Revived." In M. J. Wreen and D. M. Callen (eds.), *The Aesthetic Point of View* (pp. 188–207). Ithaca, NY: Cornell University Press.

Currie, G. (1993). "Interpretation and Objectivity." *Mind*, 102: 413–28.

Hirsch, E. D. (1967). *Validity in Interpretation.* New Haven, CT: Yale University Press.

Iseminger, G. (ed). (1992). *Intention and Interpretation.* Philadelphia: Temple University Press.

Livingston, P. (1998). "Intentionalism in Aesthetics." *New Literary History*, 50: 615–33.

Margolis, J. (1980). *Art and Philosophy.* Brighton, UK: Harvester Press.

Nehamas, A. (1981). "The Postulated Author: Critical Monism as a Regulative Ideal." *Critical Inquiry*, 8: 133–49.

Shusterman, R. (1988). "Interpretation, Intention, Truth." *Journal of Aesthetics and Art Criticism*, 45: 399–411.

Tolhurst, W. (1979). "What a Text is and How it Means." *British Journal of Aesthetics*, 19: 3–14.

ARE THERE GENERAL PRINCIPLES OF EVALUATION?

CHAPTER NINETEEN

There Are No Aesthetic Principles

Alan H. Goldman

Introduction

One cannot, except indirectly, prove or offer decisive evidence that something does not exist. The burden of proof must lie on those who claim that something does exist to show it, either by observation or explanatory inference. But we skeptics can do more than sit back and shake our heads at their attempts. We can point out that no one has ever seen one of the sort of thing in question and why, if it did exist, it would be on display somewhere. We can note that apparent sightings were illusory. Or we can show how functions thought to be served by the thing in question can be served by other things or need not be served at all. We can provide an alternative theory that takes over this explanatory role. Such counterarguments in regard to aesthetic principles should send them the way of demons and luminiferous ether. Here I will first cite some general reasons both for believing and disbelieving in such principles, then consider supposed examples, exposing them as spurious, and finally show that the legitimate functions for which principles were thought necessary can be satisfied without them.

What Aesthetic Principles Might Be If They Existed

Before embarking on this task, it will be useful to classify the different types and levels of principles that have been thought by various philosophers to exist. Genuine principles for aesthetic evaluations would link objective, nonevaluative properties of artworks to overall evaluations of the works that would be universally required by the presence of these properties. Ultimately, justifications of aesthetic judgments must appeal to such objective properties and relations and, when pressed hard enough, this is what critics do appeal to: structural properties of tones, shapes and colors, or texts, and relations between these and similar properties in other works. But the links between these and overall evaluations typically divide into two levels (appeal to the first or more basic of which, absent disagreement, might be omitted from critical speech). Appeal to objective properties justifies ascriptions of what I call middle-level evaluative aesthetic properties, such as being balanced, powerful, elegant, strident, numbing, or whining, and appeal to these in turn justifies overall evaluations. Principles could then underlie justifications at both levels, and I shall consider the two types separately, as well as presumed examples of principles that are to take us all the way from objective properties to proper evaluations.

Principles at both levels can vary in strength. The strongest state necessary and sufficient conditions for evaluative properties at the higher level in terms of properties at the lower level. In descending order of strength, weaker principles might state only necessary conditions, or might hold that properties at the lower level work in only one direction in justifying ascriptions of properties at the higher level, or finally state that appeal to lower level properties works in only one direction when the properties are isolated, in the absence of other properties with which they might interact. Different philosophers claim to recognize different principles of these sorts at different levels.

As a final preliminary to canvassing both the general reasons for believing in and denying aesthetic principles and the purported examples of these philosophers, I will briefly address the topic of the nature of aesthetic properties, since this will provide further indication of the form that aesthetic principles would have to take. As I have argued before (Goldman 1995: 21) and many aestheticians now agree, middle-level evaluative properties such as those mentioned earlier are relational properties, including typically evaluative responses of qualified observers. If ascription of these properties expresses such responses, then principles linking them to their objective bases would take the form of causal laws holding across all these qualified observers. If we could separate the evaluative and objective components of these properties and see that they nevertheless always go together for qualified observers or ideal critics, that the latter always cause the former in the same ways, or always do so absent interactions with other properties, then we would have the sought-after aesthetic principles.

But neither step in this demonstration can be completed. First, while the middle-level properties are typically evaluative in one direction, either positive or negative, they are not always so. Even properties like elegance or beauty, which involve pleasure derived from formal or sensuous properties, might be negative in particular contexts. Just as sadistic pleasure may be morally bad in itself, so the pleasure derived from particular instantiations of beauty or elegance may detract from one's overall impressions of the works. An elegant performance of the *Rite of Spring* might be worse for being so, and the beautiful prose in *The Last of the Mohicans* or *The Turn of the Screw* might detract from their overall impacts. Second, while instantiations of these properties contain both objective and evaluative (response) components, we cannot complete an analysis of the properties themselves in terms of separate objective and evaluative components. The particular objective properties that prompt the responses on different occasions or in different works do not together comprise intelligible determinable properties. And there is nothing in the phenomenology of

Alan H. Goldman

experiencing these evaluative properties to suggest an evaluatively neutral response component separable from the evaluative response (contrast Levinson 2001).

It is true that the objective components of these properties limit the types of disagreements about them that we find among competent critics. What one critic finds vibrant, another will find strident or gaudy, but not flaccid or insipid. But there is no evaluatively neutral response in common among these disputants. Furthermore, the different objective features that in each instance prompt these different evaluative responses are not themselves conceptualized as the same objective properties. The aesthetic properties are indeterminate on their objective sides, including different objective features in each instantiation, to which even ideal critics might respond differently. The terms picking out these aesthetic properties have their meanings anchored to certain paradigm uses, or to overlapping classes of paradigms for different speakers, which allows for the variations of which I have been speaking.

General Reasons for Believing or Disbelieving in Aesthetic Principles

The first motivation for believing in aesthetic principles derives simply from the fact that critics provide reasons for their judgments. An argument for principles deriving from this obvious fact goes as follows. Reasons must be general, in that if all the same relevant circumstances obtain on other occasions, the same reasons must apply. Thus, whether or not these reasons are completely articulated, whether or not the principles that underlie a judgment are immediately formulable, there must be some such principles that serve this function. More specifically, critics do appeal ultimately to objective properties of works in justifying their ascriptions of aesthetic qualities, and they appeal to the latter in justifying their overall evaluations. Since there can be no reasons without principles, however implicit, there must be principles at both these levels. Those who deny such principles owe an explanation of the normative force of aesthetic judgments and the reasons that support them.

Second, reasons for overall evaluations are given initially, we said, in terms that pick out aesthetic properties. But to apply such terms, it can be argued next, we must know the rules for their proper applications, as with any terms in the language. In the case of aesthetic terms, these rules must state the objective conditions in which they are properly applied. Hence, once more, there must be rules or principles at both levels. Skeptics will point to disagreements in the applications of these aesthetic terms and in evaluations in questioning the existence of these rules. But the very understandings that allow for these disagreements on the borderlines indicate that agreement is the norm in aesthetic judgments, even if largely unstated. Disputes over the relative merits of Verdi and Wagner may be much more visible, but agreement over the relative merits of Mozart and Manilow indicate the grounding of the use of evaluative aesthetic terms in rules for their common use.

Third, I said that aesthetic principles would take the form of causal laws linking base properties to proper evaluative responses. But since the correct ascriptions of aesthetic properties involves just such responses to just such properties, there must be causal laws underlying and explaining these responses. Hence, aesthetic principles can simply express these laws.

Finally, to turn from critics to artists, when they are creating their works, they know, at least after the initial steps, that there are right and wrong ways to proceed. The later stages of creation must follow the earlier in the right ways (and similarly, there will be right and wrong ways to attend to the works so as to appreciate this logical progression). Artists can then be said to follow rules that they create or discover in these early stages, the same rules that guide audiences in appreciating the internal meanings of elements of works in relation to other elements. According to Wittgenstein, knowing a rule just is knowing how to "go on in the right way." These rules inherent in artistic creation and appreciation for going on in the right way are also principles for creating and appreciating the aesthetic features of works. If there are right and wrong ways of proceeding artistically, such rules must exist.

On the other side, in thinking about the general reasons against believing in aesthetic principles, it will be helpful first to compare aesthetic to moral judgment on this score. Post-Kantian skeptics about aesthetic principles have often assumed a contrast here between the two domains. But in fact, genuine rules cannot capture our set of intuitive moral judgments, and for reasons similar to those that militate against aesthetic principles. It is these similarities rather than the differences between the two domains that are instructive here. In ethics, principles formulated simply enough to be usable and linking objective or nonnormative properties of situations to moral prescriptions fail to capture our set of intuitive judgments first, because there are too many morally relevant factors interacting in ways that change their priorities, and even their positive or negative values, in different actual contexts. If, for example, we define the usual moral virtues in morally neutral terms, so that honesty is simply telling the truth and courage is simply acting in the face of fear or danger, then, as Kant pointed out, virtues so conceived are not always good. Courage in this sense can be foolhardy, cold-blooded, or itself dangerous, while honesty can be tactless, insensitive, or brutal, depending on other morally relevant factors in various contexts. If, by contrast, we begin with normatively defined concepts, then we can derive moral prescriptions, but the principles linking the two will be of little use in judging actual actions in dispute. Murder, for example, is always wrong, but the condemnation of any act of killing will then depend on showing it to be a case of murder, and the principle will be useless for this crucial task. I have elsewhere termed such principles pseudo-rules, to indicate their lack of any real role in moral reasoning (Goldman 2002).

The truth of moral relativism would provide a second reason why moral evaluations cannot typically be supported by universal principles. This is not the place to establish that truth, but it is clear that if moral evaluations are relative to incompatible but equally acceptable moral frameworks – if, for example, it is permissible to sacrifice one to save more in a utilitarian but not in a rights-based moral framework – then principles for maximizing utility or protecting rights, and those that follow from them, will not be universally binding.

Corresponding to these reasons for denying that universal rules guide ordinary moral reasoning are arguments from context and taste in the aesthetic realm. Just as an open-ended list of other factors can give negative value to honesty or courage and

Alan H. Goldman

positive value to acts such as taking others' property, causing pain, or even killing, so a beautiful theme of Mozart would sound terrible in a work by Bartok. And just as what is right in one moral framework or for one moral sensibility will be wrong for another, so what is elegant for a critic with one kind of taste will be pretentious or kitsch for another with a taste for what is more lean or striking in art.

Let us first look more closely at the argument from context. If the number of potentially morally relevant factors and their possible interactions are a problem for finding usable moral principles, the problem is greater in aesthetics. Evaluatively relevant factors in general are determined by the functions of the objects that have them. Objects with one narrow function, such as knives for cutting, will be easy to evaluate, since only what serves that function, for example sharp edges, will be relevant. The functions of moral systems are quite broad – to minimize and resolve conflict, to promote cooperation, and to protect the interests of those affected by actions of others. Given these broad functions, it will be difficult or impossible to predict what features of actions or situations will be morally relevant and how they will interact. But on this ground the prospect for principles in aesthetics is bleaker still. As Kant ([1793] 1987) and others again emphasized, while art may serve basic human needs, it has no clear practical purpose whose fulfillment might provide standards of evaluation. If, as I have argued elsewhere, the function of art is simply to fully engage all our mental capacities simultaneously (Goldman 1995), then almost any feature of an artwork might contribute toward serving this function, and the set of relations among all these elements, unique to each work, will always be of primary relevance. That any change in the objective properties of a work can affect the complex formal, representational, and expressive structures that are the typical objects of aesthetic appreciation does not imply that every such change will do so. But it does indicate again that the ultimate objects of aesthetic evaluation will consist in elements, relations among them, and resultant features that differ relevantly in each case.

Accepting the problem of context, one might still maintain that at least complete descriptions of works will entail proper evaluations of them, that there are at least sufficient objective conditions in this sense. But even this claim will not do. First, it is clear that such sufficient conditions would not amount to principles of use to either artists or critics. Second, the claim ignores the problem of ultimate differences in taste, to be addressed below. Third, and most important here, the relevant context for evaluating features of artworks is broader even than complete descriptions (were that possible) of the objective properties of the works themselves, including also differing interpretations of them and their historical relations to other works. The possibility of incompatible interpretations bringing out different and incompatible aesthetic properties in works itself implies the lack of entailment from objective properties, no matter how completely described, to aesthetic ones. Preference for one or another of these interpretations may again be a matter of differing tastes for the aesthetic properties they make available.

As Kendall Walton (1970) and Arthur Danto (1981: 133–5) have shown, the aesthetic properties that works have depend also on the broader historical contexts into which the works fit. Figures that are coarse in seventeenth-century paintings might be overly refined in the context of twentieth-century painting. This means not simply that any principles linking objective to aesthetic properties would have to be historically relativized and in that sense not universal. The possibility of fitting particular works into different historical traditions implies also that even placing the works' objective properties in historical contexts, that is, dating them relative to other works, will once more not suffice for determining a unique set of aesthetic properties.

Thus, the argument from context, the interaction of morally relevant properties that militates against principles linking objective properties to proper moral evaluations, has an even stronger counterpart in aesthetics, where the number of potentially relevant factors and the contexts in which they interact are greater and broader. The other, relativist argument against the existence of moral principles, from the incompatibility of equally acceptable moral frameworks, also has a stronger counterpart in aesthetics. Whether or not there are indeed incompatible but clearly acceptable moral frameworks, it seems clear that there are ultimate differences in taste among equally highly educated and competent critics. This, together with the fact that aesthetic properties consist in relations between objective bases and (typically) evaluative responses, again implies that the same objective properties can give rise to different aesthetic properties with opposed evaluative components. And that, of course, in turn implies that there cannot be genuine principles linking objective properties to proper aesthetic evaluations.

If there were principles linking objective properties to goodness in art, and if these principles were epistemically accessible, then artists would no longer need to be artists. They could create good art without having any aesthetic sensibility, simply by knowing and following these rules. But, for better or worse, it is not so easy, and we can celebrate or lament this fact without indulging in romantic idealizations of artists. If there were such principles and they were epistemically accessible, then opposing evaluations by highly educated and equally competent critics would be inexplicable, and yet we find such disagreements even about generally acknowledged paradigms.

What are the prospects for principles on the next level, linking admittedly evaluative aesthetic properties to overall evaluations? First, as Hume recognized at the beginning of "On the Standard of Taste," such principles, corresponding to what I described as "pseudo-rules" in ethics, would be of equally little use in justifying aesthetic judgments. As Hume noted ([1757] 1987: 227), agreement that elegance is good does nothing to settle whether a given work is elegant or good. But even pseudo-principles seem harder to come by in aesthetics. Many terms for aesthetic properties are more like virtue terms in having both neutral and evaluatively charged definitions, terms like "unified," or "balanced," or "expressive." Even aesthetic terms like "elegant," which, absent further qualification, are normally used evaluatively, admit of open-ended exceptions to their normal use, as indicated earlier by the *Last of the Mohicans*, *Turn of the Screw*, and *Rite of Spring* examples. This renders such terms and the properties they pick out different from the case of "murder," which designates an act that is always wrong and hence generates a principle, although one of little use in moral reasoning or argument. I will expand on these differences in the next section.

Alan H. Goldman

Philosophers' Purported Examples

For a purported example of the strongest type of principle, stating in seemingly objective terms necessary and sufficient conditions for an aesthetic property, one must go back to Hutcheson's ([1725] 1973) equation of beauty with "unity amidst variety," a formula still endorsed by Eddy Zemach (1987: 72). Taking "unity" and "variety" to be definable nonevaluatively, this principle is easily counterexemplified. The drawing in fig. 19.1 may be a paradigm of unity in variety but is in no way beautiful. This is

Figure 19.1 Squiggles #1.

not to deny that appealing to unity in variety can explain the beauty of, say, the first movement of Haydn's string quartet Opus 76, No. 2. But as a universal principle, it fails miserably.

Peter Kivy (1973) has also proposed sufficient conditions for aesthetic properties in objective properties. His main example of an aesthetic property that is condition-governed in this way is unity itself. He points out that an orchestral movement that is monothematic will exhibit considerable unity, and in this he seems correct. Even more so a monochromatic painting. But unity in this sense is much like honesty in the moral realm. It is not always a virtue. It is in fact evaluatively neutral, as we can see from the fact that we could otherwise all produce valuable paintings in the easiest possible way. Unity in this sense may simply be boring, which is not to say that we do not marvel at the unity of certain movements by Haydn and Beethoven, at what they can do with one simple theme or motif. When speaking of the wonderful unity of such movements or works, we may be using the term evaluatively, but any plausibility to the claim that Kivy has provided a principle that links objective or nonevaluative properties to evaluative aesthetic properties simply trades on this ambiguity. It is once more true that objective properties set limits on the different aesthetic properties that different critics will perceive. What one finds wonderfully unified another will find tedious, but not chaotic. But, being evaluatively opposed, the first pair suggests no principle of evaluation.

Next in descending order of strength is Beardsley's famous proposal that unity, complexity, and intensity are always good-making features of artworks, and that other properties are of positive value only in so far as they contribute to these (Beardsley [1958] 1981: 462–6). If we add an intense chartreuse color to the squiggles in the drawing that counterexemplifies Hutcheson's proposal, it will counterexemplify Beardsley's in the starkest way as well. We will have all three of his criterial properties present without the slightest inclination to evaluate positively any of these or the work they dominate. The seeming ability of Beardsley's account to handle some counterexamples derives only from the fact that his criterial properties are often opposed. Thus, when a Mahler symphony is praised for its sprawling range of expressive qualities, it can be said not that its lack of unity is a virtue, but instead its great complexity. When a work of Rothko affects us by its powerful simplicity, this will not be said to be a lack of complexity, but a great unity. Finally, as George Dickie points out (1987: 231, 1988: 87) these properties, like other aesthetic properties, can interact in ways that reverse their usual polarities. Thus Beardsley's proposed principles, while retreating from sufficient conditions to properties that have only positive evaluative force, fare no better than their stronger counterparts.

For our next purported examples of aesthetic principles, we may turn again to Hume's "Of the Standard of Taste." Interpretations of this rich but ambiguous essay differ, but there is certainly textual support for the claim that Hume believed there are general rules of art, as evidenced by the near universal agreement in certain comparative judgments. Notoriously, he offers very few examples, limited to supposed faults and virtues in the poetry of Ariosto. These seemingly attempt to exemplify objective properties that nevertheless count only one way toward evaluations, at least when presented "singly and in high degree" (Hume [1757] 1987: 235). Among the faults he mentions are "improbable fictions" and "interruptions of narration," while

Alan H. Goldman

among the good-making features are "natural pictures of passions, especially those of the gay and amorous kind". These are supposed to be qualities that naturally please or displease, where a different response indicates only a defect in the observer or in the conditions of observation (Hume 1987: 234).

But it is painfully clear once more that these examples fail miserably to instantiate universal principles. Pictures of an obese man in the throes of hysterical laughter as well as pornographic images fit his description of an aesthetic virtue that is supposed to count only positively toward evaluation, while his first purported aesthetic blemish would condemn *Alice in Wonderland* and his second, the novels of Dickens and George Eliot. The only other kind of example he cites, the virtue of "mutual relation and correspondence of parts," comes close to exemplifying a pseudo-principle, despite his earlier dismissal of these as of no use in settling aesthetic disagreements. In fact, this phrase seems not to pick out an aesthetic property at all, let alone an objective or nonevaluative property, but to note that the formal structure of the work in question is an aesthetically good one.

Hume's own lack of confidence in his principles probably explains his failure to cite others and his turning instead to the standard of ideal critics, whose eminent characteristics he takes great pains to define. The contrast here with his position on moral judgment is eye-opening, since the nature of judgments in the two domains and the structure of the properties they pick out are supposed to be similar. The major difference in his treatment is that he is not much concerned with the characteristics of moral judges, focusing instead on the property that causes the sentiment of approbation or approval in us, namely, social utility. Here Hume proposes a genuine principle (although counterexemplified in other moral frameworks) in the form of a causal law. Moral judgments that do not satisfy the principle of approving of whatever increases social utility, those in praise of what Hume calls the "monkish virtues," are, if not untrue, at best inappropriate. In his treatment of aesthetics, Hume never comes close to defending a principle of this sort by the kind of extended argument we find in his discussion of utility. Instead, he quickly shifts emphasis from mention of rules to an extended discussion of critics and paradigm works that have withstood the test of time, making it plausible that he was uncertain of his own examples and could find no others to defend more forcefully.

The appeal to the greater expertise of ideal critics is supposed to increase uniformity among aesthetic or evaluative responses to the objective properties of works. In fact it must culminate in universal agreement among genuinely ideal critics if this appeal is supposed to support belief in unspecified universal aesthetic principles. But there is no evidence that this is the ultimate result of increasing expertise. In fact, experts are more capable of generating incompatible interpretations of the same works that, as noted, bring out incompatible aesthetic properties. And they apply their own aesthetic theories. Not surprisingly, then, we find critical disagreement in ascriptions of aesthetic properties and even in overall evaluations of works considered paradigms by the majority. Tolstoy on Beethoven and Tolstoy, Collingwood on Beethoven, and T. S. Eliot on Shakespeare are but some of the most striking examples among countless others. And we do not need widespread disagreement among ideal critics to defeat support for universal principles from this direction.

Despite Hume's own apparent doubts about his principles, support for his sort of principle has been provided in the contemporary literature by Frank Sibley and George Dickie. But their principles are in one sense weaker still, not linking objective to evaluative aesthetic properties, but stating only that normally evaluative aesthetic terms in fact pick out properties that involve only one sort of evaluative response, positive or negative, at least when considered in isolation from other properties in works. Elegance in itself, for example, only counts positively. Sibley does not endorse the former kind of principle that would link objective properties to evaluative aesthetic properties. He denies that objective properties ever constitute sufficient conditions for aesthetic properties. He allows that they might constitute necessary conditions, in that he says it might be impossible for something to be garish if all its colors are pastels (Sibley 1959: 429). If he had ever seen the hotel facades in South Miami Beach, he would not have made this concession. In a later article, he offers a nice explanation of why there are no base-level principles at all. It is that aesthetic properties do not contain fixed objective components. To use his terms, what aesthetic terms pick out in particular uses are determinate, not determinable objective properties (Sibley 1974: 11). Another way of making this point would be to say that in justifying their ascriptions of positively evaluative aesthetic properties to works, critics typically will ultimately point to objective structural properties or features not shared by other works, and which would not make those other works better if they were shared. This is why ultimate justifications of aesthetic evaluations always amount simply to descriptions of their particular objects. These varying particular objective features will be the objective components of those particular instantiations of the aesthetic properties (compare Scruton 1974: 153). (Remember that the meanings of aesthetic terms are anchored to the usual evaluative responses they express and to overlapping sets of paradigms to which they apply.) The determinate objective properties then cannot enter rules for the ascription of the aesthetic properties.

Dickie does not in general endorse rules linking nonevaluative to evaluative properties either. He probably could not consistently do so, since that sort of principle might provide rules for artists to create artworks, or at least works with many aesthetic properties that plausibly could be argued to be artworks, without the institutional support of the artworld. He does, nevertheless, offer one such example, that truth to actuality is always valuable in itself in a work, when considered in isolation from its other properties (Dickie, this volume). Can it really be the case that "grass is green" or "the sky is blue," asserted somewhere in a novel, makes it more valuable? That Dickie finds this at all plausible shows only how weak are the principles that he is proposing, since he surely does not believe that such trivial truths would add much value for being there.

When it comes to evaluative aesthetic properties, Sibley and Dickie, recognizing what I have called the argument from context, admit that their usual polarities can be reversed by interactions with other properties. Sibley seems to think that this happens only when a normally positive aesthetic property detracts from the primary aesthetic quality of a work, so that he might admit that an elegant performance of the *Rite of Spring* could be negative in detracting from its power. But there is no reason for restricting reversals to that direction or to interactions with primary or dominant features. Boredom in *Waiting for Godot* might be a positive feature. Both

Alan H. Goldman

Sibley and Dickie attempt to evade this problem by weakening their principles still further, by adding isolation clauses. Elegance, for example, is always positive when considered in isolation from other properties. This clause is stated and interpreted in somewhat different ways: one cannot say simply that a work (or performance) is bad because elegant; something cannot be aesthetically worse just for being elegant; we must consider the property as if it were the only value-relevant property.

But it seems that we can say simply, "That performance of the *Rite of Spring* was too elegant," or "James's prose in *Turn of the Screw* (or Cooper's in *Last of the Mohicans*) are too elegant." The performance and the novels are worse just for being elegant. Sibley and Dickie can reply that we can say this only because it will be understood that the negative force of the aesthetic property in these cases derives from its interaction with other properties of the works in question. The question then becomes, however, whether it is not always crucial for judging the evaluative polarity of any property to appreciate how it interacts with others in particular works, whether it is really possible to consider an aesthetic property in isolation or relevant to try to do so. Consider the most minimalist work with a minimal number of aesthetic properties, perhaps a solid red monochromatic painting. Certainly there is not only one aesthetically relevant objective property here: hue and saturation of color combine at least with shape and size of canvas to produce the aesthetic effect. Nor is there only one aesthetic property: purity of color interacts with garishness or boldness, and so on, not to mention all the aesthetic properties that result from the rejection of various richer traditions in painting or from the attempt to capture its essence.

Dickie will again reply that we can consider each of these properties in isolation, as if it were the only aesthetic property of the work. But what would be the point of doing so? It will not help at all in evaluating the work and may well distort the value of the property itself in this context. Dickie considers a singsong meter in a poem about death, admittedly bad in that context, but, according to him, nevertheless valuable in itself as a form of unity. This strikes me as similar to the hedonist utilitarian who must count sadistic pleasure as good in itself when everyone else views it as bad. Refusing as well to succumb to the argument from taste, Dickie also maintains that monotony, as a form of unity, is valuable in itself (both examples from this volume). At that point, I am tempted to say, "The defense rests."

Justification Without Principles

Before showing how the supposed functions of aesthetic principles can be fulfilled otherwise, it is perhaps worth making clearer how my view of evaluative aesthetic properties differs from that of Dickie and Sibley. I acknowledge, having called them "evaluative properties," that they usually include an evaluative response of a certain polarity, positive or negative. Therefore, normally, when we say that a performance is elegant, for example, and say nothing else, it will be understood that we intend a positive judgment. But the implication is only conversational, since there are open-ended exceptions to the usual polarities. Generalizations with open-ended exceptions cannot be used in justifications when the question is whether the particular case is an exception. There will be no independent justificatory force to such a generaliza-tion that supports only a conversational implication when nothing else is said.

In any case, when we realize how very weak are the principles for which Dickie argues – principles asserting only that evaluative aesthetic properties create some pos-sibly minimal value when considered in isolation – it is difficult to see what role they could play in the justification of any actual aesthetic judgment. I have pointed out that ultimate justifications for evaluations of artworks always point to particular objective properties or structures in the works and that if principles were to play an important role in these justifications, they would have to link those objective prop-erties to evaluative aesthetic properties and thereby to overall evaluations. Even if there were principles of the sort Dickie and Sibley endorse, they would amount to no more than what I have described as (very weak) pseudo-principles. Debate would still always center on whether works actually had the positive aesthetic properties being ascribed to them by one of the disputants, or had instead their negative counterparts. It might also center, granted Dickie's principles, on how minimal the value produced by these properties might be, since virtually anything has some value. Appeal to such principles could neither help settle critical disagreements nor help artists create good works. Of what use could they be?

In the absence of principles that could be of use to critics, we can nevertheless explain the normative force of evaluative aesthetic judgments as well as how errors in such judgments are possible. Hume showed the way in eschewing defense of prin-ciples in favor of appeal to ideal critics. In ascribing evaluative aesthetic properties or offering overall evaluations, actual critics imply that ideal critics would judge in the same way, that their audiences therefore ought to do the same. Even if we accept an ultimate relativism in aesthetic judgments, as Hume did at the end of his essay, such judgments can retain their normative force. Critics will now imply that ideal critics who share their tastes would respond in the same ways. Errors will remain pos-sible to the extent that actual judges fall short of ideal judges in knowledge, atten-tiveness, and so on. Thus we need not appeal to principles in describing how aesthetic judgments can be justified. Real critics are justified in their judgments to the extent that they approximate to ideal critics. In justifying their judgments of works they will appeal directly to the works themselves to indicate the proper responses to them, and (implicitly) to their own expertise, familiarity with the type of work, and so on.

Nor do the other general reasons offered earlier for believing in unspecified aes-thetic principles force us to accept their unverified existence. We have seen that the meanings of aesthetic terms can be anchored to overlapping paradigm uses without rules that determine correct applications in all or any cases (any, since even particu-lar paradigms can be challenged without a lapse into nonsense). That there are causal laws underlying the responses of both real and ideal critics does not imply that there are usable aesthetic principles. Given the effects of context and taste, such laws will be too fine-grained, linking works that will not be repeated to the responses of par-ticular critics, to give rise to evaluative principles.

That there are right and wrong ways for artists to proceed in their works once begun, and right and wrong ways for audiences to appreciate these quasi-logical pro-gressions, does not entail rules to distinguish right from wrong. Critics provide audi-ences with interpretations to guide their perceptions of works, but critics do not lay

Alan H. Goldman

down rules for proper perceptions. In regard to performances of works, there are some rules for right performances, such as "Play all the notes written in a musical score," but creativity and the main grounds for evaluation begin where these rules run out. Similarly artists, for example painters, learn the rules for correct perspective, but these do not even set minimal standards for evaluation. Whatever Wittgenstein may or may not have thought about the matter, not all distinctions between right and wrong imply underlying rules or principles. There is a right way for a baseball pitcher to pitch to a hitter, but if the pitcher follows rules, he will probably throw the wrong pitches. Perhaps more importantly, the arguments that should convince us that our intuitive moral judgments cannot be captured in a set of rules in no way call into question that there are right and wrong ways to judge what is morally right or wrong. Similarly for aesthetic judgments, as Kant probably indicated in his talk of purposiveness without purpose. Artworks display formal structures that seem not only right, but necessitated, without there being fixed rules (or "concepts," to use Kant's term) that determined in advance precisely what was required to complete them.

Finally, coherence in sets of judgments, and specifically in aesthetic judgments, does not require following rules or principles. A rule requires that when all the properties stipulated as sufficient for a judgment recur, the same judgment must be rendered. Coherence requires something less: that when all *and only* the same relevant properties recur, the same judgment must be made. We saw that, given how many features of artworks can be aesthetically relevant, the latter demand offers little constraint on judgments in this domain. It is very hard here to make a charge of incoherence in aesthetic evaluations stick, and I have never heard a critic faulted for failing to follow an established evaluative rule or principle.

Attempts to counter the reasons for disbelieving in aesthetic principles, the arguments from context and taste, try to broaden or narrow the relevant context for judgment and to indicate universal agreements in judgment or universal functions for art. But expanding the relevant contexts for ascribing aesthetic properties to the extent necessary results only in appeal to unique works in unique historical patterns, not in usable principles. Narrowing the context to properties in isolation results in irrelevant abstractions. One might also attempt to narrow the context to particular historical styles in order to develop evaluative principles (Davies 1990). Elegance may not be a virtue in the *Rite of Spring*, but it can be claimed to always be so in a Mozartian work. But this claim might not be universally true even in Mozart's own works under certain legitimate interpretations, in regard to certain parts of the *Jupiter Symphony* or of *Don Giovanni*, for example.

Universal judgments, other than those like "Mozart is better than Manilow," are not to be found. I shudder to say that even this one might not be universal, and if it is, I fail to see what principle emerges from it (perhaps, "Compose like Mozart, not like Manilow"?). As to universal functions, the fact that something at least approximating to art exists in all known cultures does indicate certain common basic needs underlying artistic creation – needs to represent or express; impose order, beauty, or ornamentation; exercise skill or originality, and so on. And from the side of the audience, there is the need to exercise and develop all our mental capacities – perceptual, affective, imaginative, cognitive – simultaneously "in free play." Success in fulfilling the creative needs is, of course, relevant to aesthetic evaluation, but not sufficient for judging an artwork to be great or even good. Works can succeed in representing, expressing, or even in displaying skill, originality, or beauty without being judged good as art. Success in achieving the desired effect on the audience *is* sufficient, but here we have the purest of pseudo-principles: "Create a fully engaging work." That this is the goal of the artist is not trivial, but what is wanted are principles that indicate how to achieve it. And these are not to be had.

Alan H. Goldman

CHAPTER TWENTY

Iron, Leather, and Critical Principles

George Dickie

Isenberg: The Rejection of Principles

Analytic philosophy's dispute over critical principles starts in 1949 with Arnold Isenberg's "Critical Communication." His purpose was to refute the notion that there are such principles. Unfortunately, Isenberg's mistakes still confuse this discussion. Isenberg says that, despite its deficiencies, there is a widely held notion of criticism as a deductive procedure that takes this form:

> There is the value judgment or *verdict* (V): "This picture or poem is good –"; There is a particular statement or *reason* (R): "– because it has such-and-such a quality –"; and there is a general statement or *norm* (N): "– and any work which has that quality is *pro tanto* good." (Isenberg [1949] 1979: 658)

Rewriting this view in a more usual logical form and entirely in English, it would go like this.

> NORM Any work that has a certain quality is to that extent good.
> REASON This work has that certain quality.
> VERDICT Therefore, this work is good.

The proponents of this view, Isenberg says, hold that reasons are *vindicated* by the norms in the arguments.

There appears to be a grave logical difficulty with the way Isenberg states the view he opposes. The predicate in the verdict is "is good," which suggests a *strong* overall claim that the work as a whole is good, but the predicate "is good" in the norm is qualified with "to that extent," which indicates that the quality is a good-making one that does not necessarily make the work a good one as a whole.

No doubt Isenberg intended a more plausible version of the claim he opposes, which would go:

NORM Any work that has a certain quality is to that extent good.
REASON This work has that certain quality.
VERDICT Therefore, this work is to that extent good.

This way of putting it makes the argument logically valid. It also makes it clear that Isenberg is concerned with what I would call *weak* principles, that is, principles that are about good-making or bad-making characteristics, which are principles that alone cannot underwrite a conclusion about the overall goodness or badness of a work.

Some earlier philosophers held *stronger* versions of the kind of evaluative principles that Isenberg opposes. I think Francis Hutcheson in the eighteenth century held the *strong* principle: *any work that has uniformity amidst variety is good* (Hutcheson [1725] 1973). But present-day philosophers no longer take this kind of antique view seriously. I also think Hume and Alexander Gerard, who came on Hutcheson's heels, reject the notion that there is a single master principle or a plurality of master principles that can entail a work's being good. Hume does not discuss the overall value of artworks, but Gerard does – he writes:

Our gratification must in every case be balanced against disgust; beauties against blemishes: before we have compared and measured them, we can form no judgment of the work. . . . in every performance, beauties and blemishes are to be found in different parts. [A] person of true taste forms his judgment only from the surplus of merit, after an accurate comparison of the perfections and the faults [of a work]. (Gerard [1759] 1978: 138–9)

Hume is aware of this question because he says Ariosto's poetry charms because of its many merits and in spite of its many faults. Gerard's passage suggests there are numerous small-scale principles of the kind Hume's account refers to – ones involving the merits and defects that the two eighteenth-century philosophers call "beauties" and "blemishes." Although Hume never formulated an example, he makes frequent reference to principles in "Of the Standard of Taste."

Isenberg goes on to claim that his opponents attempt to justify norms by basing them on "inductive generalization[s] which describes a relationship between some aesthetic quality and someone's or everyone's system of aesthetic response" (Isenberg [1949] 1979: 659).

Isenberg begins his argument against generalizations by citing a reason that he thinks is reasonable to give to convince someone of the beauty of Milton's line "But musical as is Apollo's lute." The reason is "the pattern of u's and l's that reinforces the meaning with its own musical quality" (Isenberg 1979: 660). He concludes there can be no norm to fit with this reason because there is no generalization "from which we might derive the prediction that such a pattern of u' and l's should be pleasing to me" (Isenberg 1979: 660).

There is no such generalization, but Isenberg is looking in the wrong place. The candidate for generalization he presents and rejects – the pattern of u's and l's – does not fit his *own* account of what such an inductive generalization should be about,

George Dickie

namely, "a relationship between some *aesthetic* quality and someone's or everyone's system of aesthetic response" (emphasis mine). In the particular case cited, the pattern of u's and l's in conjunction with a particular meaning helps generate an aesthetic quality and could do so in other cases, but the pattern of u's and l's by itself that Isenberg cites is not what Sibley or anyone else would now identify as an aesthetic quality.

Isenberg is correct that the required kind of generalizations involve a relationship between an *aesthetic* quality and a response. He, however, considers the wrong kind of characteristics as candidates for the subjects of such generalizations. It is not plausible that nonaesthetic qualities by themselves, such as patterns of u's and l's, steeply rising and falling curves, and the other examples he focuses on can evoke a response. It is plausible that aesthetic qualities such as gracefulness, elegance, and delicacy can do so.

Isenberg's misstep could result from the fact that he may not distinguish aesthetic from nonaesthetic properties as we would today. He may think of his candidate examples as aesthetic qualities. After all, he published 10 years before Frank Sibley's landmark article on aesthetic qualities.

Isenberg may show some awareness of the distinction that Sibley was to make when he says that critics cites things like patterns of u's and l's as reasons in order to get others to notice some *other* quality. Unfortunately, he focuses on the ungeneralizability of the generally nonpleasing, nonaesthetic features such as patterns of u's and l's rather than on the generalizability of things critics are trying to get their addressees to notice, which no doubt are aesthetic qualities.

Assuming terms referring to aesthetic qualities are plausible candidates for the grammatical subjects of the generalizations, how are the generalizations to be formulated? The kind of generalizations that are useful and possible will be discussed later.

Sibley: Criteria and Reasons

I set aside for the moment the question of generalizations to consider Frank Sibley's important ideas about criteria and reasons as they relate to the formulation of principles (Sibley 1983). Sibley discusses only criteria of aesthetic merit and demerit and never tries to formulate the aesthetic principles for which such criteria would be the grammatical subjects. Also, he does not discuss justifying generalizations of the kind Isenberg questions. As an example, Sibley asserts that the aesthetic quality of gracefulness is a criterion of aesthetic merit by saying that gracefulness *tout court* or *in vacuo* always has inherent positive aesthetic polarity. He asserts that the aesthetic quality of garishness is a criterion of aesthetic demerit by saying that garishness *tout court* or *in vacuo* always has inherent negative aesthetic polarity. He thinks all aesthetic qualities have inherent aesthetic polarity. (By inherent aesthetic polarity, I take Sibley to be talking about the power that certain characteristics have to produce intrinsically valued or disvalued experience.) If Sibley is right that there are such criteria, and I think he is, then they would be the obvious subjects of positive and negative aesthetic principles. How such principles are to be formulated remains to be seen.

Sibley is explicit that the aesthetic polarity of an object's aesthetic quality can be undermined if it interacts with other properties of that object, and that is why he introduces the *in vacuo* qualification. His extensive discussion of the effect on aesthetic polarity of the interaction of aesthetic qualities negatively or positively with other characteristics is very important. By the way, when Sibley speaks of gracefulness and other aesthetic qualities *in vacuo*, he does not mean that these aesthetic qualities float unrelated to anything else. Clearly, when something is graceful, for example, that aesthetic quality will depend on underlying or supporting elements. The *in vacuo* qualification is there to indicate that we are to focus on the aesthetic quality independently of its relation or relations to anything that would alter its polarity. Also, an artwork must actually have an aesthetic quality such as gracefulness in order for it to be considered *in vacuo*. If, for example, an artwork has elements which make for gracefulness but has other elements that interact negatively with the gracefulness-making elements to prevent the work from being graceful, then the work lacks gracefulness. There can be two levels of interaction: a more basic level in which elements interact positively to create or support an aesthetic quality or negatively not to create an aesthetic quality, and a higher-level interaction of the kind Sibley has in mind in which an artwork actually has an aesthetic quality that can interact positively or negatively with other properties of the work.

In my 1988 book, *Evaluating Art*, I took Sibley to be trying to justify his conclusions about criteria by using what I there called a "linguistic test" when he wrote, "One cannot intelligibly say *tout court*. . . . 'This work is bad because it is graceful,' or 'This work is good because it is garish'" (Sibley 1983: 5). I now believe he did not intend his remark as a justification of aesthetic polarity but was merely restating in another form what he had already asserted about criteria and aesthetic polarity. In any event, his remark will not work as a justification; a person could not find "This work is bad because it is graceful" unintelligible unless the person already viewed gracefulness as having positive aesthetic polarity. Still, I think that Sibley is right that aesthetic qualities have inherent aesthetic polarity even if he does not justify his claim. He probably thought it obvious that they do, and perhaps he is right.

If the question of the justification of criteria and principles is to be addressed, however, what is needed are justificatory generalizations, although not of the particular kind that Isenberg cites.

Hume: The Rules of Beauty

David Hume follows the generalization line, although what he says on the topic comes up only in passing in a discussion of another question. In "Of the Standard of Taste," Hume tries to show how cognitively insensitive persons can be shown the error of their ways. He tells the tale from *Don Quixote* of Sancho's kinsmen and the hogshead of wine that unbeknownst to everyone contains an iron key with a leather thong. One kinsman notes a slight taste of iron in the wine and the other a slight taste of leather, but no one else can detect either taste. Sancho's kinsmen are vindicated when the key with the leather thong is discovered at the bottom of the hogshead. Hume tries to

George Dickie

apply this story to the judging of artworks to show how good judges can prove to cognitively insensitive persons they are in error. He writes, "Here then the general rules of beauty are of use; being drawn from established models, and *from observation of what pleases or displeases, when presented singly and in high degree. . . .*" (Hume [1757] 1987: 235, emphasis mine). Sancho's kinsmen are vindicated because there is something everyone can see – the key and leather thong. Hume's attempt to demonstrate how good critics can prove themselves to cognitively insensitive persons fails because with art there is nothing analogous to the key with the leather thong for all to see. Even if there are rules of beauty recognized by everyone, there is no guarantee that everyone will be able to detect what a rule refers to when the referent occurs mixed (not singly) and in small degree.

Hume's remark about the rules of beauty is nevertheless a fruitful one. What he says about what pleases or displeases singly and in high degree shows how the generalizations that underlie aesthetic principles are to be discovered.

Hume's *singly* and Sibley's *in vacuo* are the same qualification, but are used by them to make different points. Sibley makes the *in vacuo* qualification because the aesthetic qualities of works of art may interact with other characteristics to change or destroy their polarity. Hume makes his *singly* and *in high degree* specification because in works of art, qualities (to use his own words) "may be found in small degree, or may be mixed and confounded with each other . . . [so] . . . that the taste is not affected with such minute qualities, or not able to distinguish all the particular flavours, amidst the disorder, in which they are presented" (Hume 1987: 235). The reason for "in high degree" comes out clearly here: presence in high degree makes it easier to focus on a *single* property. Because of the high degree of a property, one can focus on a quality in isolation from other characteristics and have a clear enough perception of it to tell if it can produce an intrinsically valued or disvalued experience or neither. Hume's clear perception factor is vital for the confirmation of generalizations that justify principles. Sibley's interaction factor, as will be shown, is crucial for the formulation of principles.

How are the observations that underlie the rules of beauty (aesthetic principles) supposed to work? Consider an artistic defect in Ariosto's poetry that Hume mentions would be involved in an aesthetic principle, namely, want of coherence. Hume gave no examples of observations and their confirmation, but he could have. Examples could have been developed on analogy with the Sancho's-kinsmen case. Suppose the hogshead had contained five pounds of rusty iron filings wrapped in a freshly tanned cowhide. In this case, everyone could have tasted the iron and leather flavors singly because of their high degree. *This* case is analogous to the way Hume's remarks show how to discover the rules of beauty, namely, by finding cases in which a characteristic in an artwork (or in nature) is so obvious (in high degree) that anyone can perceive it and react to it. Although Hume gives no examples, his forerunner, Francis Hutcheson, is explicit about how the observations were supposed to work concerning want of coherence. They are to be confirmed by thought experiments. The Humean generalization to be tested is: *want of coherence when experienced singly and in high degree produces an intrinsically disvalued experience.* There are two important factors here: (1) the subject of the generalization, the referent of which must be of sufficient magnitude that it can be clearly noticed and focused on individually and independently of the other properties of the artwork, and (2) the predicate which commits to the universal production of an intrinsic value experience – positive or negative.

Hutcheson's thought experiments are posed by asking several questions:

> [D]id ever any man make choice of a trapezium, or an irregular curve, for the ichnography or plan of his house, without necessity, or some great motive of convenience? ... Who was ever pleased with an inequality of heights in windows of the same range, or dissimilar shapes of them? Who was ever pleased with ... unequal legs and arms, eyes or cheeks in a mistress? (Hutcheson [1725] 1973: 76–7)

The implied answer is, "No one." Such architectural and anatomical features could be focused on *singly* because of their high degree. Hutcheson no doubt believed that such thought experiments were sufficient to justify the universal displeasingness of want of coherence. Hume could have produced thought experiments for generalizations about the beauties and blemishes he mentions.

An important difference between Hutcheson and Hume is that Hutcheson thought that uniformity and variety and their want are the whole story where beauty and its opposite were concerned, whereas Hume thought that there are many other beauties and blemishes.

Hume and Sibley are right that there are large numbers of positive and negative aesthetic qualities, and that, consequently, there are many generalizations of the form "Aesthetic quality X, when experienced singly and in high degree, produces an intrinsically valued (or disvalued) experience." "In high degree" occurs here to ensure that the characteristic is sufficiently noticeable so that everyone can experience it. Once an aesthetic quality has been "certified," that is, shown to be intrinsically valued or disvalued by everyone, its generalization can omit "in high degree." I use the expression "valued or disvalued" as a replacement for the eighteenth-century terminology "pleased or displeased," because it better indicates what goes on in our experience of art. I say "*intrinsically* valued or disvalued" to pick out an experience that we find valuable or disvaluable in itself, independently of anything that it might lead to. The experience of an aesthetic quality can sometimes have instrumental value, for example, be soothing. But in evaluating art, where aesthetic qualities are concerned, it is virtually always a matter of finding the experience of them intrinsically valued or disvalued.

Hume specifies the characteristics of good critics; they are free of prejudice, highly familiar with a specific art form, and the like. These issues do not arise for the confirmation of generalizations; being able to become aware of a "beauty" or a "blemish" in *some* object (in art or nature) because of its high degree is within the capacity of virtually everyone. Being prejudiced, being ignorant of an art form, and such is no barrier to a person's capacity to experience the referents of the subjects of "Humean" generalizations in one sort of thing or another (see Dickie 1996: 131–6). Thus this view of generalizations (and of principles that depend on it) does not require the notion of an ideal observer or qualified judge.

But what of the "certification" of generalizations, the showing of the universal production of the intrinsic value/disvalue experiences by Humean "beauties" and "blemishes"? Hume leaves the "certification" issue unaddressed and leaves unjustified the view that positive aesthetic qualities please universally and negative aesthetic qualities displease universally. Is he justified in doing so?

How is the capacity of aesthetic qualities for producing intrinsically valued/disvalued experiences to be shown? In the way that Hutcheson tried – by thought experiments using Humean terminology. Was anyone every pleased by unequal legs and arms, eyes or cheeks in a mistress when experienced singly and in high degree? Was anyone every displeased by gracefulness when experienced singly and in high degree?

The answer to both questions is "No," and analogous answers would hold for numerous other positive and negative aesthetic qualities if similar questions were asked. There are no doubt aesthetic qualities for which these questions fail; I suggested in *Evaluating Art* (Dickie 1988) that perhaps the negative aesthetic quality of garishness might not in some cases displease when experienced singly. In such a case, the generalization is restricted and the principle it supports would have less than universal scope.

So, there are Humean generalizations, but generalizations are not, as Isenberg aptly points out, principles. How are principles, to use Hume's words, "drawn from . . . observation"?

Principles from Generalizations

The first step in drawing principles from generalizations is to note that the generalizations are about aesthetic qualities *producing* intrinsically valued or disvalued experiences. Thus the aesthetic principles of artistic evaluation are to be formulated in terms of the *capacity* of the aesthetic qualities of works of art to produce intrinsically valued or disvalued experience. I shall discuss only positive generalizations and principles; an account of negative ones would be handled in a parallel fashion.

Understanding "instrumentally valuable" to mean "valuable for producing intrinsically valued experience," consider the following candidate principle:

Gracefulness in a work of art is always instrumentally valuable.

This formulation will not do because, as Sibley notes, gracefulness may interact with an artwork's other properties and destroy its capacity to produce intrinsically valued experience. Something's capacity, because of interaction, may function positively in one context but not in another.

So the second step in drawing principles from generalizations must take account of the possibility of interaction. This can be done by using either Hume's term "singly" or Sibley's phrase "*in vacuo*." The two philosophers use their different terms for different purposes, but both are talking about focusing on a single thing. So principles must be formulated in the following way:

Gracefulness in a work of art *in vacuo* is always instrumentally valuable.

This formulation seemed right to me in my *Evaluating Art* and elsewhere, and I tried in those places to formulate aesthetic principles in the following way:

Gracefulness in a work of art, in isolation from the other properties of the work, is always instrumentally valuable.

In order to make the language of principles mesh with generalizations smoothly and to make subsequent arguments easier, I shall reformulate this principle as follows:

All instances of gracefulness, when experienced in isolation from the other properties of the work, are instrumentally valuable in some degree.

I will illustrate, with the use of the definition of "instrumentally valuable," how the gracefulness principle, which is about an instrumentalist, normative capacity, is drawn from a generalization, which is about a property that produces intrinsically valued experience.

The general form of a positive "Humean" generalization (using my terminology) is "All instances of aesthetic quality X, when experienced in isolation from other properties, produce an intrinsically valued experience." To particularize the generalization, I will use *gracefulness* as its subject and narrow the generalization's scope to artworks. Pairing this generalization with the definition of "instrumentally valuable," the following deduction of a principle from a generalization can be made.

1   All instances of gracefulness in a work of art, when experienced in isolation from other properties of the work, produce an intrinsically valued experience.
2   Anything that produces intrinsically valued experience is instrumentally valuable in some degree (definition of "instrumentally valuable").
3   Therefore, all instances of gracefulness in a work of art, when experienced in isolation from other properties of the work, are instrumentally valuable in some degree.

A deductive argument with an aesthetic principle would go like this:

1   All instances of gracefulness in a work of art, when experienced in isolation from the other properties of the work, are instrumentally valuable in some degree.
2   This work of art is graceful or some aspect of it is, and its gracefulness does not interact negatively with any other properties of the work.
3   Therefore, this work of art is instrumentally valuable in some degree.

The second premise of this argument covers two kinds of cases: cases in which a work's gracefulness interacts positively with the other properties of that work and cases in which a work's gracefulness does not interact with the other properties of that work. It might be difficult to find an actual instance of the second kind, but it is a logical possibility. If one tried to construct another argument with the first premise of the above argument together with a second premise "This work of art is graceful or some aspect of it is and its gracefulness interacts negatively with some other properties of the work," then, without more information, no significant conclusion could be drawn.

There are, I think, as I argued in *Evaluating Art*, many aesthetic principles underwritten by universal generalizations about the production of intrinsically valued experience. I also maintained there that there may be aesthetic qualities that do not enjoy universal support. In the case of principles lacking universal support, they would have to be formulated thus: "Instances of aesthetic quality X in a work of art, when experienced in isolation from its other properties, are instrumentally valuable in some degree for some subset of persons, although not all persons." A critic using such a principle could not expect universal agreement.

Isenberg asserts that the proponents of principles believe that the reasons critics cite are *vindicated* when they are subsumed under norms. Well, it all depends on the kind of theory the principles are embedded in.

If a philosopher holds a top-down view that principles are derived from some authorizing source such as Platonic forms, pure reason, or the like, then Isenberg's claim applies. Within these philosophical pictures, principles are primary and critics discover the reasons they are to use by an examination of principles; they can then find them exemplified in artworks. For these philosophers, a reason that refers to a property in a work is *vindicated* by the occurrence of that particular property in a principle.

If a philosopher holds a bottom-up, instrumentalist view that principles are derived from experiences valued or disvalued by human beings, as the British theorists of taste and Sibley (I think) did, and as I do, then Isenberg's claim does not apply. Such philosophers may differ about how to characterize these experiences – as pleasure or displeasure, aesthetic experience, intrinsically valued or disvalued experience – but within these philosophical pictures the valued experiences are primary and are the sources of principles. What *is* vindicated within these bottom-up pictures is the consistency of the critic, which is shown by the use of a general principle.

Goldman on the Isolation Clause

In one brief paragraph in his *Aesthetic Value*, Alan Goldman makes four distinct criticisms of my account of principles. He begins, "George Dickie proposes that certain properties . . . *in isolation from others* always contribute in only one direction toward proper evaluations of works" (Goldman 1995: 141–2). So far as it goes, this is an accurate, although incomplete, characterization of my view. Goldman focuses throughout in his criticism on the isolation clause. His first criticism is

Unfortunately, this proposal makes little sense, if, as I have suggested, artworks derive their aesthetic value mainly from the ways their objective properties interact. We have little if any idea how to conceive of a painting with multiple properties as if it had only one. Even simple paintings will have degrees of several of the higher-order properties mentioned in Beardsley's theory. (Goldman 1995: 142)

Goldman sometimes writes of aesthetic properties and sometimes of objective properties. If I understand what he says elsewhere in his book, "objective properties" means "properties that objects have." Since aesthetic properties are properties that objects have, I take Goldman to mean that aesthetic properties are a kind of objective property. I assume that in this criticism, he is using "objective properties" to refer to objective properties that are aesthetic properties. In any event, since I speak only of aesthetic properties, and he is criticizing my view, he must be talking about properties that are aesthetic properties.

This first criticism gives the impression that I ignore the interaction of properties of artworks, but in *Evaluating Art*, following Sibley, I devote considerable space to this topic. Concerning Goldman's remark about the interaction of (*aesthetic*) properties to produce aesthetic value, there are several considerations.

I agree artworks may derive their *overall* aesthetic value from the interaction of their aesthetic properties. Whether they *mainly* do so I do not know, because artworks might have aesthetic properties that do not interact but nevertheless contribute to their overall value. In any event, my discussion of principles is not concerned with the *overall* aesthetic value of artworks. (That is the concern of the final chapter of *Evaluating Art*, which goes beyond the use of principles.) On my view, principles involve only the value or disvalue of the aesthetic properties that underlie the overall value or disvalue of artworks. The principles I have been concerned with have value predicates such as "valuable in some degree" and never predicates such as "good" or "excellent" which are typically used to indicate an artwork's positive overall value. Also, because he says "mainly," Goldman's remark allows for aesthetic properties that do not interact – if so, such aesthetic properties can be experienced without regard to other properties and their value can be accessed in isolation from them, although always in their presence.

On the other hand, consider a case in which some of an artwork's aesthetic value derives from the positive *interaction* of aesthetic properties, say, a poem in which its unified meter, its unified images, and its unified themes interact to produce a higher-order, overall aesthetic value. In such a case, it is easy to focus on each of the *specified*, interacting aesthetic properties and see that each is valuable even as each property interacts with the others to produce a higher-order aesthetic value. Consider a negative interaction, say, a poetic passage that has a unified meter that does not mesh with its theme, such as the one by Shelley that Beardsley cites – "Death is here, and death is there/ Death is busy everywhere." Beardsley notes that its jigging rhythm is incongruous with its subject's solemnity (Beardsley [1958] 1981: 237). In this case, one *must* focus on the unified jigging rhythm of the meter and the solemn theme in isolation from one another in order to see that the two together produce an incoherence. The unified rhythm is a valuable aesthetic property because of its unity, but its jigging character does not fit this particular context. When one focuses on – isolates on – an aesthetic property, say, the jigging rhythm of the meter, one does not cease to be aware of other properties, say, a solemn theme; it is just a matter of focusing attention. There is, thus, no problem in the cases of a work with multiple properties in focusing on its individual aesthetic properties in isolation from its other properties and assessing each's value.

In the above kind of cases, it would make no sense to say that the properties interact *unless we could see what is interacting with what*. The cases that Hutcheson cited long ago – irregular house plans, irregular windows, irregular anatomy – show that

George Dickie

an aesthetic property, even if it interacts with other properties, will stand out suffi-ciently to be seen to be disvaluable (or valuable).

I turn to Goldman's second criticism of principles, which asserts: "Where one such property dominates completely (say, formal unity with no expressive intensity or rep-resentational, or symbolic, complexity), the result is *usually* only an impoverished aesthetic experience (Goldman 1995: 142, emphasis mine). I see no reason to think that this claim is true. When one aesthetic property dominates completely, I think it might result in a powerful and satisfying experience. But even if the remark were true, one property dominating in an artwork does nothing to show that Goldman's claim that the considering of a property in isolation makes no sense. On the contrary, a dominating property, which is a good example of what Hume means by a charac-teristic "in high degree," would be particularly easy to focus on in isolation from whatever other properties the artwork might have.

Goldman's third criticism asserts: "Nor does Dickie's proposal do anything to counter the argument from taste. Even if we could consider aesthetic properties in isolation, it still seems that objective properties valued by one critic might not be valued by another" (Goldman 1995: 142).

The isolation clause is not supposed to counter such relativism; the clause is merely about focusing clearly on a property in order to react to it. Goldman's criticism is irrelevant to the significance of the isolation clause. Further, his charge of not coun-tering relativism is puzzling because I go to considerable length to point out that my view is a somewhat relativistic one, in that while I claim that many principles are undergirded by true generalizations that state there is universal accord about the sub-jects of the principles, I also clearly indicate that I am unsure whether some aesthetic qualities are so undergirded. What makes it even more puzzling that Goldman criti-cizes me for not countering relativism is that his own view is openly and explicitly relativistic.

Goldman's fourth criticism asserts: "Finally, there would be little point in consid-ering aesthetic properties in isolation, even if we could develop principles from doing so, if these properties are *always* transformed, often unpredictably, by the relations into which they enter in the aesthetic contexts in which they are actually found" (Goldman 1995: 42, emphasis mine).

I believe this claim is false. Shelley's unified jigging rhythm is not transformed by its interaction with the solemn theme of the poetic passage; it is just a unified, jigging rhythm and that is why it is inappropriate. In another kind of case, a unified meter and unified images are not transformed when they work to create a higher-order unity. These are properties that the passage has. To speak of properties being transformed is very perplexing. It sounds as though elegance might be changed into garishness or some other aesthetic property. It is true that aesthetic properties are produced by ele-ments in relation, but once the aesthetic property is thereby produced by its under-lying elements, then the work has that property. The aesthetic property may then interact positively or negatively with other aesthetic or nonaesthetic properties.

Goldman gives an argument against Beardsley that, if it worked, would also apply to my view. He writes, "the same property in a work that one critic calls unity another will call monotony" (Goldman 1995: 140–1). He thinks this is a problem for princi-ples because the property of the same set of elements is being regarded as a merit (unity) by one critic and a defect (monotony) by another critic, so that the emergent aesthetic property of a set of elements cannot be the subject of a positive principle. However, the monotony of a set of elements would be an instance of unity and would be positively, if minimally, valuable. Such unity, although valuable, becomes a liability of sorts when the artwork that has the elements has a low *overall* value. Such low overall value may come about in many ways: when the unity of a monotonous set of elements is the only value a work has, or when the work's other value properties do not add much value, or when the work's other value properties interact negatively with one another. What Goldman thinks is a problem is not one at all. It is just that when a work's unity derives from unrelieved repetition (a valuable property but of low degree), and the work has few, if any, other value properties, the work's unity is not sufficient to provide it with a high degree of overall value. "All instances of unity in a work of art, when experienced in isolation from the other properties of the work, are instrumentally valuable in some degree" is a perfectly good principle, as are many others.

Goldman's criticisms leave untouched the formulation of critical aesthetic principles with aesthetic qualities as their subjects and with their isolation clauses in place. Although Goldman does not comment on this point as a possible problem, I want to repeat here concerning the isolation clause what I said earlier about Sibley's *in vacuo* qualification: it does not mean that aesthetic qualities float unrelated to anything else; they depend on supporting elements in artworks. The isolation clause indicates that an aesthetic quality of an object is to be focused on independently of any relation to any other property of the object that would alter its polarity.

Finally, there is a way to formulate aesthetic principles without the isolation clause, using the language of interaction more directly. For example,

> All instances of gracefulness in a work of art, if they do not interact negatively with any other property or combination of properties of the work when they are experienced, are instrumentally valuable in some degree.

The interaction clause needs to refer only to negative interaction because if there were positive or no interaction, then the characteristic referred to by the subject of the principle will preserve its "instrumentally valuable in some degree" status.

Concluding Remarks

I have discussed only *aesthetic* principles here, because they are the only kind that Isenberg, Sibley, and Goldman, as well as Beardsley, were concerned with. Others, including myself, think there is another kind of principle involved in art evaluation, which I shall mention briefly to round things out. In *Evaluating Art,* I identified three kinds of cognitive value in artworks, but only two kinds of cognitive principles (Dickie 1988: pp. 101–55).

Using a mixture of Nicholas Wolterstorff's terminology (Wolterstorff 1980: 159–60) and my own, one kind of cognitive principle (the imitative) can be formulated. For example:

George Dickie

All instances of truth to actuality in some respect in a work of art, in isolation from the other properties of the work, are valuable in some degree.

I note here, as I did not in *Evaluating Art*, that this principle may have to be relativized and reformulated accordingly, because there may be some representations of actuality and truths that some persons cannot intrinsically value. So instances of this principles may have limited application, as some aesthetic principles may.

A second kind of cognitive principle is "referent-centered":

All instances of the representation in a work of art of anything valuable, in isolation from the other properties of the work, are valuable.

This cognitive principle is distinguished from the first-mentioned, accuracy-of-representation kind because it is the thing represented that is valued, not the accuracy with which it is depicted. Why the valuable thing represented is valuable is not a question for aesthetics. Such principles may also have to be relativized. The claim that there are cognitive principles should not be taken even to suggest that valuable things must be represented or that disvaluable things should not be represented.

A third kind of cognitive value is "supportive" cognitive value, which occurs when referential features of an artwork help produce a valuable aesthetic quality. In *Evaluating Art*, I did not formulate this kind of cognitive value principle, but such a principle would have the following form:

All instances of a referential feature of a work of art that are responsible for that work's having a valuable aesthetic quality, in isolation from other properties of the work, are valuable.

Robert Yanal was the first philosopher I know of to note this third kind of cognitive artistic value (Yanal 1978). The characteristics that are the subjects of cognitive principles, like those of aesthetics principles, when they occur in artworks, may not add value (when, for example, they do not work with other features of the work), may add a little value, may contribute substantial value, and so on.

My final point concerns conclusions about the specific, overall value of artworks. The evaluational principles I have defended have nonspecific, weak predicates such as "valuable in some degree." A work of art could have all the characteristics referred to by the subjects of every possible such evaluational principle, and all the statements about those characteristics together with all the statements of those principles can entail only a conclusion with the nonspecific value predicate "valuable in some degree." A conclusion with a strong, specific value predicate such a "good" or "excellent" could never be entailed in an argument involving only the evaluational principles defended here or in *Evaluating Art*.

In the last chapter of *Evaluating Art*, following Bruce Vermazen (Vermazen 1979), I tried to develop a scheme involving "comparison matrices" that can be used in a limited way to support overall conclusions about works of art with strong, specific value predicates such as "good," "excellent," "poor," "mediocre," and the like (Dickie

1988: 163–82). This scheme functions independently of critical principles and is thus not relevant to the present topic.

Note

I wish to thank Suzanne Cunningham, Ruth Marcus, George Bailey, and Robert Yanal for reading an earlier version of this paper and providing many useful comments.

George Dickie

References for Chapters 19 and 20

Beardsley, M. ([1958] 1981). *Aesthetics: Problems in the Philosophy of Criticism*. Indianapolis, IN: Hackett.

Danto, A. (1981). *The Transfiguration of the Commonplace*. Cambridge, MA: Harvard University Press.

Davies, S. (1990). "Replies to Arguments Suggesting That Critics' Strong Evaluations Could Not Be Soundly Deduced." *Grazer Philosophische Studien*, 38: 157–75.

Dickie, G. (1987). "Beardsley, Sibley and Critical Principles." *Journal of Aesthetics & Art Criticism*, 46: 229–37.

Dickie, G. (1988). *Evaluating Art*. Philadelphia: Temple University Press.

Dickie, G. (1996). *The Century of Taste*. New York: Oxford University Press.

Gerard, A. ([1759] 1978). *An Essay on Taste*, 3rd edn., ed. Walter J. Hipple. Delmar, NY: Scholars Facsimiles & Reprints.

Goldman, A. (1995). *Aesthetic Value*. Boulder, CO: Westview Press.

Goldman, A. (2002). *Practical Rules: When We Need Them and When We Don't*. Cambridge, UK: Cambridge University Press.

Hume, D. ([1757] 1987). "Of the Standard of Taste." In *Essays, Political and Literary* (pp. 226–48), ed. Eugene F. Miller. Indianapolis: Liberty Classics.

Hutcheson, F. ([1725] 1973). *An Inquiry Concerning Beauty, Order, Harmony, Design*, ed. Peter Kivy. The Hague: Martinus Nijhoff.

Isenberg, A. ([1949] 1979). "Critical Communication." In W. E. Kennick (ed.), *Art and Philosophy* (pp. 658–68). New York, St. Martin's Press.

Kant, I. ([1793] 1987). *Critique of Judgment*, trans. W.S. Pluhar. Indianapolis, IN: Hacket.

Kivy, P. (1973). *Speaking of Art*. The Hague: Martinus Nijhoff.

Levinson, J. (2001). "Aesthetic Properties, Evaluative Force, and Differences of Sensibility." In E. Brady and J. Levinson (eds.), *Aesthetic Concepts: Essays after Sibley* (pp. 61–80). Oxford: Clarendon.

Scruton, R. (1974). *Art and Imagination*. London: Methuen.

Sibley, F. (1959). "Aesthetic Concepts." *Philosophical Review*, 68: 421–50.

Sibley, F. (1974). "Particularity, Art and Evaluation." *Proceedings of the Aristotelian Society*, supplementary vol. 48: 1–21.

Sibley, F. (1983). "General Criteria and Reasons in Aesthetics." In John Fisher (ed.), *Essays on Aesthetics: Perspectives on the Work of Monroe Beardsley* (pp. 3–20). Philadelphia: Temple University Press.

Vermazen, B. (1979). "Comparing Evaluations of Works of Art." In W. E. Kennick (ed.), *Art and Philosophy* (pp. 707–18). New York, St. Martin's Press.

Walton, K. (1970). "Categories of Art." *Philosophical Review*, 79: 334–67.

Wolterstorff, N. (1980). *Art in Action*. Grand Rapids, MI: William B. Eerdman.

Yanal, R. (1978). "Denotation and the Aesthetic Appreciation of Literature." *Journal of Aesthetic and Art Criticism* 36: 472–8.

Zemach, E. (1987). "Aesthetic Properties, Aesthetic Laws, and Aesthetic Principles." *Journal of Aesthetics & Art Criticism*, 46: 67–73.

Further Reading for Chapters 19 and 20

Bender, J. W. (1995). "General but Defeasible Reasons in Aesthetic Evaluation: The Particularist/Generalist Dispute." *Journal of Aesthetics and Art Criticism*, 53: 379–92.

Dickie, G. (1997). "The Evaluation of Art." Part IV of *An Introduction to Aesthetics: An Analytic Approach* (pp. 125–66). New York: Oxford University Press.

Dickie, G. (2003). "James Shelley on Critical Principles." *British Journal of Aesthetics*, 43: 57–64.

Mothersill, M. (1984). *Beauty Restored.* Oxford: Oxford University Press.

Shelley, J. (2002). "The Character and Role of Principles in the Evaluation of Art." *British Journal of Aesthetics*, 42: 37–51.

Shusterman, R. (1981). "Evaluative Reasoning in Criticism." *Ratio*, 23: 141–57.

Urmson, J. O. (1950). "On Grading." *Mind*, LIX: 145–69.

Zemach, E. (1997). *Real Beauty.* University Park: Pennsylvania State University Press.

WHAT ARE THE RELATIONS BETWEEN THE MORAL AND AESTHETIC VALUES OF ART?

Artistic Value and
Opportunistic Moralism

Eileen John

> Paradoxical as it may seem, the only relevant qualities in a work of art, judged as art, are artistic qualities: judged as a means to good, no other qualities are worth considering; for there are no qualities of greater moral value than artistic qualities, since there is no greater means to good than art.
>
> (Bell 1915: 117).

Clive Bell here introduces us, first, to the expected autonomist distinction between judging art as art and judging it on moral grounds or, in Bell's conception, as a means to good. And he holds that the moral judgment of art is not relevant to judging art as art. But even he cannot resist building a bridge between moral and artistic value, as he asserts that the artistic judgment is relevant to the moral judgment of art, and that the artistic qualities of a work indeed have a kind of exhaustive relevance in determining its moral value. "To pronounce anything a work of art is, therefore, to make a momentous moral judgment" (Bell 1915: 115). Now, in nearly every way I disagree with Bell: I do not think of moral value in the terms of G. E. Moore, as Bell does, and one of my primary goals is to dispute the conception of judging art as art that Bell promotes. But the idea of the autonomist who is so confident that art as art has moral value is suggestive for my project. It suggests the difficulty of maintaining full separation or mutual autonomy of moral and artistic value, and it affirms a kind of global moral judgment of art that hearkens back to Plato. Though I will not affirm precisely that kind of global moral judgment, I will argue for a moral evaluation of art that is similarly ambitious in scope.

Generally, does the moral significance of works of art systematically add to or detract from their value of art? My basic answer is "No": moral significance does not systematically affect the value of art. A work that affirms moral truth can be artistically excellent, partly in virtue of its moral content, but a work that rejects moral truth can also be artistically excellent, in part because of its moral content. In this respect I endorse Daniel Jacobson's arguments against views such as Berys Gaut's that take morally commendable significance to count systematically in favor of a work's artistic value. I discuss some examples that I hope will lend support to Jacobson's claim that art can be artistically valuable in virtue of morally flawed content.

I then complicate this basic answer by considering what I think of as a statistically significant trend in the evaluation of art. The trend I assume is that, of the works of art that have moral significance, the works we tend to value *most highly* are ones that are in sympathy with the moral views we actually accept. We may value works whose moral commitments we condemn as truly excellent works of art, but I think these works are unlikely to show up on our lists of the most precious works of art, the ones we would most hope would survive as evidence of human artistic achievement. I have not done the empirical work needed to confirm the real existence of this trend, so its existence is open to challenge, but the evidence I have – of past practices of canonizing "masterpieces" and of anecdotal experience of works that people prize most highly – supports it, and I will proceed on the assumption that this evidence is representative.

One might explain this tendency in a way that had no bearing on the relation between moral truth and aesthetic value. Perhaps there simply are many more works conveying moral truth than moral error, so that works we find morally sympathetic have a statistically greater chance of showing up on "most valuable" lists. Or perhaps social pressures operate to ensure that our artistic preferences conform to our moral convictions. Those factors and others may indeed have explanatory power here, but I want to try out the idea that artistic evaluation makes room for prioritization of the moral, even while there is no systematic theory of the relation between moral and artistic value, as Jacobson argues. I call the view that allows for this prioritization "opportunistic moralism." I believe this view is true to the antitheoretical spirit, in the sense that it does not assume from the outset any particular relation between moral and aesthetic value. But it allows for the value of art to reflect the pervasive, though contingent, importance of moral truth within human life. Arguing for opportunistic moralism will require thinking about the notion of artistic value. What artistic value is, such that moral value is or is not relevant to it, needs more attention in the current debate.

Moral Flaws and Artistic Value

Let us begin by looking at how several theorists have argued, contra Bell, that moral value is relevant to artistic value. The category of narrative art, art that tells a story, has been the focus of attention. Noël Carroll argues, in defending a view he calls "moderate moralism," that

> the bottom line, aesthetically speaking, with respect to narrative artworks is that we are supposed to be absorbed by them. . . . But if it is the purpose of the narrative artwork to absorb the audience, to draw us into the story, to capture our interest, to engage our emotions, and to stimulate our imaginations, then it should be obvious that by engaging moral judgments and emotions, the author may acquit her primary purpose by secondarily activating and sometimes deepening the moral understanding of the audience (Carroll 1996: 235).

And with respect to the success of a work, "Securing the right moral response of the audience is as much a part of the design of a narrative artwork as structural components like plot complications. Failure to elicit the right moral response, then, is a failure in the design of the work, and therefore, is an aesthetic failure" (Carroll 1996: 233).

Carroll is pointing out that moral assessment is built into the project of many works of art, so that appreciating such works asks us to recognize the moral values and claims implicitly endorsed by the work and to endorse them and feel in sympathy with them ourselves. There is a scene in Jane Austen's novel *Emma* in which the heroine, Emma, says something cruel to Miss Bates, an older, impoverished woman who is a socially vulnerable target. Experiencing that as an excruciating moment – judging Emma's words to be cruel, feeling shame on Emma's behalf, and wincing at the effect on Miss Bates – are all responses that are integral to engaging with this work as it was designed. If the novel succeeds in "activating" all of these responses, because the novel's moral "take" on the scene agrees with ours, then in Carroll's view we can count the moral worth of the novel as an artistic virtue.

Along similar lines, Berys Gaut's "ethicism" argues that a work of art "manifests" its ethical or moral attitudes by prescribing moral responses in its audience (Gaut 1998). For instance, it has been argued that *Huckleberry Finn* manifests racist attitudes by calling for readers to be amused by Huck's and Tom Sawyer's treatment of Jim (Booth 1988: 465–7). Gaut argues that, "If a work prescribes a response that is unmerited, it has failed in an aim internal to it, and that is a defect" (Gaut 1998: 194). Specifically, "If these responses are unmerited, because unethical, we have reason not to respond in the way prescribed. . . . What responses the work prescribes is of aesthetic relevance" (Gaut 1998: 195). So, in Gaut's view, if a work prescribes morally virtuous responses, those responses are merited because they are morally virtuous, and meriting the responses it asks for counts in favor of the artistic value of the work. But if, on the other hand, as is claimed with *Huckleberry Finn*, the work prescribes an unethical response, that response is thereby unmerited, showing the work to fail in one of its internal aims, and so counts against its artistic value.

Gaut's argument is problematic, as others have noted (Carroll 2000: 375–6, Jacobson 1997: 177–8). Gaut seems to equivocate between notions of merited response: the response that is merited by how the artwork presents a situation and the response merited by an independent moral assessment of that situation. These responses may or may not be the same, but it seems that only the first kind of merit – whether the response is merited by what the work offers – is obviously relevant to artistic value in Gaut's sense. It would be begging the question to say that just because a response is immoral it could not be merited by what we find in the work of art.

I assume that Gaut and Carroll share an intuition that motivates their theoretical goals of integrating moral value into artistic value. They want their theories to account for the fact that they do in fact hold a work's morally flawed commitments against it as a work of art. In Gaut's case this leads to a *pro tanto* theory: a morally flawed work may still be very good, but its moral flaw counts *to that extent* against its value. In Carroll's case, as Carroll and Jacobson point out, the resulting theory does not officially rule out the contrary possibility of counting a work's moral flaws in favor of its artistic value: Carroll most centrally wants to establish that "sometimes" moral virtues and flaws are, respectively, artistic virtues and flaws (Carroll 2000: 377–8). But Carroll doubts the existence of works in which moral flaws counts as artistic virtues: "Few, if any, examples come to mind" (Carroll 2000: 380). I too often count a work's morally flawed commitments against its artistic value, but not always. The examples below are intended to suggest how experiences with narrative art might lead one not to share the moralists' motivating intuitions. These examples thus follow up on the argument made by Jacobson, in his "In Praise of Immoral Art," to the effect that moral defects can be aesthetic *merits* in a work of art (Jacobson 1997).

First consider Ernest Hemingway's story, "The Short Happy Life of Francis Macomber." The story concerns a man, Francis Macomber, who initially humiliates himself on a safari by running from a lion, and who as a result is scorned by his unpleasant, unfaithful wife and by the hunting guide (with whom the wife is unfaithful). The man finally redeems himself, however, through a courageous confrontation with a buffalo. After this moment of triumph and happiness, he dies. The moment of triumph is shown as having transformative effects on how the others see him: his wife realizes her contempt for him cannot be maintained – the balance of power in their marriage will change, and the guide reflects later that Macomber had finally grown up and become a man. I take the title of the work to be sincere: in this fictional world, these events really were a test of Macomber's worth, and he passed the test. He thus had an ultimately happy life and legitimately earned the others' respect.

Now, I do not accept either that running from a lion is truly humiliating or that confronting an angry buffalo is a genuine test of human worth. More generally, I do not see overcoming fear of this sort as crucially relevant to whether people have come into their own as persons and deserve respect. So I do not accept the moral framework that I see as supporting the whole drama of the story. But I really enjoy this work – as far as I'm concerned it is an excellent story. And I agree with Jacobson that, in a work of this type, it wouldn't make sense to say that it would be even better if it did not have this moral flaw; it just wouldn't be this story at all if it didn't celebrate precisely what it celebrates (Jacobson 1997: 182). The story needs its wrongheaded moral framework to be the excellent story that it is.

A second example: I have read Henry James's novel *The Portrait of a Lady* twice, once probably in my late teens and once in my mid-30s. The two readings elicited different responses to a morally crucial aspect of the novel: the heroine, Isabel Archer, has a nightmarishly terrible marriage, pervaded with deceit, manipulation, and unstinting efforts to break her will. At the end of the novel, she has a chance to leave this marriage and seek happiness, but she does not leave. In both readings I understood that within the novel this choice of fidelity and endurance made moral sense and was endorsed by the work. The first time around I also felt fairly strong distaste for her choice: I wished she could be a bit less dedicated to principle, a bit more lighthearted. The second time around I understood the rightness of her choice within the story more fully. I admired it, seeing her as accepting a moral challenge and taking charge of the meaningfulness of her life. But both times her choice struck me as deeply at odds with what we owe to someone else and what we owe to a vow made on the basis of deceit and manipulation. So I have a pretty sharp disagreement with one of the important moral attitudes manifested in the novel. It is a terrific novel, however, and, as with the Hemingway story, I don't see how I could count the fact of Isabel's choice and the embedded evaluation of that choice as a flaw, in the sense of being a failure of the novel on its own terms. In the second reading, I would say I came to appreciate the merit of her choice within the world constructed by the novel. But I doubt I ever had the approving emotional and moral responses that Gaut and Carroll might say the novel calls for, since I never endorsed her choice.

Finally, let's briefly consider two examples from the world of film, *Trainspotting* and *The Talented Mr. Ripley*. I take *Trainspotting* as an effort to represent a world in which a morally meaningful life is not possible. People move in an opportunistic way from one bleak and unprincipled set of habits or addictions to another, for example, from heroin addiction to middle-class consumerism. While one set of habits may be more viscerally revolting than another, it is not clear that in this world there are moral distinctions to be made between the different lives people lead. I appreciated this movie *because* it dismisses the moral commitments that I think indeed matter, and because it finds a way to convey what it might be like to live, form desires, and make choices within such an amoral world. The movie is also self-conscious about rejecting moral commitments (the characters, for instance, joke about whether knowing a lot about Sean Connery is a substitute for having moral fiber), so it asks to be treated differently than the Hemingway story or James's novel. The movie directly engages with the issue of how it may conflict with its audience's settled habits of moral response.

There is a different brand of amoralism in the film *The Talented Mr. Ripley* (and perhaps an even purer form of it in the Patricia Highsmith novel on which it is based), since in this fictional world it seems not so much that moral discernment isn't possible, but that it's not very interesting or important. The morally atrocious behavior of Ripley is portrayed at a somewhat flat psychological level: he kills people sometimes when they interfere with his desires, and he takes over another person's identity when it is a really attractive identity and he is capable of doing so. The audience's emotional responses are steered toward suspense and tension over whether Ripley will pull off his outrageously intrusive and deceptive behavior. The film's deprioritization of the moral is clearly one of the things it aims for, so it seems that to judge it as successful on its own terms we would have to count its ability to inhibit moral judgment in favor of the work. And I do count that in its favor: it is unsettling but interestingly unsettling to be worrying more about how the murderer will juggle all his deceptive schemes than about condemning his moral character.

The first point I hope to establish with these examples is that a work of art can be valued as art partly on the basis of its morally flawed commitments. Those commitments can be integral to the design of the work, to what it aims for on its own terms. If we think it works well with those commitments, I think we have to grant that the moral flaw is essential to the value of the work. It would not make the work better to remove the moral flaw, but would rather destroy the work. Gaut notes that his type of *pro tanto* moralist need not deny in such cases that removing the moral flaw would make the work worse. This kind of moralist can grant that a moral flaw may be intertwined with a work's artistic virtues in such a way that removing the moral flaw would remove those virtues as well and hence leave the work worse off (Gaut 2001: 346–8). Gaut here is interpreting the claim that the moral flaw is integral to the success of the work in terms of "nonremovability": the flaw cannot be removed without lessening the work's value. But I mean to make a claim for the flaw's positive value, as I assume Jacobson does as well. Seeing the moral flaw as part of the success of the work means that the moral flaw is pulling its weight along with the work's other virtues – it is not just a drag on the positive contributions of other features.

How could a moral flaw pull its weight in this way? A moral flaw contributes positively in precisely the ways we would usually say that morally commendable content does: the flawed content can show the meaning of events within the story; it can help one to understand characters' motivations, strengths, and weaknesses; and in general it can be one of the things one finds interesting and important in the work. Could moral evaluators like Gaut reply that the flawed content only appears to do these things? Once we confront it as mistaken, does such content lose its ability to support the meaning and interest of the narrative? Maybe it often will, but in those cases it is not the sheer mistakenness of the content that is the problem; such works fail to give us enough of a sense of how to work thoughtfully within the moral framework we reject. With regard to James's novel, the reader can get a sense of how to think of the marriage vow such that it would have a moral claim on someone even within a vile marriage. One can also see from the novel how Isabel's return to her marriage offers her a substantial, challenging, and even constructive new project in her life.

This line of thought echoes claims made by Karen Hanson, as she views a work of excellent but morally deplorable art as having the capacity to present morally deplorable ideas with cogency and to make us "understand how they fit together . . . and the relative force of the case this work makes for them." If a work thus provides "cogent thought and genuine deliberation," albeit in the service of deplorable ideas, the work has forms of power and grace that count as moral, intellectual, and artistic virtues (Hanson 1998: 221). Similarly, Matthew Kieran emphasizes the value of a work developing thick imaginative understanding, understanding that takes us beyond a superficial level (Kieran 1996, 1995). I have not given real evidence that James's novel, for instance, provides this kind of cogency, deliberation, and understanding, but that is what I would hope to do in an extended treatment. The moral flaw in an excellent work will not seem arbitrary, confused, or easily dismissable within the web of events, reasons, ideas, and feelings summoned up by that work.

Kieran has recently given a further argument for the claim that a work offering immoral experiences can be artistically valuable on those grounds (Kieran 2003). On this view, we need to understand the sources and meaning of immoral views, actions, and dispositions, in order to achieve full understanding and appreciation of moral goodness. If this cognitive need is served by experiencing a work of art – if the work makes an aspect of immorality experientially accessible and intelligible, then the immoral content of the work adds to the cognitive and artistic value of the work. Note that this "cognitive immoralism" is immoralism in the service of knowledge, both psychological and moral. A commitment to moral and psychological truth sets up the need for understanding of immorality, so perhaps this view does not grant the possibility of immoral art having value independent of our quest for moral knowledge. I will return to discuss the relation between Kieran's and my views below.

Perhaps, as Jacobson and I state that a moral flaw can be an artistic merit, while Gaut states that it cannot and Carroll doubts that it could, there is an intractable difference of taste in play. But I doubt that anyone is willing to leave matters at that level of disagreement – it seems as though there is something we can fruitfully argue about here. I want to push the burden of argument toward those who think a moral flaw cannot contribute positively to a work. I hope some of the examples sketched above are suggestive for this purpose. Why can't *Trainspotting* be valuable because it brings to life a depressing leveling of human aspirations, or *Ripley* because it shows disrespect for comfortable habits of moral condemnation? In general, there are many ways in which a story can be morally off-target, and it just seems likely that there would also be many ways to work well with those off-target moral sensibilities. It seems unreasonable to assume that artists working with divergent sensibilities, ones that at least some people would condemn, cannot work well with the moral values, concepts, and principles they endorse.

Accommodating Nonprescribed Responses

The second point I want to make, in light of the examples discussed above, involves challenging the "mismatched response principle" that Gaut, Carroll, and Jacobson share. Perhaps Jacobson's commitment to it is less central, but he says in his chapter in this volume, "Surely there is something to the thought that this sort of disparity between the responses a work prescribes and those it elicits is an aesthetic failure" (p. 347). This principle applies best to artworks that fall into familiar genre categories, where, for one thing, it is clear what responses are called for (Jacobson 1997: 167). I think there is often a much more complicated and evaluatively inconclusive relationship between the responses a work calls for and the responses it actually gets or would get from some sort of ideal audience. It often does not seem necessary for the success of a work that our responses match up with morally relevant responses prescribed by the work. Maybe this could be because a work does not prescribe such responses at all or prescribes conflicting responses. But I assume that Gaut and Carroll would say that such a work then does not manifest moral attitudes or commitments – calling for such responses is in their view just what it means for a work to manifest a moral attitude and hence to be evaluable on the basis of moral content. So for present purposes I will grant that any work that has moral commitments prescribes moral responses, but I want to read that prescription in a minimal sense. The work in some way sanctions or gives its blessing to certain responses. It makes certain moral evaluations the right ones with respect to the narrative. Even then, it does not obviously follow that provoking those responses, in us or in a morally ideal audience, is necessary for the full success of the work.

Rather, it seems most crucial that we recognize what the sanctioned moral responses are, where that can be a relatively intellectual kind of recognition. With "Francis Macomber" and *Portrait of a Lady*, it certainly matters that the reader understand what the work assumes is morally important. And probably some kind of feeling responses have to deepen and reinforce that understanding, and lend our responses the evaluative nuances that can be captured in feeling. But it seems enough of an artistic achievement if those feelings track and react thoughtfully to the moral nature of the work, while perhaps running along a "track" that is not sanctioned by the work. I think my initial strong distaste for Isabel Archer's choice, as well as my later rather grudging admiration for it, are both perfectly good reactions for James's work to provoke, meaning they are within the ballpark of responses that show the work succeeding in its aims. In each case the novel conveyed to me the moral significance of her choice, I found that significance to be coherent in relation to the work as a whole, and I found its moral significance to be interesting enough to react strongly to it. I think the novel could be a great novel even if that distaste or admiration were how morally ideal audiences would respond. With respect to the Hemingway story, for it to succeed a reader certainly has to feel the dramatic dynamic of the story, and that involves such things as feeling excitement and perhaps a sense of vicarious triumph when Macomber confronts the buffalo, and satisfaction when his wife has her rude awakening. But how morally deep do those responses have to be? Maybe I do endorse the story's vision of human fulfillment while feeling Macomber's triumph, or maybe I *try out* endorsing it, or maybe I have the dramatic responses in some way that lacks moral direction or commitment of any kind. We should consider more of the possibilities for appropriate response, ones that do not require us to be fully in sync with the story's prescriptions. Our responses should show that we grasp whatever counts as morally important within the narrative, but not necessarily that we judge and feel in the way deemed appropriate by the work.

The Contingency of Moral Value as Artistic Value

So far I have argued that neither a negative moral assessment of a work of art, nor responses that diverge from those sanctioned by the work, need interfere with the work succeeding on its own terms. I have worked with the assumption that, if we were to prove that moral value is relevant to artistic value, we would have to do so by showing that moral evaluation is relevant to the work's internal aims. Carroll makes this assumption particularly clear, as he speaks of aesthetic error as a work's failure "on its own terms, which is to say in terms of its own aesthetic aims" (Carroll 1996: 233), and he objects, for instance, to the idea of praising *Triumph of the Will* "for a use by us that it was never designed to serve" (Carroll 2000: 381). Our praise and criticism of art need to respond to the aims and design of art. This seems reasonable. Isn't that how we evaluate everything? We evaluate snow shovels based on the aims of snow shovels, and mailboxes in light of the aims of mailboxes. It wouldn't be fair to critique a mailbox because it wasn't a good snow shovel. So if a work of art doesn't have moral goals built into its aims as art, wouldn't it be inappropriate to evaluate it on moral terms? Gaut and Carroll thus argue for artistic failures that result from works not being able to achieve the moral responses they are designed to achieve.

However, this conception of artistic value as being set by a work on its own terms seems too impoverished. We can acknowledge that evaluation of art as art requires knowing how the work "conceives of itself" and what it aims for on its own terms, but that does not rule out evaluating it as art on other terms. We do this all the time, as we may evaluate a work partly by comparing it to other works that set somewhat different terms for themselves. For instance, early 1930s movie musicals with lavish production numbers look stilted and boring compared to slightly later Astaire and Rogers musicals. The earlier ones were not aiming to be casual, witty, and lighthearted in the same way, but we can still fault them for being more stilted and boring. Or consider how Casey Haskins discusses criticism of the film *Life Is Beautiful* as illustrating critics' use of evaluative standards that the film was not aiming to meet (Haskins 2001).

The acceptability of introducing perhaps unforeseen terms of evaluation for art seems in fact to be one of the things that is distinctive about art and artistic value. Works of art are not just like mailboxes with respect to evaluation. This is in part because the internal aims of works of art can be much more loosely constrained than the aims of a mailbox. There is some openness or lack of finality built into the horizon of possibilities for art: we do not assume we know in advance all there is to know about the sorts of intentions that can be realized, or how the resources of the artistic medium can be used, or what kind of expectations and interpretative practices an audience can bring to bear. This is related to a point Hanson makes in urging caution about judging the value of an experience "on its own terms," as she notes that "it is the character of those terms ... that is precisely what is often in dispute" (Hanson 1998: 219). In general, it seems that the project a work sets for itself can assume from the outset some expansiveness or innovation in the terms on which it is to be evaluated.

More broadly, though, I think that art is distinctive in that it is not content to be evaluated on its own terms, even in the more expansive sense just gestured at. It sets some terms and wants to satisfy them, but it also seeks some kind of larger, less circumscribed preciousness. By saying that art is not "content" with certain limited kinds of evaluation and "seeks" something further, I am not trying to animate art. I just mean that in our practices of evaluating art we have come to treat it as the sort of thing that rightly aims for this further preciousness. Works of art are sometimes compared to people in their uniqueness, and although I do not think art can have the value a person can have, I think there is something structurally similar in the ways a person or an artwork asks to be valued. As people, whatever the evaluative standards we actively strive to meet (trying to be more tidy, or more generous, or trying to pollute less), we are open to evaluation on criteria that we don't necessarily acknowledge or even understand. I assume that most adults have had moments of revelation of this sort: I come to see how I am failing in something I didn't even know I should have been trying to do, and I generally can't dismiss it by noting that, well, I wasn't trying to do that. We want to be valued roughly as decent members of the human race, people it was better rather than worse to have had around for a while, and that leaves us open to evaluation on a pretty unmanageable number of criteria.

In a structurally similar way, I think we pose the question of whether a work of art, whatever it may achieve on the terms it set for itself, earns a place in human life. This means that, even if greatness as a "witty, romantic, tap-dancing concoction" is exactly what a work aimed for *and* what it achieved, that does not after all make it inappropriate to assess it on other terms that it may not acknowledge or foresee. Is it worth having such concoctions? Can this object justify having a place in human experience? (And I'm not suggesting that tap-dancing concoctions cannot in fact justify their existence.)

So the idea is that there is an invitation built into the experience of art, inviting us to ask whether the work is worth having at all. We can do this sort of evaluation of a mailbox too ("why should we accommodate the delivery of mail anyway?"), but that kind of grandiose evaluation of the functional object changes the subject, takes the focus away from the virtues and vices of that mailbox to the value of the function it serves. I don't think that asking the similar question of a work of art takes the focus away from that work; it is still a question we could hope to answer by pointing out what is satisfying or not in the encounter with that work. But why include this in the "artistic value" of art? Why not call it the "all things considered" value of art, where that is something different from, bigger than, its artistic value? Basically, I do not know how to conceive of artistic value except by thinking about what seems characteristic of evaluation of art. And I think art evaluation has this distinctive character: it both takes into account explicitly aimed-for achievements and failures and spills out into something more like a justification of existence. That is the kind of terribly ambitious evaluative scope that matters to art. It seems unjustified to cordon off evaluations of how well works of art fare in this sense, as not being relevant to their value as art, if this is indeed characteristic of the value we seek in art. Let me note that the explicitly aimed-for aspects of the work are crucially relevant to the broader justification of existence. We ask whether something that achieves and fails at the particular things the work aimed for has justified its place in the world. Was it worth using the resources used by this work in this particular way? This conception of artistic value is thus distinguished from "all things considered" value, which could include such things as a work's value in stopping a bullet or its value in undermining a political movement, where those would often not be things a work of art aimed for on its own terms.

At this point the issue of moral value in art returns. I am not arguing that giving art this ambitious project automatically makes moral value central to artistic value. But I am supposing that art is in some sense an opportunist: it seizes on whatever it can in order to make itself matter to us in this larger way. If so, then seeking to convey and articulate moral truth will often be a good opportunistic choice. We happen to need to have moral matters explored and presented accurately, and we often take great satisfaction in that process as well. Presenting moral truth is thus a promising thing for a work of art to do, if it is to be valued as worth having around. Returning to Hemingway, I think he wrote an excellent story. But I will never value "Francis Macomber" as much as some other stories, including Hemingway stories, which deal well with moral challenges that I see as really weighing on us. The context for evaluation of art, in this sense, is a rich one that takes into account moral and nonmoral needs, problems, attachments, and aspirations of human beings. Kieran says, "Our evaluation of an artwork not only constitutes a judgment upon the work as art, it also substantially reflects our own concerns, goals, values, and imaginative appreciation of the world" (Kieran 1996: 348). I am not sure if Kieran is here isolating evaluation of art as art from the evaluation of art that reflects this rich context of human concerns, goals, and so on. Like Carroll, he speaks of what art aims at *qua* art, and perhaps he means to affirm the narrower notion of artistic value that is dominant in the current debate. But perhaps Kieran includes, as part of what art aims at *qua* art, the standing aim of justifying its existence as worthwhile in light of human needs and concerns. In that case our views would be very close. It seems easier to be a cognitivist, as Kieran is, and to argue for the artistic relevance of cognitive value at this rather grand level of evaluation, rather than in terms of an artwork's success "on its own terms." So I think Kieran's commitment to cognitivism should lead him to embrace this level of evaluation as properly artistic.

From the perspective of opportunistic moralism, there is no clear distinction between artistic evaluation of art and what Jacobson here calls "humanist criticism" of art. The humanist critic evaluates art in terms of its ability to serve important ethical functions, emphasizing its value as a vehicle of moral education. As long as such evaluations appeal to how a work of art uses artistic resources, the humanist praise or censure fits right into a process of artistic evaluation. If serving the humanist functions of education and cultivation of desire and perception turns out to justify a work's use of artistic resources, then those forms of humanist value would count directly toward a work's artistic value.

Let me conclude by making a few more points about what it means to think about art as an opportunistic moralist. To allow moral evaluation to contribute quite powerfully to the evaluation of art, even if a work does not aim to have moral significance and even if a work succeeds beautifully on its own no-moral terms, means being more of an old-fashioned moralist than either Gaut or Carroll. Is it so old-fashioned that it returns us to Plato's style of moralism, in which moral value appears to serve as art's primary "reason for being"? I see several related reasons why this view does not amount to a return to Plato's moralism. First, the fact that moral evaluation of art may take priority does not mean that art cannot justify its existence through realizing many other sorts of value; moral value has many competitors with respect to what can make art precious to us, such as humor, psychological insight, innovation, and sensory delight. Second, whether moral value does in fact trump various other kinds of value in the evaluation of art is a contingent matter. I take it that Plato condemned art that was morally flawed because it was morally flawed, so in his view the evaluative contribution of moral content was fixed by its very moral nature. In contrast, I am arguing that moral value is valuable in art because people care about moral value. Although the fact that we care about moral value runs extremely deep, I would say that its value is still a contingent matter, and its value in art hinges on art's need to provide something precious to us. If something other than morality became a more central preoccupation for us, that other thing could outweigh moral truth as a source of value in art. If we were, for instance, transformed into a community of perfect and perfectly invulnerable moral saints, I am not sure that moral value in art would matter at all. We might find it boring and useless. Third, on this view, even for people for whom morality is the central preoccupation, and who are quite far from being moral saints, it is not fixed in advance that moral *truth* count as a dominant source of preciousness. This view does not rule out the possibility of immoral art being the most valuable art.

Ethical Criticism and The Vice of Moderation

Daniel Jacobson

In recent work culminating in a prominent survey article, Noël Carroll (1996, 1998a, 1998b, 2000) has helped to reframe and reinvigorate debate over the ethical criticism of art. While the legitimacy of ethical criticism was for a long time suspect, it is now widely defended by philosophers of art including Carroll himself. Not every skeptic has been converted, of course, so debate once again thrives. Unfortunately, several different practices, which have diverse motivations and pose disparate philosophical problems, are often referred to as "ethical criticism." Although Carroll's work to clarify these issues has been highly influential and mostly salutary, it perpetuates certain problems afflicting this literature. I contend that the debate is in several respects confused, and that some of the most prominent positions – including Carroll's – turn out to deviate substantially from what they seem, and are claimed, to be.

The first common error is to suppose that there are two answers to the central question about the relation between moral and aesthetic values in art, when rather there are two *theories* on offer: moralism and autonomism. Roughly, *moralism* is the theory that the intrinsic moral merits and defects of an artwork also count as aesthetic merits and defects, respectively; whereas *autonomism* is the theory that such moral values are irrelevant to an artwork's aesthetic value. I will argue for the following claims here: (1) Carroll's influential taxonomy, which distinguishes between radical and moderate versions of both moralism and autonomism, is fundamentally flawed and should be discarded. (2) Moralism and autonomism fail to exhaust the philosophical possibilities on the relation between the moral and aesthetic value of works of art. Moreover, both theories are false, even in their best and most moderate formulations. (3) In fact, sometimes the very features of an artwork that render it morally dubious can contribute essentially to its aesthetic value, as I have previously argued (Jacobson 1997). Hence, while intrinsic moral defects in art *can* be relevant to its aesthetic value (contra autonomism), they *need not* be aesthetic defects – not even when they are aesthetically relevant (contra moralism). To put the claim most provocatively: the moral defects in a work of art can be among its aesthetic virtues. This claim has been called *immoralism* (Gaut 2001: 345–8, Kieran 2003), but the underlying position is better described as an antitheoretical view of the relation between moral and aesthetic value.

In her chapter in this volume, Eileen John offers some helpful reflections on the nature of aesthetic (or artistic) value – a crucial issue that is too often inadequately treated in this literature, as for instance in the present essay. She uses these reflections to advance a position that accepts my central antitheoretical claim, while perhaps challenging some of its underlying assumptions. Although I endorse several of John's arguments, I am skeptical about some of the implications for artistic value that she draws from the phenomenon she calls the "prioritization of the moral." Nevertheless, I will borrow from her "opportunistic moralism," as well as from Matthew Kieran's (2003) "cognitivist immoralism," in arguing for the antitheoretical position. Because neither John's moralism nor Kieran's immoralism is a general theory of the relation between the moral and aesthetic value of art, they are compatible with the rejection of both moralism and autonomism. Hence, my primary response to both John and Kieran is to welcome them to the fold, and to credit their contributions to the antitheoretical project.

What is Ethical Criticism?

There are several strains of ethical criticism, each of which figures in much recent work on the topic (Carroll 2000, Levinson 1998). First, the term is sometimes used to describe any moral judgment of art, including claims about an artwork's effects as well as judgments of its inherent moral character. Art might be morally dangerous, because of its bad consequences, without being immoral art properly speaking (Jacobson 1997). A second, more focused issue involves the humanist (or cognitivist) claim that art – especially narrative and dramatic art – can serve a distinctive and significant role in moral education (Carroll 2000: 360–74, Jacobson 1996). But these issues are distinct from questions about the aesthetic evaluation of artworks. One can admit the existence of immoral art without being committed to any claim about what relation, if any, the morally relevant features of an artwork bear to its aesthetic value. And one can embrace the humanist program without thinking that art need be any better aesthetically for better serving an ethical function, or reject humanism despite thinking that immoral art is deformed by its moral defects.

Most commonly, though, "ethical criticism" refers to the practice of bringing the moral praise or censure of an artwork directly to bear on its aesthetic evaluation. The fundamental question about ethical criticism and the autonomy of art concerns the legitimacy of this practice – that is Carroll's primary concern, and my own. Carroll has advanced his own program, which he calls "moderate moralism," first in an eponymous article and then in a reply to a counterargument on behalf of the view he calls "moderate autonomism" (Carroll 1996, 1998a). And Berys Gaut has contemporaneously developed a theory quite similar to Carroll's, though perhaps different in its strength and certainly defended on different grounds, which he calls "ethicism" (Gaut 1998, 2001).

Carroll's taxonomy of the debate over ethical criticism initially sorted the philosophical positions into two subdivided categories: radical autonomism, moderate autonomism, moderate moralism, and radical moralism (Carroll 1996). In his more recent survey of the literature (Carroll 2000), however, he also considers my claim that a moral defect or merit in an artwork can figure *either* as an aesthetic defect or merit, or can be aesthetically irrelevant. Though he is not persuaded of the immoralist claim that a moral flaw can be an aesthetic merit in an artwork, Carroll holds out the possibility that it can be assimilated by moderate moralism. "I'm not convinced that a moderate moralist must be antecedently committed one way or another on this issue on the basis of what the moderate moralist has said so far," he writes (Carroll 2000: 379 fn. 32). I will try to convince him otherwise. Such neutrality is impossible, because Carroll's theory has more commitments than he has yet acknowledged. Indeed, it *must* have these further commitments in order to be aptly called moralism at all.

Carroll's terminology suggests that there is a single dimension of disagreement along which the radicals and the moderates on both sides stand in an analogous relation, such that moderate moralism (MM) is to radical moralism as moderate autonomism (MA) is to radical autonomism. But that is not the case. In fact, the most salient analogy between these views undermines the taxonomy altogether: "radical moralism" is not a genuine form of philosophical moralism about art, and "radical autonomism" is not a genuine form of aesthetic autonomism. Or so I will argue. A different flaw infects the so-called moderate positions: MM is too weak and MA too strong to be perspicuously called moderate. Although I will not engage autonomism here, the debate over ethical criticism requires some attention to a problem with the way recent moralists have framed the opposing theory.

Several philosophers conflate autonomism with another, independent claim which has few if any serious philosophical defenders. For instance, Carroll claims that "philosophically, the autonomist is committed to the view that all artworks are separate from or exempted from considerations of morality" (Carroll 1998b: 127). But this somewhat murky idea is no part of the classical autonomism defended by A. C. Bradley (1959), Arnold Isenberg (1973), and others. Although Carroll's subsequent work is more accurately targeted, a vestige of this confusion lingers in his characterization of radical autonomism as the claim that "it is inappropriate or even incoherent to assess artworks in terms of their consequences for cognition, morality and politics" (Carroll 1996: 224). This is not a view about the relation of moral and aesthetic value at all; it is either a dubious moral claim (if framed in terms of appropriateness) or an unmotivated conceptual claim about morality (if framed in terms of coherence). In fact, the classical autonomists granted that the consequences of artworks can be morally assessed, and that art might be morally dangerous. As Bradley put it, "the intrinsic value of poetry might be so small, and its ulterior effects so mischievous, that it had better not exist" (Bradley 1959: 5). They simply insist that these ulterior effects are irrelevant to art's intrinsic (or aesthetic) value.

So radical autonomism is a straw man. Worse, the distinction between moderate and radical autonomism is misleading, since these are not claims of varying strength about a common subject matter. "Moderate autonomism" is simply autonomism, and "radical autonomism" is a different claim entirely. What about so-called radical moral-

Daniel Jacobson

ism, which "maintains that art should *only* be discussed from a moral point of view" (Carroll 1996: 229)? This isn't a claim about the relation of moral and aesthetic value either, nor is it a view worth taking seriously. As with autonomism, there is no basic agreement between the radical and moderate versions of moralism. The real action is between the nominally moderate versions of these theories (which will hereafter be called simply moralism and autonomism) and the denial of both theories (on so-called immoralist grounds).

How Moderate Can Moralism Get?

Consider Carroll's official definition of the nominally moderate positions, with attention to their different logical strength:

> Moderate moralism maintains that in some instances a moral defect in an artwork can be an aesthetic defect, and that sometimes a moral virtue can count as an aesthetic virtue. This opposes the view of moderate autonomism which admits that artworks can be morally defective and morally bad for that reason, but then goes on to say that the moral badness of a work can never count as an aesthetic defect. (Carroll 1998a: 419)

MM is characterized as an existential claim (that some moral defects in artworks are aesthetic defects, and some virtues aesthetic merits), whereas MA is a universal claim (that the moral defects and virtues of art never count as aesthetic values). This is a significant difference, which seems to show MM to be a much more moderate position – or at any rate a much weaker claim – than is MA.

Indeed, Carroll makes just this point when differentiating MM from Gaut's ethicism. As Gaut describes his view, "the ethicist principle is a pro tanto one: it holds that a work is aesthetically meritorious (or defective) *insofar as* it manifests ethically admirable (or reprehensible) attitudes" (Gaut: 1998: 182). The crucial difference between these views seems to be that, as Carroll puts it:

> Gaut seems willing to consider virtually every moral defect in a work of art an aesthetic defect, whereas I defend a far weaker claim – namely that sometimes a moral defect in an artwork can count as an aesthetic defect, or, as Hume would say, a blemish. Thus you can see that ethicism is a very strong position, while mine is, well, moderate. (Carroll 1998a: 419)

Carroll thus implies that ethicism is too strong to qualify as a moderate form of moralism, since it claims that artworks are inevitably blemished, to some degree, by their moral defects. In recent work, Gaut has restricted this claim somewhat, but he still frames ethicism as a universal generalization. In his view, "a work of art is always aesthetically flawed insofar as it possesses an ethical flaw which is aesthetically relevant" (Gaut 2001: 349).

One might think that, in light of this difference in logical strength between MM and ethicism, Carroll's "far weaker" view should be called moderate moralism and Gaut's view called radical moralism. But there is an obvious problem with this suggestion. Gaut's ethicism also qualifies as a version of MM according to Carroll's official definition. If *all* moral flaws in a work are (*pro tanto*) aesthetic blemishes, then *some* moral flaws are aesthetic blemishes (*a fortiori*). This isn't merely a semantic point, for it exposes a deep problem with Carroll's formulation of his view: the mere existential claim is too weak to count as moralism at all. In fact, my own view is simply that a moral defect of an artwork can figure as an aesthetic merit; I expressly allow that it can also be an aesthetic flaw or aesthetically irrelevant (Jacobson 1997). Thus my antitheoretical position too is compatible with what I'll call Carroll's *weak claim* – which presumably explains why Carroll thinks he isn't committed to rejecting it. Hence the weak claim is consistent with a view that is more naturally termed immoralism than moralism. Both titles are inapt, though, because an "ism" implies a theory. In what follows, I shall argue that there is no true *theory* of the relation between moral and aesthetic value, although there are of course some true propositions about it, such as the weak claim and its immoralist counterpart.

Consider John's suggestion in this volume that moral flaws in artworks are usually aesthetic defects, although they can also contribute positively to a work's aesthetic value. This may or may not be true; I am agnostic but will grant the claim for argument's sake. Unless there is some nontautological way to codify the relation between moral and aesthetic value, however, this claim does not amount to a theory. Compare the claim that tragedies are usually better than comedies – which, to judge by the canon (if one still can), also has some prima facie plausibility. Even is this were true, it would not make tragedy a *pro tanto* aesthetic virtue in a dramatic work; surely a great comedy is not even a little bit worse for failing to be a tragedy. We shall see that Gaut (2001) attempts to identify a specific type of moral defect that counts as a *pro tanto* blemish, while granting that other types might be aesthetically irrelevant. Were this project successful, he would have defended a view worth calling moralism – but I will argue against even this qualified version of his theory.

Yet Carroll's official gloss of MM, defined solely in terms of the weak claim, is not moderate but faux moralism. Even the most minimal version of moralism must hold that there is some kind of systematic difference between the role that the moral defects and virtues of an artwork play in constituting its aesthetic value. Carroll's problem is that he fails to acknowledge that he does indeed have such a theory: a general thesis about the relation of moral and aesthetic value. For now I will simply note that moralism about art must accept the following two propositions in order to be properly called moralism at all. First, it must hold that the moral virtues and defects of artworks are *sometimes* relevant to their aesthetic value. But this is just the rejection of autonomism, which is also compatible with the antitheoretical view. Second, moralism must hold that *whenever* a moral defect (or merit) in an artwork is in fact aesthetically relevant, it must count as an aesthetic defect (or merit). The position defined by these two claims could be called moderate or even minimal moralism, but it's most perspicuous simply to call this moralism.

Emotional Engagement and Immoral Art

Recall the official statement of MM, that "sometimes a moral defect in an artwork can count as an aesthetic defect, or, as Hume would say, a blemish" (Carroll 1998a:

419). The famous discussion to which Carroll alludes is from "Of the Standard of Taste," where Hume claims that when an artwork deviates from our moral standards, "this must be allowed to disfigure the [work], and to be a real deformity" (Hume [1757] 1987: 246). Hume's talk of blemishes, deformity, and disfigurement signal that he is speaking about the work's beauty: what we would now call its aesthetic value. He goes on to explain why moral deviation should count as a blemish when deviation from our beliefs and manners does not – an explanation that focuses on considerations about our emotional engagement with narrative and dramatic art. This story is the foundation of Humean moralism, of which both Carroll's and Gaut's theories are modern developments. They share both Hume's conception of what constitutes an intrinsic moral flaw in an artwork and why such flaws are aesthetically relevant. These are complex issues which demand more treatment than I can here afford (for a more detailed discussion see Jacobson 1997: 158–62). Although I reject the moralist conclusion, I am broadly amenable to this account, so I can accept the Humean conception of immoral art and aesthetic value not merely for argument's sake – though surely it's only a partial and simplified account of either concept.

To understand Hume's explanation of why moral defects in a work are blemishes, when they are, consider his criticism of the authors of antiquity. Hume declares, with curious confidence, that "we are not interested in the fortunes and sentiments of such rough heroes" as those sometimes portrayed even by Homer and the tragedians, and "we cannot prevail on ourselves to enter into [the author's] sentiments, or bear an affection to characters, which we plainly discover to be blameable" (Hume 1987: 246). Of course, we're not supposed to have affection for some characters, particularly the most vicious; but surely Hume does not mean to suggest otherwise. His focus is on "the author's" sentiments: those responses the work prescribes us to have (or to imagine having) toward its characters and events. When we are called upon to view vicious characters as admirable but cannot do so, we will then be unable to appreciate the work. "I cannot, nor is it proper that I should, enter into such sentiments," as these works prescribe, Hume writes; hence, "I never relish the composition" (Hume 1987: 246). Clearly this is not meant merely as an observation about his tastes: the crucial point isn't that one *cannot* but that one *should not* enter into such sentiments. Moreover, this is a general claim about how we should respond to works that prescribe emotions it would be "blameable" to feel.

Humean moralism thus involves an account both of what constitutes an intrinsic moral flaw and an aesthetic defect in art. Immoral art prescribes unethical emotional responses. This picture, though overly simplified, accords with Gaut's gloss of immoral art as "manifesting reprehensible attitudes" and Carroll's characterization of its "evil perspective" (see below). When this is the case, the Humean suggests, it is improper to respond to the work as it prescribes; and when we don't respond as prescribed, we cannot relish the work. As Carroll puts it, immoral art fails to secure *emotional uptake* (or equivalently "psychological uptake"), at least for readers like himself – Hume's vague "we." Surely there is something to the thought that this sort of disparity between the responses a work prescribes and those it elicits is an aesthetic failure. If, as Oscar Wilde remarked about Dickens's novel *The Old Curiosity Shop*, "One must have a heart of stone to read the death of Little Nell without laughing," then that must count as a blemish on the work – in this case, the flaw of sentimentality. (However, I endorse

John's caveat here that we must not take our emotional responses in aesthetic contexts at face value, especially when they have fictional objects. Such responses often seem to involve something like pretense [Walton 1990]; perhaps they are tried out, or put on, rather than truly elicited or endorsed.)

Carroll asserts quite generally that when a work fails to secure emotional uptake, this is an aesthetic flaw. For example, "[T]ragedy will fail on its own terms – terms internal to the practice of tragedy – when the characters are of the wrong sort. This failure will be aesthetic in the straightforward sense that it is a failure of tragedy *qua* tragedy" (Carroll 1996: 232). There are many ways in which the characters of a tragedy can be of the wrong sort, of course, some of which have nothing to do with morality. Sometimes, though, artworks are morally and aesthetically flawed *for the same reason*. This will be true whenever the same feature of the work explains both its moral defect (why the artwork is immoral) and its aesthetic defect (why it fails to secure emotional uptake). Then "the evil perspective [of an artwork] is an ineliminable factor in explaining why, as a matter of fact, it is morally defective and in explaining why, as a matter of fact, it is aesthetically defective" (Carroll 1998a: 423).

Although I accept the basic framework of this argument, suitably developed, I think it double-edged for Carroll. If he is right, then he must be prepared to admit that were the "evil perspective" of an artwork ever an ineliminable factor in explaining why the work is aesthetically valuable, this would show that moral defects can be aesthetic virtues in a work – which is precisely the immoralist claim. It would be ad hoc, if not flatly inconsistent, for Carroll to defend moralism this way while denying an analogous defense of immoralism. Of course, he need not grant that an artwork's evil perspective ever *is* an ineliminable factor in explaining why, as a matter of fact, the work is aesthetically valuable. And, as we shall see, he is inclined to doubt it.

This rough summary reflects a superficial problem with Carroll's exposition of the argument, inherited from Hume. He sometimes states the central claim about aesthetic value in causal or dispositional terms, for instance by writing: "An artwork that fails to secure emotional uptake is aesthetically defective on its own terms" (Carroll 2000: 377). But his view cannot really be as simple as this dictum suggests, because not every failure to secure emotional uptake signals an aesthetic flaw. Sometimes the audience, rather than the work, is at fault for its inability to respond. So the failure of a work to secure emotional uptake from its actual audience is not sufficient to show it blemished; moreover, Carroll grants that this is not a necessary condition either. Even if the work does not actually deter emotional uptake, it will be aesthetically defective "if it is such that it would daunt the work's prescribed responses for *ideally morally sensitive audiences* because it is ethically defective" (Carroll 2000: 378, my emphasis). Although this idealization is problematic, its function is clear enough: it is supposed to circumvent worries about real audiences, in order to determine what responses a work merits – which might differ from those it actually elicits.

Carroll's argument thus assumes that the *aesthetic* responses of an ideally *morally* sensitive audience will be correct. Hence, whenever a work would deter emotional uptake from a morally sensitive audience because it is morally defective, this defect counts as a blemish; but any moral defect that would not deter uptake from such an audience is aesthetically irrelevant. Carroll asserts this forthrightly:

Morally defective portrayals may elude even morally sensitive audiences and may require careful interpretation in order to be unearthed. Of course, once they are excavated, they can be ethically criticized. But the moderate moralist will not, in addition, criticize them aesthetically, if they are so subtle as to escape a morally sensitive audience. Moderate moralism is not, then, committed to the proposition that every moral defect in an artwork is an aesthetic defect. (Carroll 2000: 378).

But MM avoids this conclusion only because defects that would not deter a morally sensitive audience are irrelevant to its aesthetic value. Carroll is therefore committed to the second tenet of moralism: the claim that *whenever a moral defect is aesthetically relevant, it counts as an aesthetic defect.* So Carroll is a moralist after all, notwithstanding his official definition of MM; moreover, as I have contended, the commitments of MM exceed the weak claim and conflict with immoralism.

It's unclear whether any substantial difference remains between the two authors on whom we've been focusing. While Carroll's view is stronger than advertised, Gaut now expressly restricts his ethicism to those moral flaws that are aesthetically relevant (Gaut 2001: 349). Moreover, Gaut's merited response argument (MRA) also trades on Humean claims about emotional engagement. The following sketch is taken almost verbatim from Gaut (2001: 351):

1 A work is intrinsically ethically flawed just in case it manifests ethically reprehensible attitudes by prescribing or inviting its audience to have certain unethical responses.
2 One ground for holding a response to be unmerited is that it is unethical.
3 If an artwork prescribes responses which it does not merit, then that is an aesthetic failure in the work.

Therefore, he concludes that the ethical flaws manifested in prescribed but unethical responses are (always, *pro tanto*) aesthetic failures in the work. The first premise is the general account of immoral art with which we've been working. The second premise is more problematic, though, because it trades on an unanalyzed notion of merit for emotional responses. Of course, to judge an emotional response unethical – that is, wrong or vicious to have – is to think it in some way unmerited. But there are various ways in which such responses might fail to be merited, not all of which bear on whether its object has the evaluative property the response purports to descry. Purely instrumental (or strategic) considerations, for example, surely must be granted to bear on whether an emotional response is morally permissible. Yet Gaut grants that this sort of consideration, about the "causal powers of works to affect audiences" does not play any role in constituting an artwork's aesthetic value (Gaut 2001: 342–3).

On this point I agree with Gaut and Carroll, against John. I doubt that her "opportunistic moralism" can seize on *whatever* features justify a work's existence or make it precious to us, while continuing to maintain a focus on artistic value. Surely some purely instrumental considerations about a work – such as the role of *Uncle Tom's Cabin* in the abolitionist movement – serve to justify its existence. But the fact that the world is better for that novel does not speak to how good a novel it is. John advocates counting such instrumental considerations as part of a work's artistic value whenever they are caused by the work's deployment of artistic resources. This seems too capacious a conception of aesthetic or artistic value, however. Some things that make particular works of art precious to us – that this was "our song," say – are not features that make it worthy to "survive as evidence of human artistic achievement" (John, this volume, p. 332). Indeed, I wonder how many of our most deeply held preferences derive from such a perfectionist criterion and, hence, how much to make of John's "prioritization of the moral." Isenberg gives us reason to be skeptical of the idea that this reflects something deep about artistic value, noting that "people who are warmed by agreement with a poem or distracted by disagreement are always mistaking those reactions for perceptions of value" (Isenberg 1973: 96). However, insofar as Isenberg thinks judgments based on such reactions are always mistaken – that is, insofar as he is defending autonomism rather than attacking moralism – I consider this claim overstated. I'll say a bit more about this presently.

Gaut's merited response argument is clearly meant to concern the sort of merit that bears on a work's intrinsic, aesthetic value. He thus offers the same uncontroversial examples Carroll uses, in support of his third premise: "tragedies which do not merit fear and pity, horror films which do not merit horror, comedies which do not merit amusement, and so on, all fail aesthetically" (Gaut 2001: 351). The trouble is that not all reasons an emotional response is unethical are relevant to whether its object is as the emotion presents it: amusing, disgusting, fearsome, enviable, and so forth. Most obviously, strategic reasons not to be amused by something do not bear on whether it is funny, and arguably moral considerations concerning whether or not to have the response – to be afraid, disgusted, amused, and so forth – are not directly relevant either (D'Arms and Jacobson 2000). Consider an analogy with comic moralism: the view that a moral defect in a joke is always a comic defect, which renders it less funny. I have argued against comic moralism at length elsewhere (Jacobson 1997: 173–9), and I won't repeat those arguments except to rectify certain misunderstandings.

An analogous argument to MRA can be given for comic moralism, since jokes and comedies that do not merit amusement fail aesthetically; and one reason to hold amusement to be unmerited, according to Gaut, is that it is unethical. This puts pressure on him to accept comic moralism, which he does:

> [T]he immoralist is wrong about humor. He or she ignores the complexity of our reactions to vicious jokes. Sometimes we are indeed amused by them, but we may judge on reflection that they were not really funny: for the notion of the funny is not a merely causal one (what causes amusement) but a normative one (what merits amusement). (Gaut 2001: 348)

Despite Gaut's implication to the contrary, the argument against comic moralism is founded on the point that *funny* is a normative concept. The immoralist claim about humor is not merely that some vicious jokes do in fact amuse people – which can hardly be denied – but that some (though not all) such jokes are genuinely funny. More precisely, sometimes it is exactly what is offensive about a joke that makes it funny. Gaut, by contrast, must claim that every offensive joke is to some extent comically flawed by its moral defect. Yet surely it is no accident that so many jokes have

Daniel Jacobson

a butt, or otherwise express hostility and other dubious feelings. Much comedy transgresses the boundaries of moral propriety, and although we may judge on reflection that what amused us wasn't really funny, often we do not. A clear-eyed look at our reactions to offensive jokes shows that they are deeply conflicted. Surely Ted Cohen is right to caution readers of his recent book on jokes to "not let your conviction that a joke is in bad taste, or downright immoral, blind you to whether you find it funny" (Cohen 1999: 83). As Cohen's remark implicitly suggests, it's the moralists who fail to acknowledge the complexity of comedy, by refusing to endorse in any sense what they are unwilling to endorse morally.

Even Carroll grants not only that some immoral jokes are funny but also that they are no less funny for being offensive, because the moral indictment against them "has no bearing on [the joke's] status as an aesthetically effective species of humor" (Carroll 2000: 377). Obviously, I think Carroll is right to reject comic moralism, but he cannot shrug off the analogy with Humean moralism so blithely. Despite Gaut's uncharitable treatment of the argument against comic moralism, he seems better to appreciate why this argument puts pressure on the Humean moralist. There is a deep structural similarity between the two positions: both fundamentally involve emotional responses and advance a general claim about their warrant. This is still just an analogy, as all sides grant – notwithstanding Gaut's suggestion to the contrary (Gaut 2001: 377). Hence, it's possible that comic moralism is false but moralism about art true. Yet both jokes and pure comedies prescribe amusement and are funny insofar as they warrant it. This alone should make it uncomfortable for a Humean moralist to acknowledge the close connection between comedy and cruelty.

Indeed, this point poses a dilemma for Carroll's conception of the ideally morally sensitive audience. Would such an audience be amused by one of those jokes, which Carroll grants exist, that are no less funny for being offensive? If so, then we cannot assume that this idealized audience will always respond virtuously. It will then be an open question whether the audience might indulge in other prescribed responses to "morally defective portrayals," even when (as with the joke) these defects are not so subtle as to go undetected. This is especially problematic for Carroll because he grants, properly, that an audience can be overly moralistic – it can be "neurotically" morally sensitive (Carroll 2000: 379). On the other hand, if an ideally morally sensitive audience would inevitably be offended rather than amused by such a joke, then this idealized audience cannot be the measure of comic value. Analogously, an ideally morally sensitive audience cannot be assumed to track aesthetic value perfectly either. Thus Carroll's idealization obscures the possibility of a tension between moral and aesthetic sensitivity. Similarly, Gaut's MRA, with its undifferentiated notion of merit, conflates the different respects in which an emotional response can be endorsed or criticized.

The Rejection of Moralism

Recall Carroll's argument against autonomism: that sometimes an artwork's evil perspective "is an ineliminable factor in explaining why, as a matter of fact, it is morally defective and in explaining why, as a matter of fact, it is aesthetically defective" (Carroll 1998a: 423). My argument against moralism is analogous. If an artwork's evil perspective is ever an ineliminable factor in explaining why it is aesthetically valuable, then Carroll seems forced to acknowledge that a moral defect in an artwork can be an aesthetic virtue – and, hence, that moralism is false. Carroll and Gaut have responded somewhat differently to this argument. Carroll thinks there are few, if any, examples to be found of "immoral artworks that are aesthetically commendable because of their moral defectiveness" (Carroll 2000: 380). While Gaut doubtless agrees, he also argues that even were there incorrigible works, whose moral flaws cannot be eliminated without destroying their aesthetic value, this would not imply that moralism is false. Rather, "The moralist can consistently agree with the immoralist that removing a moral flaw might not make a work all things considered aesthetically better, but she will maintain, nevertheless, that insofar as a work is immoral, it is aesthetically flawed" (Gaut 2001: 347–8).

Gaut supports this argument with an example. Suppose your dear old aunt asks you if you like her hat – which you find dreadful. We're to imagine that there is no graceful alternative: your choice is between lying for the sake of kindness or telling the truth at the expense of her feelings. Gaut concludes that although it's best to praise the hat, your act is still morally tainted for being a lie. Nevertheless, "it does not follow that improving the act *in a particular respect* (by telling the truth) would *all things considered* improve it" (Gaut 2001: 347, his emphasis). The act is morally flawed despite being the best available option, he suggests, because lying is *pro tanto* morally bad. For the sake of argument, let's accept both Gaut's specific conclusion (which seems right) and his moral principle (about which I have my doubts). Although Gaut's example isn't unrealistic, it's important to note that the bind is a contingent feature of the circumstances. Had you thought to beat Auntie to the punch with something cleverly ambiguous ("Now *that's* a hat!"), then you could have spared her feelings without lying.

Gaut's argument thus does not speak to the central claim of immoralism, which is not merely that, as it happens, one cannot have the aesthetic value of an incorrigibly immoral artwork without its moral defect – as one cannot spare Auntie's feelings without deceiving her – but that such works cannot be morally sanitized even in principle. If what is funny about some jokes is just what is cruel about them, then their offensiveness is integral to their humor. Analogously, the immoralist claims that some works of immoral art are morally flawed and aesthetically valuable for (some of) the same reasons. John puts this point nicely. "Seeing the moral flaw as part of the success of the work means that that the moral flaw is pulling its weight along with the work's other virtues," she writes, " – it is not just a drag on the positive contributions of other features" (John, this volume, p. 336). Gaut's commitment to a *pro tanto* moralist principle forces him to deny, with Carroll, that a moral flaw can ever contribute positively to a work's aesthetic value.

Both Gaut and Carroll claim that moralism gets it right about our moral and aesthetic judgments – it best tallies with them. But tally arguments rely upon controversial value judgments. Indeed, Isenberg thought that autonomism tallies better with our aesthetic judgments than does moralism. "If factual or moral truth is the standard" of criticism, he wrote, then "some very great works will have to be condemned" (Isenberg 1973: 85). Although I cannot argue this point here, I think that several of the classical autonomists, such as Isenberg, should have contented themselves with

Daniel Jacobson

rejecting moralism rather than endorsing autonomism. Perhaps they are best understood as advocating an antitheoretical position which they never quite articulate. However that may be, Matthew Kieran has recently argued for a view he calls "cognitive immoralism" which nicely describes the position I am suggesting:

> We value many works which are morally problematic because the ways in which they are morally defective enhance our understanding. Thus there can be, and indeed are, works whose value as art is enhanced in virtue of, rather than despite, their morally defective character. What matters is not so much a question of whether the moral perspective of a work is what we take to be the right one but, rather, whether it is conveyed in such a way that we find it intelligible or psychologically credible. (Kieran 2003: 72)

Kieran here places the immoralist claim within a view of aesthetic value on which "what matters is whether an artist can get us to see, feel and respond to the [fictional] world as represented" (Kieran 2003: 72), rather than our ultimate assessment of the work's virtue.

While the antitheoretical position I've championed is amenable to this account of aesthetic value, it does not presuppose this or any other specific view. Ironically, Carroll has misconstrued my argument on exactly this point, by suggesting that the immoralist claim is based on humanist considerations about the ways in which immoral art can induce us to empathize with alien perspectives (Carroll 2001: 380–1). While I have offered some suggestions about how best to develop humanism (Jacobson 1996, 1997: 193), these considerations are tangential to the argument against moralism. Humanism must take the effects of art seriously because they are morally relevant, but my view of aesthetic value (like Carroll's and unlike John's) rules out all such purely instrumental effects of a work. The fact that some works of immoral art can serve a humanist function is indeed something like "a strategic value from a certain, perhaps liberal, point of view" (Carroll 2000: 381). Yet it is not the social or epistemic importance of such works, but the significance of the aesthetic experience itself – what artists can get us to see, think, and feel – that matters.

Because tally arguments are inherently controversial, I have primarily argued for the antitheoretical position abstractly rather than by example. Nevertheless, Carroll has challenged me to deliver a counterexample to moralism, claiming that he can find few, if any, examples of works that are aesthetically valuable for the same reason they are morally suspect. But I think such cases abound. Ironically, I find it at least arguable that *all* of Carroll's own examples of putatively disfiguring moral flaws in art qualify, even the one he considers his most unimpeachable example of a work blemished by its moral flaws: Bret Easton Ellis's infamous novel, *American Psycho*. In fact, Anthony Lane makes this argument for me in his review of Mary Harron's film version. Although the novel was "damned before it hit the stores, and all but flattened by the charge of pathological misogyny" (Lane 2000: 124), he thinks this initial response inadequate: "Now, at a distance, the book reads better than it did; it feels lit with a kind of cold hellfire, and Ellis has become our most assiduous tour guide . . . to the netherworld of the nineteen-eighties" (Lane 2000: 124).

Satire demands to be played straight, Lane observes, and requires that the author hold his nerve. Patrick Bateman, Ellis's satirical icon of the epoch, "is a type taken to the limit, and, if his story did not offend us, then Ellis and Harron would not be doing their job" (Lane 2000: 124). Moreover, Lane's ultimate praise of the film supports the rejection of comic moralism. "*American Psycho* is a fierce and timely piece of work," he writes, which "makes you laugh in ways, and at times, that should hardly be funny at all" (Lane 2000: 125). Of course, this is exactly the substance of the moralist's complaint against the work – although clearly Carroll himself is not amused. And, Gaut's defense of comic moralism notwithstanding, Lane certainly isn't saying that he found himself amused by something he judges, on reflection, not to be amusing. Rather, he suggests that we routinely do *not* respond to art as if we were real-life spectators of its events. This is a crucial insight, worthy of far more discussion than I can here afford, which raises a deep challenge to certain presuppositions of Humean moralism about our emotional engagement with art (see Jacobson 1997: 186–7).

I have argued that the notion of an ideally morally sensitive audience cannot bear the weight placed on it by Carroll's argument. Lane's argument now casts doubt on Carroll's second critical device, the "inappropriately sympathetic" character – by which he means one with whom we are prescribed to sympathize but cannot, because of his or her viciousness. The trouble is that we routinely feel things in response to works of art that would be appalling, were they responses to real-life people and events. Yet we typically don't even notice. Isenberg says: "In practical life it would be our business to correct the distorted evaluations which result from the nearness and prominence of certain objects [in works of art] . . . and not to bother about the conflicts in the soul of Macbeth when he is every day murdering innocent people" (Isenberg 1973: 84). Carroll responds as if this were an argument that *Macbeth* is therefore an immoral work of art, but that isn't the point. He claims, "the case is unconvincing because it is sympathy for a good man gone bad. The play does not prescribe that viewers exculpate Macbeth" (Carroll 2000: 380 fn. 34). But this response is far too blithe, as *American Psycho* does not prescribe that viewers exculpate Bateman either.

Although Carroll suggests that it is permissible to feel sympathy for Macbeth because he is a good man gone bad, one must wonder how bad you can go before you simply get rotten. Isenberg notes that if we took Macbeth's crimes seriously – as we do not – he would be too heinous to deserve our sympathy; hence, by Carroll's own lights, his downfall would not be tragic. Yet Macbeth and Hamlet are tragic figures, of course, partly because we just don't take seriously the moral standards we routinely and uncritically apply in responding to art. We know full well that Rosencrantz and Guildenstern aren't real people, or even fully drawn characters worthy of our emotions, but plot devices who function to illustrate that in matters not involving his father and his fate, the young prince has no problems with indecision. Perhaps this is a failure of moral sensitivity, and the correct aesthetic verdict should be harsher; but that conclusion, as Isenberg notes, would condemn some very great works indeed. Again, I am not proposing *Macbeth* or *Hamlet* to be cases of immoral art. My point is rather to demonstrate how slippery are the notions of the inappropriately sympathetic character and the morally sensitive audience.

Ethical critics need to face up to our curious habits of moral judgment and emotional response in fictional (and, more broadly, aesthetic) contexts. This would involve, among other things, dealing with the concept of an antihero and coming to grips with how ready we are to dispatch innocent but minor characters to their doom. These are

Daniel Jacobson

difficult tasks, which neither philosophical moralists nor practicing ethical critics, who tend to adopt particularly anodyne moral stances, have seriously undertaken. But as hard as it is to find critics willing to disparage virtue and the life-affirming in literature, it is much less difficult to find artworks that deliberately set themselves up against life and love. Some of these are very formidable works of art, I continue to think, not despite their problematic moral stance but because of it.

This claim ultimately rests not on the force of any specific and inevitably controversial example, but on general considerations which readers must bolster by adducing cases that fit their own evaluations. I anticipate that some readers will remain unsatisfied, however, because I have not offered them a straightforward instance of an artwork whose aesthetic value depends upon its morally dubious features. So, for those who would praise the life-affirming and morally salutary in art, and who are unwilling to accept arguments in aesthetics without a supporting example:

This Be the Verse

They fuck you up, your mum and dad.
They may not mean to, but they do.
They fill you with the faults they had
And add some extra, just for you.

But they were fucked up in their turn
By fools in old-style hats and coats,
Who half the time were soppy-stern
And half at one another's throats.

Man hands on misery to man.
It deepens like a coastal shelf.
Get out as early as you can,
And don't have any kids yourself.
(Larkin 2003: 142)

References for Chapters 21 and 22

Bell, C. (1915). *Art*. New York: Frederick A. Stokes.

Booth, W. (1988). *The Company We Keep: an Ethics of Fiction*. Berkeley: University of California Press.

Bradley, A. C. (1959). "Poetry for Poetry's Sake." In *Oxford Lectures on Poetry*, 2nd edn. (pp. 4–32). London: Macmillan.

Carroll, N. (1996). "Moderate Moralism." *British Journal of Aesthetics*, 36: 223–38.

Carroll, N. (1998a). "Moderate Moralism Versus Moderate Autonomism." *British Journal of Aesthetics*, 38: 419–24.

Carroll, N. (1998b). "Art, Narrative, and Moral Understanding." In J. Levinson (ed.), *Aesthetics and Ethics: Essays at the Intersection* (pp. 126–60). Cambridge, UK: Cambridge University Press.

Carroll, N. (2000). "*Art and Ethical Criticism : an Overview of Recent Directions of Research.*" *Ethics*, 100: 350–387.

Cohen, T. (1999). *Jokes: Philosophical Thoughts on Joking Matters*. Chicago: University of Chicago Press.

D'Arms, J. and Jacobson, D. (2000). "The Moralistic Fallacy: on the 'Appropriateness' of Emotions." *Philosophy and Phenomenological Research*, 61: 65–90.

Gaut, B. (1998). "The Ethical Criticism of Art." In J. Levinson (ed.), *Aesthetics and Ethics: Essays at the Intersection* (pp. 182–203). Cambridge, UK: Cambridge University Press.

Gaut, B. (2001). "Art and Ethics." In B. Gaut and D. Lopes (eds.), *The Routledge Companion to Aesthetics* (pp. 341–52). London: Routledge.

Hanson, K. (1998). "How Bad Can Good Art Be?" In J. Levinson (ed.), *Aesthetics and Ethics* (pp. 204–26). Cambridge, UK: Cambridge University Press.

Haskins, C. (2001). "Art, Morality, and the Holocaust: the Aesthetic Riddle of Benigni's *Life Is Beautiful*." *Journal of Aesthetics and Art Criticism*, 59: 373–84.

Hume, D. ([1757] 1987). "Of the Standard of Taste." In *Essays Moral, Political, and Literary*, ed. E. Miller (pp. 226–48). Indianapolis: Liberty Classics.

Isenberg, A. (1973). *Aesthetics and the Theory of Criticism*. Chicago: University of Chicago Press.

Jacobson, D. (1996). "Sir Philip Sidney's Dilemma: on the Ethical Function of Narrative Art." *Journal of Aesthetics and Art Criticism*, 54: 327–36.

Jacobson, D. (1997). "In Praise of Immoral Art." *Philosophical Topics*, 25: 155–99.

Kieran, M. (1995). "The Impoverishment of Art." *British Journal of Aesthetics*, 35: 15–25.

Kieran, M. (1996). "Art, Imagination, and the Cultivation of Morals." *Journal of Aesthetics and Art Criticism*, 54: 337–51.

Kieran, M. (2003). "Forbidden Knowledge: the Challenge of Immoralism." In J. Bermudez and S. Gardner (eds.), *Art and Morality* (pp. 56–73). London: Routledge.

Lane, A. (2000). "To the Limit." *The New Yorker*, April 17.

Larkin, P. (2003). *Collected Poems*. London: Faber and Faber.

Levinson, J. (ed.). (1998). *Aesthetics and Ethics: Essays at the Intersection*. Cambridge, UK: Cambridge University Press.

Walton, K. (1990). *Mimesis as Make-believe*. Cambridge, MA: Harvard University Press.

Further Reading for Chapters 21 and 22

Anderson, J. C., and Dean, J. T. (1998). "Moderate Autonomism." *British Journal of Aesthetics*, 38: 150–66.

Eaton, M. (2001). *Merit, Aesthetic and Ethical*. Oxford: Oxford University Press.

Gass, W. (1996). "The Baby or the Botticelli." In *Finding a Form* (pp. 272–92). New York: Alfred A. Knopf.

Kieran, M. (2004). *Revealing Art*. London: Routledge.

Kieran, M. (2003). "Art and Morality." In Jerrold Levinson (ed.), *The Oxford Handbook to Aesthetics* (pp. 451–70). Oxford: Oxford University Press.

Mamet, D. (1986). "Decadence." In *Writing in Restaurants* (pp. 57–9). New York: Viking Penguin.

Nehamas, A. (1982). "Plato on Imitation and Poetry in Republic 10." In J. Moravcsik and P. Tempko (eds.), *Plato on Beauty and the Arts* (pp. 47–78). Totowa, NJ: Rowan and Littlefield.

Tolstoy, L. (1994). *What is Art?* London: Duckworth.

Walton, K. (1994). "Morals in Fiction and Fictional Morality." *Proceedings of the Aristotelian Society*, supplementary vol. 68: 1–24.

Index

affect
and aesthetic experience 26, 71–6, 82, 93
fictive 223–6, 230–1, 233
Alberti, Leon Battista 152
Alter, Robert 217–18
Ammons, A. R., "Beautiful Woman" 90
anticognitivism 115–16, 121–2, 125–6
anti-intentionalism 269, 283–93
criticism 283–7
proving 291–3
appearance and representation 146, 158–9,
162–3, 172
appearance emotionalism 179, 180–4, 196–9
criticisms 184–8
appreciation
as aesthetic state of mind 99–101, 102–3,
109–10
and interpretation 270–1
literary 133–6
and sensibility 107–8
and value 22, 23–4, 47–8, 104–7
Aquinas, St Thomas, and the senses 94 n.2
architecture (built), cognitive value 128
architecture (mental), cognitive 227, 231,
232, 242–3
Ariosto, Ludovico 306–7, 314, 317
Aristotle 59, 138–9
and cognitivism 117, 126, 131–2
and emotional responses to fiction 245,
252
Poetics 58, 117, 131
art
and aesthetic state of mind 108–10
and cognition 115–26
arts, fine/liberal 109–10
artworks
and aesthetic experience 69–70, 71–2,
78–9, 81–3
and aesthetic objects 7–8
and critical judgment 173
defective 72, 75, 332–7, 341, 342–3, 344,
345–6, 347–52
and imagination 209
and interpretation 270, 272
and location 12–13, 33–4
association, and music 179–80
assumption, and judgment 210
attention
and engagement 18–19
joint 216

audience appreciation 7
Austen, Jane, *Emma* 121, 333
authenticity, and fakes 11–12, 15–16, 18
authors, and characters 214–15, 217–21
autonomism 331, 342, 343–6, 350, 352–3
aversion 59–61, 63
paradoxes of 58–9, 60
axiology
and aesthetic experience 81–8, 90, 91–2,
93, 101–4, 106
empiricist 22–3, 25–7, 31, 33–4

Bach, J. S., *Well-tempered Clavier* 201
Baumgarten, Alexander 70, 71, 98, 107–10
Beardsley, Monroe C.
and aesthetic experience 75, 101, 107
and aesthetic properties 54, 306, 322, 323,
324
and intention and interpretation 42,
283–4, 287, 292
and noncognitivism 116, 139
and ready-mades 33
Beardsmore, R. 116
beauty 5, 39–50, 51–63, 317
and cognitive contextualism 43–50
definition 52–3
differing intuitions 39–40
easy and difficult 57–8
formal 41–2, 53–6
and Kant 5, 16–17, 40–2, 43–4, 50, 51, 55
and morality 5
nonsensory 50
out of context 40–3
and pain 51–2, 53, 58–61, 135
as paradox 58–9
and pleasure 5, 41–2, 43–8, 51, 53–8,
73–4, 109, 300, 316–17
and prettiness 55, 57, 59, 63
and sublimity 56–7, 58–9, 63
and taste 40, 44, 54
terrible 5, 51–63
as unity in variety 54, 305–6, 314, 318
Bechara, A. et al. 248
Beckett, Samuel, *Waiting for Godot* 308
Beebe, M. 134–5
Beethoven, Ludwig van, Fifth Symphony
201
behavior, human
and emotions 224
and music 181–3, 196–7

belief
- and action 242, 255
- and character identification 227–8
- false 259–60
- and fictional emotion 241–2, 246–7, 250–1, 253, 254–5
- and imagination 222–3, 224–7, 231–2, 233
- instrumental 255
- and judgment 210
- and recognition 170
- simulated 2, 211–13, 215–16, 226, 229
- and valuing 105–7

Bell, Clive 42, 71, 75, 78, 101, 331, 332
Berg, Alban, *Wozzeck* 100, 101, 105
Bogart, Humphrey 230
Boghossian, Paul 202–3
Bonzon, Roman 23
Bosanquet, Bernard 57–8, 59, 60, 62
Bosch, Hieronymus 61
Bradbury, Ray, "There Will Come Soft Rains" 228
Bradley, A. C. 344
Brahms, Johannes, First Symphony 193
Breughel, Pieter (the Elder), *Wedding Dance in the Open Air* 286–7
Britten, Benjamin, *War Requiem* 51
Brontë, Anne, *The Tenant of Wildfell Hall* 218–21
Brooks, C. 136
Budd, Malcolm 23, 181, 195–6
Bullough, Edward 75
Burke, Edmund 53–4, 57, 60

Cacoyannis, Michael 55
Cage, John, *4′33″* 18
Campbell, John 216
Cantor, Jay, *Great Neck* 87
Caravaggio (Michelangelo Merisi), *The Doubting of St. Thomas* 62
Carlson, Allen 44, 47, 92
Carroll, Noël
- and aesthetic experience 6, 69–93
- and aesthetic state of mind 98–9, 101–6, 107–8
- and cognitivism 116
- and interpretation 275, 282, 287, 288–9
- and moral value 332–6, 337, 338, 340, 342, 343–4, 345–6, 347–54
- and simulation theory 212–13

Cavell, Stanley, *The World Viewed* 230
character, artistic 7–8
character, fictional
- and genuine and rational emotion 241–53, 254–64
- and identification 227–8, 229, 232, 234–5: imaginative/doxastic 236
- and moralism 354–5
- and paradox of fictional emotions 241–4
- simulation 213–15, 216–17: and empathy 217–21, 235
Cheever, John 293
Clark, Kenneth 27–8
cognition
- cognitive architecture 227, 231, 232, 242–3
- and emotion 122, 187, 188–9, 257
- and imagination 116–21, 122–3, 126, 222–35
cognitivism 19–21, 26, 33
- aesthetic claim 115, 121–6
- and appreciation 100, 106–7, 108, 133–6
- broad 254
- epistemic claim 115, 116–21
- and essentialism 124–5, 135
- and falsehood 137–9
- minimal nondoxastic 224–6, 227–32, 235
- narrow 254–5, 257, 259–60
- and nature 44–50
- and pain 60–1
- and pluralism 123–4
- strong 47–8
- and theme and subject 124–6, 136–7, 138–9
- and value 6, 26, 115–26, 127–39, 324–5, 340–1
Cohen, Ted 351
coherence, as aesthetic principle 139, 317–18, 322, 338
Coleridge, Samuel Taylor 245
Collingwood, R. G. 130, 209, 307
comedy
- and beauty 58
- and moralism 350–1
communication
- aesthetic 110
- aural 185, 194
- and intention 271–2, 276, 278, 290
- interpretation as 288
- visual 145, 151, 154, 156, 173–4

and the senses 94 n.2
and the sublime 59
Kantianism, and cognitivism 19–21, 24, 48
Keats, John, "Ode on a Grecian Urn" 135–6
Kieran, Matthew 1–8
  and cognitive immoralism 336, 340–1,
    343, 353
  and enlightened empiricism 23, 25–6, 31
  and imagination 212–13
  ugliness and beauty 56
Kivy, P. 116, 137, 186, 197, 306
knowledge
  and the aesthetic 1, 76–80, 100, 106–7,
    108, 115–26, 127–33, 137
  and beauty 44–50, 58
  and imagination 116–21, 126; and
    cognitive imagination 70, 222–35
  nonpropositional 129–30
  propositional 128–9
knowledge of intention dilemma 276–7
Korsgaard, C. M. 105
Korsmeyer, Carolyn 5, 51–63
Kovakovich, Karson 4, 241–53, 257, 260, 262
Kripke, S. 105
Kristeller, P. O. 109
Kruger, Barbara 171
Kundera, Milan 117, 123

Lamarque, P. 6, 116, 124–6, 127–39
Lamarque, P. and Olsen, S. H. 116
landscape, beauty and ugliness 44, 47–8, 53
landscapes (painted) 130, 131
Lane, Anthony 353–4
Langer, S. 181
Language Artists 79
Larkin, Philip 355
Leavis, F. R. 263
Lessing, Alfred 30–1
Levinson, Jerrold
  and enlightened empiricism 23, 25–7, 29,
    31
  and musical expressiveness 5, 188, 190,
    192–204
Lewis, D. 244–5
liberal arts 109–10
literature
  and aesthetic experience 70, 77, 91
  and cognitivism 115–26, 128, 131–6
  and critical practice 133–6
  and expressiveness 200

and falsity 137–9
and fiction 132–3
Livingston, Paisley 94 n.12
location, and aesthetic value 12–13, 33–4
Locke, John 51
Lopes, Dominic 7, 154, 156–7, 159, 160–74
Louis, Morris 28, 31
Lucie-Smith, Edward 28
Lukács, Georg 131–2

MacLeish, Archibald, "Ars Poetica" 42
Magritte, René 172
Marinetti, Filippo Emilio 31
Matisse, Henri 55, 57, 59
Matravers, Derek 4, 254–64
meaning, and interpretation 269, 270,
  272–8, 279–80, 281, 282–93
Meinong, Alexius 244
Melville, Hermann, *Moby Dick* 287
mental state *see* state of mind
merit *see* value
Meskin, Aaron 2, 104, 222–35
metaphor, and intention 284–5
metaphysics 3–4
metarepresentational theory 225, 232
methodology
  piecemeal approach 1–2, 3
  programmatic approach 2–3
Miller, J. Hillis 125
Miller, Richard 96 n.27
Milton, John 314–15
  Paradise Lost 123–4, 130
mimesis, and representational art 58, 130–1
mind, aesthetic state 98–110
Miró, Juan 19
mistakes
  of imagination 117
  literary 137–8
MNC *see* cognitivism, minimal nondoxastic
Moore, G. E. 106, 331
Moore, Ronald 47
moralism
  comic 350–1, 354
  and contingency of moral value 338–41
  and emotional engagement 346–61
  and mismatched response principle 337–8
  moderate 332–3, 343–51
  opportunistic 331–41, 343, 349–50
  radical 344–5
  rejection 351–5

morality
and aesthetic experience 90
and aesthetic value 3, 49–50, 331–41,
342–55
and beauty 5, 49
and emotions 252, 263–4
and objectivity 4, 303–4
movement, in music 181–2, 193, 196
Mozart, Wolfgang Amadeus
Don Giovanni 311
Sinfonia Concertante 28–9
Symphony No. 41 *(Jupiter)* 99, 100, 311
Muir, K. 136
Murdoch, Iris 129
music
and aesthetic experience 82–3
and aesthetic principles 299–300
and appearance emotionalism 179, 180–8,
196–9
and association 179–80
cognitive value 115, 116, 128–9
and contextualism 20
and expression 5, 179–91
and hearability-as-expression 192–204
and hypothetical emotionalism 179,
188–90, 199–200
pure 5, 115–16, 179–91
and response-dependent properties 180–2
and unity 306

narrative art
and aesthetic experience 26
and moral value 332–4, 343, 347
Nassauer, Joan 46–7
Nathan, Daniel O. 5, 7, 282–93
nature
aesthetic appreciation 19, 44–7, 53,
99–101
and aesthetic experience 92–3
and cognitive contextualism 44–50
Neal, J. and M. 48
Nietzsche, Friedrich 209
noncognitivism 115–16, 121–2, 125–6
Novitz, D. 116
Nussbaum, Martha 116, 137, 252
Nyman, Michael 28–9

object, aesthetic 7–8
objectivity 4
and aesthetic experience 83–5, 102

and aesthetic properties 4, 300–1, 303–4,
305–8, 310, 321–2
and beauty 51, 53–5
and expressiveness 182–3, 195, 202
and literary criticism 217–18
and values 32, 303–8
ontology
of art 24, 26
of beauty 52
of fictional characters 244–5, 246
originality 1, 15, 30–1, 130

pain, and beauty 51–2, 53, 58–61, 135
painting
and authorial intention 286–7
cognitive value 128, 130–1
experienced resemblance theory 130–1,
147–50, 151–9, 161–3
recognition theory 154, 155, 156–9, 160,
169–71
representational 130–1, 145–59, 160–74
and seeing-in 90, 147, 150, 151, 154,
155–6, 158–9, 163–8
paradigms, aesthetic 1–2, 44, 70
paradox of fictional emotions 241–4
belief condition 241–2, 246–7, 250–1,
253, 254–5
coordination condition 241–2, 243, 246–7,
253, 257
resolution 246–52, 253
response condition 241–2, 243, 246–7,
253
traditional formulations 245–6
paradoxes of aversion 58–9, 60
particularism, and objectivity 4
pastiches, and fakes 1, 11–12, 15–16,
20
Pater, Walter 6
Peacocke, Christopher 3
perception
and cognitivism 48–50
and experience 5–6, 25, 71, 77, 107–8
and recognition 170
perfection 107–8
performance art 79
Perkins, V. F. 230–1
Perrett, D. I., May, K. A. and Yousikawa, S.
50
personae, in music 5, 188–90, 193–4, 199,
201, 203–4

objective resemblance theory 169
and outline shape 147–50, 151, 152–4, 158, 162–3, 164–9, 171
and point of view 145–6, 158–9, 163, 172
recognition theory 154, 155, 156–9, 160, 169–74
and seeing-in 90, 147, 150, 151, 154, 155–6, 158–9, 163–8
subject and theme 124–6, 131
and truth 130–1
verbal 145–6
visual 130–1, 145–59, 160–74
resemblance
and music and emotion 181–3, 195–9
and pictorial content determination 155–7, 158, 160–2, 163, 166–8, 169–71, 173
and representation 130–1, 147–50, 151–9, 160–3
Richards, I. A. 129
Ricks, Christopher 137–8
Riefenstahl, Leni, *Triumph of the Will* 100, 101, 338
Rite of Spring (Stravinsky) 300, 304, 308–9, 311
Robinson, Jenefer 189, 199
Rodin, Auguste, *The Burghers of Calais* 51
Roesen, Severin 54
Romanticism 7
Rousseau, Jean-Jacques 263
Rowe, M. W. 135, 137–9
rules, aesthetic 302, 310–11
Russolo, 31
Ryle, Gilbert 60

Saarinen, Eero 54
St. Denis, Ruth 71
Santayana, George 51
Sartre, Jean-Paul, *No Exit* 75
Savile, A. 287
Schier, F. 156–7, 159
Schopenhauer, Arthur 74
Scruton, Roger 202, 203–4
sculpture
cognitive value 128
as representation 146–7, 157–8, 172
seeing-as 123
seeing-in 147, 150, 151, 154, 155–6, 158–9, 163–8
and aesthetic experience 90
semantics 3, 244–5

sensibility, and aesthetic experience 70, 71, 107–8
sentimentality 130, 261–4, 347
Shaftesbury, Antony Ashley Cooper, 3rd Earl 73
Shakespeare, William
Hamlet 256, 354
King Lear 51, 118–19, 136
Macbeth 136, 354
Much Ado About Nothing 99–100
Othello 234
sonnets 132
shape
outline 147–50, *148*, *149*, *150*, 151, 152–4, 158, 162–3, 164–9, *166*, 171
three-dimensional 147, 149–50, 152–3, 158
Sharpe, R. A. 29–30
Shelley, Percy Bysshe 322, 323
Sibley, Frank 308–9, 310, 315–16, 317, 318, 319, 321, 322, 324
simulation theory 121, 211–13
and character-simulation 213–15
and empathy 215–21
and folk psychology 229–30, 234
and imagination 2, 211–13, 226–31
impersonal 228–9
Sircello, Guy 286–7
Smiley, Jane, *Good Faith* 87
Sober, E. and Wilson, J. 216
Socrates, and beauty 39, 50
Sophocles, *Oedipus Rex* 286–7
ST *see* simulation theory
star power 230–1, 232
state of mind 98–110
and character-simulation 2, 213–14, 216–17
and expression 192–4, 199–201, 203–4
and fictional emotion 254–6, 262
Steadman, P. 29
Stecker, Robert 5, 7, 199, 269–81
Steinberg, Saul 171–2
Stewart, James 230–1, 232
Stolnitz, J. 116
Stone, Robert, *A Flag for Sunrise* 62
Stravinsky, Igor, *Rite of Spring* 300, 304, 308–9, 311
style, and adverbial imagining 209–10
subject and theme 124–6, 131, 133–5, 136–7, 138–9

subjectivity
  and aesthetic experience 83, 85, 92, 101–4
  and beauty 41, 53, 54–5
  and empathy 217–18
  and literary criticism 217–18
sublimity, and beauty 56–7, 58–9, 63
Swift, Jonathan, "A Modest Proposal" 285
symbol systems, pictorial 155–6
sympathy
  and empathy 215, 219
  transfer 230–1

The Talented Mr Ripley (film) 335, 337
Tanner, Michael 262–4
taste 4
  and aesthetic principles 303, 304, 309,
    310, 323
  and beauty 40, 44, 54
  and judgment 210
  in Kant 16–17, 44, 52
Tate Modern, opening exhibition 12
terror
  and pleasure 59–61
  and the sublime 5, 56–7, 58–9, 63
theme
  and falsity 138–9
  and literary appreciation 124–6, 133–5,
    136–7
  in representational art 131
Titian (Tiziano Vecellio), Diana and Actaeon
    131
Tolkien, J. R. R., The Lord of the Rings 224
Tolstoy, Leo 43, 307
  Anna Karenina 242, 244–5, 246, 249
  War and Peace 287
tragedy 58–9, 135, 138, 234, 346, 348
Trainspotting (film) 335, 337
Trilling, Lionel 135–6
truth
  as aesthetic value 6, 127–30
  and beauty 40, 135–6
  and falsity 137–9
  and imagination 222, 245
  and literature 124–6, 132, 135–7
  moral 331–2, 340–1
  and representation 130–1
Turner, J. M. W., Snowstorm 27–8, 31,
    32
Turner Prize 13
Twain, Mark, Huckleberry Finn 333

ugliness 39–50
  in context 43–7
  as contrast 56–7
  and disgust 61–3
  in nature 44, 47–8
  out of context 40–3
understanding
  and interpretation 270, 282
  as source of value 128–9
unity/uniformity, as aesthetic property 54,
    89, 305–6, 309, 314, 318, 322–4
universalism
  and beauty 41, 52
  and morality 117, 345
utility, social, as aesthetic principle 307

value 1–2, 11–21
  and aesthetic empiricism 14–21, 22–4,
    27–8
  and aesthetic experience 1, 22–34, 69–70,
    81–8
  and aesthetic principles 299–312,
    313–26
  and beauty 42, 43
  cognitive 6, 26, 115–26, 127–39, 324–5,
    340–1
  cultural 31
  extrinsic 105
  and fakes 11–12, 14, 19
  instrumental 82–8, 102, 105–6, 263–4,
    318, 319–21, 349–50
  intrinsic 81–8, 90, 92, 102–7, 108, 127,
    260, 262, 303, 318–19, 320–1, 350
  moral 3, 49–50, 331–41, 342–55
  and pluralism 123–4
  and ready-mades 12–14, 19, 33
Van Eyck, Jan, Arnolfini Marriage 29
Van Meegeren, Han 12, 15, 20
  Disciples at Emmaus 11, 29, 30–1
Vermazen, B. 194, 199, 324
Vermeer, Jan 11, 20, 29, 30–1
Verne, Jules, Mysterious Island 275
voluntarism, imaginative 232

Walsh, D. 129
Walton, Kendall
  and aesthetic properties 303
  and fiction and emotion 224, 245–6,
    248–50, 251, 255, 264
  and intention 284, 289